SOCIETY FOR NEW TESTAMENT STUDIES
MONOGRAPH SERIES
General Editor: R. McL. Wilson F.B.A.
Associate Editor: M. E. Thrall

38
'LOVE YOUR ENEMIES'

'Love your enemies'

Jesus' love command in the synoptic gospels and
in the early Christian paraenesis

A history of the tradition and interpretation of its uses

JOHN PIPER

Associate Professor of Biblical Studies
Bethel College, St Paul, Minnesota

CAMBRIDGE UNIVERSITY PRESS

CAMBRIDGE

LONDON NEW YORK NEW ROCHELLE

MELBOURNE SYDNEY

Published by the Press Syndicate of the University of Cambridge
The Pitt Building, Trumpington Street, Cambridge CB2 1RP
32 East 57th Street, New York, NY 10022, USA
296 Beaconsfield Parade, Middle Park, Melbourne 3206, Australia

First published 1979

Printed in Great Britain at the University Press, Cambridge
Typeset by H Charlesworth & Co Ltd, Huddersfield

Library of Congress Cataloging in Publication Data
Piper, John, 1946-
    'Love your enemies.'
  (Society for New Testament Studies. Monograph series; 38)
  Revision of the author's dissertation, Ludwig-Maximilians-Universität, 1974.
  1. Love (Theology) – Biblical teaching. 2. Jesus Christ – Teachings. 3. Bible.
N.T. Gospels – Criticism, interpretation, etc. 4. Christian ethics – Early church,
ca. 30–600. I. Title. II. Series: Studiorum Novi Testamenti Societas. Monograph
series; 38.
BS2417.L7P56 1979   241'.6'77   77-95449
ISBN 0 521 22056 4

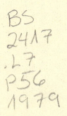

To Noël

CONTENTS

Preface   xi
Abbreviations   xii

Introduction   1

1   **In Search of the Paraenetic Tradition of a Command of Enemy Love**   4
I   The Pertinent Texts   4
II Literary Dependence or Common Traditional Source?   5
III Determining the Form of the Command in the Paraenetic Tradition   8
    A. I Thess 5:15   8
    B. Rom 12:17 and I Pt 3:9   14
IV Conclusion   17

2   **The Origin of the Command of Enemy Love in the New Testament Paraenetic Tradition** 19
I   The Question and the Approach   19
II Hellenistic Philosophy   20
    A. Seneca   21
    B. Epictetus   25
III The Old Testament   27
IV Hellenistic Judaism   35
    A. Works from the Apocrypha and Pseudepigrapha   35
    B. Philo   39
V   Qumran and Works in the Region of its Influence   39
    A. Manual of Discipline   40
    B. The Book of Jubilees   42
    C. The Testaments of the Twelve Patriarchs   43
VI Palestinian Judaism outside Qumran   45
    A. The Wisdom of Jesus Son of Sirach   45
    B. Josephus   46
    C. The Rabbis   47

VII	The Teaching of Jesus	49
	A. The Question of Q	49
	B. The Question of the Antitheses	51
	C. Analysis of the Individual Sayings	56
VIII	Conclusion	63
3	**Jesus' Command of Enemy Love in the Larger Context of His Message**	**66**
I	Preliminary Remarks	66
	A. The Hermeneutical Problems	66
	B. The Validity of Systematizing	67
	C. The Content of the Chapter	68
II	Jesus' Command of Enemy Love and the Kingdom of God	69
	A. Four Recent Studies and One Older Work	69
	B. Jesus' Command of Enemy Love and the Coming Kingdom: Condition?	76
	C. Jesus' Command of Enemy Love and the Present Aspect of the Kingdom: Enablement	80
	D. Jesus' Command of Enemy Love as a Sign of the Kingdom	86
III	Jesus' Command of Enemy Love and the Law	89
	A. Non-Resistance (Mt 5:39–42) vs the *Lex Talionis* (Ex 21:24)	89
	B. Enemy Love (Mt 5:44 par Lk) vs Neighbor Love (Lev 19:18)	91
	C. Abolition vs Continuation of the Law	95
4	**The Use and Meaning of Jesus' Command of Enemy Love in the Early Christian Paraenesis**	**100**
I	Preliminary Remarks	100
II	The Motivation of the Command of Enemy Love	101
	A. A Brief Survey of the Previous Research	101
	B. Paul	102
	C. I Peter	119
III	The Content of the Command of Enemy Love	128
	A. The General Features of Enemy Love	128
	B. Love and the Command of Enemy Love and the Institutions of Society	130
5	**The Gospel Tradition of Jesus' Command of Enemy Love and its Use in Matthew and Luke**	**134**
I	The Gospel Tradition of Jesus' Command of Enemy Love before the Gospels	134
	A. Determining the *Vorlage*	134
	B. Determining the *Sitz im Leben* of the *Vorlage*	136

Contents

II The Gospel Tradition of Jesus' Command of Enemy Love in the Gospels — 139

A. The Approach and Methodology — 139

B. Matthew's Use of the Gospel Tradition of Jesus' Command of Enemy Love — 141

C. Luke's Use of the Gospel Tradition of Jesus' Command of Enemy Love — 153

Conclusion — 171

Notes — 176

Bibliography — 235

Index of passages cited — 249

Index of modern authors — 267

Index of subjects — 271

PREFACE

This book is a slightly revised and updated version of my doctoral dissertation which was accepted by the Protestant theological faculty of Ludwig-Maximilians-Universität, München, in the summer of 1974.

I want to express my gratitude for, if not to, my gracious and highly esteemed 'Doktorvater' Professor Dr Leonhard Goppelt who died seven months prior to the completion of my studies in Munich. His exemplary scholarship, humility and hospitality provided the guidance and encouragement needed to complete this work. His influence upon the conception of the book will be obvious even though we did not always agree.

At Professor Goppelt's untimely death Professor Dr Georg Kretschmar, in addition to his many other responsibilities, generously agreed to supervise the finishing touches on the dissertation which was at that time substantially complete. For his time and help he deserves more praise than many know because of the unusual burden he was carrying.

I also owe thanks to the Evangelisch-Lutherische Landeskirche Bayern for a monthly stipend which together with my parents' generosity enabled me and my family to do research in Munich for three years. My good friend Scott Hafemann should be mentioned for his help in compiling the indexes.

The debt I owe my wife is only symbolized but not exhausted by the fact that she typed the full manuscript at least three times through the stages of its emergence (sometimes with infant Karsten in her lap). For her prayers and her timely 'You can do it,' I give thanks to her and to the Lord whom we serve together – who loved us 'while we were yet enemies,' reconciling us to himself and giving us a ministry of reconciliation.

ABBREVIATIONS

ATD	Altes Testament Deutsch
ATLA	American Theological Library Association
ATR	*Anglican Theological Review*
BEvTh	Beiträge zur evangelischen Theologie
BFChTh	Beiträge zur Förderung christlicher Theologie
BL	*Bibel und Leben*
BNTC	Black's New Testament Commentaries
BR	*Biblical Research*
BSGNT	United Bible Societies Greek New Testament
BSt	Biblische Studien
BZ	*Biblische Zeitschrift*
BZNW	Beihefte zur *Zeitschrift für neutestamentliche Wissenschaft*
CBQ	*Catholic Biblical Quarterly*
EK	*Evangelische Kommentare*
Encycl Jud	*Encyclopaedia Judaica*
ET	*Expository Times*
EvTh	*Evangelische Theologie*
FRLANT	Forschungen zur Religion und Literatur des Alten und Neuen Testaments
FZTP	*Freiburger Zeitschrift für Theologie und Philosophie*
HNT	Handbuch zum Neuen Testament
HThK	Herders theologischer Kommentar
HTR	*Harvard Theological Review*
ICC	International Critical Commentary
IDB	*The Interpreter's Dictionary of the Bible*
JBL	*Journal of Biblical Literature*
JBR	*Journal of Bible and Religion*
JR	*Journal of Religion*
JTS	*Journal of Theological Studies*
KuD	*Kerygma und Dogma*
LZ	*Lebendiges Zeugnis*

MK	Meyer Kommentar
MNTC	Moffatt New Testament Commentaries
NovTest	*Novum Testamentum*
NTD	Neues Testament Deutsch
NTA	*Neutestamentliche Abhandlungen*
NTS	*New Testament Studies*
PTR	*Princeton Theological Review*
RB	*Revue Biblique*
RGG	*Religion in Geschichte und Gegenwart* (3rd edition)
SacMun	*Sacramentum Mundi*
SBT	Studies in Biblical Theology
SNTS	Society for New Testament Studies
StTh	*Studia Theologica*
TDNT	*Theological Dictionary of the New Testament*
ThEx	*Theologische Existenz Heute*
ThGl	*Theologie und Glaube*
ThLZ	*Theologische Literaturzeitung*
THNT	Theologischer Handkommentar zum Neuen Testament
ThP	*Theologie und Philosophie*
ThQ	*Theologische Quartalschrift*
ThR	*Theologische Rundschau*
ThStKr	*Theologische Studien und Kritiken*
ThZ	*Theologische Zeitschrift*
TU	Texte und Untersuchungen zur Geschichte der altchristlichen Literatur
UNT	Untersuchungen zum Neuen Testament
WMANT	*Wissenschaftliche Monographien zum Alten und Neuen Testament*
WUNT	Wissenschaftliche Untersuchungen zum Neuen Testament
ZEE	*Zeitschrift für evangelische Ethik*
ZKT	*Zeitschrift für katholische Theologie*
ZNW	*Zeitschrift für neutestamentliche Wissenschaft*
ZSTh	*Zeitschrift für systematische Theologie*
ZThK	*Zeitschrift für Theologie und Kirche*

INTRODUCTION

The Question and the Approach

'Love your enemies!' is one of the few sayings of Jesus, the authenticity of which is not seriously questioned by anyone. Nor is it disputed that this command is crucial in understanding what the earthly Jesus wanted to accomplish. It is further evident in the paraenetic[1] portions of the New Testament epistles that commands are found which, while not rendering Jesus' command of enemy love[2] word for word, nevertheless aim in the same direction and at times echo the phraseology of Jesus. In view of these facts it is surprising that (to my knowledge) no monograph exists which treats in a thorough way the history of this command in the various levels of the New Testament tradition. Therefore, as the title indicates, the present work aims to analyse the history of the tradition of Jesus' command of enemy love and to interpret the way it was understood in the various stages of early Christian tradition within the New Testament.

The peculiarity and limitation of my approach can perhaps be clarified by contrast with the approach taken in a related study: *The Love Command in the New Testament* (1972) by Victor Furnish. Dr Furnish distinguishes his own approach from those of James Moffatt's *Love in the New Testament* (1929), Ceslaus Spicq's *Agape dans le Nouveau Testament: Analyse des Textes* (1958), and Viktor Warnach's *Die Liebe als Grundmotiv in der neutestamentlichen Theologie*[3] (1951) in that 'each of these . . . seeks to cut a broad swathe through *all* aspects of "love" in the New Testament,'[4] not focusing as such on the love command, while his work, being more limited, 'focuses on the love *ethic,* the love *command*.'[5] But even Furnish's focus is very broad and the content of the book shows that the emphasis in the above quote falls on 'ethic' rather than 'command'. The subtitles of the Pauline section reveal that Furnish's focus is broader than the love *command*: 'Love and the New Creation,' 'Love and the Law,' 'Love and Freedom,' 'Love in the Deutero-Pauline Letters.' A fitting subtitle for Furnish's book may have been, to use Furnish's own description of its content, 'what the New Testament teaches and otherwise reflects about earliest Christianity's view of loving one's brother, one's neighbor, and one's enemy.'[6]

In contrast, the focus of the present work is narrowed in two ways: the love *command* which is the object of my attention is specifically *Jesus'* love command and further it is Jesus' command of *enemy* love. This narrowing of focus onto a particular command of Jesus is necessitated by the history-of-traditions viewpoint which has governed the work from the beginning. It is the history of the tradition and the various understandings and applications of this one command of Jesus that I intend to investigate.[7] While Furnish does say his intention is 'to trace and define the *various ways* the love command has been received, interpreted and applied,'[8] he does not define which precise command he means nor, therefore, in what sense that particular command is 'received'. In other words his work is not governed by the history-of-traditions viewpoint and that is its fundamental difference from mine.

It is my hope therefore that, although its general subject matter has been the object of countless studies, my work will not merely retrace the steps of its worthy predecessors, but add its own fresh contribution to the understanding of Jesus' command of enemy love.

The Content

The title of this work anticipates in part the results of the investigation, namely, that the tradition of Jesus' command of enemy love may be traced not only in the 'gospel tradition'[9] which in the New Testament formed the core of the synoptic gospels, but also in the 'paraenetic tradition'[10] which left its deposit in the paraenetic portions of the New Testament epistles. That Jesus' love command was transmitted along lines which led to the synoptic gospels is not disputed.[11] That it was taken up into the paraenetic tradition is disputed. Therefore, the first task before me is to isolate the elements of the paraenetic tradition which *possibly* represent the reception and application of Jesus' command of enemy love (Chapter 1). Whether or not these elements of the paraenetic tradition do *in fact* rest on Jesus' command is the question I try to answer in Chapter 2. The approach in that chapter is to pursue a history-of-religions investigation of the teaching on enemy love in the environment of the early church which may have influenced the formation of the New Testament paraenesis. This investigation culminates with the interrelated attempts to determine on the one hand the genuineness and scope of Jesus' command of enemy love and on the other hand its relation to the corresponding elements in the New Testament paraenesis.

The remaining three chapters form a triad in which I try to interpret the function of Jesus' command of enemy love first in his own earthly ministry (Chapter 3), then in the New Testament paraenesis (Chapter 4) and finally in the gospel tradition and synoptic redaction (Chapter 5). The concern in these three chapters is to go beyond merely formal and purely historical observations to the fundamental intention of Jesus and of those in the New Testament who used his command of enemy love. The questions which govern my investigation at each stage of the tradition are, therefore, very basic: Wherein consists obedience to this love command? and, How shall this obedience be realized?

The Concern of the Author

Every scholarly work on the New Testament is preponderantly an intellectual exercise. The work of thinking which the production of a book like this demands from the author is demanded also from its reader. But because of the nature of the reality with which this work has to do, the *necessary* preponderance of intellectual work can nevertheless frustrate the goal for which the work is done. For that reality is and demands far more than thinking. Adolf Schlatter has warned: 'Thought can become scholasticism, a mere jangle of words, if the concept replaces the essence, or dogma replaces reality.'[12] The reality from which Jesus' command of enemy love springs and the reality at which it aims is not exhausted by correct thinking about the command. If a book about this command does not ultimately lead beyond mere thinking to an active realization of what the command intends, then that thinking itself, in all of its possible technical accuracy, becomes worthless. 'Though I understand all mysteries and all knowledge . . . and have not love, I am nothing.'

1

IN SEARCH OF THE PARAENETIC TRADITION OF A COMMAND OF ENEMY LOVE

Our first task is to isolate the elements of the paraenetic tradition which possibly represent the reception and application of Jesus' command of enemy love. To do this we must, first, focus on those commands in the paraenetic portions of the New Testament which have a similarity to Jesus' command of enemy love; second, we must determine whether these commands were a part of the early Christian paraenetic tradition which existed prior to and alongside the New Testament epistles; and third, we must try to determine what form the command(s) had in that tradition. The existence of such a tradition is not one of my assumptions, but is to be demonstrated by the investigation.

I. The Pertinent Texts

Since we are concerned not with commands to love in general, but only with commands of enemy love, our attention may be confined primarily to three texts:

> *Rom 12:14,17–20*
>
> Bless those who persecute you; bless and do not curse them.
> . . .
> Pay back no one evil for evil.
> Take thought for what is good before all men.
> If possible, so far as it depends on you, be at peace with all men.
> Do not avenge yourselves, beloved, but give place to wrath
> for it is written: Vengeance is mine, I will repay, says the Lord.
> But if your enemy hunger, feed him;
> If he thirst, give him drink;
> for, doing this, you will heap coals of fire on his head.

The structure of the paraenetic material in Rom 12 and 13 will be discussed in Chapter 4, p 103. Anticipating that discussion, we may simply note here that Rom 12:14,17–20 is part of a fairly long chain of admonitions which are grouped roughly with regard to the problems Paul is addressing. Rom 12:3-8 deals with the functioning of the body of Christ; Rom 12:9-21 begins with the phrase 'Let love be genuine,' and deals more generally with the Christian's relations to his brothers and to outsiders; and Rom 13:1-7 deals with the Christian's relation to the state. That gives the general context in which the command with which we are concerned is found.

I Thess 5:15

See that none of you pays back evil for evil,
but always pursue good to each other and to all.

This text too comes in the midst of a series of short, crisp imperatives. It is preceded by admonitions concerning the relations between Christians and their church leaders, and it is followed by admonitions concerning the individual Christian in his relation to God: 'Rejoice always, pray constantly, give thanks in all things' (5:16ff).

I Pt 3:9

Do not pay back evil for evil or reviling for reviling,
but on the contrary, bless;
for to this you were called in order that you might inherit a blessing.

This text comes at the end of I Pt's 'Haustafel'.[1] I Pt 2:13-17 deals with the Christian and the 'human institution' or governmental authority. I Pt 2:18-25 deals with Christian servants and their masters. I Pt 3:1-7 deals with wives and husbands. I Pt 3:8 is usually taken to refer to relationships among Christians, while 3:9 goes farther and refers to the Christian's relations to his non-Christian neighbors.[2] The text is then followed by an Old Testament quote from Ps 34 which grounds the command of 3:9.

Other texts relating to love (such as I Cor 4:12) will come into view only insofar as they stand in textual or essential proximity to these.

II. Literary Dependence or Common Traditional Source?

A detailed comparison of these three texts reveals some very close parallels in Rom 12:14,17; I Thess 5:15; and I Pt 3:9. These parallels can be recognized most readily from the following diagram. Following the diagram is a detailed list of the similarities and differences among Rom 12:14,17; I Thess 5:15; and I Pt 3:9.

Rom 12:14

εὐλογεῖτε τοὺς διώκοντας
εὐλογεῖτε καὶ μὴ καταρᾶσθε

I Thess 5:15	Rom 12:17	I Pt 3:9
ὁρᾶτε μή τις <u>κακὸν ἀντὶ κακοῦ</u> <u>τινι ἀποδῷ</u>	<u>μηδενὶ</u> <u>κακὸν ἀντὶ κακοῦ</u> <u>ἀποδιδόντες</u>	<u>μὴ</u> <u>ἀποδιδόντες</u> <u>κακὸν ἀντὶ κακοῦ</u> ἢ λοιδορίαν ἀντὶ λοιδορίας τοὐναντίον δὲ
ἀλλὰ (πάντοτε τὸ ἀγαθὸν διώκετε εἰς ἀλλήλους καὶ εἰς πάντας)	(προνοούμενοι καλὰ ἐνώπιον πάντων ἀνθρώπων) [Prov 3:4 LXX]	(εὐλογοῦντες)

A. Similarities
   1. Common to all three commands:
      a. Each contains the identical phrase κακὸν ἀντὶ κακοῦ.
      b. The verb governing this phrase in each is a form of the verb ἀποδίδωμι.
      c. Each contains a form of the negative μή.
   2. Common to Rom and I Pt:
      a. Each has the imperative participle ἀποδιδόντες.
      b. Each has the command to bless, though not in the same order or form.
   3. Common to Rom and I Thess:
      In each the verb ἀποδίδωμι has a dative object.
   4. Common to I Thess and I Pt:
      a. In each the verb ἀποδίδωμι is negated by μή.
      b. In each the negative command is followed by an adversative particle (ἀλλά, τοὐναντίον δέ) and a positive command (which are different in content and length).

B. Differences
   1. Unique to I Pt:
      a. I Pt is unique in adding to κακὸν ἀντὶ κακοῦ the phrase λοιδορίαν ἀντὶ λοιδορίας.
      b. It attaches an Old Testament quotation (3:10–12) in order to ground the command.
      c. It reverses the order of κακὸν ἀντὶ κακοῦ/ἀποδιδόντες.
   2. Unique to Rom:
      a. Rom is unique in separating the elements of the command by other admonitions (cf Rom 12:14,17,19).

    b. It precedes κακὸν ἀντὶ κακοῦ ἀποδιδόντες with its positive counter-
    part (εὐλογεῖτε, 12:14).
    c. It uses the negative μηδενί.
  3. Unique to I Thess:
    a. I Thess is unique in using a subjunctive form of the verb ἀποδίδωμι.
    b. Its ἀποδῷ clause is dependent on the introductory ὁρᾶτε.
    c. It attaches to the negative command the positive command to
    pursue good toward all.
(Other minor differences may be inferred from the list of similarities.)

The similarities in these three texts demand an explanation. The three
possible explanations from which we can choose are: (1) these commands
are the writers' own formulations and are only coincidentally similar; (2)
there was a literary dependence of one writer upon the other; (3) the
writers drew from a common paraenetic tradition.

The first of these three possibilities may be dismissed right away. The
coming together in the same command of the identical phrase κακὸν ἀντὶ
κακοῦ with the same verb ἀποδίδωμι is not to be explained by coincidence.
Thus the question remains whether there was literary dependence of one
writer on another or dependence on a common tradition. Since I Pt is
later than Rom and I Thess, the question may be formulated: Was I Pt
dependent on either Rom or I Thess? In view of the identical imperative
participle ἀποδιδόντες in Rom 12:17a and I Pt 3:9a, Rom and not I Thess
is the more likely candidate if we are to choose a literary source for I Pt.
Thus our question is finally: Was I Pt 3:9 dependent on Rom 12:17 or
were they both dependent on a common paraenetic tradition? In spite of
Beare's assertion to the contrary,[3] the scale has been tipped in favor of a
common paraenetic tradition rather than literary dependence. In the first
place, while the core of the command in Rom 12:17a and I Pt 3:9a is
strikingly similar, the *differences* listed above eliminate the possibility of
simple transcription. In the second place, if we compare the immediate
contexts in both epistles, the *imprecise similarities amidst wide divergences*
make direct dependence improbable:

Rom	*I Pt*
12:10 τῇ φιλαδελφίᾳ...φιλόστοργοι	3:8 φιλάδελφοι
12:14 εὐλογεῖτε	3:9 εὐλογοῦντες
12:16a τὸ αὐτὸ...φρονοῦντες	3:8 ὁμόφρονες
12:16b ταῖς ταπεινοῖς συναπαγόμενοι	3:8 ταπεινόφρονες
12:17 μηδενὶ κακὸν ἀντὶ κακοῦ ἀποδιδόντες	3:9 μὴ ἀποδιδόντες κακὸν ἀντὶ κακοῦ
12:18 εἰρηνεύοντες	3:11 ζητησάτω εἰρήνην

In the third place, Dodd has made the point well that the paraenetic sections like I Thess 5:14-18; Heb 13:1-3; I Pt 3:8-9 (and we may surely add to his list Rom 12:9-21) are *alike in style but differ from the style of their authors.* 'They are all marked by a concise staccato style. They use the fewest words possible. They have a kind of sing-song rhythm that helps the memory.' He concludes, 'It seems probable on general grounds that we are here indirectly in touch with the common tradition.'[4] In the fourth place, since the texts in question (Rom 12:17a; I Pt 3:9a) contain a participle used as an imperative, David Daube's argument is pertinent, namely, that behind this use of the participle in the New Testament lie early Christian Semitic ethical codes, probably in Hebrew.[5] On the basis of these four arguments it is more probable that the similarity of Rom 12:17a and I Pt 3:9a is to be traced back to a common paraenetic tradition than that it stems from literary dependence.[6] This conclusion has met widespread scholarly acceptance.[7]

III. Determining the Form of the Command in the Paraenetic Tradition

What was the form(s) of this command as it appeared in the tradition behind I Thess 5:15;[8] Rom 12:17; and I Pt 3:9? In trying to answer this question my procedure will be first to treat I Thess 5:15 in an attempt to account for its divergences from both Rom 12:17 and I Pt 3:9; then to investigate Rom 12:17 and I Pt 3:9 in order to ferret out more precisely the wording of the traditional command.

A. I Thess 5:15

I Thess 5:12-22 appears least likely to offer the original traditional context of the command, and 5.15 appears least likely to be its traditional form. I do *not* mean that in I Thess 5:12-22 Paul did not draw upon the paraenetic tradition, but rather that, while drawing upon it, his own hand is evident, especially at 5:15. The following paragraphs are an attempt to support this contention.

Above I argued that the presence of the imperative participle in Rom 12:17 and I Pt 3:9 is a clue to their traditional origin. It is noteworthy, therefore, that *none* of the admonitions in I Thess 5 employs an imperative participle (such as we find, for example, in Rom 12:9-13, 16,17,19 and I Pt 3:1,9). This is not to be explained by supposing that the admonitions in I Thess 5 have a different content from those admonitions which elsewhere use the imperative participle. The opposite is the case: as the following table shows, the traditional commands in Rom 12 which use the imperative participle have their essential counterparts in the commands of I Thess 5 which do not use the imperative participle.

I Thess	Rom
5:21f τὸ καλὸν κατέχετε, ἀπὸ παντὸς εἴδους πονηροῦ ἀπέχεσθε	12:9b ἀποστυγοῦντες τὸ πονηρόν κολλώμενοι τῷ ἀγαθῷ
5:19 τὸ πνεῦμα μὴ σβέννυτε	12:11b τῷ πνεύματι ζέοντες
5:16 πάντοτε χαίρετε	12:12a τῇ ἐλπίδι χαίροντες
5:17 ἀδιαλείπτως προσεύχεσθε	12:12c τῇ προσευχῇ προσκαρτεροῦντες
5:15 ὁρᾶτε μή τις κακὸν ἀντὶ κακοῦ τινι ἀποδῷ	12:17a μηδενὶ κακὸν ἀντὶ κακοῦ ἀποδιδόντες
5:13 εἰρηνεύετε ἐν ἑαυτοῖς	12:18 μετὰ πάντων ἀνθρώπων εἰρηνεύοντες

This fact suggests that, even though Paul was in I Thess 5 depending on the tradition, he was nevertheless more thoroughly reworking the traditional material in I Thess 5 than he was in Rom 12. As Charles Talbert observes, 'It is far easier to see these non-participial imperatives [in I Thess] as Paul's selection and rendering into proper Greek of certain individual rules from a unit of Semitic tradition than to see Rom 12:9ff as a Pauline collection and rendering in a Semitic style of individual injunctions, many of which he uses elsewhere in a non-participial form. It is easier to see Paul moving away from the participle used as an imperative than in [sic] moving to it.'[9]

A second clue for seeing the hand of Paul in shaping the context of I Thess 5:15 is found when we consider whether the admonitions of 5:14 may have been especially formulated for the specific Thessalonian situation. Dibelius asserts to the contrary: 'There is not the slightest trace of evidence that precisely these admonitions would have been especially appropriate for this church.'[10] It seems to me, however, that Dibelius has here carried a correct insight too far: *in general* vv 14–18 reflect traditional admonitions which are binding on every church but this does not exclude the possibility that Paul could have adapted the tradition to meet the specific Thessalonian need.[11]

Verses 14f read: 'We exhort you, brothers, admonish the idle, encourage the fainthearted, help the weak, be patient with all. Watch lest someone pay back evil for evil, but always pursue good for each other and for all.' The word ἀτάκτους ('the idle') and its cognates (ἠτακτήσαμεν, II Thess 3:7; ἀτάκτως, II Thess 3:6,11) are unique to the Thessalonian epistles in the New Testament. From one standpoint the rarity of the word could suggest that it is not typically Pauline and was thus taken over by him from the tradition. That would support Dibelius' contention. But from

another standpoint, the rarity of the word *in the paraenetic tradition*
with which we are acquainted could suggest that it was not taken over
from the tradition but was occasioned by a specific problem in Thessalonica.
These two ways of arguing from the rarity of ἀτάκτους reveal the ambiguity
which usually accompanies literary judgments of this nature. How shall we
proceed?

The uniqueness of a word is not by itself enough to determine whether
the word is merely a quote from the tradition or not. But when there is
other evidence that precisely this word is called for by a specific situation,
then the uniqueness of the word together with this evidence is a good indication that the word represents not a mere rehearsal of tradition but a
concern of the author to meet a particular need. The 'other evidence' that
the command 'admonish the idle' was specifically called for in Thessalonica
comes from 4:11[12] where Paul exhorts the Christians 'to aspire to live
quietly, to mind your own affairs and *to work with your hands* as we
charged you in order that you might walk respectfully before outsiders
and not have need.' With the words 'as we charged you' Paul lays emphasis
on the admonition 'to work,' that is, not to be 'idle.' That this admonition
was especially needed at Thessalonica may also be the reason Paul in 2:9
stresses his own manual labor: 'For you remember our labor and toil,
brethren; we worked night and day that we might not burden any of you
while we preached to you the gospel of God.' The singularity of the command 'admonish the idle' together with this other evidence is sufficient
support, I think, for the contention that Paul is not merely being carried
along by the tradition here but is at this point writing specifically for the
Thessalonian situation.[13]

Somewhat less persuasive but perhaps worthy of note is the uniqueness
of the command 'encourage the fainthearted' (5:14). While ὀλιγοψύχους
is a *hapax legomenon* in the New Testament, the verb παραμυθεῖσθε
occurs in one other place in the New Testament, namely in 2:12 of this
epistle: 'You know how, like a father with his children, we exhorted each
one of you and *encouraged* and charged that you might walk worthily of
the God who called you into his Kingdom and glory.' In a sense 2:12 is an
admonition to the Thessalonians to 'encourage' each other since Paul is
here describing his own behavior as exemplary. Therefore παραμυθέομαι
is used twice in I Thess in a similar sense but nowhere else in the New
Testament paraenesis. This could suggest again that Paul's composition is
being controlled not merely by the tradition but also by his concern for
the Thessalonian situation.[14]

A third clue that I Thess 5:14-22 may not offer the original traditional
context of the command in 5:15 is found when we consider vv 16ff. The

vv 16-22 are distinguished from the preceding in content and in form. They deal not with relationships between men but with the personal religion of the believer: 'Rejoice always, pray constantly' etc. Dibelius' judgment (see above, p 9) applies well to these verses: they are taken from the tradition and seem to have no special application to the Thessalonian situation.

But if we observe the context of the commands as they occur in other paraenetic contexts we are given no reason to think that they were attached to the command of I Thess 5:15 in the tradition. In Rom 12 the parallels to the command to rejoice (I Thess 5:16 = Rom 12:12a), to pray (I Thess 5:17 = Rom 12:12c) and to hold fast to the good (I Thess 5:21 = Rom 12:9) are *not* directly connected to the command in Rom 12:17a (= I Thess 5:15). The parallels between I Thess 5:14-21 and Phil 4:5-8 may be tabularized as follows:

I Thess	*Phil*[15]
5:14d be patient (μακρο- θυμεῖτε) with all	4:5 let all men know your for- bearance (ἐπιεικές)
5:16 always rejoice	4:4 rejoice in the Lord always and again I say rejoice
5:17 pray without ceasing	4:6 in everything with prayer and supplication . . . let your requests be known to God
5:18 in everything give thanks	4:6 with thanksgiving
5:21 test everything and hold fast to the good	4:8 whatsoever is true . . . think on these things

As the first parallel in this table shows, the admonitions of I Thess 5:16-21 may have been connected with an admonition on patience or forbearance in the tradition. Were this the case, I Thess 5:15 would thus be a redactional insertion into the traditional unit. But this is very speculative. Let it suffice to note that we have no evidence outside I Thess 5 that I Thess 5:15 was transmitted in its present context.

The best evidence that the form of I Thess 5:15 is due to the hand of Paul and not to the tradition is found in the verse itself. To this we now turn our attention.

Given the agreement of Rom 12:17a and I Pt 3:9a on the participial form of ἀποδιδόντες plus the traditional character of the imperative participle, we have a good case against the originality of ἀποδῷ in I Thess 5:15a. Paul's form of the verb is accounted for by its subordination to the verb ὁρᾶτε. The inference then that ὁρᾶτε is to be attributed to Paul and not to the tradition finds support in the observation that this kind of construction is less characteristic of the New Testament paraenetic material than it is a frequent stylistic device of Paul.[16] Besides injecting this initial verb ὁρᾶτε Paul (we may suppose) employs the subject τις and dative object τινι. Is it possible to explain these redactional variations from the context in I Thess 5?

We must decide first whether ὁρᾶτε is addressed to the leaders of the church referred to in v 12 (τοὺς κοπιῶντας ἐν ὑμῖν καὶ προϊσταμένους ὑμῶν)[17] or whether it is addressed to the congregation as a whole.[18] For Paul's construction would be explained if the presence of ὁρᾶτε here was intended to remind the leaders to watch over the congregation lest the members avenge themselves. However, the relationship between the two halves of v 15 seems to be decisive here against this view. The ἀλλά following ἀποδῷ introduces the positive counterpart either of ὁρᾶτε or of ἀποδῷ; since διώκετε is indicative like ὁρᾶτε and not subjunctive like ἀποδῷ, the ἀλλά sentence is grammatically the counterpart of ὁρᾶτε. But from the meaning it is obvious that Paul intends to give the positive counterpart not of overseeing the church (ὁρᾶτε) but of rendering evil for evil (ἀποδῷ). The conclusion, therefore, is that ὁρᾶτε is to be taken not as a separate command to the leaders but as united with ἀποδῷ and thus addressing the whole church.[19] The command would thus read, 'All of you take heed lest someone avenge another.'

But if Paul is addressing the whole church why did he not merely say μὴ ἀποδίδοτε κακὸν ἀντὶ κακοῦ? Why the extra verb, and why particularly ὁράω which he uses nowhere else in this way? The three closest analogies to this construction, where Paul uses βλέπω instead of ὁράω (I Cor 8:9; 10:12; Gal 5:15), constitute warnings to the church of unexpected pitfalls. Paul attempts to alert them to an incipient error to which they may be oblivious. We may only surmise from this that in addressing the Thessalonians whose particular problem was idleness or disorderliness (ἀτάκτους, 5:14; 4:11f) and faintheartedness (ὀλιγοψύχους, 5:14) Paul considered it especially needful to make a special call for alertness as he brought this section of his exhortations to a climax with this command against revenge in 5:15. The preference of ὁράω over βλέπω may have merely stemmed from the stylistic desire for assonance (note the 'o' and 'a' sounds in the preceding and following phrases). As for the use of τις and τινι, we can only guess that if Paul's intention really was to create a special alertness to this command, the insertion of the unusual τις and τινι in the familiar traditional phrase (μὴ ἀποδιδόντες κακὸν ἀντὶ κακοῦ) would probably elicit even more attention as well as sharpening the individual thrust of the demand.[20] Since I Thess 5:15a has proved to be so heavily redactional we must wait until we examine Rom 12:17a and I Pt 3:9a before we determine the precise form of the tradition.

We must now ask whether I Thess 5:15b (ἀλλὰ πάντοτε τὸ ἀγαθὸν διώκετε εἰς ἀλλήλους καὶ εἰς πάντας) or some core of it was attached to the command against revenge (5:15a) which Paul found in the tradition. Portions of this positive command are probably Paul's own additions for this particular letter. In the first place, the phrase εἰς ἀλλήλους καὶ εἰς πάντας occurs only once again in the New Testament and that is in 3:12 of this same epistle: 'May the Lord make you increase and abound in love εἰς ἀλλήλους καὶ εἰς πάντας.' The absence of this phrase from the other New Testament paraenetic material and its double occurrence in I Thess point to its occasional rather than to its traditional character. This is not to say that ἀλλήλους or πάντας could not have been found in this connection in the tradition (ἀλλήλους: Rom 12:10,16; 13:8; I Pt 4:9; 5:5; πάντας: Rom 12:17b,18; Phil 4:5), it is merely to say that the present combined construction is probably Paul's own formulation for this occasion.[21] In the second place, the occurrence of πάντοτε may possibly be viewed as Paul's attempt to bring this command into line with the abundant use of πᾶς or πάντοτε in 5:14d,16 (ἀδιαλείπτως, v 17), 18,21,22. However, since one of the features of traditional paraenesis is superficial catchword connections,[22] this chain of words could itself point to the original traditional coherence of these exhortations. Whether πάντοτε in 5:15b was an original element of the tradition or was Paul's own contribution remains open. Most important is whether the positive command τὸ ἀγαθὸν διώκετε was found by Paul in the tradition already attached to the negative command against revenge (v 15a).

To answer this question we may notice first that the command τὸ ἀγαθὸν διώκετε is not attached to the command against revenge in either Rom 12:17a or in I Pt 3:9a. If it had originally been attached to this command, it has been dropped in these two texts. Yet it is precisely these two texts which follow most closely the tradition of the command against revenge. In both Rom 12:17 and I Pt 3:9 the negative command *is* followed by a positive one, but in each case it is different (Rom 12:17b, προνοούμενοι καλὰ ἐνώπιον πάντων ἀνθρώπων;[23] I Pt 3:9b, τοὐναντίον δὲ εὐλογοῦντες). Secondly, we may notice that the two words ἀγαθός and διώκειν are common in the paraenetic material, and that their use probably stems from Ps 33:15 (LXX) which is quoted from the LXX with only minor grammatical changes in I Pt 3:11:[24]

Let him turn away from evil and do good,
ἐκκλινάτω δὲ ἀπὸ κακοῦ καὶ ποιησάτω ἀγαθόν,

let him seek peace and pursue it.

ζητησάτω εἰρήνην καὶ διωξάτω αὐτήν.

Both the command to do good[25] (ποιησάτω ἀγαθόν) and the command to pursue peace[26] (διωξάτω αὐτήν) became integral constituents of the paraenetic tradition. The poetic parallelism between *pursuing* peace and doing *good* in Ps 33:15 (LXX) is certainly enough to suggest Paul's combined construction 'pursue good'. Whether it had been suggested to someone before him, we have no way to be sure. Therefore, while the vocabulary and, as we shall see later, the attachment of a positive command to the command against revenge are traditional, the precise wording of this verse cannot be assigned to the tradition with much certainty.

B. Rom 12:17 and I Pt 3:9

Turning now to a treatment of Rom 12:17 and I Pt 3:9 we may orient ourselves in the discussion with a short critique of a recent attempt to determine the tradition behind Rom 12:14–21.

In an article entitled 'Tradition and Redaction in Romans 12:9–21' (1969) Charles Talbert attempts to show that, in accord with David Daube's general thesis, there is a primitive Semitic code (composed of vv 19a, 16a, 17a, 18, 19a, and 21) behind Rom 12:14–21 into which a Hellenistic redactor, probably Paul, has inserted Hellenistic material (namely 14, 15, 16c, 17b, 19b) (p 91). If his conclusions are correct he will have provided us with a fixed traditional context for the command in Rom 12:17a.

Talbert describes four problems which he says make it virtually impossible for 12:14–21 in its present form to go back to a Semitic source (p 87). (1) He sees echoes of the sayings of Jesus in vv 14, 17a, 18, 19a, but such sayings are unlikely to occur in such a code formulated in Palestine because 'the use of a form of language for Jesus' sayings which was associated in a Semitic milieu with rules of derived and secondary authority [namely, the imperative participle] would be an acute problem for the Semitic church' (p 88). (2) Vv 14ff 'contain a large number of perfectly acceptable Greek forms for the imperative' (p 88). (3) The quotations from the Old Testament are primarily from the LXX (p 88). (4) 'The presence of Greek link words . . . presents yet another problem for any theory of a Semitic source' (p 89). Talbert's methodology of determining what is traditional and what is redactional is to say that any part of 12:14–21 against which two or more of these objections can be raised must be peeled away and regarded as redaction (p 90). The result is that he discovers a two-strophe pattern of three lines each which he considers to be more likely a fragment of a traditional code than a coincidence.

In spite of the splendid clarity which characterizes Talbert's work, I find his reconstruction unconvincing for the following reasons. In trying to explain the redaction one must claim either that Paul took a fixed well-structured two-strophe code and at random stuck in other exhortations or that he consciously chose and inserted his material with a new structure in mind. The first alternative is highly unlikely. Talbert opts for the second. He maintains, 'The result of this redaction of the Semitic code was a well-ordered paragraph' (p 93). This, I submit, is simply not true. To illustrate: he says that verses 14 and 21, which are concerned with returning good for evil, form an inclusion. But there is no mention of good and evil in v 14 whereas v 9 forms a closer parallel to v 21. He says vv 16–21 form an a (v 16) b (v 17) a' (v 18) b' (vv19–20) pattern, the 'a' being commands relating to living in harmony, the 'b' being commands against revenge. But v 15 is left completely unexplained and v 17b is slipped in with 17a when it really means something quite different.[27]

A serious problem lies in Talbert's criterion for eliminating redactional material. He conceded that each one of the four objections (listed above) to a Semitic origin of vv 14–21 as they stand is not in itself prohibitive. Therefore his criterion is that redactional material must be opposed by *two* objections. While it is not altogether illegitimate, yet it is at least questionable to claim that two indecisive arguments make a decisive one. The peculiar result of this criterion reveals, I think, its inadequacy: he eliminates as redactional v 14 because (1) it echoes the words of Jesus, and (2) has Greek imperatives (p 91), while he retains as traditional v 17a, just as much a saying of Jesus, and v 21 which contains two Greek imperatives. The problem can be seen from another angle when we look at v 17b. It is excluded 'because of the use of the LXX text and the Greek link words made possible by the insertion of πάντων . . .' (p 90). This verse he says 'comes from Hellenistic or Greek-speaking Christianity' (p 91). But nowhere does he explain why we have here a Semitic imperative participle which does not stem from the LXX. In fact he says (p 87) it is very unlikely that Paul himself would convert Greek imperatives into imperative participles. For these reasons I think Talbert's attempt to determine a fixed Semitic code behind Rom 12:14–21 has failed. He has made more obvious than ever the complexity of the background of the passage and the curious inter-mingling of Hellenistic and Semitic influence.

If we have become skeptical about the existence of such a fixed ethical code behind Rom 9:14–21 as Talbert suggests, we must now press on either to confirm or to contradict this skepticism by our own limited cross-sectional method of investigation. We will do this indirectly by continuing our quest for the traditional form of the command behind I Thess 5:15; Rom 12:17; and I Pt 3:9.

We observed earlier that the similarities between Rom 12:17a and I Pt 3:9a point not to literary dependence but to a common tradition behind both verses (cf pp 7–8). In treating I Thess 5:15 we tried to establish that the form which this common tradition received in I Thess 5:15 is not its traditional form, but rather the traditional form must be sought in the wording of Rom 12:17a and I Pt 3:9a. On the basis, therefore, of the elements common to both Rom 12:17a and I Pt 3:9a we may conclude that the original form of the tradition contained the phrase κακὸν ἀντὶ κακοῦ along with the imperative participle ἀποδιδόντες and a negating particle (see the table p 6).

Which of these two texts preserves the tradition more precisely: Rom 12:17a (μηδενὶ κακὸν ἀντὶ κακοῦ ἀποδιδόντες) or I Pt 3:9a (μὴ ἀποδιδόντες κακὸν ἀντὶ κακοῦ)? Decisive in answering this question is the occurrence in Joseph and Asenath 28:4 of the form which we have in I Pt 3:9. (See Chapter 2, pp 37-9 for a discussion of the Jewish-Hellenistic background of this command.) We must, of course, reckon with the possibility that this traditional exhortation had itself undergone some variation and specification so that it may have existed in a number of similar forms. It is possible then that the minor alterations found in Rom 12:17a are due not to Paul, but to a variant of the tradition.

We focus now on the remaining commands of I Pt 3:9 (ἢ λοιδορίαν ἀντὶ λοιδορίας, τοὐναντίον δὲ εὐλογοῦντες), referred to now as v 9b. The key parallel here is I Cor 4:12: 'When reviled we bless, when persecuted we endure, when slandered we try to conciliate.' Paul describes his response to opposition with the words λοιδορούμενοι εὐλογοῦμεν, 'when reviled we bless.' He adds that he is writing this to 'admonish' them (v 14) and he urges them to 'imitate' him (v 16), and then he refers to his 'ways in Christ' (v 17) which he 'teaches everywhere in all the churches' (v 17). Probably, therefore, λοιδορούμενοι εὐλογοῦμεν reflects the catechetical teaching common among all the churches. The combination of λοιδορίαν and εὐλογοῦντες in I Pt 3:9b is almost certainly, then, traditional. Moreover, on the basis of I Pt 3:9 we may suppose that the connection of the command not to return evil for evil with the command to bless is also traditional. An analysis of Rom 12:14-17 supports this supposition.

Rom 12:14-17 reads:

Bless those who persecute you, bless and do not curse. (15) Rejoice with those who rejoice, weep with those who weep. (16) Be of one mind among yourselves; do not set your mind on high things, but be carried away with the lowly. Don't think yourselves wise. (17) Render to no one evil for evil but take thought for what is good before all men.

Michel observes, 'Between v 16 and v 17 there is no bridge, but rather v 14 and vv 17-21 are closely connected to each other. While v 16 has relations within the church in view, v 14 and vv 17–21 are admonitions of a more general kind with a stronger traditional connection; they put relations with non-Christians in the foreground.'[28] It is not unlikely, therefore, that vv 14 and 17 were originally connected in the paraenetic tradition and that v 14 was drawn away from v 17 because of the catchword connection between v 13 (τὴν φιλοξενίαν διώκοντες) and v 14 (εὐλογεῖτε τοὺς διώκοντας). Thus there is no evidence either from Rom 12:17 or from I Pt 3:9 or from I Thess 5:15 that the command μὴ ἀποδιδόντες κακὸν ἀντὶ κακοῦ ever circulated among the churches without a positive counterpart (such as 'bless' or 'pursue good toward all').

From all of this I would propose that the situation was something like the following. The saying μὴ ἀποδιδόντες κακὸν ἀντὶ κακοῦ became a fixed rule early in the Christian paraenetic tradition. As the community reflected upon this rule and endeavored to apply it to life-situations a process of specification occurred. Κακὸν ἀντὶ κακοῦ is defined more closely, for example in I Pt 3:9b, as λοιδορίαν ἀντὶ λοιδορίας. Another example is Polycarp (2:2) who, after quoting I Pt 3:9, adds ἢ γρόνθον ἀντὶ γρόνθου ἢ κατάραν ἀντὶ κατάρας ('blow for blow, curse for curse'). Along with this specification of the negative side, that is, what must *not* be repaid, there was probably a corresponding specification of the appropriate Christian response to these specific forms of opposition. We have already seen the εὐλογοῦντες of I Pt 3:9b (cf Rom 12:14) and the τὸ ἀγαθὸν διώκετε of I Thess 5:15b, to which may now be added the closely connected command to 'seek peace' (I Pt 3:11; Rom 12:18; I Thess 5:13; see note 26) and the extended list in I Cor 4:12ff: 'when reviled we bless, when persecuted we endure, when slandered we try to conciliate.'

IV. Conclusion

In conclusion, this portion of our study has turned up the following information. The command μὴ ἀποδιδόντες κακὸν ἀντὶ κακοῦ belongs to the early Christian paraenetic tradition. This command was probably taught in close connection with certain specifications such as λοιδορίαν ἀντὶ λοιδορίας as we have, for example, in I Pt 3:9. These negative commands were always accompanied by a positive counterpart and here is where the emphasis fell. This must be stressed for, as we shall see, in this consists the distinction between the New Testament command of enemy love and many similar commands in the environment of the early church. The negative command to renounce retaliation is never found in the New Testament paraenesis without a positive command of some sort. The command to bless was a certain constituent of the tradition, as seen from I Pt 3:9; I Cor 4:12; Rom 12:14; Lk 6:27; and was versatile enough to counter a wide variety of antagonisms. Other such positive traditional commands in the immediate context of the prohibition of revenge were very likely 'pursue/do good toward all' (see note 25) and 'pursue peace' or 'live at peace' (see note 26).

Our study has not encouraged us to postulate fixed codes (such as Talbert sees) behind the New Testament paraenesis. Rather there appears to have been a fund of oral traditional material systematized only loosely under different themes (e.g., church order, behavior toward Christians, behavior toward non-Christians, personal piety). In these thematic groupings there was apparently much variation. From this fund of paraenetic material the New Testament writers with whom we are concerned drew out what was useful and within certain essential limitations adapted it freely.

2

THE ORIGIN OF THE COMMAND OF ENEMY LOVE IN THE NEW TESTAMENT PARAENETIC TRADITION

I. The Question and the Approach

The question I will try to answer in this chapter is whether or not the elements of the New Testament paraenetic tradition, determined in Chapter 1, do *in fact* rest in some way on Jesus' command of enemy love. My approach here is to pursue an investigation of the teaching on enemy love in the environment of the early church which may have influenced the formation of the New Testament paraenesis. This investigation culminates with the interrelated attempts to determine, on the one hand, the genuineness and scope of Jesus' command of enemy love and, on the other hand, its relation to the corresponding elements in the New Testament paraenesis.

This investigation has brought up far more questions than can be answered in the limited space available here. In a number of cases the complex problems of origin and composition make it very difficult to draw even probable conclusions about the relationship between certain documents (e.g., the Testaments of the XII Patriarchs and the Slavonic Book of Enoch) and the early Christian paraenetic tradition. Where this is so I have been very hesitant to make any remarkable claims even if the subject matter suggests fascinating possibilities. Others who have more expertise than I can at these points pursue the matter further.

The documents discussed were not read with a view toward their teaching on love, but rather with a view toward their teaching on how *enemies* (in a broad sense) should be treated. Documents which have nothing very explicit to say on this are not included. The investigation begins with the pervasive Hellenistic philosophy, Stoicism. It is unique among the possible spheres of influence discussed, in that it in no way emerges from Old Testament thought or tradition. We focus next on the Old Testament upon which, in various degrees of directness, the rest of the documents depend.

In treating the relation between the Old Testament and the New Testament paraenetic tradition we should be aware that the Old Testament's influence impinged upon the early church in more than one way. Alongside the direct influence of the Old Testament canon were its scribal interpretation and elaboration (which reached the ordinary people in the synagogues), its peculiar adaptations in contemporary movements like Qumran, its absorption into the other intertestamental literature and its formation of the unwritten inherited piety of the people. However, it is beyond the scope of this work to trace each Old Testament statement on enemy love through the various channels by which it may have come to the early church. Rather, my procedure has been to treat the Old Testament as a direct influence but also to stay alert in my investigation of the other documents for instances where explicit Old Testament material has been preserved or has been taken up and given a new form. At such points the traditional connections will be brought out (see especially Joseph and Asenath, and Qumran).

Following the discussion of the Old Testament material come the spheres of Hellenistic and Palestinian Judaism, the latter being divided into the works inside and outside the influence of Qumran. With regard to the locale of the documents discussed, the consensus of the standard introductory works has been followed.

II. Hellenistic Philosophy

Here I intend no survey of all the Greek ethical systems. Rather I will restrict myself to that ethical school, the teachings of which could most immediately have influenced the young church in the formation of the paraenetic tradition, namely, the school of the Stoics. Stoicism had spread throughout the empire before the birth of Jesus and there is little doubt that the soil from which the church sprang up had been watered by the Stoic philosophy.[1] The ethics of the classical era of Greek philosophy were not only temporally at a greater distance from the first century, but they also had a 'lower' view of enemy love than did the Stoics.[2] Epicureanism, which Max Pohlenz describes as 'der weltanschauliche Antipode'[3] of Stoicism, was too contrary to Christian teaching to be a source of paraenetic material.[4] It is generally recognized 'that among all the manifold philosophical views of life which stamped the Greek world, none stood nearer to Christianity than the Stoic view.'[5]

Leaving aside the earlier Stoics (Zeno, *c*. 336-263 B.C.; Cleanthes, *c*. 331-232 B.C.; Chrysippus, *c*. 280-205 B.C.; Posidonius, *c*. 135-51 B.C.) and those after the New Testament period (e.g., Marcus Aurelius, A.D. 121-180), our focus will be on the two main representatives of Stoic thought who flourished in the first century A.D.: Epictetus of Hierapolis (*c*. A.D. 55-135) and Lucius Annaeus Seneca (*c*. 4 B.C.-A.D. 65).

A. Seneca

The dates of Seneca's birth and death plus his activity in Rome could make one wonder whether a direct contact between him and the Christians existed. Such a contact, however, cannot be asserted on the basis of the evidence: nowhere does Seneca mention the Christians[6] and the alleged correspondence between Paul and Seneca which has come down to us is of little historical value.[7] Our investigation of his views on enemy love will confirm (at least) the ethical distance between the two men.

Perhaps the most commonly quoted passage with regard to enemy love is *De Otio* 1.4 where the Stoics say: 'We shall engage in affairs to the very end of life, we shall never cease to work for the common good, to help each and all, to give aid even to our enemies when our hand is feeble with age.'[8] To this we may add the instruction in *De Beneficiis* VII.30.2 and 5:

> And so let your thoughts follow this trend: 'He has not repaid me with gratitude: what shall I do?' Do as the gods, those glorious authors of all things, do, they begin to give benefits to him who knows them not, and persist in giving them to those who are ungrateful . . . Let us imitate them: let us give even if many of our gifts have been given in vain; none the less let us give to still others, nay, even to those at whose hands we have suffered loss.

However, as a norm for determining right behaviour the imitation of the gods is secondary and relative, as the following discussion of the same problem shows (*De Beneficiis* IV.26):

> If you are imitating the gods, you say, 'then bestow benefits also upon the ungrateful; for the sun rises also upon the wicked, and the sea lies open to pirates (*nam et sceleratis sol oritur et piratis patent maria*).' This point raises the question whether a good man would bestow a benefit upon one who was ungrateful, knowing that he was ungrateful . . . Understand that according to the system of the Stoics, there are two classes of ungrateful persons. One man is ungrateful because he is a fool . . . Another man is ungrateful, and this is the common meaning of the term, because he has a natural tendency to this vice. To an ingrate of this first type . . . a good man will give his benefit . . . To the ingrate of the second type . . . he will no more give a benefit than he will lend money to a spendthrift, or entrust a deposit to a man whom many have already found false.

One does not just do what the gods do. One calculates what kind of person he is dealing with and treats him appropriately. There are some persons to whom it is simply not fitting to give benefits. But we cannot overlook that at times Seneca insists that one should not return evil for evil. The instances are numerous. For example in *De Ira* II.32.1ff we read:

> 'But of course there is some pleasure in anger,' you say, 'and it is sweet to return a smart.' Not at all; for it is not honorable as in acts of kindness to requite benefits so to requite injuries with injuries. In the one case it is shameful to be outdone, in the other not to be outdone. 'Revenge' is an inhuman word and yet one accepted as legitimate; and 'retaliation' is not much different except in rank; the man who returns a smart commits merely the more pardonable sin.

On the surface this sounds much like the Christian teaching on enemy love. But what lies behind this concern to be 'honorable' (*honestus*)? And in what sense is it 'shameful' (*turpis*) to be outdone? The immediately following illustration of Seneca's ideal man, Marcus Cato, reveals the proper understanding of the preceding quotation.

> Once when Marcus Cato was in the public bath, a certain man, not knowing him struck him unwittingly . . . Later when the man was making apology, Cato said, 'I did not recall that I received a blow.' It is better, he thought, to ignore the incident than to resent it . . . Only a great soul can be superior to injury; the most humiliating kind of revenge is to have it appear that the man was not worth taking revenge upon . . . He is a great and noble man who acts as does the lordly wild beast that listens unconcernedly to the baying of tiny dogs.[9]

Evidently it is 'honorable' to disdain the lowly and foolish man who cannot control his passions as Cato can, and to requite him by humiliation, and above all to preserve and manifest the lofty tranquility of 'the great and noble man'.

With this we hit upon the motivating force of Seneca's ethics: good and wise behavior is behavior that springs from and thus displays mastery over one's passions and a freedom from external threats and rewards. The cultivation and exercise of such mastery is the aim of the good life and the only way to peace and happiness. How one behaves toward friend or foe is simply a reflex of the 'great soul's' calculation of how to be master of the situation and thus stay unperturbed. This concern with one's own self may be further illustrated by Seneca's argument against hate in *De Ira* III.42.3,4; III.43.1,2:

> Why do we, forgetting our weaknesses, take up the huge burden of hate, and, easily broken as we are, rise up to break? Soon a fever or some

other bodily ill will stay that war of hatred which we now wage with such unrelenting purpose. Soon death will step in and part the fiercest pair of fighters . . . That hour you appoint for the death of another is perchance near your own.

Why do you not rather gather up your brief life and render it a peaceful one to yourself and all others? Why do you not rather make yourself beloved by all while you live and regretted by all when you die? . . . Why do you try with all your might to crush the man who rails against you, a low and contemptible fellow but sharp-tongued and troublesome to his betters? Why are you angry? . . . Wait a little. Behold death comes who will make you equals . . . Can you wish for the victim of your wrath a greater ill than death? . . . You waste your pains if you wish to do what needs must be.[10]

Should a wise man render evil for evil, injury for injury? Seneca would say the question is wrongly conceived. The question is: Can a wise man be injured in the first place?

'What then,' you will say, 'will there be no one who will attempt to do the wise man injury?' Yes, the attempt will be made but the injury will not reach him. For the distance which separates him from contact with his inferiors is so great that no baneful force can extend its power all the way to him (*De Constantia* 4.1).

Belonging to this 'distance' above one's 'inferiors' is an appropriate scorn which we saw already in Cato: 'Whoever scorns his tormentors removes himself from the common herd and towers above them. The mark of true greatness is not to notice that you have received a blow' (*De Ira* III.25.3).[11] How is it to be explained that the wise man cannot be injured? It is very logical: 'That which injures must be more powerful than that which is injured; but wickedness is not stronger than righteousness; therefore it is impossible for the wise man to be injured' (*De Constantia* 7.2). Or to look at it from another angle, 'the wise man can lose nothing. He has everything invested in himself' (*De Constantia* 5.4). Should a man return evil for evil? The answer is evident: 'The really great mind, the mind that has taken the true measure of itself, fails to revenge injury only because it fails to perceive it' (*De Ira* III.5.8).

What is liable to go unnoticed is that the wise man 'fails to perceive' injury *only* in the sense that he is not perturbed or unsettled by it. He indeed *does* perceive it in the sense that he knows that a common rascal has done a reprehensible thing. Therefore it is not too surprising to read that 'The wise man . . . will admonish them and inflict suffering and punishment not because he has received an injury but because they have committed one, and in order that they may desist from doing so' (*De Constantia* 12.3; 13.1). Again it is evident that how one treats his enemy is quite secondary to the overarching concern to maintain a sovereign tranquility of mind. Such a stance relativizes interpersonal ethics in such a way that Seneca, when discussing the problem of how to overcome the anger of another, can say, 'Some matters are cured only by deception' (*De Ira* III.39.4), and can assert that 'if any man's power is so great that he can assail anger from an eminent position, let him deal with it harshly' (*De Ira* III.40.5).

We may now sum up briefly the similarities and differences between Seneca's teaching on enemy love and that of the New Testament paraenesis. Seneca admonishes non-retaliation and good deeds toward one's enemies. This behavior is occasionally based on an imitation of the gods. In this he stands remarkably close to the New Testament. From one standpoint Seneca's ethics may be classified with the admonitions of the wisdom literature, in that he argues from experience and aims to provide insight into how one can lead a happy life. His hero is often called a wise man. The New Testament paraenetic tradition too contains elements of wisdom (cf. Rom 12:16-19).

The paraenetic tradition of the New Testament differs formally from the long reasoned discourse of the Stoics. It is characterized by a concise, staccato style, linking together a chain of short imperatives. The more substantial differences reveal that the similarities mentioned above are superficial and do not extend to the essence of the New Testament paraenesis. The paraenesis starts from the *mercies of God* in Christ (Rom 12:1,2) which the Christian has encountered and by which he has been transformed. This unique Christian starting point gives rise to a deep divergence from the Stoics in motive and eventually in conduct.

We saw that for Seneca 'the principal motive behind the conduct he advocates is always the keeping intact of the wise man's inner imperturbability. In Seneca every description of the wise man's conduct towards those who abuse, insult or do him an injustice only serves to magnify the inviolate wise man who is raised far above common mortals.'[12] But the paraenetic tradition of the New Testament has no praise for Seneca's 'great soul' or 'noble man.' On the contrary the man who loves aright is 'not boastful or puffed up' (I Cor 13:4), he is 'not high minded but is concerned with the lowly' (Rom 12:16). He 'weeps with those who weep' (Rom 12:15). In the New Testament paraenesis love is not motivated by a concern for one's own greatness and nobility. It is motivated by the freeing mercies of God and the concern is for the other person's good. While

Seneca's wise man may ignore, humiliate, punish and deceive his enemy, the Christian is commanded with regard to his enemy, do not render evil for evil but do good, bless, seek peace.

B. *Epictetus*

In his book *Epiktet und das Neue Testament,* Adolf Bonhoeffer says that his criterion for gathering parallels between Epictetus and the New Testament was not in 'the verbal correspondences which force themselves on us' but was rather the 'relationship of thought lying deep within and penetrating to the center of the whole life-view.'[13] It is highly instructive, therefore, that the best parallel he can find to I Pt 3:9: 'Do not repay evil for evil or reviling for reviling' (λοιδορίας) is *Encheiridion* 42: 'If therefore you start from this point of view, you will be gentle with the man who reviles (τὸν λοιδοροῦντα) you.' The 'point of view' referred to, from which this gentleness springs, is the awareness that the reviler is mistaken and 'the man that suffers is the man who has been deceived.'[14] In other words the good man will not be harsh with those unlike himself 'because he knows well the saying of Plato, that "every soul is unwillingly deprived of the truth"' (*Discourses* I.22.36).

The 'deep lying' disparity between Epictetus and the New Testament paraenetic tradition is unmistakable. Plato's quote stands in diametrical opposition to Paul's conception of men's ignorance: 'They hold down the truth in unrighteousness' (Rom 1:18). The Christian's love for his enemy is not grounded in any amelioration of the enemy's evil.

Another difference between Epictetus and the New Testament paraenesis is that gentleness toward an enemy generally has the purpose of cultivating the 'moral purpose' (προαίρεσις) of the Stoic rather than achieving the good of the enemy (cf Mt 5:44; Lk 6:28, 35; Rom 12:14; 1 Thess 5:15 etc.). Epictetus advises the Procurator of Epirus who had taken the side of a comic actor and thereby incurred the reviling of the citizens: 'No one is dearer to me than myself; it is absurd, therefore, for me to let myself be hurt in order that another man may win a victory as a common actor' (*Discourses* III.4.9). And if I cannot avoid being reviled, I can still make good use of the occasion to train my own character:

Is it possible, then, to derive advantage from these things? Yes, from everything. – Even from the man who reviles me? – And what good does his wrestling-companion do the athlete? The very greatest. So also my reviler becomes one who prepares me for my contest, he exercises my patience, my dispassionateness, my gentleness (*Discourses* III.20.9).

While there is some similarity here to a text like Rom 5:3ff, nevertheless, unlike the New Testament, 'dispassionate' is here the key word. Indeed when Epictetus reaches for a metaphor to picture his ideal, his choice is a stone: 'Take your stand by a stone and revile it; and what effect will you produce? If, then, a man listens like a stone, what profit is there to the reviler?' (*Discourses* I.25.29). So it is with the man who has learned the lesson of the philosophers:

> He will feel no pain, no anger, no compulsion, no hindrance but . . . will pass [his life] in tranquility and in freedom from every disturbance . . . He contemplates and reflects; 'Now no evil can befall me, for me there is no such thing as an earthquake, everything is full of peace, everything full of tranquility; every road, every city, every fellow-traveller, neighbor, companion, all are harmless' (*Discourses* III.13.11, 13).[15]

As with Seneca the important thing is not so much to avoid avenging an insult or injury; what is really important is to be so completely the master of yourself that you cannot be insulted or injured.[16]

It is against this background that we should probably understand Epictetus' commendation of enemy love in the true Cynic:

> For this too is a very pleasant strand woven into the Cynic's pattern of life; he must needs be flogged like an ass, and while he is being flogged he must love ($\phi\iota\lambda\epsilon\hat{\iota}\nu$) the men who flog him, as though he were the father or brother of them all (*Discourses* III.22.54).

It is difficult to know in just what sense this love is meant. To give Epictetus the benefit of the doubt we could argue from *Discourses* III.22.81, 82 that the Cynic has a real concern for the best welfare of his enemy:

> Man, the Cynic has made all mankind his children . . . ; in that spirit he approaches them all and *cares for them all* ($\pi\acute{\alpha}\nu\tau\omega\nu\ \kappa\acute{\eta}\delta\epsilon\tau\alpha\iota$). Or do you fancy that it is in the spirit of idle impertinence he reviles those he meets. It is as a father he does it, as a brother and as a servant of Zeus, who is Father of us all.

But this concern for the good of the enemy seems greatly overshadowed by the delight the Cynic takes in appearing sovereignly serene in adversity.[17] One could also add that this particular motive of the familial bond with all humanity is foreign to the New Testament which pictures a new humanity and brotherhood in Christ. Yet there is at least a superficial parallel between the Cynic's acting as the servant and son of Zeus and the Christian's acting as his Father in heaven (Mt 5:45, 48; I Pt 1:14f).

Bonhoeffer assesses the relation between Epictetus and the New Testament so: 'At one point in its social ethics Christianity seems to deserve superiority over the Stoics, namely in its practice of active deeds of neighbor love.'[18] His judgment that Epictetus possesses a disposition which is completely free of hate and vengefulness exactly to the same degree as the New Testament[19] may be misleading unless one remembers Epictetus' metaphor of the stone: it too is completely free of hate and vengefulness. Our investigation of Epictetus' teaching on enemy love has shown it to be not essentially different from Seneca's. We have seen certain external similarities between the Stoics and the early Christian paraenetic tradition but are not able to speak of any kind of dependence or deeper harmony.

III. The Old Testament

There is no question that the early church drew from the Old Treatment in forming its paraenetic tradition concerning enemy love. The tradition which we isolated in the preceding chapter contains explicit Old Testament elements and stands in loose relation to Old Testament quotations: Rom 12:16b = Prov 3:7 (Is 5:21); Rom 12:17a = Prov 17:13;[20] Rom 12:17b = Prov 3:4 (LXX); Rom 12:19b = Dt 32:35; Rom 12:20 = Prov 25:21f; I Pt 3:10–12 = Ps 34 (LXX 33): 12–16.[21] Therefore, the following investigation of the Old Testament's teaching on enemy love does not aim to determine whether the Old Testament *was* a source for the New Testament paraenesis; rather the aim is to determine whether the Old Testament as a source is adequate to account for the understanding of enemy love in the New Testament paraenetic tradition.

The *meanings of the words* 'love' and 'hate' should not be rigidly predetermined, for, as the following discussion shows, the immediate context is all-important in discovering the intention behind the concept of love and hate in the Old Testament. It is appropriate, however, to keep in mind that the connotations of love and hate which we bring to the text from our own experience may not correspond to the meaning intended by the Old Testament author. We must be open to that which is new for us if we hope to learn from, rather than distort, the Old Testament. The articles by Quell[22] and Michel[23] in *TDNT* are helpful to this end.

We may mention briefly several dimensions of love and hate in the Old Testament in order to give some idea of the range of meanings. The *active side* of love is seen in such favorite combinations as: to love Yahweh and keep his commandments (Ex 20:6; Dt 5:10; 7:9; 11:1; I Kg 3:3; Dan 9:4; Neh 1:5); to love him and serve him (Dt 10:12; 11:13; Is 56:6); or to love him and walk in his ways (Dt 10:12; 11:22;

19:9; 30:16; Josh 22:5; 23:11). But while the focus here is on active obedience, *feeling* is not excluded: Jeremiah recalls the days when Israel loved God as a bride (2:2). God is to be loved with all the heart and with all the soul and with all the might (Dt 6:5). In fact, only from a tender heart of flesh, not a heart of stone, can God's commands be obeyed (Ez 11:19; Jer 31:33). 'To love God is to have pleasure in him and to strive impulsively after him' (Quell, p 28). Similarly in human relationships, the active (cf Dt 10:18,19) as well as passionate (II Sam 1:26; Song of Sol 8:6f) side of love is evident.

Similarly, hate can refer to the *active* execution (Mal 1:3) of ill against someone, as well as the *disposition* of heart (Lev 19:17; Dt 4:42; Ps 41:7) from which such action proceeds. What measure of passionate feeling is intended must be determined from the context, for it is possible that 'hate' can mean merely 'love less' as for example in the case of Jacob's 'hate' of Leah (Gen 29:31ff; cf Michel, p 690, note 23f). Similarly in the laws of divorce in Dt 24:1–3, to hate a wife means that she finds no favor in the eyes of her husband, i.e., she is probably an unsatisfactory sexual partner (cf Dt 21:15–17; 22:13). But hate can also include very extreme distaste (II Sam 13:15) and strong desire for someone's total ruin (Ps 139:19–22).

This very brief survey should alert us to the breadth of connotation possible in the words 'love' and 'hate' in the Old Testament, and should sensitize us to the need to be open in our treatment of the various contexts in which the words or the concepts occur.

The Old Testament statements and stories about enemies are very diverse. We will begin with the more positive and proceed toward the negative. In Ex 23:4,5 we find:

> If you meet your enemy's (אֹיִבְךָ/ἐχθροῦ) ox or ass going astray, you shall bring it back to him. If you see the ass of one who hates you (שֹׂנַאֲךָ / ἐχθροῦ) lying under its burden, you shall refrain from leaving him with it, you shall help him to lift it up.

The word for enemy here אֹיֵב (*poēl* of אָיַב) occurs 53 times in the Pentateuch and means uniformly the national enemy of Israel (cf the nearest example, Ex 23:22,27). We shall see, when dealing with Philo (p 39) and the Rabbis (p 48), that these verses have been understood to the effect that one is here seeking his own advantage (Philo) or that the 'enemy' is only another Israelite (Rabbis). Standing alone in its specificity with no ground- or purpose-clause, the command is subject to such (mis-?) interpretations. But Schmauch is surely correct when he describes these verses as 'an embryo of the rule of enemy love.'[24]

Two instances where revenge is denounced are Prov 24:29,

> Do not say, 'I will do to him as he has done to me,
> I will pay the man back for what he has done.'

and I Kings 3:10ff. In the latter instance Solomon has just prayed for wisdom to determine right and wrong and to govern his people well; God responds to his prayer:

> Because you have asked this and have not asked for yourself long life or riches or *the life of your enemies* but have asked for yourself understanding to discern what is right, behold I now do according to your word.

It is significant to note here that God is pleased that Solomon did not *pray* for the destruction of his enemies. This stands in contrast to certain prayers of the psalmists and to King David's attitude on his death bed (see note 30). Nevertheless one could even from this text maintain that revenge is not eliminated but is only less desirable than wisdom.

Another example of positive treatment of the enemy is the book of Jonah. The book is consciously directed against an exclusivism which restricts God's mercy to Israel. It intends to drive home the point that God is 'gracious and merciful, slow to anger, and abounding in steadfast love' *even toward non-Israelites* (4:2). Though the emphasis of the story is on God's love, the implications are obvious for Jonah and men in general. The answer to God's question to Jonah is clear: 'Do you do well to be angry?' (4:4). He does not do well. The conclusion is not ambiguous: Jonah would do well if he, like his Lord, abounded in steadfast love toward his enemies in Nineveh.

Next we may cite Prov 24:17,18:

> Do not rejoice when your enemy falls,
> and let not your heart be glad when he stumbles,[25]
> lest the Lord see it, and be displeased,
> and turn away his anger from him.

Are we to suppose with some that the last line of this proverb ruins the whole thing? Was the wise man really describing a subtle method for securing the destruction of one's enemy? I think not. So interpreted the proverb admonishes a psychological impossibility. Verse 17 demands that *in your heart* you not *desire* the destruction of your enemy (for it is the attainment of what we desire that makes us *glad*). If v 17 excludes the inner disposition that desires the enemy's destruction, then v 18 cannot be an appeal to that disposition. Verse 18 must be understood another way. I would suggest that v 18 supports v 17 in this way: there is a bit of irony; if a man does not obey v 17 but instead exults over his enemy's trouble, God will be displeased with him and he will show this displeasure in a very effective way; he will remove the man's cause of exultation, that is, he will restore the fortunes of the enemy so that the man who exulted will be humiliated for his sin. He who laughs last laughs best, we would say today.

While Prov 24:17f was only a prohibition, Prov 25:21f is a positive command to do good to the enemy and is taken over by Paul in Rom 12:20 almost in its entirety:

Prov 25:21f (LXX)	*Rom 12:20*
ἐὰν πεινᾷ ὁ ἐχθρός σου τρέφε	ἐὰν πεινᾷ ὁ ἐχθρός σου ψώμιζε
αὐτόν, ἐὰν διψᾷ πότιζε αὐτόν,	αὐτὸν ἐὰν διψᾷ, πότιζε αὐτὸν
τοῦτο γὰρ ποιῶν	τοῦτο γὰρ ποιῶν
ἄνθρακας πυρὸς σωρεύσεις	ἄνθρακας πυρὸς σωρεύσεις
ἐπὶ τὴν κεφαλὴν αὐτοῦ	ἐπὶ τὴν κεφαλὴν αὐτοῦ.
ὁ δὲ κύριος ἀνταποδώσει	
σοι ἀγαθά.	

For our present purpose it is important only to notice that the proverb is not taken over in its entirety. Omitted from the Christian paraenesis is that which would suggest that the good deeds are being done for private advantage.

We pose the question next as to the extent of the Old Testament command to love your *neighbor*. The meaning of Lev 19:18 where this well-known command occurs becomes clear when seen in its immediate context:

You shall not go up and down as a tale bearer among your people (בְּעַמֶּיךָ/ἐν τῷ ἔθνει σου),
and you shall not stand forth against the blood of your neighbor (רֵעֶךָ/τοῦ πλησίον σου): I am the Lord.
You shall not hate your brother (אָחִיךָ/τον ἀδελφόν σου) in your heart.
You shall surely reprove your neighbor (עֲמִיתֶךָ/τὸν πλησίον σου), and not bear sin because of him.
You shall not take vengeance nor bear any grudge against the children of your people (בְּנֵי עַמֶּךָ/τοῖς υἱοῖς τοῦ λαοῦ),
but you shall love your neighbor (לְרֵעֲךָ/τὸν πλησίον σου) as yourself: I am the Lord (Lev 19:16–18).

In this context all of the objects of the action are members of the Israelite community. The word רֵעַ/πλησίον occurs twice and in both instances is coordinate with עַמְּךָ, 'your people'. Consequently, there is general agreement that 'neighbor' in Lev 19:18 is a command to love, not men in general, but fellow Israelites.[26] Lev 19:34 then explicitly broadens the object of love:

> The sojourner (הַגֵּר) who sojourns with you will be to you as a native
> (כְּאֶזְרָח, cf Ex 12:19),
> and you shall love him as yourself; for you were strangers in the land of Egypt: I am the Lord your God.

Here again the commandment to love falls short of including the average non-Israelite, for גֵּר denotes a non-Israelite who has become part of the Israelite community.[27]

In order to see this Old Testament teaching on love of the neighbor in its proper perspective the following observations should be made. Dt 10:18,19 offers a close parallel to Lev 19:34:

> He [God] executes justice for the fatherless and the widow, and loves the sojourner, giving him food and clothing. Love the sojourner therefore; for you were sojourners in the land of Egypt.

The two texts are bound together in that they both command love for the sojourner and both refer to the Israelites' sojourn in Egypt. Most important, however, is that the statement in Lev 19:34, 'I am the Lord your God,' has its counterpart in Dt 10:12–22 in a full description of God's love, justice and mighty deeds on behalf of his people. The Israelites are to show the same kindness to the sojourner as God had shown them. Similarly Lev 19 begins with the command, 'You shall be holy; for I the Lord your God am holy.' The repeated phrase 'I am the Lord' (15 times) which follows the individual commands of Lev 19 shows that the intention of the chapter is to give specific instances of how to be holy as God is holy. Accordingly the command to love the neighbor (19:18) and sojourner (19:34) are instances of being holy as God is holy. Seen in the wider context of Dt 10:12–22 this means that the command to love is grounded in the nature of God and the way he acts toward his people. The love which the Israelites are to render is a love which springs from the greater love they have already been shown by God (Dt 10:15ff).

God's love for Israel was free, unmerited by any peculiarity in the people (Dt 7:7,8). One might expect that Israel would conclude that she too should love without placing prior conditions on non-Israelites (cf Jonah). But Israel did not as a rule draw this conclusion. Rather the conclusion was more commonly drawn: since God has established his covenant with us alone and showered his love upon us, it is right that others should place themselves under the terms of his covenant (i.e., take the yoke of the law upon them) before we show them love. We shall see how the Qumran sect follows this line of argument to its vivid conclusion:

love for those in the sect, hate for those outside, *even though* they know themselves totally dependent on God's mercy (1QS 1:9,10; 10: 9–13)!

Looking more closely at what love means in Lev 19:18,34 we see that it is not merely activity but is also a condition of the heart: 'You shall not hate your brother in your heart' (19:17). Accordingly it excludes both the *deed* of vengeance and the bearing of a *grudge* (19:18). Further, it should not be overlooked (as is already hinted in the command not to bear a grudge) that Lev 19:18 does include love of enemies if they are Israelites, that is, personal enemies. Nevertheless, the non-Israelite enemies are not in view in Lev 19.

From this limitation of the love command implied in the term 'neighbor,' we move now to a consideration of those texts where the enemy is the object of hate or destruction.[28] We may begin with Israel's conquest of Canaan. According to Dt, when the people had taken possession of the land and defeated the seven nations greater than themselves, they were to make no covenant with them, show no mercy to them and utterly destroy them (Dt 7:1,2; cf Dt 25:17–19; Ex 34:12). Concerning the Ammonites and Moabites, Israel was not to seek their peace or their prosperity all their days, because they did not offer bread or water to Israel when Israel came out of Egypt (Dt 23:3–6). The word 'hate', however (שָׂנֵא, שָׂטַם) does not occur at all in Dt (or Josh) with reference to enemies. The reason given in Dt for the utter destruction of the enemy is two-fold. First, 'that they may not teach you to do according to all their abominable practices which they have done in the service of their gods, and so to sin against the Lord your God' (Dt 20:18). Second, the destruction is not only a protection of Israel from sin, but also a punishment of the nations for sin: 'Because of these abominable practices the Lord your God is driving them out before you' (Dt 18:12). Since it is *God* who is driving out the enemy, the command to destroy the enemy is a command to be a weapon in God's hands. This is the picture we have of the actual conquest in the book of Joshua. 'One man of you puts to flight a thousand, since it is the Lord your God who fights for you, as he promised you' (Josh 23:10).[29]

We may include here two other texts related to the above only by the theme of conquest. In II Chr 19:2 Jehoshaphat returns from a rather poor showing in battle with the Syrians. Jehu goes out to meet him and rebukes him with the words, 'Should you help the wicked and love those who hate the Lord?' The obvious meaning is that love is a completely inappropriate response to the enemies of God's people. In II Sam 19:6 David is found weeping over his son Absalom whom Joab had killed. He is thus humiliating his servants who were prepared to rejoice over the victory. Joab accuses

David of covering the faces of his servants with shame: 'because you love those who hate you and hate those who love you.'[30]

Turning to the Psalms, the clearest statement on hate which we find is Ps 139:19-22:

> O that thou wouldst slay the wicked, O God,
> and that men of blood would depart from me,
> men who maliciously defy thee,
> who lift themselves up against thee for evil!
> Do I not hate them that hate thee, O Lord?
> and do I not loathe them that rise up against thee?
> I hate them with perfect hatred;
> I count them my enemies.

Here the object of hate is not nations, but individuals, and the cause for the hate is not national allegiance, but religious devotion. The last line, 'I count them my enemies,' discloses the process of the psalmist's thought: he does not hate them because they are his enemies but rather he declares them to be his enemies, i.e., the objects of his hate, because they are already God's enemies. The psalmist seeks to align himself with God,[31] and he subjects himself to God in that he does not seek vengeance himself, but asks God to slay the wicked. For the psalmist the declaration of his hate is the proof of his purity. The psalm begins and ends with the acknowledgment that God searches the heart and knows all of a man's thoughts (vv 3,4,23,24). To hate those who hate God is the negative demonstration of the psalmist's confession (vv 17,18):

> How precious to me are thy thoughts, O God!
> How vast the sum of them!
> If I would count them, they are more than the sand.
> When I awake, I am still with thee.

In the light of this psalm taken alone it would be quite natural for a devout Jew to conclude that to hate the wicked is a virtue, indeed an obligation.

It is not obvious, however, how this pious declaration of hate actually worked itself out in personal relations. If one probes more deeply into the psychology of the Psalms, one encounters a complexity that makes questionable any simple opposition of love and hate. Ps 109 presents the most astounding sequence of maledictions in the psalter. For fifteen verses the psalmist calls down every sort of curse on his accusers. They are a plea for God to act on his behalf (v 21) for he is poor and needy (v 22). If the psalmist does not avenge himself, how does he relate to his enemy? Immediately preceding the table of curses we have these words (vv 4,5):

In return for my love they accuse me,
even as I make prayer for them.
So they reward me evil for good,
and hatred for my love.

Thus we have an expression of the psalmist's love for his enemies side by
side with merciless curses. In Ps 35 we find a similar pattern. The writer
prays (v 1):

Contend, O Lord, with those who contend with me;
fight against those who fight against me!

But as for his own *action* he says (vv 12-14):

They requite me evil for good;
my soul is forlorn.
But I, when they were sick – wore sackcloth,
I afflicted myself with fasting.
I prayed with head bowed on my bosom,
as though I grieved for my friend or my brother.

Thus even the psalms of revenge contain within themselves the diversity
of attitude toward the enemy which we said at the beginning characterizes
the Old Testament as a whole.[32] (On the theological problem see note 54.)

The question we posed at the start was: Can the Old Testament as a
source account for the understanding of enemy love in the New Testament paraenesis? In answer to this we may draw the following conclusions.

We have no grounds for asserting that the God of the New Testament is
any other than the God of the Old Testament – a God of mercy *and* of
judgment who, in the end, does indeed take vengeance on his enemies
(Rom 2:8; 12:19; Rev 20:9,15; Mt 13:30). The difference between the Old
and New Testaments does not consist in any weakening of a proper
abhorrence of evil by God and man (Rom 12:9).[33] Moreover we have seen
the seeds of enemy love sown widely in the Old Testament (Ex 23:4f; Prov
24:29; I Kg 3:10; Jonah; Prov 24:17f; 25:21f; Dt 10:18f etc.), some of
which have taken root in the New Testament paraenesis (e.g. Prov 25:21f
= Rom 12:20; Prov 17:13 = Rom 12:17; Ps 34:12-16 = I Pt 3:10-12 etc.).
What is unique in the New Testament paraenesis is the new eschatological
context in which the teachings on enemy love are put (cf Rom 1:1,2; I
Thess 5:1-10; I Pt 1:13; 2:9f) and the selective use of the Old Testament
(see on Prov 25:21f; p 30) to avoid possible misunderstandings to which
the Old Testament admixture of love and hate was so susceptible (cf
rabbinic teaching, p 48). As a source the Old Testament alone cannot

entirely account for the understanding of enemy love in the New Testament paraenesis. The followers of Jesus had heard a new word which guided them in the proper use of the old word.

IV. Hellenistic Judaism

A. Works from the Apocrypha and Pseudepigrapha[34]

The works discussed in this section are arranged in chronological order so far as this can be determined. The problems surrounding their origin and traditional relation to Christianity will be discussed in turn as we investigate each document.

1. In the *Book of the Words of Tobit,* which according to Eissfeldt reflects a 'realistic picture of the conditions in the eastern Jewish diaspora in about 200 B.C.,'[35] there is no mention of enemy love. Tobit's exhortation to his son Tobias is rather a negative form of the Golden Rule and an admonition to be generous with his surplus *only* to the righteous, thus preserving the restrictive side of the Old Testament love command.

> Take heed to thyself, my child, in all thy works and be discreet in all thy behavior. And what thou thyself hatest, do to no man . . . Give of thy bread to the hungry, and of thy garments to them that are naked: of all thine abundance give alms; and let not thine eye be grudging when thou givest alms. Place your bread on the grave of the righteous, but give none to sinners (Tobit 4:14-17).

2. The *Letter of Aristeas*[36] contains a banquet conversation (187-294) by which the author intends to show the superiority of the virtue and knowledge of the Jewish envoys over that of 'the philosophers' (Aristeas 200). The superiority results from the fact that the Jews 'all made God the starting point of their words' (220, 235). However, a closer examination of the content of the Jewish responses at the banquet conversation shows that the wisdom of the Jews is not essentially different from that of 'the philosophers' and shows distinct Stoic influence (211, 222, 235, 256). Consequently in its teaching relating to enemy love, the Letter of Aristeas reflects some of the same features we found in Seneca and Epictetus: e.g., expediency for the sake of one's own advantage, and a high estimation of the mind's tranquility. This may be found in the following excerpts. See the discussion of this kind of wisdom on pp 23f.

> The King . . . said, 'What is the teaching of wisdom?' And the other replied, 'As you wish that no evil should befall you, but to be a partaker of all good things, so you should act on the same principle towards your

subjects and offenders, and you should mildly admonish the noble and the good. For God draws all men to Himself by his benignity' (207).

The King . . . asked another How he could despise his enemies? And he replied, 'If you show kindness to all men and win their friendship, you need fear no one. To be popular with all men is the best of good gifts to receive from God' (225).

The King asked the next, 'To whom ought a man show liberality?' And he replied, 'All men acknowledge that we ought to show liberality to those who are well disposed towards us, but I think we ought to show the same keen spirit of generosity to those who are opposed to us that by this means we may win them over to the right and to what is advantageous to ourselves' (227).

The King asked another How he could be free from grief? And he replied 'If he never injured anyone, but did good to everybody and followed the pathway of righteousness, for its fruits bring freedom from grief' (232).

3. In the *Fourth Book of Maccabees*[37] we encounter another author whose aim is to stimulate faithfulness to the law and to show that the Greek ideal of virtue can be realized only by Judaism.[38] As with the Stoics, so here 'Reason is in the position of master over the passions or affections' (IV Macc 2:9). While Reason controls the love of wife, children and friends so that a man rebukes and punishes them at times (2:10-12), 'do not think it a paradoxical thing when Reason through the Law is able to overcome even hatred, so that a man refrains from cutting down the enemy's orchards, and protects the property of the enemy from spoilers, and gathers up their goods that have been scattered' (2:13,14). As we saw in the Stoics, so here it is primarily the mastery of self and not the good of the enemy which is at stake.

4. In the *Slavonic Book of Enoch*[39] revenge against neighbor and enemy is explicitly forbidden, because God will be the avenger on the day of judgment:

Endure for the sake of the Lord every wound, every injury, every word and attack. If ill-requitals befall you, return them not either to neighbor or enemy because the Lord will return them for you and be your avenger on the day of great judgment, that there be no avenging here among men (50:3; cf 51:3; 60:1).

Here the command is negative and recalls Rom 12:19; 'Never avenge yourselves but leave it to the wrath of God.' But Slavonic Enoch also gives a positive love command, once expressed in a form of the Golden Rule and once as an admonition to universal charity especially to the needy:

> Just as a man asks (sc. something) for his own soul from God, so let him do to every living soul (61:1).

> Blessed is the man who does not direct his heart with malice against any man, and helps the injured and condemned and raises the broken down, and shall do charity to the needy because on the day of the great judgment every weight and every measure . . . will be as in the market, that is to say they are hung on the scales and stand in the market, and everyone shall learn his own measure and according to his measure shall take his reward (44:4,5).

One is tempted to see in these quotes the echoes of Christian tradition. The unrestricted nature of the admonitions stands in tension with a command like 'Hide not your silver in the earth, help *the faithful man* in affliction, and affliction will not find you in the time of your trouble' (51:2). But we are in no position to draw secure conclusions about Christian influence on Slavonic Enoch or vice versa. We may simply say that there are material parallels. It is not impossible that the enemy love in this book represents a further development of Old Testament commands like Lev 19:18 and Dt 32:35.

5. More important for our purpose than the other Hellenistic writings is *Joseph and Asenath*.[40] In the final chapters of this work (23-29) the son of Pharaoh plots to kill his aging father and Joseph so that he may possess the throne and marry Joseph's wife Asenath. To this end he attempts to enlist the support of two of Joseph's brothers, Simeon and Levi: he threatens to kill them if they do not join his conspiracy. Simeon is so enraged that he reaches for his sword to strike the son of Pharaoh. But Levi restrains him with these words (23:9):[41]

ἵνα τί σὺ ἐθυμώθης κατ' αὐτοῦ;	Why are you angry at him?
διότι ἡμεῖς ἀνδρὸς θεοσεβοῦς	For we are sons of a godly
παῖδές ἐσμεν, καὶ <u>οὐ</u> προσήκει	man, and it is not seemly
ἀνδρὶ θεοσεβεῖ <u>ἀποδοῦναι κακὸν</u>	for a godly man to repay
<u>ἀντὶ κακοῦ</u> τῷ πλησίον αὐτοῦ.	evil for evil to his neighbor.

Pharaoh's son manages, however, to persuade the sons of Bilhah and Zilpah to attempt to kidnap Asenath with a band of men. In the fight that ensues this band of men is wiped out (Benjamin being the decisive defender); the four rebellious brothers of Joseph plead with Asenath to have mercy on them. She responds to them (28:4):

θαρσεῖτε καὶ μὴ φοβεῖσθε,	Be of good courage and
διότι οἱ ἀδελφοὶ ὑμῶν εἰσιν	fear not for your brothers
ἄνδρες θεοσεβεῖς καὶ μὴ	are godly men and do not
ἀποδιδόντες κακὸν ἀντὶ κακοῦ	repay evil for evil to
τινι ἀνθρώπῳ.	any man.

Asenath then intercedes for the fearful brothers and tells the others to be content with their victory. Simeon, who has not learned his lesson, is irritated and asks, 'Why is she speaking good words on behalf of her enemy?' (28:12). She answers for herself (28:14):

μηδαμῶς, ἀδέλφε, ἀποδώσεις	In no way, brother, shall
κακὸν ἀντὶ κακοῦ τῷ πλησίον	you repay evil for evil to
σου, διότι κύριος ἐκδικήσει τὴν	your neighbor, for the Lord
ὕβριν ταύτην.	will avenge this insolence.

Finally, Benjamin, in his eagerness to complete the defeat which he had largely brought about, is about to slay the wounded son of Pharaoh, when Levi intervenes with these words (29:3):

μηδαμῶς ἀδέλφε, ποιήσῃς τὸ	In no way, brother, shall
ἔργον τοῦτο, διότι ἡμεῖς ἄνδρες	you do this deed, for we
θεοσεβεῖς ἐσμεν, καὶ οὐ	are godly men, and it is
προσήκει ανδρὶ θεοσεβεῖ	not seemly for a godly man
ἀποδοῦναι κακὸν ἀντὶ κακοῦ ...	to repay evil for evil ...
οὐδὲ ἐκθλίψαι τὸν ἐχθρὸν ἑως	neither to crush his enemy
θανάτου.	to death.

In 28:4 above we have the exact wording of the tradition which in the preceding chapter we determined lay behind I Thess 5:15a; Rom 12:17a and I Pt 3:9a (μὴ ἀποδιδόντες κακὸν ἀντὶ κακοῦ). Three other instances of the clause occur with minor variations. Dieter Lührmann drew attention to this phrase in Joseph and Asenath in reference to the Christian abolition of the *lex talionis* in Mt 5:38f.[42] But, to my knowledge, its relation specifically to the New Testament paraenetic tradition has not been treated in any detail.[43]

That this parallel is the result of New Testament influence on Joseph and Asenath is not probable (see note 40). Any other Christian feature is missing from the contexts. The ethical framework is Jewish, characterized by the οὐ προσήκει sentences and the use of ἀνὴρ θεοσεβής. The word θεοσεβής occurs in the New Testament only in Jn 9:31 and then in the first-century Christian literature only in I Clement 17:3 (a quote of Job 1:1). However, in the diaspora Judaism, it had become almost a technical term for the self-designation of a Jew.[44]

Moreover, the author's use of the phrase 'do not repay evil for evil' does
not indicate that it is original with him, but already has the character of a
common tradition. In each instance it is brought forth in stereotype fashion
as if it is a well-known proverb: a God-fearing man does not repay evil for
evil. Therefore we need not suppose that the New Testament paraenetic
tradition was directly dependent on Joseph and Asenath. But we may say
with confidence that the saying behind I Thess 5:15a, Rom 12:17a and
I Pt 3:9 was taken over from previously existing Jewish paraenetic tradition.
Johannes Thomas suggests reasonably that the tradition stems ultimately
from Prov 17:13 (ὃς ἀποδίδωσιν κακὰ ἀντὶ ἀγαθῶν, οὐ κινηθήσεται κακὰ
ἐκ τοῦ οἴκου αὐτοῦ) and represents a further development of the principle
developed there.[45]

In spite of the verbal parallel between Joseph and Asenath and the New
Testament paraenetic tradition we cannot conclude that the same ethic is
present in both. This Hellenistic Jewish element was not merely taken over
by the early church; it was put into the context of the gospel by which a
man is made new (Rom 12:2; I Pt 1:3,23; cf I Thess 2:13) and it was
expanded so that it became only the negative counterpart to the positive
love command.[46] In Joseph and Asenath the commands relating to neighbor
(Joseph's brothers) and enemy (Pharaoh's son) are all prohibitions.[47]

B. Philo

Philo's indebtedness to the Stoics is explicit. They are the best (*De
Migratione Abraham* 128) and first (*De Plantatione* 49) philosophers.
Their influence is especially evident in his ethics.[48] We need not, therefore,
devote much space to his teaching on enemy love. The following exposition
of Ex 23:5 will suffice to show out of what tradition he lives:

> By this he [Moses] implies a further lesson: that one should not take
> pleasure in the adversities of those who have shown him hatred ... Again
> if you see an enemy's beast straying, leave the points on which you
> quarrel to serve as incentives for other more vindictive dispositions and
> lead the animal away and restore it. You will benefit yourself more
> than him: he gains an irrational and possibly worthless animal, you the
> greatest and most precious treasure in the whole world, true goodness.
> And this, as surely as the shadow follows the body, will be followed by
> a termination of the feud (*De Virtutibus* 116-118).[49]

V. Qumran and Works in the Region of its Influence

Fragments of each of the documents discussed here have been found in the
caves of Qumran.[50] They are discussed here in chronological order insofar

as this can be fixed. Even if the composition of the Testaments of the Twelve Patriarchs preceded the composition of the Book of Jubilees, the text as it has come down to us is certainly later (see below).

A. *Manual of Discipline*[51]

The Manual of Discipline opens with the most explicit command to hate in the environment of the early church. The sectaries are instructed:

> to seek God with [all their heart] and [all their soul]
> . . .
> and to love all that he has chosen[52]
> and to hate all that he has despised
> . . .
> and that they may love all the sons of light
> each according to his lot in the council of God
> and that they may hate all the sons of darkness
> each according to his fault in the vengeance of God (1:2,4,9,10).

This commitment to hate those outside the community must not lead us to think, however, that the perfect sectary was vindictive in his *actions*. To the contrary, he expresses himself in this way:

> To no man will I render the reward of evil,
> With goodness I will pursue each one;
> For judgment of all the living is with God,
> And He it is who will pay to each man his reward.
> . . .
> As for the multitude of men of the Pit
> I will not lay hands on them till the Day of Vengeance (10:17-19).

The man of understanding apparently saw no contradiction between hating a man and pursuing him with goodness until the Day of Vengeance. This strange combination may find an explanation in the source of the sectary's hate. His hate does not spring from a feeling of superiority:

> As for me I belong to wicked humanity
> To the assembly of perverse flesh
> . . .
> For is man master of his way?
> No, men cannot establish their steps,
> For their justification belongs to God,
> And from his hand comes perfection of way (11:9-10).

For the sectary, love and hate are an inevitable reflex of God's absolutely sovereign and eternal election:

> Truly the Spirits of light and darkness were made by Him:
> . . .
> The one God loves everlastingly
> And delights in all his deeds forever
> But the Counsel of the other he loathes
> And he hates all his ways forever (3:25; 4:1).[53]

The destiny of the just and the unjust is fixed from all eternity. The lot of the one is to share in the 'Council of God' (1:10); the lot of the other is to endure the 'Vengeance of God' (1:11). Therefore, the sectary's hate for the unjust is simply an aligning of himself with God and an affirmation of the rightness of God's decrees.

In spite of the sectary's willingness to pursue his enemy with good deeds, it is hate for the outsider that brings satisfaction:

> I will not withdraw my anger far from perverse men,
> I will not be content till he [God] begins the Judgment (10:20).

As with certain parts of the rabbinic literature (see p 48) Qumran apparently represents a further development of that side of the Old Testament seen in Ps 69:21-28; 109; 139:19-22.[54] From God's absolute election follows the clear division of those to be loved and those to be hated. Paul too, who was one of the chief bearers of the early Christian paraenetic tradition, had a conception of God's absolute election (Rom 9-11). Indeed he could say, 'Jacob I loved, but Esau I hated' (Rom 9:13). But unlike Qumran, Paul does not conclude from this that the non-Christians are to be hated. On the contrary he says, 'I have great sorrow and unceasing anguish in my heart. For I could wish that I myself were accursed and cut off from Christ for the sake of my brethren my kinsmen by race' (Rom 9:2,3). Paul's 'heart's desire and prayer to God for them is that they might be saved' (Rom 10:1). This is a different atmosphere than we find in Qumran. The election of God is here realized in the hearing of faith (Rom 10:17; Gal 3:2), not in the adherence to a strict community code. The result is that 'the mercies of God' 'transform' the believer (Rom 12:1f) and move him to bless those who persecute him (Rom 12:14). That Qumran did not develop an ethic in this direction *even though* it confessed its absolute dependence on God for justification (1QS 11:10) is perhaps due to its focus on the primacy of legal perfection as a demonstration of piety.

B. The Book of Jubilees[55]

When the Book of Jubilees speaks to Israel about other nations it has one dominant thing to say: stay separate. Abraham admonishes Jacob in 22:16:

> And do thou my son Jacob remember my words
> And observe the commandments of Abraham, thy father:
> Separate thyself from the nations,
> And eat not with them:
> And do not according to their works
> And become not their associate.

Separation from unbelievers (II Cor 6:14-18; Eph 5:7; II Jn 10) and from disobedient believers (II Thess 3:6; Rom 16:17; Tit 3:10) had a place in the paraenetic teaching of the early church. To this extent the church preserved this Jewish custom. It differed, however, in two ways: it was never to be based on nationality or pride in any natural quality; and it was not an absolute separatism. The command to be separate is relativized by freedom in Christ, so that Paul can say, 'If an unbeliever invites you (to dinner) and you want to go, eat whatever is set before you . . .' (I Cor 10:27). In this Paul follows the freedom of his Lord who 'received sinners and ate with them' (Lk 15:2; 5:30; 19:7). Therefore Christians could not properly conclude from the admonitions to separate, that unbelievers are not to be loved. On the contrary such a conclusion is specifically contradicted when Paul prays that the believers in Thessalonica might 'abound in love to one another *and to all men*' (I Thess 3:12) and when he commands, 'do good to one another *and to all*' (I Thess 5:15; cf Gal 6:10). Differently from this, the Book of Jubilees only commands love to the brother, i.e., the fellow Israelite. In Isaac's farewell address he commands his sons with these words:

> And love one another, my sons, your brothers as a man who loves his own soul, and let each seek in what he may benefit his brother and act together on the earth; and let them love each other as their own souls . . . And if either of you devises evil against his brother, know that from henceforth everyone that devises evil against his brother shall fall into his hand, and shall be rooted out of the land of the living and his seed shall be destroyed from under heaven (36:4,9; cf 7:20).[56]

Even here the notion of 'falling into the hand of the brother' seems to condone a revenge which brother will execute on brother.

C. The Testaments of the Twelve Patriarchs

The difficulties in deciding how and when the Testaments came into being complicate tremendously our discussion of their teaching on enemy love and their relation to the New Testament paraenetic tradition. Jacob Jervell writes: 'The state of the research can be described as follows: At this time (1969) it is not possible to find a solution on the basis of literary criticism.'[57] The same conclusion may be drawn from the *Introduction* by Denis (1970), for in discussing the date of the Testaments and their Christian interpolations[58] he simply gives the various possibilities ranging from R. H. Charles to M. De Jonge.[59] According to Charles the Testaments date from 109 B.C. and were written originally in Hebrew. The ethical teachings, he claims, belong to the essence of the work and form its warp and woof; they must be distinguished from the 'dogmatic Christian inter- polations' which are of a different color and texture from the original material.[60] De Jonge, on the other hand, in his older work asserts that the Testaments 'may no longer be reckoned to the pseudepigraphic literature of the Old Testament. They must be classified among the literary products of the early Christian Church . . . The Testaments, because they contain notions which seem to be generally accepted in the time of Irenaeus, Hippolytus and Tertullian and are not found earlier, were written *c.* A.D. 200.'[61] However, since fragments of the Testaments of Levi and Naphtali have been found at Qumran (see note 50) De Jonge now maintains that 'the Testaments, though perhaps not composed by a Christian author using much Jewish traditional material of all kinds (as I thought in my book), underwent at any rate a thoroughgoing redaction.'[62] Similarly Leonhard Rost views the Testaments of Naphtali and Levi as pre-Christian and related indirectly to Qumran while, according to his view, the remainder of the Testaments originated in the first century A.D. This Jewish work was then reworked by a Christian around A.D. 200.[63]

A. Dupont—Sommer, however, maintains that all twelve Testaments originated in Qumran before the Christian era since parallels to all but one of the Testaments have been found in the Damascus Document.[64] About the same time that Dupont-Sommer's book appeared, M. Philonenko published his little book, *Les Interpolations chrétiennes des Testaments des Douze Patriarches et les Manuscrits de Qoumrân* (1960), in which he argued (following Dupont–Sommer) that the Testaments are very closely related to Qumran and that Christian influence on them is almost negligible.[65] This work, however, along with the work of A. S. van der Woude[66] received a detailed and telling critique by M. De Jonge whose position has been greatly strengthened.[67] It would seem to me that in view of the work of De Jonge and Becker (see below) we may tentatively say that the Testaments originated in the sphere of Qumran in the first pre-Christian centuries but then underwent expansion with Hellenistic influence and finally a large-scale Christian redaction (see Becker's view below in support of this).

Given this uncertain state of affairs in contemporary scholarship relating to the Testaments, we should proceed very cautiously as we examine their teaching on enemy love. The most important texts for our purposes are the following:

> For the good man hath not a dark eye, for he showeth mercy to all men, even though they be sinners, and though they devise evil intent concerning him, by doing good he overcometh evil, being shielded by God (Benjamin 4:2f).

> If anyone seeketh to do evil unto you, do well unto him, and pray for him and ye shall be redeemed of the Lord from all evil (Joseph 18:2).

> And if he [your enemy] be shameless and persist in his wrongdoing even so forgive him from the heart, and leave to God the avenging (Gad 6:7).

> I loved the Lord, likewise every man with all my heart (Issachar 7:6).

> Do you, therefore, my children from that which God bestoweth upon you, show compassion and mercy without hesitation to all men and give to every man with a good heart . . . I know that my hand found not the wherewithal to give to him that needed, and I walked with him weeping seven furlongs, and my bowels yearned towards him in compassion (Zebulun 7:2–4).

Neither De Jonge nor Philonenko discusses these ethical texts. So we turn for help to a work by Jürgen Becker. In his *Untersuchungen zur Entstehungsgeschichte der Testamente der Zwölf Patriarchen* (1970) Jürgen Becker devotes a good deal of space to the specific problem facing us here and I am largely dependent on his work in the following discussion. According to Becker's analysis the origin of the Testaments occurred in three stages: (1) a Hellenistic Jewish *Grundstock*, (2) later Hellenistic Jewish expansions, and finally, (3) a Christian redaction.[68] Concerning the love command in the earliest stage he says, 'Like a red thread the theme of neighbor love extends through the entire *Grundschrift* of the Testament.[69] The demand is for 'Agape, to be free from oneself, one's life, will and possessions and to be there wholly for the other person.[70] 'With this radicalization the *Grundstock* of the Testaments stands alone within Judaism.'[71]

In spite of the apparently unique character of this love command within Judaism there may still be a restriction of love to one's neighbor (Reuben 6:9, neighbor = brother). 'The love command is valid for the Israelite community. The neighbor is not simply everyone.'[72] This comes out clearly in Zebulun 8:5 - 9:2. Becker asserts that the places where love is commanded toward 'all men' are later additions because they have 'an especially strong Hellenistic stamp. One must assume the background consists of popular philosophical ideas, especially stoical thoughts about the equality of man's honor and nature.'[73] Besides this restriction of love to the neighbor, Becker notes two other features of the love command in the *Grundstock* which set it off from the New Testament view. The expression of love is viewed in Zebulun 8:5 - 9:2 as a means of preventing the dispersion of the Jews[74] and in Joseph 18:1-4 as a meritorious act that God repays on this earth with well-being.[75]

On the basis of Becker's work we may conclude the following. The Testaments do not present a unified view on neighbor love (in Reuben 6:9 the neighbor is a brother; in Zebulun 6:6 and 8:3 the neighbor refers to 'all men'). The universal expressions of love are probably, therefore, expansions under the influence of Stoicism. Nevertheless the remaining admonitions to have mercy upon, forgive, and pray for one's 'enemies' (Gad 6:7; Joseph 18:2) are singular in the literature we are investigating. If the 'enemy' here is not intended to be restricted to fellow Jews, then these admonitions come nearer than any we have found to the New Testament paraenetic commands of enemy love. However in view of De Jonge's and Becker's arguments for a Christian redaction of the Testaments, we can make no dogmatic assertions about which direction the influence may have gone between the early Christian paraenetic tradition and the Testaments of the Twelve Patriarchs.[76]

VI. Palestinian Judaism outside Qumran

Before discussing the early church's living contemporaries (Josephus and the Rabbis), we will take a brief look at Sirach which was probably written around 190 B.C. in Jerusalem.[77]

A. *The Wisdom of Jesus Son of Sirach*

Like each of the sources we will examine in this section on Palestinian Judaism, Sirach's ethic is characterized by a limitation of who should be loved. This narrowness which in Sirach restricts the doing of good deeds to the godly is seen most clearly in 12:1-7:

> If you do a kindness, know to whom you do it,
> and you will be thanked for your good deeds.
> Do good to a godly man, and you will be repaid –
> if not by him, certainly by the Most High.
> . . .
> Give to the godly man, but do not help the sinner.

Do good to the humble, but do not give to the ungodly;
hold back his bread, and do not give it to him,
lest by means of it he subdue you;
for you will receive twice as much evil
for all the good which you do to him.
For the Most High also hates sinners[78]
and will inflict punishment on the ungodly.
Give to the good man, but do not help the sinner.

Here the author argues in good wisdom fashion by appealing to experience
and to the desire for a good life in the world: 'Hold back his bread . . . lest
by means of it he subdue you.' We have seen in our discussion of the Stoics
that the early Christian paraenetic tradition has an element of wisdom too,
although here the substance is quite different. This difference is even
clearer when Sirach turns to argue theologically: 'For the Most High hates
sinners and will inflict punishment on the ungodly.' That God would
inflict punishment on the ungodly, the Christians did not deny. But that
this work of God should be imitated by men is emphatically rejected (cf
Rom 12:19). The argument of Sirach 12:6f is the precise opposite of Jesus'
argument in Mt 5:44f.

B. Josephus[79]

Although Josephus may on some counts be reckoned as belonging to
Hellenistic Judaism we include him here primarily because of the kinship
his view of enemy love has to the rabbinic view. His terminology (e.g.,
φιλανθρωπία and ἀρετή) may at times reflect the influence of the philosophers, but it is his allegiance to the law which controls his teaching on
enemy love.

Apion levels a blow to Judaism claiming that Jews take an oath not to
show good will to a single alien, especially to Greeks. Josephus responds to
this charge:

> From the Greeks we are severed more by our geographical position than
> by our institutions, with the result that we neither hate nor envy them.
> On the contrary, many of them have agreed to adopt our laws; of whom
> some have remained faithful, while others, lacking the necessary endurance,
> have again seceded (*Against Apion* II.123).

The opposite of hating the Greeks is to extend to them an invitation to
become proselytes. There is a generous provision for aliens (enemies) in
the law, namely a welcome to any who will accept it:

The consideration given by our legislator to the equitable treatment of aliens also merits attention. It will be seen that he took the best of all possible measures at once to secure our customs from corruption, and to throw them open ungrudgingly to any who elect to share them. To all who desire to come and live under the same laws with us, he gives a gracious welcome, holding that it is not family ties alone which constitute relationship, but agreement on the principles of conduct (*Against Apion* II.209f).

How a Jew relates to a non-Jew depends on 'agreement on the principles of conduct,' that is, it depends on the non-Jew accepting the law, or becoming a proselyte. That this possibility exists for the non-Jew is proof of the Jews' φιλανθρωπία.

We, while we have no desire to emulate the customs of others, yet gladly welcome any who wish to share our own. That, I think, may be taken as a proof both of humanity and magnanimity (φιλανθρωπίας ἅμα καὶ μεγαλοψυχίας; *Against Apion* II.261).

On Josephus' terms it is understandable that he views an invitation to obey the law as a magnanimous act, for 'the only wisdom (φρόνησιν) and the only virtue (ἀρετήν) consist in refraining absolutely from every action, from every thought that is contrary to the laws originally laid down' (*Against Apion* II.183). Without the Jewish law the gentiles are hopelessly ignorant and immoral.

Among these laws there are, incidentally, some duties to be carried out toward your enemies, even when you have done battle with them:

We must furnish fire, water, food to all who ask for them, point out the road, not leave a corpse unburied, show consideration (ἐπιεικεῖς) even to declared enemies. He does not allow us to burn up their country or to cut down their fruit trees, and forbids even the spoiling of fallen combatants (*Against Apion* II.211f).

This behavior, as with the welcome to the proselyte above, is called φιλανθρωπία. The moral edge is taken off this word, however, when, in the following section, the law's concern with brute beasts is also viewed as an evidence of φιλανθρωπία.[80] Thus for Josephus enemy love means primarily offering the enemy a chance to become a proselyte.

C. *The Rabbis*

The lawyer's question in Lk 10:29 ('Who is my neighbor?') shows that in Jesus' day the reference to loving your neighbor in Lev 19:18 was not unequivocal. In fact in the synagogue at that time 'only the Israelite counted as a רֵעַ ; the others, i.e., the non-Israelites, are not included in this term.'[81] Further, the גֵּר , mentioned in Lev 19:34 as the object of Israel's love, is interpreted to exclude those non-Israelites who do not become full proselytes within the first twelve months they spend among the Israelites.[82] It is evident here, as Michel says, that 'The election of Israel, the covenant made with her, and the fact of the Law determine the concept of "neighbor".'[83]

We should not think, however, that the Rabbis presented a unified front on these matters.[84] The literature itself is often a record of debate. In the Talmud, Ex 23:4f (helping your enemy with his ox) was debated as to whether the 'enemy' here is a gentile or not.[85] And the command to give bread and water to your enemy (Prov 25:21) is given primarily an allegorical interpretation: the 'enemy' is the 'evil impulse' in man which, through the bread and water of the Torah, can be stilled.[86]

Along with the debate over who the 'neighbor' and 'enemy' are (and the generally narrow conclusions) there are also some very unloving comments regarding gentiles[87] and even the admonition to hate certain ones:

> A man should not direct his mind to say, 'Love wisdom (the scholars) and hate the pupils, love the pupils and hate those ignorant of the law,' rather, 'hate the Epicureans (free thinkers), the seducer, likewise the informer.' David also said, 'Should I not hate those who hate you, Lord, should I not abominate those who raise themselves up against you? With perfect hatred I hate them, they have become my enemies' (Ps 139:21f). But does it not say, 'You shall love your neighbor as yourself; I am the Lord; (Lev 19:18) I have created him'? Yes, when he behaves according to the conduct of his people, you should love him, but when he does not, you should not love him (Aboth R. Nathan 16:7).

Here we see how it is possible to develop an ethic from the Old Testament quite unlike that of the New Testament paraenesis. Why the early Christian paraenetic tradition did not develop a similar conception on enemy love even though it drew upon the Old Testament is a question we will try to answer when dealing with the teachings of Jesus.

The Rabbis could also speak positively about behavior toward non-Jews.[88] Hillel is credited with the statement, 'be of the disciples of Aaron, loving peace, and pursuing peace, loving mankind and bringing them nigh to the law' (Aboth 1:12). R. Joshua ben-Hananiah (around A.D. 90) said, 'An evil eye, the evil inclination, and hatred of the fellow-creatures put a man out of the world' (Aboth 2:11). More important for our purposes is the interchange between R. Jochanan and R. Simeon b. Abba (middle of third century). The former began his address with Prov 17:13: 'If a man returns evil for good, evil will not depart from his house.' But the latter responded: Not that alone – 'if a man returns evil for good' – but also, 'If a man returns evil for evil, evil will not depart from his house.' R. Meir (around A.D. 150) said, 'God said to Moses, Be like me, as I repay good for evil, so you also repay good for evil.' Here we have a confirmation of J. Thomas' suggestion cited above (p 39) that the command not to repay evil with evil (I Thess 5:15a; Rom 12:17a; I Pt 3:9) is a further development of Prov 17:13. The saying (μὴ ἀποδιδόντες κακὸν ἀντὶ κακοῦ) should not be confined either to Hellenistic or to Palestinian Judaism. It was apparently a common proverb in the environment of the early church which she adapted to her own purposes (see note 46).

VII. The Teaching of Jesus

The last and most important step in our survey of the environment of the early Christian paraenetic tradition is to pose the questions: What did Jesus teach concerning love of enemies? and, How likely is it that this teaching was taken over by and accounts for the character of the early church tradition on love of enemies? The first of these two questions draws the discipline of synoptic criticism into our history-of-religions survey. The key teaching of Jesus on enemy love, upon which we will focus, is found in two different forms: one in Mt 5:38–48, the other in Lk 6:27–36. The effort to determine as precisely as possible the teaching of Jesus which stands behind these accounts involves us in a detailed synoptic comparison. This effort and its accompanying synoptic analysis cannot be separated from the possible influence Jesus had on the New Testament paraenetic tradition because this influence itself figures in the determination of what Jesus taught.

A. The Question of Q

Dieter Lührmann has published the table on p 50 in two different works;[89] its importance for this study makes another showing worthwhile. A glance at this table reveals (1) that almost the entirety of Lk's Sermon on the Plain is contained in Mt's Sermon on the Mount and (2) that the ordering of the subject matter (with minor exceptions) is the same in both.

In view of this it would be unreasonable to maintain that Mt and Lk independently constructed their sermons with no dependence on a common pattern.[90] But neither is it correct to speak simply of Q as the common source with which Mt and Lk worked.[91] To do so with no qualification is to overlook differences between Mt and Lk that cannot reasonably be attributed to the redaction of the evangelists.[92] If we

Lk	Mt	
6:20	5:3	
6:21a	5:6	Beatitudes
6:21b	5:4	Lk 6:20–23/Mt 5:3–12
6:22f	5:11f	
6:24–26		Woes Lk 6:24–26
6:27f	5:44	
6:29f	5:39b–42	
6:31	*7:12	Enemy love
6:32f	5:46f	Lk 6:27–35/Mt 5:39b–47
6:34	–	
6:35	5:44f	
6:36	5:48	
6:37a	7:1	
6:37b, 38a	(12:36?)	
6:38b	7:2b	Judging
6:39	15:14	Lk 6:36–42/Mt 5:48; 7:1–5
6:40	10:24	
6:41f	7:3–5	
6:43	*7:18	The fruits
6:44	7:16	Lk 6:43–45/Mt 7:15–20
6:45	12:35, 34b	
6:46	7:21	Hearing and doing
6:47–49	7:24–27	Lk 6:46–49/Mt 7:21–27

*signifies a different sequence in Mt.

designate the common pattern which underlies the Sermon on the Mount and the Sermon on the Plain as Q, then we must think in terms of two distinct forms of Q in order to account for the divergences between Mt 5:38–48 and Lk 6:27–36.[93] These intermediate stages make our effort to determine the oldest single tradition all the more complex.

As I have weeded my way through the extremely detailed literature on these texts I have become aware of the speculative and conflicting nature of the results which the various critical analyses frequently yield (see for example notes 144, 170, 171). The attempts to penetrate behind the evangelists have become ever more complicated. Accompanying this increased complication is a rise in the frequency of suppositions, guesses, conjectures and assumptions. It seems to me, however, that the value of arguments and conclusions overburdened with speculation is at least questionable.[94] It is even more questionable when an author ceases to insert the guarded 'probably' or 'supposedly' and instead presents as facts what are only guesses. I am not pretending myself to be free from the difficulties which prompt speculation. I make these observations rather as an attempt to justify my hesitancy in the following analyses to press for conclusions where the evidence for such does not suffice. Even if we are dissatisfied with the information available to us, it is still more valuable to utilize that to the full than to spend our time and energy supposing what we do not know.

B. The Question of the Antitheses (Mt 5:38-39a, 43-44a)

We will consider Mt 5:38-42 with Mt 5:43-48 because they are bound together by the common theme of the stance one should take toward his enemies and because the Lukan parallel unites the material of Mt 5:38-48 under the love command.

Our first question in comparing Mt 5:38-48 with Lk 6:27-36 is the origin of the last two antitheses in Mt. Jeremias has shown that the common division[95] between the first, second and fourth antitheses as original and the third, fifth and sixth antitheses as secondary is questionable.[96] With regard specifically to the fifth and sixth antitheses, which concern us here, we may consider the pertinent data. Bultmann writes, 'The introductory forms in vv 31, 32a, 38, 39a, 43, 44a are obviously moulded on the pattern of the antithetical forms in vv 21f, 27f, 33-37 . . .'[97] From the standpoint of *form* this is not obvious, however: the antithetical half of all six antitheses begins with the identical phrase ἐγὼ δὲ λέγω ὑμῖν which in itself speaks as much for common origin as for any secondary formulation. With regard to the initial words of the thesis half of the antitheses, no uniform structure appears in the so-called original antitheses. The second, fifth and sixth antitheses begin with Ἠκούσατε ὅτι ἐρρέθη. This phrase distinguishes itself from the other 'secondary' antithesis (third: Ἐρρέθη δέ) *and* from two of the 'original' antitheses (first: Ἠκούσατε ὅτι ἐρρέθη τοῖς ἀρχαίοις; fourth: Πάλιν ἠκούσατε ὅτι ἐρρέθη τοῖς ἀρχαίοις). Moving beyond the introductory words to the form of the antithetical statements themselves, we notice that the infinitive form of the fifth antithesis (5:39 μὴ ἀντιστῆναι) sets it off from the other two 'secondary' antitheses (5:32, 44) and parallels only one of the 'original' antitheses (fourth: 5:34, ὀμόσαι). The imperative form of the sixth antithesis (5:44, ἀγαπᾶτε . . . προσεύχεσθε) has no parallel in the 'original' *or* 'secondary' antitheses.[98] The thesis half of the fifth antithesis (5:38 *lex talionis*) is a simple Old Testament quote. As such it is similar to the second and fourth[99] (but not the first) of the 'original' antitheses and is similar to the third (but not the sixth) of the 'secondary' antitheses. On the other hand, the sixth antithesis is an Old Testament quote with a non-Old Testament addition, and as such is unlike the other two 'secondary' antitheses (third and fifth) and is like only the first of the 'original' antitheses.[100] The supposition, therefore, that the third, fifth and sixth antitheses were secondarily formulated on the pattern of the first, second and fourth antitheses does not account for the complicated mixture of similarities and divergences of form.

Bultmann's argument from the *subject matter* is that the three 'original' antitheses have a prohibition which is not abolished but surpassed, whereas in the 'secondary' antitheses there is no prohibition but an instruction (or concession, 5:31) which is not surpassed but abolished.[101] However, the fourth antithesis does not fit this scheme. 5:34 (μὴ ὀμόσαι ὅλως) is not an intensification of the command not to swear falsely (5:33 ἐπιορκήσεις), but an abrogation of the command to perform to the Lord your oaths (5:33 ἀποδώσεις δὲ τῷ κυρίῳ τοὺς ὅρκους σοῦ). It must, therefore, on this count be included with the 'secondary' antitheses which overthrow the meanings given their individual Old Testament quotations. Thus if we insist on the criterion that only those antitheses are original which surpass but do not overthrow the theses, then only the first two antitheses remain as original.[102] And there are notable discrepancies even between these two.[103] Moreover as Lührmann points out, the first and second theses (5:21,27) *cannot* be abolished, and as for the third antithesis we have a limitation, not an abrogation of the possibilities of divorce (differently from Lk and Mk).[104] Are we justified in insisting that every genuine antithesis conform so closely to a single pattern of negative thesis, intensified antithesis?

This argument from the subject matter does not, however, stand alone. It is buttressed by at least two other significant observations: first, that the 'original' antitheses *could not* have been formulated from non-antithetical statements because the second halves of the antitheses are not intelligible except in the antithetical context; and, second, the antithetical halves of the 'secondary' antitheses have all been handed down in an independent form by Lk.[105] A closer examination of the fifth antithesis (Mt 5:38,39a) from the perspective of these two arguments reveals, however, that they support rather than contradict its originality. Jeremias has pointed out that the fifth antithesis (ἐγὼ δὲ λέγω ὑμῖν μὴ ἀντιστῆναι τῷ πονηρῷ) has no parallel in Lk 6:27-36 or anywhere else in the synoptics.[106] The change of person from plural to singular between 5:39a and 5:39b shows that the basic antithesis was probably restricted to 5:38,39a. Lk 6:29,30 parallels not the antithesis but its expansion in Mt 5:39b-42.

If the fifth antithesis (Mt 5:38,39a) is *not* original, there are two possibilities: (A) Mt invented the command not to resist evil (μὴ ἀντιστῆναι τῷ πονηρῷ);[107] (B) he found it as an isolated saying of Jesus in the tradition.[108] Against A are the following considerations: (1) Mt did not need to invent it; he could have said with good effect, 'But I say to you, "Whoever strikes you on the cheek turn to him also the other." ' (2) If he created the fifth as well as the sixth, why is the fifth welded to the antithetical form by the infinitive (of indirect address) structure while the sixth is a loosely connected imperative? (3) The command is extreme, drastic, pointed, risky; as such it sounds more like a saying of Jesus than a creation of the evangelist. Against B (that Mt found the saying isolated in the tradition) there are also objections: (1) First of all, the possibility that the saying originated in the church may be excluded because, wherever $\dot\alpha\nu\theta\dot\iota\sigma\tau\eta\mu\iota$ appears in connection with some sort of evil in the paraenesis, the command is 'Resist' (Gal 2:11; Eph 6:13; Ja 4:7; I Pt 5:9).[109] (2) As we already noted above the saying in its present infinitive form is integrally bound to the antithetical form and does not look like a free-floating saying (cf Mt 5:34). (3) Most important is to notice that the argument of Bultmann and others that the second halves of the 'original' antitheses are not intelligible if separated from their antithetical contexts, applies even more so to the fifth antithesis. That the command 'Do not resist evil!' circulated without some counterpart to give it concrete direction is virtually unthinkable.

But if Mt did not invent 5:39a and did not find it as an isolated saying in the tradition, then the explanation lying nearest at hand and with the fewest problems is that Mt 5:38,39a existed from the beginning in antithetical form.[110] I do not claim certainty for this conclusion but I do maintain that it is just as probable as any other possibility.[111] In support of this conclusion we may cite first Ja 5:6 which, while not rendering the Matthean form of 5:39a, nevertheless offers an essential parallel and may well be an application of Jesus' command. The rich condemn ($\kappa\alpha\tau\epsilon\delta\iota\kappa\dot\alpha\sigma\alpha\tau\epsilon$) and murder ($\dot\epsilon\phi\sigma\nu\epsilon\dot\nu\sigma\alpha\tau\epsilon$) the righteous man, but 'he does not resist ($o\dot\nu\kappa$ $\dot\alpha\nu\tau\iota\tau\dot\alpha\sigma\sigma\epsilon\tau\alpha\iota$) them.' Second, it is noteworthy to recall that a prominent element in the early church paraenesis was the rejection of the $\dot\alpha\nu\tau\dot\iota$ principle of retaliation. The memory of Jesus' *explicit* denunciation of the $\dot\alpha\nu\tau\dot\iota$ principle in Mt 5:38,39a (. . . $\dot\sigma\phi\theta\alpha\lambda\mu\dot\sigma\nu$ $\dot\alpha\nu\tau\dot\iota$ $\dot\sigma\phi\theta\alpha\lambda\mu\sigma\dot\nu$ $\kappa\alpha\dot\iota$ $\dot\sigma\delta\dot\sigma\nu\tau\alpha$ $\dot\alpha\nu\tau\dot\iota$ $\dot\sigma\delta\dot\sigma\nu\tau\sigma\varsigma$, . . $\mu\dot\eta$ $\dot\alpha\nu\tau\iota\sigma\tau\dot\eta\nu\alpha\iota$) would have offered the incentive and criterion for the early church's frequent use of the Jewish saying $\mu\dot\eta$ $\dot\alpha\pi\sigma\delta\iota\delta\dot\sigma\nu\tau\epsilon\varsigma$ $\kappa\alpha\kappa\dot\sigma\nu$ $\underline{\dot\alpha\nu\tau\dot\iota}$ $\kappa\alpha\kappa\sigma\dot\nu$ (Rom 12:17a; I Thess 5:15a; I Pt 3:9a).

The origin of the sixth antithesis (Mt 5:43,44a) is more difficult to decide. In this case, unlike Mt 5:39a, the second half of the antithesis is found word for word in Lk 6:27 without the antithetical form ($\dot\alpha\gamma\alpha\pi\dot\alpha\tau\epsilon$ $\tau\sigma\dot\nu\varsigma$ $\dot\epsilon\chi\theta\rho\sigma\dot\nu\varsigma$ $\dot\nu\mu\dot\omega\nu$). The question poses itself: Did Lk (or Q-l)[112] eliminate the antithesis already found in Q, or did Mt (or Q-m) build the sixth antithesis secondarily from the simple command in Q to love your enemies? To bring this question into sharper focus let us reconstruct the processes of redaction[113] which would probably have occurred in each of the two instances. (In the following two paragraphs Lk = 'Lk or Q-l,' and Mt = 'Mt or Q-m.')

In the first instance Lk has before him material in the form of Mt 5:38-48. Having no intention to polemicize against 'what has been said of old' he purposes to omit the antithetical form. This leaves Mt 5:39b-42 without a context. The verses must be brought within the material of Mt 5:44-48. The only suitable slot for their insertion is right after the imperatives of 5:44. This breaks off the promise of sonship (Mt 5:45) from the love command so that the promise must be temporarily omitted. The opening which is left allows Lk to gather in another semi-related saying, the Golden Rule. After the Golden Rule (Lk 6:31) Lk continues with the Matthean order, i.e., the rhetorical questions (Mt 5:46/Lk 6:32-34). The promise of sonship is too important to omit altogether and yet it must be attached to the love command. Therefore Lk restates the love command, molding it so that it symmetrically recalls each of the three preceding rhetorical questions. To this command he now attaches the promise of sonship which he earlier had to omit in order to insert vv 29,30.[114] He closes with a command to be like God.

In the second instance Mt finds before him in Q the material of Lk 6:27-36. He decides to close his program of antitheses with this material on the love command. He notices that Lk 6:29,30 are not well at home in their present context but that they would provide an admirable expansion for the fifth antithesis. After excerpting Lk 6:29,30 he sees too that the Golden Rule is not directly related to the real concern of enemy love and takes it out for later use. Seeing no need to repeat the love command as Lk 6:35 does and desiring all attention to be on the antithesis of Mt 5:43,44, Mt drops the second love command and brings forward the promise of sonship which was attached to it and attaches it to Mt 5:44.[115] Then he continues with the rhetorical questions and closes with a command to be like God.

While these two hypotheses are over-simplified because they do not take into account the various levels at which these changes occurred or the complex differences between the individual sayings, nevertheless a process akin to one of these two must have taken place between Q and the final redaction of the evangelists. The question of the originality of the sixth antithesis is the question: Which of these two processes is more probable?

In support of the first process (that Lk has eliminated the original fifth and sixth antitheses) are the following arguments: (1) Lk 6:35a is so artfully designed on the pattern of the preceding three verses that its repetition of Lk 6:27 really does appear calculated, as Bultmann suggests (see note

114), to allow for the connection of the promise of sonship. Is not the displacement of the promise of sonship by the insertion of Lk 6:29,30 and the subsequent need to attach it to the love command the best explanation for Lk's calculated repetition of Lk 6:27? (2) Because of the relatedness of the subject matter it is likely that in the early gospel tradition Lk 6:29,30/ Mt 5:39b–42 first became attached to the fifth antithesis and was later disengaged from this context in order to become part of a whole paragraph on love. (3) Ernst Percy points out that while Lk has dropped the antithetical form, nevertheless he cannot get away from its intention, for the command to love your enemies in Lk 6:35 is stated as the antithesis (πλήν) of the neighbor love in the three preceding verses. The command to love your enemies demands a contrasting background.[116] Finally J. Jeremias and P. Gaechter maintain that the Ἀλλὰ ὑμῖν λέγω . . . of Lk 6:27 reflects a remnant of the antithetical form itself.[117]

In support of the second process described above (that Mt formed two paragraphs out of one and created the sixth antithesis) are the following arguments: (1) D. Lührmann and H. Schürmann have pointed out that common elements[118] in the love command and in the beatitudes suggest that these two passages were at one time directly connected. It is hardly conceivable that the material of Mt 5:38–42 would come between the beatitudes and the love command. 'Rather opening with the command of enemy love, as it is preserved in Lk, offers a meaningful beginning.'[119] (2) Lk is characteristically less prone to alter the Q material. (3) The antitheses are an important part of Mt's program and reflect a pattern set in Mt 5:20. Thus a motivation is close at hand why he should want to reconstruct the material of Lk 6:27ff into antitheses.[120]

Which of these two sets of arguments shall we follow? In my judgment the evidence is not adequate for us to make a certain decision. However, we can now say that those scholars[121] who, against the current, have maintained the originality of the fifth and sixth antitheses have as much evidence in their favor as the majority who deny it. This does not, however, hinder us significantly in understanding Jesus' command. Ernst Percy's insight is worth repeating, namely, that, even in Lk where the *formal* antithesis is gone, Jesus' command of enemy love demands a contrasting background of restricted neighbor love (Lk 6:35 over against 6:32–34) against which Jesus' command is antithetical. Therefore, even if Jesus never expressed this command in the 'you have heard . . . but I say to you' form, nevertheless this form in Mt 5:43, 44a interprets precisely the antithetical accent which the command 'Love your enemies!' must have had in Jesus' preaching.[122]

C. Analysis of the Individual Sayings (Mt 5:39b–42, 44b–48/Lk 6:27–36)

Our aim in this section is not *primarily* to determine the origin and intention of redactional variants or to reconstruct Q, but to penetrate as directly as possible to Jesus' teaching. Where literary analysis reaches its limits, we will attempt to go beyond this point by way of the subject matter itself. As we mentioned already (p 49), this effort cannot be separated from the influence Jesus had on the New Testament paraenetic tradition. Consequently in the following analyses we will endeavor to bring to light simultaneously what Jesus taught and its effect on early Christian paraenesis.

Lk 6:27,28/Mt 5:44

The command to love your enemies (Mt 5:44a/Lk 6:27a) is identical in both gospels. The next two commands in Lk are missing in Mt; then both close the group with a command to pray. Διωκόντων is to be attributed to Mt (or Q-m).[123] Bultmann observes that Lk's 'is more likely to be the original form since he gives otherwise parallel elements in abridged form.'[124] Further Seitz argues that the synthetic parallelism of Lk 6:27,28 shows that these four lines are preserved 'with great fidelity' and 'are probably of Palestinian origin.'[125] Lührmann, however, argues that Mt's two-line form is more original,[126] and that from these two lines only the first (Mt 5:44a) is original.[127] From the standpoint of form Schulz, it seems to me, has drawn the most acceptable conclusion: 'A secure decision as to whether here [Lk 6:27,28] we have Q is scarcely possible.'[128]

From the standpoint of *content* what may be said concerning these four commands? There need be no doubt that Jesus commanded ἀγαπᾶτε τοὺς ἐχθροὺς ὑμῶν: the command is identical in both gospels; we found nothing so explicit and unequivocal in our survey of Jesus' environment;[129] nor is it thinkable that the early church should invent the saying and thus impose upon themselves such a troublesome requirement. On the contrary it was Jesus' unflinching stand against the ἀντι principle of retaliation (Mt 5:38,39a; see p 53) and his insistence upon enemy love which stamped the paraenesis of the church. Nevertheless, we do not find anywhere in the New Testament paraenesis the command 'Love your enemies.' In Jesus' own environment, where Rabbis discussed 'Who is my neighbor?' (Lk 10:29) and where nationalistic feelings ran high, the command 'Love your enemies!' struck home with discomforting concreteness. As such it was a penetrating, concrete element of Jesus' eschatological call to repentance (see Chapter 3). In the early church the situation was different. Neither nationalistic allegiance nor rabbinic exegesis formed the immediate backdrop for the love command. The question the early church faced was: How shall we act toward the unbeliever, the hostile townspeople, the ridiculing old friends? 'Love your enemies' would not strike home here like it did in Jesus' situation. Therefore the 'enemies' were specifically described: revilers (I Pt 3:9; I Cor 4:12), persecutors (Rom 12:14), those who do evil to you (I Thess 5:15; Rom 12:17; I Pt 3:9).

This specification in the early church paraenesis raises the question whether the three remaining commands in Lk 6:27b,28 might be the paraenetic commentary of the early church. At least the command προσεύχεσθε ὑπὲρ τῶν ἐπηρεαζόντων goes back to Q. While praying for one's enemy is not unknown in the Old Testament, its occurrence in the literature of Jesus' day is very rare.[130] In the New Testament the words προσεύχη or προσεύχομαι occur nowhere else with regard to an enemy of any sort.[131] The word ἐπηρεάζω is found only once more in I Pt 3:16 where the context is a Christian suffering abuse unjustly. The command to pray for your abusers was apparently not a favorite in the early church. There appears to be no good reason why we should deny that Jesus himself gave this command.

With the remaining two commands the situation is different. The command to 'do good' (καλῶς ποιεῖτε/ἀγαθοποιεῖτε Lk 6:27b/35), as we showed in Chapter 1 (p 14), is an Old Testament command (Ps 33:15 LXX), and was drawn into the early church paraenesis in its Old Testament context (cf I Pt 3:10-12). The command 'Do good!' is common in the paraenesis although it never has an object as it does here in Lk 6:27b.[132] With regard to the word μισοῦσιν, nowhere in the New Testament outside the gospels is there a reference to outsiders hating Christians. That Jesus himself used the words καλῶς/ἀγαθὸν ποιεῖν on other occasions is shown by Mt 12:12/Mk 3:4/Lk 6:9. However, whether it was Jesus' command in Lk 6:27b which gave the early church the incentive and criterion for taking up the Old Testament command to do good, or whether the early church took it up and put it here in Jesus' mouth as a specification of his love command, remains an open question.

The command εὐλογεῖτε τοὺς καταρωμένους (Lk 6:28a) does not in this form occur in the paraenesis, but Rom 12:14 offers a very close parallel: εὐλογεῖτε τοὺς διώκοντας/εὐλογεῖτε καὶ μὴ καταράσθε. In I Pt 3:9 blessing is commanded in response to reviling (λοιδορίας, cf I Cor 4:12). There are no other comparable uses of εὐλογέω or καταράσθαι in the New Testament paraenesis (cf Ja 3:9-12). The far more common use of εὐλογέω in the New Testament is God's blessing and being blessed. Therefore it is not likely that this command in Lk 6:28a would be created by the church. Rather Rom 12:14 looks like a free reconstruction of Jesus' saying of which Paul was aware.[133]

From our analysis of Lk 6:27, 28 par and in anticipation of the following analyses we may suggest that in these verses we have the substance of Jesus' teaching on enemy love. Viewing it in relation to the New Testament paraenetic tradition has revealed how thoroughly Jesus' commands determined the early church's teaching on this matter. His sayings were quoted, interpreted and applied; they also constituted the criterion according to which Jewish paraenetic elements were taken over.

Lk 6:29-30/ Mt 5:39b-42

The change of person from plural to singular between Mt 5:39a and 39bff, and between Lk 6:28 and 29f suggests the original independence of this sayings group.[134] Although Mt 5:41 is not found in Lk we may with good reason assign all of Mt 5:39b-42 to Q.[135] That the content of these sayings is probably more original in Mt follows from the observation that it is more probable that Lk (or Q-l) has simplified the text by eliminating the legal technicalities suggested by δεξιάν (Mt 5:39b), κριθῆναι (Mt 5:40), and ἀγγαρεύσει (Mt 5:41) than that Mt (or Q-m) complicated with legal details a more simple text in Q.[136] But the priority of Lk is maintained by some because it is 'in strict poetic form, showing parallelism and – on translation into Aramaic – rhyme and rhythm.'[137] However, a distinct poetic form is also seen in Mt 5:39b-42 in which Semitic influence is evident.[138] Therefore, we cannot from the standpoint of form decide with any reasonable degree of certainty what the earliest wording of these commands was.[139] Nor is it certain whether the individual commands were originally in this manner grouped together.[140]

The 'imaginative quality', the 'realism and dramatic power' that shines through the words of Mt 5:39b-42 par is a mark of Jesus' teaching, not of the early church paraenesis.[141] While these sayings have the appearance of wisdom proverbs, nevertheless, they 'reach out beyond popular wisdom and piety and are yet in no sense scribal or rabbinic nor yet Jewish apocalyptic. So here if anywhere we find what is characteristic in the preaching of Jesus.'[142]

With all the variety in wording between Mt and Lk, the point of the teaching comes through: retaliation against physical abuse is rejected (Mt 5:39b); more than that, positive generosity is commanded toward the one who makes harsh demands on your possessions (Mt 5:40) and your time and energy (Mt 5:41). One must be ready to give and to loan without a view to one's own financial advantage (Mt 5:42). This teaching continues and elaborates the emphases we isolated in the preceding section: Jesus renounces unconditionally the ἀντί principle of revenge and stresses the positive response of love precisely toward the one who seems least likely to deserve it, the enemy.

The paraenetic tradition of the early church does not employ these sayings of Jesus directly. His commands were so specific that they were apparently unsuitable for moral instruction in the congregation. Even so his commands control the development of the paraenesis: 'Never avenge yourselves!' (Rom 12:19); 'Give your needy enemy food and drink!' (Rom 12:20); 'Suffer an unjust beating patiently!' (I Pt 2:20); 'Suffer wrong and be defrauded rather than go to court, especially with a brother!' (I Cor 6:7).

Lk 6:32-34/Mt 5:46,47

A group of rhetorical questions in connection with the love command may be assumed in Q. Again it is Mt's form which is likely to be the more original. We have already noticed the stylized symmetry between Lk's rhetorical questions and his repeated love command in 6:35a (see p 54). Lk's third question (6:34) separates itself from the others by describing a different kind of situation.[143] It may thus be a secondary addition to reintroduce the δανίσασθαι omitted in Lk 6:30b (cf Mt 5:42b).[144] Concerning the second rhetorical question, if Mt 5:47 and Lk 6:33 did not both stand in Q then Mt's ἀσπάσησθε is probably primary.[145] The first question concerning loving those who love you is common to Mt and Lk.

It is a common opinion that Mt's μισθόν is more original than Lk's χάρις.[146] But the meaning of both expressions is probably the same so that they may be merely stylistic variations of a common Aramaic original.[147] The bringing together of 'tax collectors' and 'gentiles' in Mt 5:46,47 calls to mind this pair in Mt 18:17, which suggests that the combination may be Mt's in both places. Moreover, the word for gentiles in these two texts is ἐθνικός, a word occurring only three times in the synoptics. The other occurrence is in Mt 6:7, which is unparalleled in Mk and Lk. On the other hand 'sinners' in Lk 6:32,33,34 may be an accommodation to gentile readers.[148] But again in any case, the meaning is essentially the same.[149] The περισσόν of Mt 5:47 is probably Mt's adaptation under the influence of 5:20 (περισσεύσῃ).[150]

The rhetorical questions did not likely circulate as an independent unit but were attached from the time of their origin to the love command as the Q context shows. Lührmann, while agreeing with this, denies however that the questions go back to Jesus. He argues that the reference to 'tax collectors,' 'gentiles' and 'sinners' is a *Qualifizierung der anderen* which contradicts Jesus' love command and therefore did not form a part of his teaching. 'If the "Neighbor" can even be the "enemy" then such talk is no longer possible.'[151]

This argument is, in my opinion, not convincing. If Lührmann means that Jesus did not make distinctions between men with regard to salvation or morality, then I think the synoptic tradition shows him wrong.[152] If he means, however, merely that the distinctions Jesus made would not have been made *in this way*, i.e., with the words τελῶναι, ἐθνικοί, or ἀμαρτωλοί, then the objection is superficial. Whether a man is *speaking* in accord with Jesus' love command will not hang on something so outward as the titles he uses for people. In Jesus' situation few words would have driven his point home to a pious Jew like τελῶναι, ἐθνικοί,[153] or ἀμαρτωλοί. Such people love those who love them; therefore, if you do no more than this, you class yourselves with those who, *even by your own standards,* will receive no reward. There seems to be no reason to deny that Jesus addressed his hearers in this way.[154]

The element in Jesus' teachings here which we have not yet encountered is the idea of reward (see further pp 76ff). Does this aspect of Jesus' teaching, which is not restricted to this text,[155] reduce Jesus' command of enemy love to a mere expedient whereby his disciples, by using others, satisfy their own desires? The 'reward', as the context here (Mt 5:45; Lk 6:35c) shows, is 'to be sons of God' or, as the wider context of the beatitudes (cf Mt 5:9,3/Lk 6:20) shows, 'to attain the blessings of the Kingdom of God.'[156] Does Jesus mean then that a man earns his way into the Kingdom, that God is waiting to see who deserves to enter on account of his superior moral effort? A text like Mt 6:15 seems to suggest this: 'If you do not forgive men their trespasses, neither will your Father forgive your trespasses.' But the parable of the unforgiving servant (Mt 18:23-35)[157] makes explicit a principle which underlies Jesus' command to forgive and love: the forgiveness and love of God precedes the servant's forgiveness of his brother. Therefore loving one's enemies is not the test by which one proves to God that he is worthy to be forgiven and accepted into the Kingdom; the reverse is the case: God first forgives and accepts in order that a man through faith in his acceptance may pass the test of loving his enemies.[158] When Jesus calls for a man to love those who do not love him, he is not calling for heroes who, by the sheer will to self-surrender, act for the good of others. He is calling for insecure and self-indulgent children (cf Mt 18:3) to trust their Father and thus find the security (cf Mt 6:25ff, μὴ μεριμνᾶτε) and gladness (cf Mt 5:12, χαίρετε καὶ ἀγαλιᾶσθε; Lk 6:23, χάρητε καὶ σκιρτήσατε) which will enable them to take patiently whatever pain or humiliation may come from loving their enemies.[159] Having his own longings satisfied in God's acceptance, the disciple is freed to satisfy the longings even of his enemy. But a man who does not love his enemy will not enter into the Kingdom of

God: a good tree *cannot* bear evil fruit (Mt 7:18; cf 24:12f). That Jesus'
call to this newness of existence is first concealed in the form of an ethical
command corresponds to the hiddenness of his mission and to the fact
that an ethical transformation must accompany a response to his call.

Following Jesus the early church did not urge enemy love with
the promise of earthly reward. As we have already noted, when Prov
25:21 was taken up into the Christian paraenesis (Rom 12:20), the last
phrase, 'and the Lord will reward you,' was omitted. The early church
is pre-eminently conscious of the priority of God's love and forgiveness in
accomplishing all that is necessary for a man's salvation (Rom 5:6-8;
I Thess 2:12,13; I Pt 1:3-5, 18-21, 23; 2:24; 3:18). But, also like Jesus,
the threat of losing one's 'reward' is an inextricable part of the New Testament paraenesis. To the believer who, instead of bearing the fruit of love,
does the works of the flesh, Paul warns (Gal 5:21), 'I say to you, as I have
said before, that those who do such things will not inherit the Kingdom of
God.' To the believer who may be tempted to 'transgress or wrong his
brother' in the matter of immorality, Paul warns (I Thess 4:6), 'The
Lord is an avenger in all these things as we said before and testified.'[160]
Finally, the function of the Old Testament quote in I Pt 3:10-12 is to
provide incentive for loving one's enemies (I Pt 3:9); it does so by
reminding that 'life' is contingent upon the way one uses his tongue (v 10),
and by warning that the Lord looks favorably on those who do good but
turns his face against those who do evil (v 12).[161]

Each of these three instances of warning/promise manifests a similar
pattern of the divine saving work. In Gal the key is found in the phrase
'faith working through love' (5:6b). In I Thess, 'the word of *God* is at
work in the believers' (2:13) and it is the *Lord* who makes believers abound
in love to one another and to all (3:12). In I Pt the believer has been
'brought to God' by the death of Christ (3:18), 'born anew' through
the living and abiding word of God, so that he can 'do good' and even
suffer for it because 'he trusts his soul to a faithful creator' (4:19). The
priority of the divine saving work is stressed in each case. As in Jesus'
teaching there is a reward for loving your enemies, but it is not a reward
of mere human achievement. It is not a reward which encourages the
manipulation of the enemy to meet my own needs, on the contrary it
will be given only to him whose needs have been met in the saving work
of Christ.

Lk 6:35b/Mt 5:45

The saying on sonship was connected to the love command already in Q
and it probably did not ever exist independently since it demands that the

deed be mentioned which results in sonship. The original form of the divine name and the verb for 'be/become' cannot with confidence be determined.[162] Lk sums up Mt's sending of sunshine and rain in the word χρηστός. This condensation is theologically more abstract; Mt's more lively, realistic form is probably original.[163] Whether one accepts as primary Lk's 'ungrateful and evil' or Mt's 'evil and good . . . just and unjust' will depend on whether one thinks the sixth antithesis is original in which Mt's 'good and evil' is paralleled by 'neighbor and enemy' (see my conclusion, p 55).

The saying in both Mt and Lk affirms that sonship of God depends on acting like God: God is kind to his enemies; therefore anyone who wants to be a son of God must do the same. There is nothing specifically Christian in the command to imitate God.[164] In fact the saying as we have it here looks very much like a popular proverb attributed to the Stoics: 'If you are imitating the gods then bestow benefits also upon the ungrateful; for the sun rises also upon the wicked and the sea lies open also to pirates' (Seneca, *De Beneficiis* IV.26.1).[165] Nevertheless the early church did not use this kind of lively realistic language so that there is no decisive objection to Jesus' having taken up the proverb and putting it to his own use.[166]

The ὅτι of Mt 5:45 does not introduce an observation of nature which intends to prove in this instance the kindness of God; it introduces an absolute statement about the kindness of God which is realized, among other ways, in rain and sunshine. In other words, the concern of the verse is not to deal with the problem of how we *know* God is kind to his enemies, but rather, by the assertion that he *is* kind to his enemies, to provide the pattern for his sons' behavior.[167]

How did this pattern function for the early church? It is not immediately obvious that to imitate God means always to love one's enemy. God is the one who having killed has the power to cast into hell (Lk 12:5/Mt 10:28; cf Mt 5:29f). He will judge those on whom he has sent sun and rain (Mt 5:22). Does this mean that for the believer the love command is accordingly qualified? In the New Testament paraenesis the imitation of Christ overshadows the imitation of God (cf Rom 15:3,7; I Cor 11:1; Phil 2:5ff; I Thess 1:6; I Pt 2:21). But the imitation of God does come to expression in Eph 4:32-5:2 where forgiveness is commanded. In all of the places where Christ is the example, loving, self-giving behavior is exhorted.[168] Nowhere does the paraenetic tradition suggest that the imitation of God or Christ could be a justification of abusing or injuring someone. While the early church knew God as judge of his enemies, it was precisely this divine prerogative of which imitation was explicitly forbidden (Rom 12:19). Thus the church employed the concept of imitation in a way not essentially different from the way Jesus did. It developed the concept, further focusing on the kindness shown by God 'in Christ' (Eph 4:32), but it never transferred the notion of imitation to his wrath.

Lk 6:36/Mt 5:48

This parallel shows that a command to be perfect/merciful like God closed the section on enemy love in Q.[169] The primary difference between the two forms of the command is the difference between τέλειοι in Mt and οἰκτίρμων in Lk. While good arguments are not lacking for the originality of Mt's form,[170] the Matthean addition of τέλειος in 19:21 makes Mt's τέλειοι here more probably redactional.[171]

In the early church paraenesis the believer is exhorted to be both τέλειος (I Cor 14:20; Phil 3:15; Col 1:28; 4:12; Heb 5:14; Ja 1:4, cf 3:2) and οἰκτίρμων (Phil 2:1; Col 3:12); but nowhere is either of these words directly connected with an imitation of God as here in Mt and Lk. If Lk is original here, then Lk 6:36 only makes more explicit the direction which Jesus gave to the concept of imitation; mercy not judgment is to be imitated.[172]

VIII. Conclusion

The over-arching concern of this chapter has been to determine whether or not the elements of the New Testament paraenetic tradition, worked out in Chapter 1, rest in some way on Jesus' command of enemy love. In the course of our investigation we have seen that, as far as the *raw material* of the paraenetic tradition is concerned, the early church did draw from the sayings of Jesus as it did also from the Old Testament and Jewish Hellenistic sources. We may summarize these adaptations as follows.[173]

'*Bless those who persecute you, bless and do not curse*' (Rom 12:14; for 'persecute' see I Cor 4:12; II Cor 4:9; Gal 5:11; 6:12; II Tim 3:12; Rev 12:13). This is likely a free construction of Jesus' command, 'Bless those who curse you.'[174] The focus on persecution is a result of the young church's experience (see pp 56–8).

'*Do good (to all)*' (I Pt 3:11; I Thess 5:15; Gal 6:10; cf Rom 2:10; 13:3; Eph 6:8; I Pt 2:14f,20; 3:6,13,17; 4:19; III Jn 11). The same may be said here as with the preceding command. We should emphasize here, however, that the widespread utilization of this element of Ps 34 and its expansion to 'do good *to all*' (Gal 6:10; I Thess 5:15) probably was prompted by Jesus' own use of the command to do good (Lk 6:33,35) even to those who hate you (Lk 6:27). Such a traditional connection would be supported by I Pt 2:20 which recalls clearly Jesus' rhetorical question in Lk 6:33[175] (see pp 13, 57).

'Seek peace (with all)' (I Pt 3:11; Rom 12:18; I Thess 5:13; cf Rom 14:19; Heb 12:14). This command and its variations probably entered the Christian paraenetic tradition directly from Ps 34:15 (LXX 33:15) as the quote in I Pt 3:10–12 (cf 2:3 = LXX Ps 33:8) shows. In this the church may well have been following the teaching of her Lord, Mt 5:9; Mk 9:50 (see p 14).

'Do not return evil for evil' (Rom 12:17; I Thess 5:15; I Pt 3:9). The phrase occurs repeatedly in Joseph and Asenath and was rendered also by R. Meir (A.D. 150). It appears to be a further development on the thought in Prov 17:13 (cf 20:22 Mas) and was a common possession of Palestinian and Hellenistic paraenesis (see pp 39, 49).

It was natural that the early church should preserve in its paraenetic tradition, certain elements of its Jewish inheritance. But we noted earlier that, at those points where the church took up raw material from the Old Testament and from Jewish Hellenistic sources (cf the section on Joseph and Asenath), it did not do so without distinction. Therefore, the elements taken up do not merely reflect the character of the sources. They were chosen because they suited a Christian purpose and they were altered by the context into which they were put (cf p 39).

Our investigation of Jewish and Hellenistic sources revealed that they could not alone account for the precise character of the command of enemy love in the early Christian tradition, because they were characterized by one or more of the following features: a command or permission to hate another person; a qualification of enemy love so that it is not always or in every case demanded; an ambiguous mixture of unrelated directions to love and hate; a ground and aim in 'loving' which is irreconcilable with the New Testament paraenesis.[176]

The early Christian paraenesis, on the other hand, answers the question, 'How shall I treat my enemy?' with the unequivocal and unqualified demand upon the believer not to repay evil with evil but, positively, to do good, bless, pray for, seek peace, in short, to love. This love is grounded in the mercies of God experienced by the believer in Christ and it aims ultimately at the enemies' enjoyment of that mercy.

That which sets the early church off from its environment, however, is that which it has in common with Jesus. The paraphrased, interpreted and applied sayings of Jesus form the center of the paraenetic teaching on enemy love. Therefore it is the peculiar character[177] of Jesus' command of enemy love which constituted the unique criterion according to which the non-Christian paraenetic elements were taken up into the early Christian paraenetic tradition. (This conclusion will be further tested in Chapter 4.)

With this conclusion our study aligns itself with those who find the roots of the early Christian paraenetic tradition in the teachings of Jesus.[178] The notion that Paul and others involved in the gentile mission and in the formation of this tradition were either unaware of or deliberately ignored the words of the earthly Jesus is, in view of our conclusion, untenable.[179]

3

JESUS' COMMAND OF ENEMY LOVE IN THE LARGER CONTEXT OF HIS MESSAGE

I. Preliminary Remarks

A. *The Hermeneutical Problems*

It is a hermeneutical axiom that the part can only be properly understood in relation to the whole. For us that means: Jesus' command of enemy love can only be properly understood in relation to the message of Jesus as a whole. But every whole, including Jesus' message, is the sum of its parts and is accessible to the investigator only through its parts. We are, therefore, at the outset, confronted by the venerable problem of the hermeneutic circle: one must have some conception of Jesus' over-all intention in order to construe correctly his individual sayings, and one cannot have a proper conception of Jesus' over-all intention until one perceives in some degree the meaning of his individual sayings.

This is a problem that every interpreter of any document faces. But it is exacerbated in the case of Jesus' message because, as the form critics have shown, the sayings of Jesus, preserved for us in the gospels, are not always preserved in their original historical context. In other words the 'whole' in which we now find the words of Jesus (= parts) and which would normally shed light on these individual sayings has been shown in many cases to be the work of the evangelists.

The hermeneutical circle is also made more difficult by the shadow of uncertainty that has been cast across the individual sayings themselves. J. Jeremias has argued that 'In the synoptic tradition it is the inauthenticity and not the authenticity of the sayings of Jesus that must be demonstrated.'[1] But this conclusion has not put an end to the opposite one: 'The nature of the synoptic tradition is such that the burden of proof will be upon the claim to authenticity.'[2] Regardless which of these two views is correct, it is evident that the problem of determining the meaning of Jesus' love command in the larger context of his message is not merely the problem of the hermeneutic circle. Modern research has thrown into question both the part and the whole of Jesus' message as we have it in the gospels.

In view of this, our task in this chapter has involved an investigation of the authenticity of a number of Jesus' sayings besides his command of enemy love. But the reader should be made aware in advance that this work has, as a rule, been consigned to the notes. Its position there signifies that, while needful, it is of secondary importance to the purpose of the chapter. I stress the fact that the question of authenticity is handled in the notes so that the uninterrupted flow of the text will not give the impression that the sayings cited are employed without an awareness of the problems they raise.

Even if due consideration has been given to the question of the authenticity of the individual sayings, the problem remains as to how these shall yield a total picture of Jesus' message. There must be a careful and judicious attempt to piece the parts together in view of their essential content and the historical milieu and the clues offered by the gospel contexts. As the picture begins to take shape, we have a tentative 'whole' by which we can construe other individual sayings and judge more appropriately their genuineness. Thus while we do not escape the hermeneutic circle, our emerging interpretation is hopefully guarded from arbitrariness by the mutually corrective interplay of the whole and the parts.

From this short sketch of the hermeneutical problems encountered in this chapter it has become clear that a *thorough* understanding and demonstration of the meaning of Jesus' love command requires that we view the command within the total picture of Jesus' message. But to develop such a total picture would demand more than a whole monograph itself. The limitations of this chapter will, therefore, be evident in two ways. The 'total picture' of Jesus' message will be considered only as it comes to expression in two of its major components: the Kingdom of God and the law. And further we will lean more heavily on the secondary literature where we must develop the themes of Jesus' message more distant from our limited topic.

B. *The Validity of Systematizing*

The attempt to present Jesus' own understanding of his command of enemy love raises the question of the appropriateness of systematizing. Jesus did not write a systematic theology, nor did he spend a lifetime developing any theological system. To use an analogy of the late Leonhard Goppelt, Jesus' ministry was like a thunder-shower that comes over the land with its rain and is then quickly gone. He left many issues unaddressed and many of our questions unanswered. Due to the nature of his mission much of what he wanted to communicate was implicit and hidden. The questions, then, are: How much of Jesus' implicit intention should we make explicit? How many unanswered questions can we legitimately attempt to answer? How far can we carry a proper systematization of Jesus' message?

My stance on these questions may be summed up in the following way. If Jesus made two seemingly contradictory statements with no effort to reconcile them, the task of the exegete is three-fold: (1) to acknowledge the apparent contradiction openly; (2) to inquire if there is an underlying unity between the two statements and what it is; (3) to explain why Jesus did not try to reconcile them in his own ministry. So far as I can see it is legitimate and necessary to seek the unity behind Jesus' words and work if such exists. Without a perception of this *under*lying unity one can scarcely claim to have *under*stood Jesus.[3] Insofar as a presentation of this unity must appear 'systematic', to that extent is systematization legitimate. What is important is to distinguish the system from the explicit message of Jesus and to make as plain as possible why Jesus expressed himself as he did.

C. The Content of the Chapter

The first major section (II) of the chapter focuses on the relationship between Jesus' command of enemy love and that reality called the Kingdom of God. After hearing five voices on this relationship in Section A, we turn to our own presentation. Section B brings the love command into connection with the coming Kingdom. Specifically the question is posed: Is the love command a condition for entrance into the Kingdom, and, if so, in what way? We pursue this question because Jesus' sayings behind Mt 5:43-48 and Lk 6:32-36 put it unavoidably in our path and because it provides a point of contact with Jesus' call to repentance. Section C brings the love command into connection with that aspect of the Kingdom which is present in Jesus' ministry. We limit ourselves here to the manifestation of the new age in Jesus' acceptance and forgiveness of sinners. A contact with Jesus' love command is more easily observable here than in his healings and exorcisms. Section D is a discussion of the widespread designation of the love command as a 'sign' of the Kingdom of God.

The second major section (III) of the chapter focuses on the relationship between Jesus' command of enemy love and the law. Section A deals with the conflict between the love command and the *lex talionis* (Ex 21:24).

Section B deals with the positive relationship between the command of enemy love and the Old Testament command of neighbor love (Lev 19:18). Finally in Section C we struggle with the difficult question of whether, in view of Jesus' radical command of enemy love, a disciple can or should ever follow the path of resistance.

In the Introduction (p 3) we said that the questions governing our study throughout are: Wherein consists obedience to Jesus' command of enemy love? and, How shall this obedience be realized? The emphasis of this chapter falls heavily upon the latter of these two questions. Jesus himself gives the clearest and most concrete illustrations of what he means by 'Love your enemy!' It is not my intention to develop from these an extensive casuistry (though I believe there is a place for such reflection). This does not mean that nothing is said concerning the nature of obedience to Jesus' love command. On the contrary, in stressing the 'how' of the love command's realization, we uncover the decisive element of that obedience.

The essence of Jesus' ministry was such that if we stressed a specific pattern of behavior in daily life instead of stressing the enabling source of that pattern, we would misrepresent it as a new legalism. It is our conclusion that if the question of enablement can be properly answered, the concrete nature of obedience will emerge naturally, just as a good tree naturally brings forth good fruit.

II. Jesus' Command of Enemy Love and the Kingdom of God

Milan Machoveč states clearly our hermeneutical starting point in seeking to understand Jesus' love command: 'If one is to understand and interpret it, one must surely guard himself from arbitrariness. The only correct basis of interpretation is without doubt found only by answering this question: What place do these expressions in the Sermon on the Mount have in the total structure of Jesus' thought, what place alone could they have?'[4] At the center of the 'structure of Jesus' thought' is the Kingdom of God. The question concerning the place of Jesus' command of enemy love in the whole structure of his thought is, therefore, chiefly the question concerning the role this command played in his proclamation of that reality called the Kingdom of God.

A. Four Recent Studies and One Older Work

Almost everyone who writes seriously about the message of Jesus discusses his teaching on the Kingdom of God and at least mentions his love command. There is, therefore, a vast literature from which we could take a sampling. The studies I have chosen to discuss briefly were not chosen because they represent all the main options for understanding Jesus' love command. They do not present a very broad spectrum.[5] I chose them rather as timely expressions of the recent radical and dramatic trends in biblical studies, and because they all[6] raise in a radical way the question whether *God* is necessary to a proper understanding of Jesus' command of enemy love.

Milan Machoveč is chosen as a representative of the contemporary (and sympathetic) Marxist treatment of Jesus' message. Although *Jesus für Atheisten* does not stem from a member of the establishment of biblical and theological studies,[7] it is nevertheless characteristic of a significant interchange between Christians and Marxists which is definitely affecting that establishment. Herbert Braun represents the radical and influential development inside German New Testament scholarship. Kurt Niederwimmer is one of the periodic non-conformist voices which bring to bear upon Jesus' message some contemporary discovery – in this case depth psychology. Dieter Lührmann is included primarily because his is one of the most recent detailed studies dealing strictly with Jesus' command of enemy love. Finally, one can still not overlook Bultmann's view because it has left its mark on each of the above and is thus still widely influential.

1. Milan Machoveč's 'Jesus für Atheisten'

I have cited Machoveč as one who states well my own methodological starting point for interpreting Jesus' love command. This does not mean we come to the same conclusions; rather the fact that we come to such radically different conclusions starting from the same point[8] shows how carefully the synoptic tradition must be handled. How does Machoveč view the relationship between Jesus' command of enemy love and the Kingdom of God? 'The basic thought . . . is for Jesus undeniably the idea of the nearness, the actuality and the binding claim of the so-called "Kingdom of God".'[9] His love command 'is an anticipation of the "Kingdom of God" through demand, change and mental transformation' (p 133). 'It has to do with a claim and a demand upon the "I" of the believer, the man completely grasped by the Kingdom' (p 130). All the details of the Sermon on the Mount 'have their authenticity only insofar as we conceive them as details of the foundational message about transformation for the Kingdom of God' (p 100). Jesus was not effective, however, in that he proclaimed a *future* Kingdom: 'Jesus swept men along with him as one who laid a present claim upon men from the standpoint of this future age' (p 99).

But what is this future age that has the power to grasp a man? 'The future is your own affair . . . Jesus brought the future down from the heavenly clouds . . . The future is not something that is "coming" from somewhere independently of us . . . rather *the future is our own affair* in every moment; it is the *demand of the present,* the challenge to human ability to exploit every moment as fully and as exactingly as possible' (p 101). The key phrase in this quote is that which summarizes the future age as the 'challenge to human ability (*Herausforderung der menschlichen Fähigkeit*).' Accordingly it must be said of Jesus' love command, which is

an 'anticipation of (*Vorgriff auf*) the Kingdom of God,' 'It does not have
to do with casuistic rules for daily behavior; what we are dealing with are
examples of maximum claim upon *possible human activity*' (p 130, my
italics). It is a necessary consequence of Machoveč's atheism that man is
made the measure of the Kingdom of God. The man who is 'completely
grasped by the Kingdom' is grasped and empowered by nothing more than
the challenge to make himself a morally better person. Accordingly the
'believers' are defined as 'those already changing themselves' (p 113) and
'metanoia' means 'Strive for your own inner transformation' (p 100).
Jesus' preaching is the challenge of a great man with a great ideal to other
men to do and be the best they can with the human powers at their disposal. Machoveč summarizes this way: 'If we dispense with the mythical,
time-bound garb, it would be possible to render the basic message of
Jesus (Mt 4:17) as follows . . .: "Demand much from your life, for perfect
humanity is possible." It is near, that is, one can grasp it, one can become
morally better, purer, one can be more human and *one can do it on his
own* (*durch eigenes Zutun*)' (p 102, my italics). Machoveč's answer to
the question concerning the relationship between Jesus' love command
and the Kingdom of God is not only that the love command anticipates
and corresponds to 'the ideal of the future age' but, more basically, that
the love command is the challenge to realize that ideal in every moment
of one's own existence by one's own human power.

2. Herbert Braun's 'Jesus'

The second study representative of the current positions being taken on
the subject of enemy love and the Kingdom of God is Herbert Braun's
Jesus. According to Braun, 'The Kingdom of God is the center of Jesus'
end-time proclamation.'[10] This Kingdom is not present, rather ' "nearing"
and "coming" are the appropriate verbs to describe its place in time'
(p 54). The end was expected within one generation but this was an error
as the New Testament itself implies (p 60). No attempt is made to
recalculate a new time for the end of the world, 'because Jesus does not
aim to teach about the near end but to summon men in view of its
nearness' (p 61). 'The actual burden of Jesus' end-time proclamation is . . .
an unimaginable sharpening of human responsibility' (p 59). The warning
which Jesus expresses by the coming of the Kingdom of God must be
expressed by us today in a new way. With the sinking away of Jesus'
apocalyptic preaching of the Kingdom, the 'essential parts of his proclamation maintain their validity' (p 61).

What is this that remains? 'The right conduct toward one's neighbor is
for Jesus the main issue' (p 122). 'Love of one's neighbor is in fact the

center of the life which Jesus demands' (p 132). If we ask now about how
this relates to the Kingdom of God we receive no explicit answer, for there
exists no longer a Kingdom of *God*. God has been deposed by his subjects:
in the decisions and opinions of Jesus 'The neighbor already reigns . . . as
the secret king' (p 132). God is not the source, ground or goal of Jesus'
love command; God 'is an expression for this path along which a man can
obediently and humbly go' (p 171).[11] God is permitted to exist (but in no
sense as king) to the extent that I accept myself and then serve others
(p 169).[12] There is, therefore, no essential connection between Jesus' love
command and the Kingdom of God, which was entirely an illusion.

3. Kurt Niederwimmer's 'Jesus'

The third book to consider is Kurt Niederwimmer's *Jesus,* which, according to the blurb on the back of the book, aims to utilize the 'secured
results of depth psychology' in interpreting the preaching of Jesus. How
does Niederwimmer relate Jesus' love command to the Kingdom of God?
Of Mt 5:43–48 and other radical demands of Jesus, Niederwimmer
comments: 'What is peculiar consists . . . in this: that the level of legalism
is totally abandoned and man is put before the unconditional and fathom-
less demand, a demand which can only be proclaimed in connection with
hope for the *eschaton* and which is absurd outside the *eschaton.*'[13] Here
we see the present and future aspects of the *eschaton:* Jesus' radical
demand is absurd unless it is made inside the *eschaton* and yet is made
in hope of the *eschaton.* What is this *eschaton* which makes Jesus' radical
demand possible?

Another name for this *eschaton* is the Kingdom of God. Niederwimmer
defines this aspect of Jesus' teaching in the following way. 'Speech about
the coming Kingdom of God can and must be unmasked as an illusion, if
it is interpreted as a temporal Nearness approaching in the immediate
future. Rather it must be understood as the objectification of a collective
process of consciousness (*Bewusstseinsprozess*); it points to the fact that
this consciousness is about to take on a new attitude (*Neueinstellung*)'
(pp 87f). The coming of the *eschaton* or the Kingdom of God is the
approach of a 'new adjustment' in the human psyche. Our hope for this
change in our consciousness plus its fragmentary present reality is the
ground of Jesus' love command. This change which we are hoping for may
be described as a 'final self-realization,' a fulfilment of all that which our
fragmentary human experience promises (p 87). The eschatological sym-
bols in Jesus' preaching show that man in his existential crisis is open to
this goal of history (p 51).

The guarantee that there is such a goal of history is Jesus himself. In his freedom he certifies 'that man – in spite of everything – is on the way to himself' (p 87). In Jesus 'the man has already appeared toward whose realization all of history is flowing' (p 87). Jesus is thus the present personification of that 'Neueinstellung des Bewusstseins' which constitutes the coming of the *eschaton* or the Kingdom of God. He is, therefore, also the legitimation of his own love command. The fragmentary fulfilment which his disciples may achieve is possible only because of the hope he awakens in them for an eventual complete self-realization. However, Jesus was completely ignorant of the fact that these psychological phenomena were occurring in his ministry and that his love command related to the Kingdom of God in this way: 'Jesus did not see through the mythological character of his concepts, he did not see through the myth as myth and therefore lived in the illusion of the myth' (pp 87, 42).

4. Dieter Lührmann's 'Liebet eure Feinde'
The fourth study is Dieter Lührmann's article, 'Liebet eure Feinde.' The scope of this article is more limited than that of the previous three studies which we have examined, so that there is no broad discussion of the Kingdom of God in which Jesus' love command might take its place. The article was, after all, written by request 'with special attention given to method.'[14] Nevertheless Lührmann does comment summarily on the relationship between Jesus' love command and the Kingdom of God. His last sentence says of Jesus' love command, 'Its eschatological horizon lies not in its exegetical coordination with Jesus' βασιλεία proclamation, but rather in its *Macht gegenüber aller Aktualisierung.*'[15] Jesus' love command is, therefore, eschatological in that it is always beyond our attempts to understand exegetically its relation to the Kingdom of God. It seems to me that if we were to accept Lührmann's conclusion then in effect we could no longer speak of *Jesus'* command. The moment we attach any concrete meaning to the command, it ceases to be *Jesus'* command which, according to Lührmann's definition, is always tearing itself loose from our exposition. On the other hand, if all interpretations of Jesus' command are accepted as legitimate, then the possessive noun 'Jesus'' becomes meaningless, for with the word 'Jesus'' we imply that there is a single unified intention behind the command 'Love your enemies!'

5. Rudolf Bultmann's 'Theology of the New Testament'
After discussing these fairly recent statements concerning the relationship between Jesus' love command and the Kingdom of God it is fitting to include here a noteworthy earlier position, the influence of which has been unmistakable in the works previously cited; the position is that of

Rudolf Bultmann. For Bultmann 'the dominant concept of Jesus' message is the Reign of God.'[16] 'Thus Jesus takes over the apocalyptic picture of the future . . . But what is new and really his own about it all is the certainty with which he says, "Now the time is come! God's Reign is breaking in! The end is here!" ' (p 6). Besides announcing the presence of God's reign Jesus also called for radical obedience to the will of God. 'What positively is the will of God? *the demand for love* . . . There is no obedience to God which does not have to prove itself in the concrete situation of meeting one's neighbor' (p 18).

Jesus' demand for love and his announcement of the presence of God's reign are not unrelated, for the proclamation of the will of God 'must be described as an eschatological ethic' (p 19). It is not eschatological in that it is motivated by reference to the impending end of the world (p 20). The expectation of the near end of the world is only the mythological clothing of the prophetic consciousness 'that man's relation towards God decides his fate and that the hour of decision is of limited duration . . . The absoluteness of God's will is so overpowering that before it the world sinks away and seems to be at an end' (p 22)[17] Therefore the proclamation of the will of God, that is, the demand for love, is eschatological in that it directs man into the Now of his encounter with his neighbor, a Now which always has the nature of a final hour of decision: either God or this world (pp 19, 21).[18]

The demand for love appears, then, to be almost identical with the announcement of the arrival of the Kingdom. Bultmann puts it this way: 'The unity of the eschatological and ethical message of Jesus may be so stated: fulfilment of God's will is the condition for participation in the salvation of his reign' (p 20). However we must not consider the fulfilment of this condition as one thing and the salvation of God's reign as something else added later. They are one: when one exists, so does the other. The person who fulfils God's will, that is, who loves his neighbor, is manifesting that he is experiencing the present reign of God, because he is deciding for God who confronts him in the person of his neighbor. The eschatological proclamation and the ethical demand of Jesus are really one. 'Both things . . . direct man to the fact that he is brought before God, that God stands before him; both direct him into his Now as the hour of decision for God' (p 21)[19] The difference between the two is that the love command makes explicit the fact that this decision for God is always a decision for the neighbor.

6. Summary

To sum up: For *Machoveč* the 'Kingdom of God', as the title of his book already announces, has nothing to do with God. It is an expression of the 'future' which Jesus snatched out of the clouds and made the business of men. It is thus the challenge to exploit every moment to the full. Jesus' love command is a 'Vorgriff auf das Königreich Gottes.' It thus gives expression to the challenge of the Kingdom to become morally better, purer, more human. *Herbert Braun* also sees no place for God in his discussion of Jesus' proclamation: 'Der Nächster regiert bereits . . . als der geheime König.' The love command, therefore, has no essential relation to the Kingdom of God for Jesus; the love command is merely a sharpening of the call to live responsibly towards one's neighbor. According to *Niederwimmer* the Kingdom of God must be understood as 'Objektivierung eines kollektiven Bewusstseinsprozesses.' The love command is grounded in our hope for this total alteration of the human psyche and in our fragmentary experience of it already. Jesus could command love like this because he was a preliminary appearance of that human toward which all history is tending. *Lührmann*'s study is small but would seem to offer an explanation for all the different conceptions of the relation between Jesus' love command and the Kingdom of God: Jesus' love command shows its eschatological horizon 'in seiner Macht gegenüber aller Aktualisierung.' This horizon is not to be found by exegetically seeking its relation to Jesus' βασιλεία proclamation. But with this assertion we are reminded of our methodological starting point with Machoveč: the only way to avoid caprice in our interpretation of Jesus' love command is to investigate its place in the larger structure of Jesus' thought which means first and foremost an exegetical attempt to determine the role it played in Jesus' proclamation of the Kingdom of God.[20] Finally for *Bultmann* Jesus' love command is essentially one with his preaching of the Kingdom of God because the apocalyptical conception of the coming Kingdom is only a mythological way of stressing the urgency of the demand for love. The real manifestation of the reign of God is when a man loves his neighbor. This is very much like Braun's view, but Bultmann never explicitly equated *God* with neighbor love as Braun does (see notes 11 and 12).

As this selective survey has shown, the question of the relationship between Jesus' command of enemy love and the Kingdom of God is crucial because it is the question of *God*. L. Goppelt's comment in his essay 'Das Problem der Bergpredigt' is today still keenly relevant: 'Perhaps the key question today in the interpretation of the Sermon on the Mount is, what these instructions which are directed entirely to men (do not kill, do not lust, do not lie, show only love) have to do with God.'[21] The most direct approach to this question as it bears on our study is to pursue now our own investigation of the relationship between the love command and the Kingdom of God in Jesus' ministry.

B. Jesus' Command of Enemy Love and the Coming Kingdom: Condition?

We have examined briefly Jesus' claim that the one who obeys his love command will be rewarded (pp 60-1).[22] We will now investigate this idea from the standpoint of our present problem: the relationship between the love command and the Kingdom of God. Specifically, we may ask the question: Is Jesus' love command a *condition* for entrance into the Kingdom of God, and if so in what way?

> In asking this question it is important to make clear what we mean by '*condition*'. Depending upon one's theological preconception, the word 'condition' may imply a legalistic view of salvation in which man, by his native powers, fulfils certain requirements before God performs any work in his life. But this is not a necessary implication of the word 'condition' (as our discussion of Bultmann's view above shows, p 74), and our use of the word in the above question should not prejudice the answer in this direction. All that is meant here by 'condition' is this: the condition of anything is that without which it does not occur or exist. Should we determine that the fulfilment of Jesus' command of enemy love is a condition for entrance into the Kingdom of God in this sense, then the question would not yet be answered, whether there is an inner, essential relationship between the two or whether they are only arbitrarily connected. That is why we must ask: *In what way* is the love command a condition? If entering into the Kingdom of God were compared to the enjoyment of a symphony we would have to ask: Is the fulfilment of Jesus' love command a condition in the sense that a good ear and a high appreciation of music is a condition for enjoying a symphony? Or is the love command a condition in the sense that buying a ticket is a condition for enjoying a symphony?

As a result of our analysis of Lk 6:35/Mt 5:45 (pp 61f) we determined that Jesus promised those who loved their enemies that they would thereby become sons of God because God is kind to his enemies. We concluded also (p 59) that in this same context belong Jesus' rhetorical questions (Lk 6:32f/Mt 5:46f). In these Jesus says in a negative form what the promise of sonship declares positively. That is, if you do not obey the command to love your enemies, you will have no reward at all. 'If you love those who love you, what reward do you have?' Answer: none. To love your enemies is to receive the reward of sonship; not to love your enemies is to be denied the reward of sonship. The fulfilment of Jesus' love command is a condition for sonship of the heavenly Father.[23]

To become a son of God and to enter into the Kingdom of God are closely related events.[24] One cannot be a son of God and be excluded from his Kingdom, nor can one be included in the Kingdom of God and be denied sonship.[25] Sonship of God is a blessing which all those and only those enjoy who will enter the Kingdom of God. This is confirmed by the Matthean form of the beatitudes where to be called the sons of God (5:9) is one of the blessings of belonging to the Kingdom of heaven (5:3,10).[26] Consequently the reward spoken of in Jesus' rhetorical questions (Mt 5:46f par) is nothing less than entering into the Kingdom of God.[27] Accordingly the fulfilment of Jesus' love command is in some sense a condition for entering into the Kingdom of God.[28]

The way in which the fulfilment of the love command is a condition for entrance into the Kingdom is suggested by a seemingly unrelated saying of Jesus concerning those who are rich, but nevertheless a saying of which Schniewind says, 'What is spoken here is a key saying for the entirety of Jesus' moral instructions.'[29] In Mk 10:23-28 Jesus interprets for the disciples the underlying meaning of his encounter with the rich young man.[30] Jesus told this man the condition he must meet in order to inherit eternal life: 'What must I do to inherit eternal life?' . . . 'Go, sell what you have, and give to the poor, and you will have treasure in heaven: and come, follow me' (Mk 10:17,21). The man refused to meet the condition and Jesus draws the general conclusion, 'How hard it will be for those who have riches to enter the Kingdom of God' (10:23). As if to confirm the disciples' amazement at this statement, Jesus goes farther and says that it is hard for *anybody* to enter the Kingdom (10:24). Indeed, as the disciples rightly conclude from Jesus' saying about the camel and the needle's eye, it is humanly *impossible* for a man to be saved, i.e., enter the Kingdom of God.[31] But on the other hand, 'with God all things are possible' (10:27). In other words the *sine qua non* of salvation is the action of God doing the humanly impossible. An indispensable condition for entrance into the Kingdom is the power of God.

How is this condition of divine intervention related to the conditions contained in Jesus' commands, specifically, the command of enemy love? Jesus was prompted to say that rich men cannot enter the Kingdom of God when a particular rich man did not obey Jesus' command to sell all he had, give to the poor and follow him. That is, the rich man's inability to enter the Kingdom of God was his inability to meet the condition which Jesus set. A man *cannot* abandon that which he loves the most (cf Lk 14:26,[32] δύναται). He *cannot* choose against what he values most highly. He *cannot* give his heart to that which he does not treasure (Mt 6:21 par). Therefore, as long as a man treasures that which is on earth, whether it be riches (Mk 10:17-22), family (Lk 14:25f), religious practices (Lk 18:9-14 Mt 6:1ff[33]), wisdom (Mt 11:25 par[34]), political power (Mk 10:42ff[35]) or his own life (Mk 8:34f par[36]), it will be impossible for that man to inherit the Kingdom of God. Jesus' belief that this impossibility does in fact exist is based on his conviction that men do in fact naturally set their hearts on these earthly things rather than on the Kingdom of heaven (Mt 6:32; cf Jn 5:44).[37]

Therefore, if any man is to enter the Kingdom, he must experience a thoroughgoing inversion of values. Instead of clinging to his riches he must give them to the poor, instead of loving his family he must hate them, instead of parading his religiosity he must practice his piety in secret, instead of depending on his wisdom he must become a baby, instead of lording it over others he must be the servant of all, instead of saving his own life he must lose it. Only when a man carries through this radical reversal of where his treasure is, can he enter the Kingdom of God. Since no mere human can accomplish this transformation, Jesus pronounces entrance into the Kingdom impossible.

But then he implies that God, for whom nothing is impossible, has the power to perform this transformation. Apparently God alone can free a man so completely that the man can and will fulfil the conditions for entering the Kingdom.[38] If it is not precisely at this point that the omnipotence of God is at work, namely, the point of enabling men to fulfil the conditions of entrance into the Kingdom, and if men nevertheless are to enter the Kingdom, then either the commands and warnings of Jesus are not what they claim to be (i.e., conditions for participation in the Kingdom), or a man really can on his own power work his way into the Kingdom of heaven. But if we take seriously both the commands of Jesus and his sober pessimism about man's moral ability,[39] the only conclusion we can come to is that, if a man is to enter the Kingdom of heaven, God must enable him to fulfil the conditions contained in the command. What God demands he gives.[40]

Jesus' command of enemy love must be obeyed, we have said, if one is to enter into the Kingdom of God. Thus, as a condition for entrance into the Kingdom, it is a part of the scheme we have just sketched. It may, therefore, be said of Jesus' love command, 'With men it is impossible.' It is not therefore a condition in the sense that the Kingdom of heaven is a prize granted to a contestant who by great personal effort has won the contest. Rather it is a condition which when fulfilled in no way reflects the superiority or merit of the disciple (cf Lk 17:10[41]). On the contrary, it reflects the power of God. It is for this reason that when men see the disciple's good works they glorify not him but his Father in heaven (Mt 5:16[42]).

The connection between the commands of Jesus and the enabling power of God is never made so *explicit* by Jesus as we have described it here. Jesus never says, for example, 'You must love your enemies because God will enable you.' Such a statement would tend to misrepresent Jesus' intention which is to grant the divine enablement through calling men into discipleship to himself (see below, p 85). Nevertheless this connection is *implicit* in Jesus' message, for the Kingdom of God is 'good news' (Lk 8:1; 4:18; Mt 11:5), it is a gift (Mk 10:15; Lk 12:32) and yet it is conditional.[43]

In saying that one fulfils the love command by the power of God we imply an even closer relationship between the love command and the Kingdom of God than we have so far described (and here we begin a transition into the topic to be discussed in the next section). This power of God to transform a man and enable him to obey his will as Jesus commands is itself the power of the new age, the blessing of the Kingdom of God.[44] We are therefore compelled here to distinguish between the Kingdom of God as a future, yet to be fully consummated reality[45] and as a present already effective reality[46] (Lk 11:20; 17:21; Mt 11:2-6). The fulfilment of the love command is on the one hand that without which one will not enter the future Kingdom of God when it is consummated, and on the other hand, that which is *impossible* if one has not in a sense already entered the Kingdom, or better, been entered by the powers of that Kingdom.

Therefore the love command, as a condition for entrance into the Kingdom, is of one piece with that for which it is a condition. Until now we have treated the connection between Jesus' love command and the Kingdom of God merely as external, as if there were no essential unity between the Kingdom of God and this condition for entrance into it. Now we must stress that there is a unity, and that the love command is not just accidentally the condition of entrance into the Kingdom of God.[47] The earthly fulfilment of the love command does not happen apart from the powers of the Kingdom, nor will final entrance into the future Kingdom mean that the conditions of entry are left behind. Life in the consummated Kingdom will not, therefore, be essentially different from the action and attitude demanded by the love command. Only that person will enter the Kingdom whose living has already reflected the life and power of the Kingdom. That life and power are reflected most clearly when a man loves his enemy, for in doing this he acts most contrary to the natural pattern of human relations in this age (cf Lk 6:32-34. See pp 86ff).

To round out this section we may bring our two conclusions into association with Jesus' central concern summed up in the thematic command: 'Repent, for the Kingdom of Heaven is at hand' (Mt 4:17; cf Mk 1:15). First, we saw that obedience to Jesus' love command, which is a condition for entering the Kingdom, requires a man's transformation. This transformation, which in fact all of Jesus' commands demand, is what is meant by repentance, μετάνοια.[48] Second, we saw that this transformation, i.e., repentance, which is demanded by the love command is the work of God. Jesus' call to repentance, is therefore a call[49] to recognize one's hopeless situation and to appeal to the omnipotent kindness of God for present help in making a radically new beginning as a disciple of Jesus.[50] Jesus' call to repentance, expressed concretely in the love commandment, is, therefore, not grounded merely in the future and hastening judgment day. That such a day is coming Jesus taught. In fact, its certainty and seriousness give Jesus' commands their grave importance.[51] But the prospect of the approaching end of the age cannot of itself effect in man the repentance Jesus was calling for. If the Kingdom is only future and men are left to themselves to get ready, no one will enter it. Jesus, however, calls a man to repentance not just because it is important for this future, but also because it is possible in the present. God is now at work in Jesus' ministry to effect repentance and thus enable obedience.

> Martin Hengel ('Leben in der Veränderung,' 1970) provides a good summary statement for this section: 'In the message of Jesus the demand which is radicalized by the nearness of God's Kingdom is the consequence of salvation not a *condition* of it to be achieved by man (*nicht vom Menschen zu leistende 'Bedingung'*) . . . Not the imperative but the indicative is the point of departure and the goal of Jesus' proclamation. The epiphany of the love of God in his person proclaims the "justification of the godless" . . . Viewed from Jesus' message and work, the Sermon on the Mount becomes . . . the instructions for a new existence of "lived faith" (*gelebten Glaubens*), which is no less grounded in God's free grace than the imperative of the pauline paraenesis' (p 650f).

> One qualification may be necessary in view of our discussion. Jesus' command of enemy love *is* a condition for entrance into the coming Kingdom (in the sense developed above) but, as Hengel says, it is not a '*vom Menschen zu leistende*' condition. Only people who love their enemies will enter the Kingdom of God but no one who boasts of his achievements will enter.

C. Jesus' Command of Enemy Love and the Present Aspect of the Kingdom: Enablement

In the final paragraphs of the previous section we touched upon a theme that cannot be passed over because of its importance but also cannot be handled in detail because of its size: the presence of God's reign in the ministry of Jesus. The powers of the new age are not randomly present; they are present in Jesus. All of our talk about the present effect of the

Kingdom which enables repentance and obedience is qualified by the fact that this effect is not realized apart from the person[52] and work of Jesus. We will eliminate from discussion the present aspect of the Kingdom manifest in Jesus' casting out of demons (Lk 11:20) and his healings (Mt 11:2-4). We focus instead on another aspect of Jesus' ministry by which men were granted the renewal of heart which Jesus demanded, namely, Jesus' fellowship with sinners and his forgiveness[53] of their sins.

This facet of Jesus' ministry and the scandal it caused come to expression in the saying, 'Behold a glutton and a drunkard, a friend of tax collectors and sinners!' (Mt 11:19).[54] His task which caused many to take offence (Mt 11:6)[55] was the delivering of good news to the poor (Mt 11:5/ Lk 4:18; cf Lk 7:22), that is, 'poor' in the prophetic sense of oppressed, afflicted, ostracized and helpless.[56] The result of his bringing good news to the poor was that Jesus could say to the religious leaders in Jerusalem, 'Tax collectors and harlots go into the Kingdom of God before you' (Mt 21:31).[57] In other words, 'Blessed are you poor, for yours is the Kingdom of God' (Lk 6:20).

One of the concrete encounters with these 'sinners'[58] in which Jesus brings them the good news is the shared meal. 'The Pharisees and scribes murmured, saying, "This man receives sinners and eats with them"' (Lk 15:2; cf Mk 2:15-17 par). 'To understand what Jesus was doing in eating with "sinners," it is important to realize that in the east, even today, to invite a man to a meal was an honor. It was an offer of peace, trust, brotherhood and forgiveness; in short sharing a table meant sharing life.'[59] Jesus did not eat with sinners because he took pleasure in sin, a fact which the Pharisees could not grasp; he was among sinners as a physician among the sick (Mk 2:17).[60] His presence with them at table was an offer of acceptance and forgiveness and this forgiveness insofar as it was accepted was the healing of the 'sick'.[61]

The acceptance and forgiveness which Jesus offers tax collectors and sinners by eating with them is the very acceptance and forgiveness of God as Lk 15 shows.

A summary of the discussion concerning the unity of the parable of the prodigal son may be found in the brief debate between E. Schweizer (*ThZ* 4, pp 469ff)[62] who maintains that vv 25-32 did not belong to vv 11-24 originally and J. Jeremias (*ThZ* 5, pp 228ff) who maintains that vv 11-32 are an original unit. Judging from the standpoint of the original *intention* of the parable the unity of it may be denied if one sees the older brother scene as extraneous to the point about the father's love in vv 11-24. (On the original intention, see below.) Judging from the standpoint of *form*: 'Vv 25-32 are not an allegorical fabrication, but remain completely within the parable' (Bultmann, *History*, p 196).

As Charles Smith observes, 'The effort to divide the parable into two seems unnecessary and impossible. The place of the older son in the narrative is secured by references in vv 11–13. There would be no point in this if the older son were to play no part in the story' (*Parables*, p 100).

Not essentially different from Jülicher, Bultmann sees the intention of the parable: 'to make plain the fatherly goodness of God, which unconditionally forgives self-condemning remorse.' The second half of the parable is not really different from the first, 'but rather makes plain by contrast the paradoxical character of divine forgiveness' (*History*, p 196; cf Jülicher, *Gleichnisreden* II, p 363). This interpretation alone, however, does not do justice to the entreaty of the father to the elder son in which the parable culminates. In Jesus' situation it is inevitable that the Pharisees or scribes be seen in the figure of the older brother.[63]

It would correspond then to Jesus' usual practice of confrontation (as opposed to merely speaking *about* someone) if we were to assume that the hearers of this parable included the Pharisees or scribes. This inference from the content of the parable corresponds in fact with the Lukan setting for the parable in chapter 15. Here the parable is told in response to the Pharisees' and scribes' murmuring, 'this man receives sinners and eats with them.' In keeping with this correspondence it would seem arbitrary to ignore Lk's setting, according to which the parable intends to say something about Jesus' ministry as it relates both to sinners *and* to Pharisees.

Schottroff's contention, 'Lk 15:1–3 cannot at all depict the setting in Jesus' life for the parable of the prodigal son' (*ZThK* 68, p 51), is, I think, inadequately grounded. Her first argument is: 'The Pharisees to whom Jesus was opposed could not recognize themselves in the figure of the oldest son, because they could scarcely have reprimanded Jesus that his company with sinners was for them an undeserved gift of God (or of Jesus); for in that case they would have had to recognize him as the bringer of salvation' (*ZThK* 68, p 50). That the Pharisees had to be able to see themselves in the older son is not a prerequisite for the son's being an accurate representation of them. Of course the Pharisees do not admit Jesus is the bringer of salvation but the parabolic form does not demand that every element of the historical situation have a counterpart in the parable. The parable is here not a *description* of what is happening between Jesus and the sinners and the Pharisees, but rather an *interpretation* and thereby a summons to the Pharisees to see Jesus and themselves in the true light of the parable.

Her second argument is: 'The Pharisees could not recognize themselves in the older son because they do not find here their own theological conception . . . The self-assurance with which the older brother boasts in his achievement is not the portrayal of a Pharisee, and the dependence on the grace of God which the prodigal son accepts would not have been foreign to a Pharisee' (*ZThK* 68, p 50). The argument here against finding the *Sitz im Leben* of this parable in Jesus' own situation seems to miss one important point. Whether or not the Pharisees were as bad as the gospels picture them is not the key issue here, but whether, from what we know of Jesus, he thought they were. In order to strike this parable from the genuine Jesus tradition one cannot simply appeal to the contemporary witness of the Pharisees (showing they were not so bad as the parable says); one must show that the parable pictures the Pharisees other than *Jesus* did (whether he was right or wrong). This I do not think has been done, for this picture (*Karikierung*?) of the Pharisees is the same one Jesus paints everywhere.

L. Goppelt, I think, does greater justice to the parable in the following: 'This parable is not an enlightenment about the love of God, as Liberalism thought . . . Rather in accord with its introduction in Lk 15:1f (which in any case is appropriate to the parable's subject matter) it explains what happens where Jesus offers his fellowship to sinners: acceptance into fellowship with Jesus means forgiving acceptance into fellowship with God and, indivisibly connected with that, the conversion to obedience, which becomes visible in the case of Zacchaeus (Lk 19:8) and the sinful woman (Lk 7:45ff)' (*Christentum*, p 50).[64] This is not merely a justification of Jesus' questionable practice of eating with sinners, but, as 15:25–32 shows, it is also a call for the Pharisees to repent: 'Jesus invited the Pharisee to leave the courtyard where he serves like a slave and to come into the father's house, into the fellowship of saved sinners (15:28–32). This entrance into joy with those who are saved . . . is the conversion of the righteous. It means giving up one's boasting in achievement and reward, giving up the attitude of a slave toward God, longing for the graciously given fellowship with the father, and a forgiving love toward the sinful brother!' (*Christentum*, p 51)[65]

Goppelt's interpretation does justice both to the parable taken as an independent unit and to the Lukan context. This interpretation tallies with the essential features of Jesus' work which we are here sketching. Therefore it is justifiable to affirm that the acceptance and forgiveness which Jesus offers sinners are the very acceptance and forgiveness of God. It is the recognition of this hidden reality that binds the repentant sinner to Jesus in discipleship.

The forgiveness of sin and acceptance with God which happen in Jesus' fellowship with repentant sinners are the first rays of the dawn of the new age. The rejoicing of God over the recovery of the lost in Lk 15:7,10 could be seen as the fulfilment of Is 65:19 and Zeph 3:17.[66] Schniewind points out that the forgiveness Jesus vouchsafed was the highest hope of the prophets for the new age (Is 33:24; 53:5f; Jer 31:34; Ez 36:25–27; Zech 13:1).[67] Besides these indirect indications of the presence of the Kingdom of God in Jesus' ministry, we have the description of his own ministry as the delivering of good news to the poor (Mt 11:5b)[68] – a fulfilment of the prophetic word for the new era (Is 61:1), albeit, a fulfilment which did not correspond one-to-one with the Old Testament prophecies.

By granting to a sinner in this way forgiveness and acceptance with the Father, Jesus was granting what we have called the power of God to transform the sinner and enable him to obey his commands (pp 78f above).[69] An excellent quote from Schlatter focuses our attention on Jesus' command to love as seen through Jesus' forgiveness: 'Jesus saw the power of forgiveness to stand a man upright and to heal him in this: forgiveness produces love. And when he was reproached for forgiving he justified with the fact that it brings forth not hardening and new guilt but rather love.'[70] Jesus did not think that the forgiveness he imparted had only a negative effect: the elimination of punishment and the removal of a bad conscience. Surely he intended that the forgiveness he granted have a positive and visible effect. It was to be 'the foundation of a new behavior with new norms and new obedience.'[71] It aims at changing the one forgiven into the one who forgives, that is, who loves, who is merciful as his Father in heaven is merciful. This aim finds expression in the parable of the unforgiving servant (Mt 18:23–35).

The emphasis of this parable is not first to instruct about the theological possibility of being a forgiving person but rather to admonish and warn that it is necessary to be such a person if one is to experience mercy on the judgment day. Linnemann (*Gleichnisse*, p 113) sees v 35 as a wrong interpretation of Jesus' parable because it 'lets the parable appear as a threat which it really is not.' She therefore takes issue (p 172) with Bultmann (*History*, p 177) and Klostermann (*Matthäus-Evangelium*, p 153) who view v 35 as a correct interpretation of the parable. However, while seeing the whole point of the parable in v 33 ('We should allow ourselves to enter into the order of mercy with our whole life,' p 118), she must admit that v 34 is a kind of threat: 'There is such a thing as too late' (p 116). Further Linnemann disagrees with Schlatter (*Matthäus*, p 560f) that the parable refers to forgiveness received by the disciples through Jesus. She argues first that the parable was not addressed originally to the disciples and second, 'The understanding of the gospel as a message of forgiveness is an early Christian concept, but may not be put in the mouth of Jesus' (p 173). To the second point Jeremias (*Gleichnisse*, p 210) protests rightly: 'One comes to such mistaken judgments when one sticks to the concordance (s.v. ἀφιέναι) and does not take into account that Jesus, differently from Paul, preferred to use not theological vocabulary so much as word pictures, parables, and parabolic acts, in short, symbol-language.' To the first point one can only admonish caution since we are dealing here with *Sondergut*. We have no control by which to determine how the parable might have been differently used. Viewing the parable from the subject matter we may say, however, that if it was directed to the Jewish people as a whole on the basis of Yahweh's mercy in history, then the principle would apply *a fortiori* to the disciples who perceived that precisely in Jesus' ministry Yahweh was graciously at work.

That Jesus' own loving reception and forgiveness of sinners is the means by which they are enabled to fulfil the love command is not a new insight.[72] However, the frequency with which scholars make this observation must not lead us to think that it lies plainly on the surface of Jesus' message. As we have already mentioned (p 79) Jesus does not openly expound upon the connection between his love command and his own gracious work of forgiveness. On the one hand he commands enemy love and makes entrance into the Kingdom of God dependent on it, and on the other hand he receives sinners and eats with them, thus offering his forgiving fellowship unconditionally. He gives no discourse on the connection of these two sides of his ministry. Such an explication would have apparently contradicted the mystery of his eschatological work.

Our claim that the connection we have described does in fact exist, rests on an attempt to penetrate beneath the surface of Jesus' message.[73] We have tried to show that Jesus' love command is a call for a man's transformation, a transformation which, however, only God can perform. We have also tried to show that Jesus himself personally granted God's forgiveness and acceptance. And we have finally drawn the conclusion that Jesus did not view God's work of transforming a man, on the one hand, and his own impartation of divine forgiveness, on the other hand, as two unrelated events. Mt 18:23ff and Lk 7:41ff, as well as the nature of the events themselves, point in the opposite direction. The transforming work of God which enables obedience of the love command, and the forgiving fellowship of Jesus with sinners form a unity. In this way we may penetrate beneath the surface of Jesus' teaching and see the fundamental connection between his love command and his forgiving fellowship with sinners. Jesus grants what he commands. The *conditions* for entering the coming Kingdom are *enabled* by the hidden, powerful presence of that Kingdom in Jesus.

We may take a quick glance back to the question raised by our survey at the beginning of the chapter (p 75); What does Jesus' command of enemy love have to do with God? The answer of Machoveč, Braun and Niederwimmer is that the love command can be adequately explained without reference to God. But in the light of our study we may seriously doubt whether it is *Jesus'* love command which is there being explained. If the main lines of our study have been correct, then *Jesus'* love command is unintelligible apart from its relation to the heavenly Father. In the first place it is the nature of *God* which determines the content of the love command. Second, the love command aims at repentance – the transformation of a man which sets him in a new relationship to *God* as well as to men. And finally it is the omnipotent kindness of *God* which enables the fulfilment of the love command.

D. Jesus' Command of Enemy Love as a Sign of the Kingdom

After seeing that Jesus' love command is not an accidental condition for
entry into the Kingdom of God, but is determined by the nature of the
Kingdom itself (p 79), and having seen that it is the powers of the new
age in Jesus' ministry of forgiveness which enable the fulfilment of his
commands, it is not surprising to find that in discussions of Jesus' ethic the
love command (along with the rest of Jesus' message and work) and its
fulfilment is frequently called a *sign* of the Kingdom of God.[74] In this
section we will ask in what sense this designation of Jesus' love command
is appropriate.

It is instructive to broaden our textual base here by drawing into consideration the saying of Jesus which describes the disciples' obligation as
'servants' (Mk 10:43f). 'If anyone would be first, he must be last of all
and servant of all.'

> Flender (*Botschaft*, p 63) states in this context: 'The pre- and post-
> Easter traditions of the numerous synoptic sayings about service are
> not easy to distinguish. For to the early church Jesus was a servant
> (Lk 22:27) above all through the sacrifice of his life (Mk 10:45). The
> sayings about hierarchy (of least and greatest) seem to me most clearly
> to be attached to the earthly Jesus. With regard to the table regulations
> in Lk 14: 7–14 [he excludes vv 12–14 from the original] the fact that a
> marriage feast is in view, the OT picture of the time of salvation (Mk
> 2:19; Mt 22:2), speaks for the originality of the saying. If one takes this
> as the basis, then vv 7–11 describe in a parable (v 7) the eschatological
> order which God establishes by the humbling of the proud and the
> exalting of the lowly . . . The question of hierarchy is taken up in Mk
> 9:33–37 and reveals there the transition to the concept of service. Thus
> it is evident that the church applied the (*diesseitige*) eschatological
> hierarchy of Jesus' proclamation to its own arrangements of serving.'
> But if it is granted that Lk 14:11 ('everyone who exalts himself will be
> humbled, and everyone who humbles himself will be exalted') is original
> (as do also Jeremias, *Gleichnisse*, p 50; and Dibelius, *From Tradition to
> Gospel*, p 248), then the *subject matter* of Mk 10:43,44 belongs in the
> teaching of Jesus. The question is whether Jesus spoke in terms of
> *'serving'* and *'servants'* (διακονέω, διάκονος). First, we note that the
> word group applied to Jesus or his disciples is not restricted to any one
> level in the tradition (M – Mt 25:44; L – Lk 12:37; 17:8; Mk – Mk
> 10:43f). Second, we must pose the question to Flender: Where did the
> church's *Dienstordnung* come from? In the early church 'service' is an
> esteemed function (I Cor 12:5; Rom 12:7) and even the apostles know
> themselves as 'servants' (I Cor 3:5). But this esteem of διακονία is not
> the attitude of the church's environment (cf *TDNT* II, p 83). Is it not
> more probable that Jesus' own teaching on service influenced the
> church than vice versa?

It is not illegitimate to view the *service* referred to here as a paraphrase of the *love* which Jesus commands elsewhere (Mt 5:43–48). Both involve self-renunciation for the sake of another. Both are promised a reward. Love is related to the love of God (Mt 5:45,48; Lk 6:36); service is related to the mission of Jesus (Mk 10:45). Both set the disciples off from the gentiles (Mt 5:47; Mk 10:42). This distinctiveness from the gentiles makes it possible that love/service could be a *sign* of the inbreaking Kingdom of God. 'With those who serve rather than rule, with the disciples of Jesus, the new order of God's Kingdom appears as a sign (*zeichenhaft*) in this world.'[75] But how is the sign-quality to be understood?

> In the following, when we refer to the behavior of the disciples, we mean the behavior Jesus was aiming at in his love command rather than the behavior the disciples actually produced during Jesus' earthly days. We know too little about the disciples' daily lives and what we do know is not always exemplary (e.g., Lk 9:54–56). What we are interested in is whether in Jesus' understanding of his love command there was that which justifies the designation of the command of enemy love as a sign of the Kingdom of God.

The disciple who obeys Jesus' command of enemy love and is thus the 'servant of all' would have already begun to live as he will live in the consummated Kingdom, and therefore his behavior would be now a sign of how it will be then. But according to Jesus the experience of the disciple who loves and serves now is not the same as it will be in the coming age. If he is last now, he will be first then (Mt 19:30; 20:16; Mk 10:31; Lk 13:30).[76] If he is humbled now, he will then be exalted (Lk 14:11; 18:14). What he loses through service he will gain back a hundredfold (Mt 19:29; Mk 10:30f). That is to say the Kingdom of God will be an age of glory and gain, not disgrace and loss. In this sense the present experience of one who obeys Jesus' love command and is thus humiliated and hurt by a blow on the cheek is anything but the reflection or sign of how it will be in the coming age of glory. Commenting on Mk 10:42 Beyer says, 'The aim of Jesus and his disciples is not to set up human orders in this world. Their concern is with the Kingdom of God and the age of glory. But the way to this goal leads through suffering and death.'[77] The sign of the age of glory is apparently, then, *not* glory. In this sense the breaking in of the Kingdom is not a breaking in of precisely that which will be. Thus the question becomes the more urgent. How can obedience to the love command which is characterized by service, humiliation, suffering be a sign of the age of glory?

The glory of the new age consists at least in the abolition of all evil. For the glory of the new age is the glory of God. This glory will mean exaltation and reward for the followers of Jesus insofar as the glory of their heavenly Father is their greatest delight (Mt 6:9b par; cf 5:16).[78] But where evil has not yet been abolished, to delight in the glory of the Father does not mean exaltation and reward but humiliation and suffering; for the essence of evil and the character of this evil age is that men seek not God's glory but their own (Mk 10:42; Mt 6:1ff; 23:12; Lk 18:9-14; Jn 5:44). Where this fundamental contradiction of life goals exists among men, conflict is inevitable (Lk 12:51-53 par[79]). In this conflict those who follow Jesus' teaching, that is, those who have their treasure in heaven (Mt 6:20 par), who trust their heavenly Father to supply all their needs (Mt 6:30-33 par), and who desire that their good works give glory to their Father in heaven (Mt 6:9b par; 5:16), will not seek to preserve their own honor, safety or possessions at the cost of another (Mt 5:39-42). They will serve rather than be served, for in this they set themselves off from the sons of this age and manifest the sufficiency and willingness of their heavenly Father to give them all 'good things' (Mt 7:11).[80]

Therefore, when the disciple obeys Jesus' love command, he *signifies* that his own hardness of heart[81] with its bondage to evil has been overcome and that the powers of the future age of glory are already effective in him enabling him to renounce earthly esteem and security. To the degree that one's life goal is determined by his hardness of heart, by the evil of this age, to this degree will one see such behavior as offensive. On the other hand, to the extent that one's hardness of heart is overcome, to this extent will one see clearly that this behavior is a sign of the Kingdom of God.

The command of Jesus and the fulfilment at which it aimed are thus seen to be a reflex of Jesus' own mission. While he proclaimed that in his work the Kingdom of God had come (Lk 11:20 par) yet he did not assume the role of a king. Although the Kingdom was in the midst of the people (Lk 17:21) and the new age of salvation had dawned (Mt 11:2-6), the signs of glory which the Jews demanded were missing (Lk 17:20; cf Mt 12:39/Lk 11:29; Mt 13:31f). Jesus' ministry was a real sign of the inbreaking Kingdom of God. But just as Jesus' ministry contradicted the expectations of the Jews, so also his command of enemy love and its fulfilment contradict the natural inclinations of the human heart. The sign may, therefore, be seen and not perceived, heard and not understood. It may be an offence rather than a revelation.

III. Jesus' Command of Enemy Love and the Law

A. Non-Resistance (Mt 5:39–42) vs the Lex Talionis (Ex 21:24)

Jesus' command not to resist evil (Mt 5:39–42) demands the opposite of the Old Testament legal principle, 'an eye for an eye and a tooth for a tooth' (Mt 5:38; cf Ex 21:24; Lev 24:20; Dt 19:21). If and when Jesus' word is binding, then the other is not. Jesus makes no effort here to integrate the two commands into a consistent whole. As the individual interpretative examples in Mt suggest, Jesus' command applies to both personal (5:39b,42) and legal (5:41) affairs, to both physical (5:39b) and property (5:41) damage. The antithesis between this Old Testament legal principle and Jesus' command is real. Taken absolutely they exclude each other; they are contradictory. Jesus was in some sense abolishing the *lex talionis*.[82]

But on what basis could Jesus lay aside a commandment in the Old Testament? For he explicitly recognized the divine origin and authority of the Old Testament (Mk 1:44; 7:13; 10:18 par; cf Mt 5:17ff; 23:3).[83] He has harsh words for others who 'reject the commandment of God' (Mk 7:9[84]). What makes the difference in this case? In order to answer this question it will help to take into consideration another text in which Jesus lays aside another Old Testament commandment but in this instance justifies his procedure. It is fitting to consider this text here, for as Jeremias has said it is 'the key to the understanding of all Jesus' ethical demands.'[85] I am referring to Mk 10:2-9.[86]

Here the Pharisees ask Jesus if it is lawful for a man to divorce his wife (v 2). Jesus asks in turn what Moses had commanded (v 3). They answer that Moses allowed a man to write a bill of divorcement and put his wife away (v 4). Jesus' own command, in contrast, is: 'What God has joined together let not man put asunder' (v 9). Jesus offers a two-fold defense of his response: he describes Dt 24:1 as a 'commandment' made to the people as a concession on account of the hardness of their hearts (πρὸς τὴν σκληροκαρδίαν ὑμῶν, v 5) and he supports this description by appealing to two other Old Testament texts (Gen 1:27; 2:24) which reveal that God's original intention in creating male and female was that they become one in an indissoluble marriage (vv 6-8).

The most important conclusion we can draw from this incident for our purpose is this: whereas once God made concessions on account of the hardness of man's heart and thus provided a control of the evil effects of that hard heart, Jesus now abolishes such concessions.[87] The explanation for this action lying nearest at hand is that Jesus presupposes that a change is taking place so that men no longer have hard hearts.[88] His appeal to the pristine period of human history (Gen 2:24) supports this explanation, as does the conclusion reached earlier (pp 78f) that Jesus' radical commands aim at the transformation of a man, i.e., at repentance, or we may now say, at a new heart.[89]

Does the argument which Jesus uses here to justify his setting aside an Old Testament commandment also lie tacitly behind his rejection of the *lex talionis*? Let us approach the fifth antithesis (Mt 5:38f) via the fourth (Mt 5:33f). As Jesus abolishes the *lex talionis* in the fifth antithesis, so he abolishes the Old Testament rule of swearing to the Lord (Num 30:2; Dt 23:21) in the fourth antithesis.[90] But in Mt 5:37 Jesus goes so far as to say that anything more than 'Yes, yes' and 'No, no' is from evil (ἐκ τοῦ πονηροῦ).[91] That is, he does not just set aside the Old Testament rule; he says that it springs from evil. Schlatter asks: 'How could Jesus have seen a Satanic element in the law?'[92] He finds the answer by relating this saying of Jesus to the one we have discussed in Mt 19:8 (= Mk 10:5). Just as there the bill of divorcement was a concession to man's hardness of heart and a partial control of its evil effects, so here 'The law wrestles with the sinfulness of man and erects the oath as a dam against lying.'[93] But again this means that Jesus' elimination of all oaths presupposes that the source of oaths is also being eliminated, namely the evil in men's hearts which causes lying.

We may, therefore, in the same way, understand Jesus' rejection of the *lex talionis* in the fifth antithesis.[94] Even more obviously than divorce and oath-taking is the *lex talionis* an accommodation to the evil in men's hearts and a curb on the effects of that evil.[95] The *lex talionis* stipulates 'life for life' (Ex 21:23; Dt 19:21), but God's will is 'You shall not kill' (Ex 20:13); you *are* your brother's keeper (Gen 4:9). Due to man's hardness of heart he injures and kills his fellow man. God therefore gives by concession a legal regulation as a dam against the river of violence which flows from man's evil heart. Therefore the abolishing of this legal principle, upon which the order of society rests (see notes 114, 115), evidently also has in view the overcoming of man's hardness of heart.

A change of heart which makes superfluous the written law of Moses is proclaimed by the prophet Jeremiah (31:31-34; 32:37ff). It is a part of the 'new covenant' which Yahweh is to make with his people. Ezekiel (36:26; cf 11:19) describes this change as a replacement of a heart of stone (τὴν καρδίαν τὴν λιθίνην, LXX) with a heart of flesh.[96] The sins of the people would be forgiven (Jer 31:34; Ez 36:25) and there would be perfect obedience of God from the heart (Jer 31:33; Ez 36:27). With the fulfilment of such a prophecy a new age must begin. We have seen that Jesus presupposed the elimination of the hardness of men's hearts when he made his radical demands. If Jesus saw this change in men's hearts as a fulfilment (even if partial) of the Old Testament prophecy of Jeremiah and Ezekiel then he must have seen a new age beginning. More than that, the beginning of this new age is, therefore, the presupposition of his radical commands.[97]

Jesus' command to love your enemy and not to resist evil is thus a call for a new heart[98] – a call grounded in and released by the mysterious dawn of the new age of salvation. That Jesus took a critical stance toward the law and eliminated certain aspects of it is a result of the eschatological situation he was bringing. What he denounced was not the perfect will of God which he also saw in the Old Testament (Mk 7:8,9), but rather any compromise of this will of God for the sake of man's hardness of heart. Insofar as the law was an instrument by which men regulated their lives in coexistence with evil, it is being abolished in view of the inbreaking Kingdom of God. Jesus' command of enemy love was a summons to advance this abolition and a call to experience the power and blessing of the new era which he was bringing.

B. Enemy Love (Mt 5:44 par Lk) vs Neighbor Love (Lev 19:18)

Turning to the sixth antithesis we may ask whether a similar attitude to the Torah is expressed by Jesus here. Because of the uncertainty of the background of the sentence, 'You shall love your neighbor and hate your enemy,'[99] we shall proceed not from the stated antithesis of Mt 5:43f but rather from an attempt to see Jesus' words in their historical setting. The situation into which Jesus spoke his command was one in which love was a very limited affair. Josephus witnesses to the hate the Jews had for the Romans.[100] Within Judaism, the Pharisees tended to exclude the non-Pharisees.[101] In Qumran, hate was commanded for all 'the sons of Darkness' (1QS 1:10). In the synagogue, the Old Testament command 'Love your neighbor as yourself' (Lev 19:18) was interpreted so that neighbor excluded the non-proselytized non-Israelite (see 47f). Thus the widespread attitude of non-love to outsiders was ostensibly grounded in an Old Testament regulation.

The question we must raise is this: when Jesus in this situation demanded, 'Love your enemies,' was he attacking only the scribal interpretation of the Old Testament command in Lev 19:18, or was he also attacking the Old Testament command itself? We have seen earlier that Jesus did not hesitate to oppose parts of the Torah (Mk 10:5; Mt 5:33f, 38f), so that it is not impossible that he is in similar fashion here opposing a commandment of the law. The perceptive Jew must have viewed Jesus' love command as an attack on the Torah, first, because it contradicted his understanding of Lev 19:18 and, second, because it seemed in general to devaluate the distinction between Jew and gentile – a distinction grounded in the Torah. Jesus' command to love the enemy as well as the friend contained the seed for the dissolution of the Jewish distinctive.[102]

The Jews were not completely mistaken about Jesus' attitude toward the law. Lev 19:18 really did refer to neighbor in a limited sense (see pp 30f). There were other commands relating to love, some more positive, some less; but it was just this mixed collection of regulations on love and non-love which provided the soil in which the scribal casuistry flourished. As long as the Old Testament was seen merely as a collection of varied and equivocal sayings, the scribes were, in fact, able to ground their limited love command in Lev 19:18. Therefore, when Jesus commanded 'Love your enemy!', he attacked not only the scribal limitation of love but also its ostensible Old Testament support. As a source of a legal regulation in which men seek a feasible course of action which allows for human weakness and dilutes the perfect demand of God, Lev 19:18 must be contradicted, abolished.

Jesus' attitude to the law in this matter will become clearer if we bring in the double love command (Mk 12:30f par) alongside the conclusion we have just come to. All three evangelists record that Jesus combined (or approved of the combination in Lk) Dt 6:5 and Lev 19:18, offering the two commands as the will of God without criticism. After the conclusion we have come to above, is it possible that Jesus could express himself so positively with regard to Lev 19:18? To answer this question we will enter into a brief discussion with a recent attempt to determine the origin of the tradition of the double love command.

A recent detailed study of the double command of love is Christoph Burchard's 'Das doppelte Liebesgebot in der frühen christlichen Überlieferung.' His conclusion concerning the authenticity of the double command: 'The double love command was not created by Jesus and did not come into the Christian tradition through him.'[103] A brief outline of his argument runs as follows. Neither Mt nor Lk represent older tradition than Mk, so that we are dependent on Mk for our probe behind traditions (pp 50f).[104] The question of the scribe in Mk 12:28, 'Which commandment is the first of all?' and Jesus' answer, which gives a 'first' and 'second' commandment (12:29, 31), do not correspond to the Palestinian view of the law. There were attempts to summarize the law and to break the commandments down into small and great, but each always retained absolute validity.[105] 'The Rabbis appear never to speak of a first commandment' (p 54). However, while the Palestinian sources do not help, 'There is in the tradition of the Diaspora a series of places which explicitly or substantially combine the attribute "first" with the sentence about one God [Mk 12:29], about God as creator, etc.' (p 54). He cites a quote from

Josephus *Against Apion* II.190, and then concludes that in Mk 12:28, 29 'The question and the answer are/were conceived together. That would mean that there was no freely circulating double love command which constituted the germ of the tradition' (pp 54f).

Burchard concedes, however, that the authenticity of at least the mere double love command 'could nevertheless be right, especially if the double love command as such or its function with respect to the Torah were a Novum' (p 55). In fact, as Burchard notes, the combination of quotations from Dt 6:5 and Lev 19:18 *is* unparalleled in the Jewish sources. Apart from this formal uniqueness, however, he attempts to show that the *substance* and *function* of the double love command is found already in Hellenistic Jewish sources (p 55). He cites Test. Iss. 5:2 (ἀλλὰ ἀγαπήσατε τὸν κύριον καὶ τὸν πλησίον πηνέτα καὶ ἀσθενῆ ἐλεήσατε) and Test. Dan 5:3 (ἀγαπήσατε τὸν κύριον ἐν πάσῃ τῇ ζωῇ ὑμῶν καὶ ἀλλήλους ἐν ἀληθινῇ) as the nearest in formulation to Mk 12:30f, 33. As he admits, the commands are not called 'first' or 'second' nor do they provide a sum of all the other commandments. Then he cites Philo, *De spec. leg.* II.63, wherein Philo refers to δύο τὰ ἀνωτάτω κεφάλαια, τό τε πρὸς θεὸν δι' εὐσεβείας καὶ ὁσιότητος καὶ τὸ πρὸς ἀνθρώπους διὰ φιλανθρωπίας καὶ δικαιοσύνης. As Burchard interprets, 'The ἀνωτάτω κεφάλαια are superscriptions for the two tables of the Decalogue . . .' (p 56). Here we have, then, something like a summary of the law but the summary is not expressed in commands nor is there any reference to love of God or neighbor. On the basis of these parallels Burchard concludes that the double love command is not new and therefore was taken up by the early church from Hellenistic Judaism and put in Jesus' mouth (p 57).

Burchard seems to have left out a very significant part of the demonstration of his contention mentioned above, namely, that the *'Substanz'* of the double love command is 'jüdisch vorgebildet.' Nowhere does Burchard probe into what the double love command in itself is *substantially* commanding. The result of this exclusively formalistic approach is that he can say, 'The double command (like the whole OT) is to be sure the common possession of Jews and Christians, but the Jews do not keep it, as the parable of the Samaritan shows' (p 59). What does he mean that the double love command is the 'common possession' of Jews and Christians? By his own concessions the *formal* divergences are clear (see above). But if we probe into the substantial *meaning* of the two conceptions (which Burchard does not do) the divergences appear again.[106] If we use the command 'Love your neighbor as yourself' as a point of reference, is it possible to describe the double love command merely as a common possession of Jews and Christians? Did the evangelists understand it thus?

First, *Lk* is not merely saying in the parable of the good Samaritan that Christians obey the double love command and the Jews do not. He is saying also that the lawyer has fundamentally missed the point of his own command by asking 'Who is my neighbor?' In other words, the lawyer's understanding of the double love command and Jesus' under-

standing are *not* identical. Second, *Mt* sees the whole law and prophets
hanging on the double love command (22:40). But after his severe
criticism of mere neighbor–love in Mt 5:43–48, are we to think that, for
Mt, Jesus' double love command is merely a common possession with
Judaism? Does Mt think that Jesus and the scribes meant the same
thing by 'Love your neighbor as yourself'? Third, while in *Mk* Jesus
does *approve* of the scribe's response (12:34), his own statement, 'You
are not far from the Kingdom of God,' probably means not that there is
something more besides these two commands,[107] but rather that the
scribe is on the brink of penetrating to Jesus' real intention in these two
commands.[108]

For the evangelists, therefore (at least Mt and Lk), Burchard's statement
does not hold. Jesus' double love command is not for them a mere
common possession between Jews and Christians. For the Christians
'Love your neighbor as yourself' meant far more than it did for the
Jewish contemporaries. For them Jesus abolished the rabbinical
nationalistic interpretation of 'neighbor' (see pp 47f). Nor can the
Testaments of the Twelve Patriarchs or Philo[109] account for the substance of the *Christian* double command of love (see pp 39, 43ff).

The question of authenticity is whether the evangelists have Christianized
a Jewish double commandment on the basis of what they knew of Jesus'
teaching, e.g., on enemy love; or whether Jesus himself used the double
love command, transforming it in accordance with his other teaching.
In favor of the latter alternative – that Jesus used the double love
command – is, first, that nowhere in the Jewish literature do we find
Dt 6:5 and Lev 19:18 joined like this;[110] and, second, as Bornkamm
observes, 'The summarizing of the whole Torah in the command to
love God and neighbor may be designated . . . as a distinctive of the
proclamation of Jesus.'[111] And we may suggest, third, that the parable
of the good Samaritan (Lk 10:29–37), although its context in Lk may
not be original,[112] nevertheless renders the essence of Jesus' understanding of neighbor love and, therefore, shows that the words 'Love
your neighbor as yourself' in the double love command would have in
Jesus' mouth constituted the 'Novum' which Burchard says is the *sine
qua non* of authenticity.[113]

It is not our purpose to go beyond this to determine the various
redactional usages of Jesus' double love command, nor shall we try to
specify the exact context(s) into which Jesus spoke it. It is sufficient for
our present purpose to conclude merely that it is probable that Jesus did
express himself in the double love command – he did so positively with no
outward criticism of the two elements of the Torah which he was quoting.
In other words, in the double commandment Jesus took up Lev 19:18 and
proclaimed it as the perfect will of God.

In Section III.A, we faced the problem that Jesus, who at times sees
the perfect will of God in the Old Testament commandments, at other

times sees other Old Testament commandments in one sense as imperfect compromises of this will. The one he affirms, the other he rejects. Here in Section B the problem is different: the same Old Testament commandment is both affirmed and rejected. Lev 19:18 stands in conflict with Jesus' command of enemy love and yet he announces this Old Testament command along with Dt 6:5 as the unadulterated will of God. What lies behind this paradoxical attitude toward Lev 19:18?

A part of the explanation for Jesus' procedure is his rejection of the limited meaning of 'neighbor' in Lev 19:18. In the parable of the good Samaritan (Lk 10:29-37) and in the command of enemy love (Mt 5:44-47 par Lk) Jesus denies that it is God's will that the command of love be limited to friends or countrymen.[114] Therefore, when Jesus commands enemy love on the one hand and neighbor love on the other, he is not contradicting himself. But why did Jesus choose to formulate the positive will of God by attaching to Dt 6:5 a commandment which was at least ambiguous, and the accepted meaning of which was contrary to his intention?

We may suppose that Jesus used the Old Testament commandment, first, because he *does* intend for the 'neighbor' in the Old Testament sense, the fellow Israelite, to be loved; this *is* the will of God. But he uses it also as a criticism of the restriction on love which was assumed to be in the commandment. This criticism could be better accomplished by employing the command in a new sense than by ignoring it. Jesus could take up this element of the Torah and make it the expression of the perfect will of God only because he had abolished it as an equivocal, legal regulation by which a man, through casuistic application, could justify himself. Jesus' new usage of the command excluded the possibility of even asking the question 'Who is my neighbor?' (Lk 10:29). Therefore, Jesus' announcement of the will of God in the double love command was at the same time an implicit criticism of the contemporary understanding of the apparently equivocal Old Testament command of neighbor love.

C. Abolition vs Continuation of the Law

I admit from the outset that the question I will try to answer in this closing section is one which Jesus neither asked nor explicitly answered. Nevertheless it is a question which any Christian who takes seriously the contemporary importance of the teaching of his Lord cannot avoid. The general problem we are dealing with is the abiding validity of the law in view of Jesus' criticism of it. We will limit ourselves to one small question which is yielded by the following facts. Jesus' command of enemy love abolishes the *lex talionis* on the presupposition that the hardness of men's hearts is being overcome (pp 90f); the love command is thus no less than a command that this renewal of heart happen. We saw earlier that this renewal or conversion is possible because the powers of the Kingdom of God are already at work in Jesus' ministry. The specific question posed by these conclusions is: Can or should a disciple of Jesus under the influence of these powers ever render an eye for an eye or a tooth for a tooth?

We have described the *lex talionis* (along with the bill of divorcement and oaths, p 90) as a divine accommodation to the evil in men's hearts for a curb on the effects of that evil. Looking more closely we see that the *lex talionis* exists not merely to restrict retaliation but also to restrict crime. The evil society that gave rise to the need for this statute was *both* the evil that makes a man put out your eye *and* the evil that makes you then want to put out both of his. The entire elimination of this legal principle from human society must presuppose that not only those who are injured can return good for evil, but that also no one will do evil in the first place. In other words its *entire* elimination presupposes the overcoming of *all* hardness of heart in *all* men. It presupposes the glorious new age, the consummation of the Kingdom of God. Until that time the complete elimination of this 'foundation of all civil order'[115] would mean the destruction of human society.[116]

At this point the problem of Jesus' love command is most acute – at the point, namely, where we must decide its intention for our *action* in the face of the human reality of evil (i.e., in the face of the *lex talionis* which is the legal counterpart of this evil). At this point, therefore, the various interpretations of the feasibility of Jesus' radical demand divide most clearly.[117] An 'interim ethic' takes seriously the heroic, literal fulfilment of Jesus' command without regard to the societal effects because society for Jesus is unimportant, the end is so near. A 'Gesinnungsethik' takes seriously the realistic historical possibilities and tends to reduce fulfilment of the love command to the development of a loving disposition. The classic Catholic view takes sober account of human ability and the effect on society if all Christians literally followed Jesus' love command, and so it construes the literal fulfilment of the command as a special task for a few. Luther attempts to preserve both society and the strict fulfilment of the love command by restricting literal fulfilment to those instances where only *my* concern is at stake. Visionary literalists see the love command as the standard of all personal, social and national action which should transform all spheres of human life. In this array of opinions no consensus is reached on whether the disciples of Jesus can or should ever act according to the *lex talionis*.

To attempt an answer to this question which will accord with Jesus' intention (which is all we can hope to do, since he did not address the problem directly) we should state clearly again the two seemingly contradictory elements of his preaching. The one we have already elaborated: Jesus' radical demands abolish certain elements of the Torah (Mk 10:2-9; Mt 5:34,39). The other element is Jesus' conviction that the Torah is valid in its entirety.[118] In all likelihood the saying (in Q?) behind Lk 16:17 and Mt 5:18 goes back to Jesus himself and is intended to stress the enduring validity of the law down to its smallest details.[119] For our study the contrast can be put thus: Jesus said in effect that the law (which includes the *lex talionis*) has enduring validity, but he also said that, when one strikes you on the cheek, you are not to strike back, you are to do good to those who hate you and bless those who curse you. The *lex talionis* is valid and it is not valid.

Were this the only such paradox in Jesus' message and ministry we would be hard put to offer an explanation for it. But it is not the only one. Jesus' proclamation of the Kingdom of God, as we have seen, involves a similar paradox: the Kingdom of God is present and active but is also not yet present (p 79). It is reasonable to expect that the paradox of the abolition and continuing validity of the law will find its solution, if at all, in relation to this central paradox of the present and yet future Kingdom of God. In fact, as it appears, the former is an inevitable reflex of the latter. The present breaking in of the Kingdom in a hidden way begins to overcome evil, thus making all elements of the law which stem from this evil (p 90) unnecessary; the remaining future of the Kingdom means that evil and historical life are not eliminated and that those same elements of the law still serve in part the purpose they always did.[120]

Here we must make two qualifications of this eschatological tension. (1) Since the Kingdom of God in Jesus' ministry was hidden and partial, the chronological categories of present and future are not fully adequate to explain the Kingdom's work. It is true to say the Kingdom is present, but you have not thereby determined where it is present, or at what particular moments its powers are being displayed, or how it looks when it is manifesting itself. (2) Because the Kingdom is hidden and partial we cannot think of individual people as completely and consistently under the powers of the age to come such that their behavior would always and unequivocally be distinguished from the behavior determined by this age.

For these two reasons, which are grounded in Jesus' fundamental message of the mysterious inbreaking of the Kingdom, we *cannot* say that a disciple of Jesus, who has come under the powers of the new age, cannot or should not at times act according to the *lex talionis*. Since God has willed to accomplish redemption through a hidden working of his power without the dissolution of the world and historical life, therefore he must have a purpose in preserving the world. To be called into God's Kingdom can mean nothing less than acknowledging the rightness of God's purposes and placing oneself at his disposal for their accomplishment. This means that a disciple of Jesus serves God not merely as a witness to the inbreaking new age through a radically new way of life (free from fear and worry in dependence on God), but also as an obedient agent of the creation who contributes to the preservation of this world as long as God wills. Because the Kingdom of God is now hidden, there are no ethical manifestos that everyone can consult to determine when to denounce retaliation and when to execute it. The eschatological tension into which the disciple is placed by Jesus' love command is thus a continual challenge to become a 'good tree' which *naturally* bears good fruit, i.e., it is a challenge to repent and set one's whole treasure in God alone.

The apparent conflict between non-resistance of evil on the one hand and resistance for love's sake on the other has been discussed in an excellent article by Luise Schottroff, 'Gewaltverzicht und Feindesliebe in der urchristlichen Jesustradition: Mt 5:38–48; Lk 6:27–36' (1975). She approached the problem differently from me. Instead of seeing the conflict between the law (*lex talionis*) and the command of Jesus (Mt 5:38), she sees it between the command not to resist evil (Mt 5:38) on the one hand and the command for 'active love' (Mt 5:44) on the other (pp 202, 219). 'If one takes his starting point from Mt 5:44f par and an interpretation of enemy love as an active love, then the demand to put up with injustice becomes a riddle. Abstaining from resistance, i.e. a total submission to unjust demands of one's enemy, cannot be called love' (p 219). 'Why is resistance forbidden and next to it active enemy love commanded? What is the act of love supposed to be when one simply offers the enemy the other cheek? – His wrong will only be made greater' (p 203).

Nevertheless Schottroff insists that the context demands that non-resistance and active enemy love be held together. She seeks a solution through a socio-political analysis of the text. Reflection upon the content of the command of enemy love shows 'the active necessity of a *sozialgeschichtlichen Fragestellung*. The ones who love and the enemies in Mt 5:44ff par cannot be viewed as separated from their social reality' (p 202). Therefore a specific occasion in the social relations of early Christianity is sought in which the prohibition of resistance would have concrete significance. The solution of the riddle must be found in the concrete social relations because 'on the level of a timelessly valid ethic the riddle is unsolvable' (p 219).

Following the direction of P. Hoffmann[121] and M. Hengel,[122] Schottroff sees a political situation in which zealotism is rejected. 'Mt 5:39–41 par would then be – directed inwardly – a demand to make no plans for a rebellion or for violent resistance and – directed outwardly – an asseveration of peaceful intentions, a political apologetic: we are not revolutionaries' (p 219). In other words only 'a definite kind of resistance' is being rejected but not '*every* kind of resistance' (p 220).

In response to Schottroff's argument I would first observe that her sense for the tension between active enemy love and total non-resistance to evil is accurate. Also it is wholly appropriate to pose the socio-political question so that commands bound to one social relationship are not unthinkingly transferred to another. And it is a needed corrective that she has laid all the stress on the active practice of love for the sake of the loved enemy[123] as opposed to an over-emphasis on the inner freedom of the one loving (pp 197f, 216). Finally, that Jesus was no zealot and rejected that path (Lk 22:38, 51) makes it feasible that his commands of non-resistance would, at least in part, be understood in that context as a rejection of political rebellion. But the context of Mt 5: 38–48 par, as well as the paraenetic use of this material in the epistles, suggest that the political situation does not provide the crucial context into which these commands were spoken.[124] Rather the specific details of turning the other cheek, being sued for a coat, giving to beggars, loaning freely, praying for persecutors, greeting the unfriendly, etc. reflect a context of ordinary daily life on the one hand and religious hostility on the other.

The resolution of the tension between active love and non-resistance lies then not only in recognizing a possible limiting political context but also in recognizing that even at the most personal level the commands of non-resistance and acquiescence are not absolute prescriptions with no exceptions, but rather are pointed, concrete illustrations of how enemy love may and should often look in the life of a disciple. That these illustrations are not always the way enemy love acts is clear from Jesus' own behavior[125] and from the nature of love itself as that which aims at the best life for the beloved.

4

THE USE AND MEANING OF JESUS' COMMAND OF ENEMY LOVE IN THE EARLY CHRISTIAN PARAENESIS

I. Preliminary Remarks

We concluded at the end of Chapter 1 that the tradition behind the written New Testament paraenesis probably did not consist of fixed codes. We suggested, rather, that there was a large fund of oral,[1] traditional material systematized only loosely under different themes (e.g., church order, behavior toward fellow Christians, behavior toward non-Christians, personal piety). In these thematic groupings there was apparently much formal variation. From this fund of paraenetic material the New Testament writers drew out what was useful and, within certain essential limitations, adapted it freely.

Our purpose in this chapter is to investigate the use and meaning of Jesus' command of enemy love in this paraenetic tradition. We have touched on this subject already in Chapter 2 (cf Section VI). There we put forward that the paraenetic teaching of the early church on enemy love is set apart from its environment by that which it has in common with Jesus (p 64) and that, therefore, the peculiar character of Jesus' love command constituted the unique criterion according to which the non-Christian paraenetic elements were taken up into the early Christian paraenetic tradition. In Chapter 2 (Section VI) this proposition grew out of our analysis of the history of the tradition of Jesus' sayings on enemy love and was thus grounded largely in *formal* and *historical* observations. In this chapter the aim will be to test this proposition from the standpoint of the *meaning* of the paraenetic love command within its theological framework. This chapter, therefore, forms the counterpart to Chapter 3 and seeks ultimately to ascertain whether the motivation and content of the command of enemy love in the paraenetic tradition is essentially the same as the motivation and content of this command in Jesus' earthly ministry.

We have seen that it is possible to isolate distinct, small elements in the pre-written paraenetic tradition on enemy love (see Summary, pp 63f). But the larger meaning of these elements cannot be determined so long as they are isolated. Only within a larger context and within a theological framework do they manifest their specific character. Such a context and framework in the oral paraenetic tradition is not immediately accessible to us. We must take as our starting point the larger contexts into which the command of enemy love has been put in Paul's letters and in I Pt. This does not mean that the New Testament writers were the first to put the isolated paraenetic elements into a theological framework. That such a framework existed already in the living tradition has been shown by Philip Carrington and E. G. Selwyn.[2] It means, rather, that as far as our investigation is concerned, we must deal first with the texts that lie before us and only then make statements about the larger meaning of the love command in the oral tradition. If common motifs and patterns emerge between Paul and I Pt we may then be able to draw conclusions about the common tradition lying behind them.

II. The Motivation of the Command of Enemy Love

In anticipation of one of our conclusions we propose at the outset that the decisive motivation for the command of enemy love in the New Testament paraenesis is the kerygma of Jesus Christ, the good news of his death for sins and his resurrection. Before developing our support for this contention we shall take a short look at the history of the pertinent research.

A. A Brief Survey of the Previous Research

Martin Dibelius' criticism of Alfred Seeberg's *Der Catechismus der Urchristenheit* (1903) provides a provocative starting point: 'Seeberg's thesis suffers from the fact that he wants to subsume under his hypothetical catechism not only the paraenesis but also the preliminary stages of the confession of faith. But the development of the kerygma and the paraenesis do not run on the same tracks, which is obvious from the fact that the kerygma is an original Christian formation but the paraenesis to a large degree consists of borrowed material.'[3] Dibelius, therefore, draws the conclusion in another place, 'Thus we see that the hortatory sections of the Pauline epistles have nothing to do with the theoretic foundation of the ethics of the apostle, and very little with other ideas peculiar to him. Rather they belong to tradition.'[4] Dibelius' work has had a strong influence on the modern German research into the New Testament paraenetic tradition.[5] The trend has not, however, gone unchallenged. Wolfgang Schrage, while not using the form critical method, shows the weakness of Dibelius' standpoint,[6] and Ferdinand Hahn has more recently criticized Dibelius and his followers with these words: 'Important viewpoints, which Alfred Seeberg had already observed, have for him fallen fully into the background. The specifically Christian elements are not brought out; rather it is stressed how strongly these are leveled out. The total context is judged negatively and the connection with baptism motifs plays no role.'[7]

In the English-speaking world, research into the New Testament paraenesis has followed more closely the way pointed by Seeberg which sees a closer connection between kerygma and paraenesis. Philip Carrington (*Catechism,* 1940) and E. G. Selwyn after him (*I Peter,* 1947) have attempted to reconstruct a pattern of teaching behind the New Testament epistles which includes both unique Christian elements and borrowed paraenetic material.[8] C. H. Dodd recognized that not all the paraenetic material is specifically Christian but tried to show how 'ethical ideas are transformed by being brought into a context which is religious through and through being defined by the Gospel itself as it is contained in the *kerygma.*'[9] In the same vein W. D. Davies says of Paul's hortatory sections, 'All the traditional material has been baptized by Paul into Christ.'[10]

In the following two sections (B and C) we will focus on the letters of Paul and on I Pt and we will inquire what the relationship is there between the command of enemy love and the kerygma. Is the kerygma the decisive motive for the love command? How is this relationship to be understood?

B. Paul[11]

We may limit ourselves for the sake of brevity to Paul's epistle to the Romans. To discuss Paul's use of the command of enemy love in I Thess[12] would add little to his more developed and programmatic treatment in Rom 12. The text at the center of our discussion is Rom 12:14,17-21:

> Bless those who curse you,
> bless and do not curse.
> Do not repay anyone evil for evil;
> take thought for what is good before all men.
> If possible, so far as it depends on you live at peace with all men.
> Do not avenge yourselves, beloved,
> but give place to wrath.
> For it is written: Vengeance is mine, I will repay, says the Lord.
> But if your enemy hungers, give him food,
> and if he thirsts, give him drink;
> for doing this you will heap coals of fire on his head.
> Do not be overcome by evil,
> but overcome evil with good.

1. The 'Mercies of God' (Rom 12:1f)
In *Der Brief des Jakobus* (pp 19-23) Dibelius gives five characteristics of the literary form paraenesis: (1) eclecticism, (2) the absence of context,

(3) catchword connections, (4) repetition of the same motif in different places, (5) the admonitions do not fall within the bounds of one particular situation. Each of these paraenetic features is found in Rom 12 and 13 but the second feature, the absence of an ordered progression of thought, must be qualified. While it is true that the admonitions of Rom 12:9-21 cannot be grouped *perfectly* so that 'relations to outsiders' follows 'relations to fellow–Christians,'[13] nevertheless a rough outline is visible in the paraenesis if we take into account the larger context of Rom 12:3-13:7.[14] Rom 12:3-8 deals with the functioning of the body of Christ; 12:9-21 deals more generally with the Christian's relation to his brothers and then to outsiders (although the sequence here is imprecise); and 13:1-7 deals with the Christian's relation to the state. All of the material in these three sections is grounded in the fundamental admonition of Rom 12:1,2.[15]

This means that the paraenetic tradition on enemy love (Rom 12:14, 17-21) is not treated by Paul in isolation; it is rather subsumed under the appeal of Rom 12:1f.[16] Without going into a detailed exegesis of these two verses we may make three concise observations. *First,* the transition to the paraenetic section is made with the conjunction οὖν (12:1; cf Eph 4:1; I Cor 4:16) which grounds the following admonitions in what has preceded in the epistle. Paul sums up this preceding ground as 'the mercies of God' (12:1).[17]

Since we are dealing here with the ground of the love command (Rom 12:14,17ff) it is appropriate to specify these 'mercies of God' (12:1) as Paul does elsewhere. Parallel to Rom 12:1, 'I appeal to you, therefore, brothers, through the *mercies of God,*' is Rom 15:30, 'I appeal to you, brothers, through our *Lord Jesus Christ* and through the *love of the Spirit.*' Here the 'mercies of God' are explained in terms of 'the Lord Jesus Christ' and 'the love of the Spirit'. That these terms stand for the mercies of God and, as such, ground the following appeal is suggested by Rom 5:5,8, 'Hope does not put us to shame because the *love of God* has been poured out in our hearts *through the Holy Spirit* which is given to us . . . God shows his love to us in that while we were still sinners *Christ died for us.*' In view of Rom 5:5 it is possible to take 'the love of the Spirit' in 15:30 to mean essentially the same as 'the love of God poured out through the Spirit.'[18] That is, it is the Spirit who opens us to the love of God and applies it sensibly to us so that we are assured of it. But this work of the Spirit is not a merely mystical affair, for that which he certifies to our hearts is 'shown' in a historical event: the death of Christ. The 'love of God' which is *poured out* through the Spirit is *demonstrated* in history 'by the death of his Son' (5:10). Therefore Paul's appeal 'through the mercies of God' is very appropriately specified as an appeal 'through the Lord Jesus Christ and through the love of the Spirit'; for those mercies are supremely demonstrated in the person of Jesus in his dying for sinners,[19] and those mercies, i.e., God's love, are poured into or made sensibly manifest to, the heart of the believer by the Holy Spirit. On the basis of this objective and subjective aspect of God's mercies Paul summons believers to obey the love command.

Moreover, the love of God which has been shown in the death of Christ and poured into the heart of the believer is stated clearly to be enemy love: 'For if *while we were enemies* we were reconciled to God by the death of his son . . .' (Rom 5:10). 'Enemies' is also rendered 'helpless,' 'godless,' 'sinners' (5:6,8). The point of 5:6,7 is that God's love surpasses human love at its best (dying for a good man) precisely in this: that it will die for enemies – not converted enemies but those who were *still* enemies when Christ died for them (cf ἔτι in vv 6,8 and concessive present participle ὄντες in v 10). In view of this 'the mercies of God' (12:1) take on a new significance as the ground and motive of the command of enemy love in Rom 12:14,17ff. The Christians are being called upon to let their enemies experience what they experienced while they were still God's enemies: namely, 'blessing and not cursing' (Rom 12:14). How can believers do otherwise with the Spirit of God himself rendering their hearts full of and responsive to God's love?

Second, the admonition 'to present (παραστῆναι) your bodies as a living sacrifice to God' (12:1) recalls Rom 6:13, 'Do not present (παριστάνετε) your members to sin as weapons of unrighteousness but present (παραστήσατε) yourselves to God as those who are alive from the dead.' As Michel observes, 'Röm 12,1 setzt die Mahnungen von Röm 6,13 fort.'[20] Rom 6:13 is grounded (cf οὖν, 6:12) in the believer's death with Christ through baptism. Thus the admonitions of Rom 6 and Rom 12:1f presuppose not only 'the mercies of God' but also the appropriation of this mercy by faith in baptism. *Third,* the aim of Rom 12:2 is that the church members be able to determine the will of God. The prerequisite to this is an experience of God's mercy and consequent transformation (μεταμορφοῦσθε) which includes a renewal of the mind (12:2). We conclude, therefore, that, along with the rest of Rom 12, the tradition on enemy love is addressed to baptized believers who live 'in Christ' and experience 'the mercies of God,' specifically, the unique excellence of God's mercy in loving his enemies (Rom 5:5-10). The individual commands are given on the basis of the eschatological saving work of God in Christ, and are therefore a summons to live from the powers of the new age which this saving work has inaugurated.

We may confirm this understanding of the ground of the individual commands of Rom 12 by examining how one of these commands was developed by Paul in a less traditional context. One of the commands under the subheading 'Let love be genuine!' (12:9)[21] is 'Share in the needs of the saints' (12:13). Paul's aim in writing II Cor 8 and 9 is to prepare the Corinthian church to share generously in the needs of the saints when Titus comes to make the collection among them for the poor saints in Jerusalem (8:4,14,19f;9:1,5,12; cf Rom 15:26–28). As in Rom 12:9 he insists that this appeal is merely a proving of 'the genuineness of your love' (τῆς ὑμετέρας ἀγάπης γνήσιον, 8:8; cf 8:24). A careful examination of Paul's argumentation in II Cor 8 and 9 reveals a number of substantial similarities with Rom 12:1,2. The following parallels are based on the essential subject matter and not on linguistic features. They show that the foundation of the imperative in Rom 12:13 and in II Cor 8 and 9 is essentially the same.

Rom		II Cor	
12:1	Paul appeals 'by the mercies of God.'	8:9	Paul appeals by 'the grace of our Lord Jesus Christ' and by 'the grace of God' (8:1).
12:1	He calls them to present their bodies to God.	8:5	By way of example for the Corinthians he recalls that the Macedonians 'gave themselves first to the Lord.'
12:1	This sacrifice to God is a λογικὴν λατρείαν.[22]	9:12	The Corinthians are to follow the generosity of the Macedonians in a διακονία τῆς λειτουργίας[22] which abounds in thanksgiving to God.
12:2	They are to be transformed by a renewal of their mind.	8:9	They are to recall that through Christ's poverty on their behalf they have been transformed from poor to rich (cf 9:7).
12:2	The aim is 'to prove the will of God.'	8:5	The exemplary Macedonians' pattern was 'through the will of God.'

The structure is the same in both: prior and fundamental to all doing of God's will is the grace ('mercies') of God which renews the mind of the believer. Perhaps the clearest statement in these two passages which shows that the gracious work of God is that which precedes and enables any good work of the Christian is II Cor 9:8: 'God is able to cause all grace to abound unto you *in order that* . . . you might abound in every good work.' This is why Paul grounds the entirety of Rom 12:3 – 13:7 in 'the mercies of God.' What Paul states in a less personal and more compact form in Rom 12:1f as the ground of the following paraenesis is precisely that which came to expression spontaneously and functionally in II Cor 8 and 9 as the ground of his appeal for the poor saints in Jerusalem.

Having ascertained that the command of enemy love in its paraenetic context in Paul is grounded on the one hand in the mercies (or love,

Rom 5:5ff) of God manifest in Christ and, on the other hand, in the consequent renewal of the Christian (Rom 12:2) by faith through baptism
(Rom 6:6), the question arises: in what sense is it grounded? It is not
immediately obvious why the eschatological work of God in Christ and the
newness of the believer should ground the love command – should it not
rather eliminate the need of such a command? Why must a new creature
be commanded to walk the new way of love? In trying to answer this
question in the following section we are drawn necessarily into wider considerations of Paul's thinking. I acknowledge the risk of spreading myself
too thin and touching on areas that would demand more discussion than
I can give them here; but, in my opinion, apart from these wider considerations the command of enemy love in the paraenetic tradition cannot
be properly understood. The view through the microscope is valuable, but
it is often impossible even to know what you are looking at until you pull
out the slide and look at the whole piece.

2. The Necessity of the Command of Enemy Love

The Christian's newness can be described from two different standpoints.
In both cases the question rises: Why is the love command any longer
necessary? *First,* he can be described as one who has been mastered by a
new power – the Holy Spirit. He is led by the Holy Spirit (Rom 8:14;
Gal 5:18); he bears the fruit of the Holy Spirit (Gal 5:22). He is 'taught
by God to love' so that he needs no one to write to him (I Thess 4:9).
So the question rises: Why does the believer need any 'leading' from men;
why does he need to be instructed by men to love his enemy? The *second*
way to describe the newness of the believer is to say that he has been
'washed, sanctified, justified' (I Cor 6:11) or, in other words, he died with
Christ in baptism (Rom 6:4) 'in order that the body of sin might be
abolished so that he might no longer serve sin' (Rom 6:6). He now walks
'in newness of life' (Rom 6:4); sin will have no dominion over him (Rom
6:14). The love of God has been poured into his heart (Rom 5:5). He is
a new creature (II Cor 5:17; Gal 6:15). Why must this man be commanded
to love his enemy? He is enslaved to righteousness (Rom 6:18); can he do
otherwise?

The newness of the believer in both of these descriptions is essentially
the same: in both cases his newness consists in a new *relation to God.* This
is obvious in the first case where the Christian is now led by the Holy
Spirit, the Spirit of God. But it is true of the second also, for Paul can
substitute 'you have become slaves of God' (Rom 6:22) for the phrase
'you have become slaves of *righteousness'* (Rom 6:18). And in Gal 2:20
the result of being crucified with Christ is that 'Christ lives in me and the

life I now live in the flesh I live by faith . . .' This is essentially the same as being led by the Holy Spirit (cf Rom 8:9f,14).[23] Consequently the basic thing about the Christian's newness is his living faith in Christ and the presence of Christ's (Holy) Spirit in him to 'lead' him. Therefore the question why Paul thought it necessary to address Christians with the love command is the question how he understood the 'leading' or 'fruit-bearing' work of the Holy Spirit.

The standard work which deals with the problem of the individual commands in Paul is Wolfgang Schrage's *Die konkreten Einzelgebote in der paulinischen Paränese* (1961). The work is of immense value and I am grateful for what I have learned from it – a great deal. In the 50-page *Forschungsbericht* Schrage gives his critique of the major attempts to explain the existence of individual commands in Paul's writings: (1) the commands are a result of a de-eschatologizing process; (2) they are a compromise between ideal and reality, relapses into Jewish legalism; (3) they are temporarily necessary and valid, but in the long run superfluous; (4) they are exclusively concrete and situational. I consider Schrage's critique of these views valid so that it is unnecessary here to redo his excellent work.

The body of Schrage's work is a descriptive analysis of Paul's paraenesis. He makes clear that for Paul there can be no thought of eliminating the individual commands. He sees that there is a tension between viewing love as a *fruit of the Spirit* and as a *command* or duty (p 249f); neither side can be done away with. He devotes a sizable section ('Das Verhältnis von Gebot und Geist,' pp 71–93) to the solution of this apparent contradiction. His argumentation may be summed up in the following sentences. 'The Spirit in no way stands . . . in opposition to authority and tradition' (p 89, cf I Cor 7:40). Against Lietzmann, it is not true that 'Where life moves in the Spirit, no command has a place' (p 75; Lietzmann, *Römer*, p 71). On the contrary, 'The Spirit . . . admonishes in, with and under "external" admonition, and precisely this is a charismatic function. As the Spirit does his work in general through the apostolic office (II Cor 3:8), so he admonishes and commands through the apostolic paraenesis (cf I Cor 7:40)' (p 86). 'The Spirit works and leads not directly but rather makes use of the human understanding as a means' (p 92). But even this spiritual understanding is not an individualistic affair: 'Leading from the Spirit is found only in the sphere of and in relation to the church' (pp 90, 174).[24]

In a similar vein Anton Grabner-Haider stresses in his book *Paraklese und Eschatologie bei Paulus* (1968) that there is no inconsistency between the work of God in the believer and the need for human tradition: 'All Paul's tradition receives a completely new stamp through the fact that he understands his admonition not as man's word but as God's word' (p 29). 'It is actually God himself who speaks' (p 37). 'Christ is the mediator of the paraklesis of God' (p 48).

This is essentially the line of thinking which I will attempt to develop in the following pages in a somewhat different manner and with an application to Jesus' command of enemy love as it was used in the paraenetic tradition (preserved by Paul).

I have intentionally posed the problem of the individual commands without reference to the usual indicative-imperative tension.[25] Such a grammatical description of what we find in Paul tends to conceal the fact that what is here called 'indicative' is in reality the living God. This is what I meant earlier when I said that the essential newness of the Christian consists in his new *relation to God* by faith. The personal or relational character of the 'indicative' comes to expression most clearly in Paul's statements about the work of the Holy Spirit. This is why I have formed the question as I have: If the almighty Spirit of Christ is leading the Christians and yielding fruit, why does Paul and the early Christian tradition with him think it necessary to command them specifically and repeatedly to love their enemy?

The presupposition underlying this question is that the leading of the Holy Spirit takes place through a private communion with the divine in which the Christian is informed of the right and motivated to do it apart from human influences. This, however, was not Paul's understanding of the way the Spirit worked. This may be illustrated first from II Cor 5:20. Here we find the well-known imperative, 'Be reconciled to God!' Nevertheless, it is a clear element of Paul's theology that a man's reconciling himself to God is the work of the Spirit (I Thess 1:5); it happens only when the creator 'shines in our hearts to give the light of the knowledge of the glory of God in the face of Christ' (II Cor 4:6; cf II Cor 4:16,17; Rom 9:16; Eph 2:8).

From a false preconception of how the Spirit of God works one could theoretically deny the need for the imperative 'Be reconciled to God!' on the ground, namely, that God is great enough to accomplish our salvation without humans stepping in to inform us of our need and God's offer. This objection fails to see that man does not merely step in; he is called in, indeed he is drawn in even before his birth (Gal 1:15). He is made an ambassador of the risen Christ (ὑπὲρ χριστοῦ οὖν πρεσβεύομεν, II Cor 5:20), and thus speaks on Christ's behalf (δεόμεθα ὑπὲρ χριστοῦ). Indeed, it is not merely man but God who says, 'Be reconciled.' In other words God has chosen not to do his saving work privately with an individual; rather he makes his appeal through men (ὡς τοῦ θεοῦ παρακαλοῦντος δι' ἡμῶν). Here we do not see a conflict between a human imperative and God's work in the heart. Rather we see a single working of God, from one side, making his appeal through men and, from the other side, enlightening the heart (II Cor 4:6). The fact that God's speaking is here called παρακαλοῦντος (II Cor 5:20) suggests that this same pattern may characterize the παράκλησις in general.[26]

Rom 12 begins: παρακαλῶ οὖν ὑμᾶς ἀδελφοί. Parallel with this in 12:3 we read: λέγω γὰρ διὰ τῆς χάριτος τῆς δοθείσης μοι. The former recalls the divine παρακαλοῦντος of II Cor 5:20; the latter is a *terminus technicus* referring to Paul's apostolic commission (Rom 1:5; 15:15; I Cor 3:10; Gal 2:9; Eph 3:2,7). Paul therefore considered that the paraenesis which he addressed to the Roman church was a function of the same ambassadorial commission which he exercised on Christ's behalf in the kerygmatic appeal: 'Be reconciled to God!' Because he is speaking 'through the grace given to him' it is not only he who speaks but 'God is admonishing through him.'[27] As with the gospel, so with the paraenetic tradition of the command of enemy love; it is not a mere human influence in tension with the divine influence in the renewed mind of the believer; the command of enemy love is an element of the divine renewing word.

The point at which this divine word meets the believer effectively is in the 'body of Christ.' The paradoxes of Christian ethics find their practical solution in the local community of believers. This is suggested by the following observations. For the Christian 'all things are permitted.'[28] This does not mean for Paul that the question of sin no longer exists for the Christian. The question of good and evil still exists but is answered not by referring the Christian to legal codes or to his own private experience of the Holy Spirit, but rather by placing him in the body of Christ. 'All things are permitted but not all things συμφέρει' (I Cor 6:12). But in the body of Christ 'each is given the manifestation of the Spirit πρὸς τὸ συμφέρον' (12:7). 'All things are permitted but not all οἰκοδομεῖ' (10:23). But in the body of Christ 'the one who prophesies speaks to men οἰκοδομήν' (14:3), indeed 'all things are to be done for the οἰκοδομήν' (14:26). In other words, the ethical question for the completely free man is answered not with a legal code which specifies what is permitted, nor by mere private communion with the Spirit, but rather with his incorporation into the body of Christ in which the Spirit of Christ 'leads' his people through the apostolic paraenesis, the prophetic utterance[29] and the enlightenment of the heart.

To the body of Christ, Paul says, 'Let the word of Christ dwell in you richly, teaching and admonishing (νουθετοῦντες) each other in all wisdom' (Col 3:16; cf Rom 15:14). Into such an instructing, admonishing body each believer was baptized by the Holy Spirit (I Cor 12:13); this body is also the temple of God in which God's Spirit dwells (I Cor 3:16). The Spirit creates the body, inhabits the body, indwells the members of the body

(I Cor 6:19), admonishes the body through the members, and, to the degree that 'the Lord is the Spirit' (II Cor 3:17), the body of Christ is also the body of the Spirit. Therefore, to talk of being led by the Holy Spirit in the sense of being informed privately on the question of morality stands in contradiction to Paul's understanding of the Spirit's work. The Christian is led by the Holy Spirit not only in the renewing of his mind to prove the will of God but also by being placed into a community of believers where he hears the paraenetic admonitions which are the voice of the Spirit himself.[30] This hearing is not once for all but happens repeatedly in the normal life of the community as the various members 'teach and admonish each other' (Col 3:16).[31]

That this human activity of teaching the paraenetic tradition is not, for Paul, inconsistent with, but a necessary part of the divine pneumatic instruction of the believer, is shown further by the command of enemy love in I Thess.[32] Paul reminds the Thessalonian Christians how he had handed over ($\pi\alpha\rho\epsilon\lambda\acute{\alpha}\beta\epsilon\tau\epsilon$) to them the tradition 'how you are to walk and to please God' (4:1). A part of this tradition was doubtless the command of enemy love which is alluded to more than once (5:15; 3:12; 4:9; cf 1:6). Nevertheless, Paul says, 'You yourselves have been *taught by God* to love one another' so that they have no need that he write them (4:9). Thus the love command delivered by human means (ultimately from the sayings of Jesus) is not in conflict with the fact that the Thessalonians are $\theta\epsilon o\delta\acute{\iota}\delta\alpha\kappa\tau o\iota$. The tradition of the command of enemy love is rather an essential part of the means God uses to teach. This is suggested also when Paul says that he gave his instructions originally 'through the Lord Jesus' (4:2), that is, as a divine word. Thus when Paul prays in 3:12, 'May the Lord cause you to increase and abound in love to one another and to all' (cf 5:15), he is praying that the *living* Lord may continue to speak creatively within his 'body' through the paraenetic tradition which is rooted in his earthly teaching.

On the basis of these observations it is not inconsistent to say, on the one hand, that a Christian is a new man, led by the Spirit of the living Lord and bearing the fruit of this Spirit, and, on the other hand, to say that the Christian must be admonished often with the concrete command to love his enemy. By means of this and other commands the Spirit has chosen to lead his people, to cultivate his fruit and to bring every man to maturity in Christ.[33] To put it in a picture: the command of enemy love, as part of the New Testament paraenesis given 'by grace' and 'through the Lord,' is a seed sown by the Spirit's gifted servants, in the ground of the renewed heart, which the Spirit himself has created, so that the fruit which springs up in the attitude and action of the Christian is indeed the fruit of the Spirit.[34]

3. Implications for the Use of Jesus' Command of Enemy Love

The saying of Jesus on enemy love was not a curious relic of mere historical interest in the early church. It was a vivid illustration of the will of the *living* Lord who is one with the *earthly* Jesus. It was inevitable, therefore, and proper that the paraenetic tradition on enemy love, while having its roots in the words of the earthly Jesus, should be delivered and applied as if spoken by the resurrected Lord. This does not mean that the early church made no distinction at all between a prophetic utterance from the Spirit of the Lord and the traditional sayings of the earthly Jesus. On the contrary, the 'words of the Lord' explicitly cited by Paul[35] have a unique character in relation to his other statements. 'While on the one hand he subjected all his pneumatic judgments and instructions to the Spirit at work in the church for discussion (I Cor 14:37) the words of the Lord on the other hand functioned as criteria of the Spirit (I Cor 7:10).'[36] Nevertheless, the historical sayings of Jesus were uniquely authoritative not merely because they were spoken by the earthly Jesus but because the earthly Jesus who spoke to them is the present living Lord whose will has not changed.[37]

But there is a difference between Jesus' command of enemy love as it is taken up in the paraenetic tradition and the command as it went forth from Jesus' mouth. This difference is evident first in the *form* of the command (see pp 56f). It is also evident in the *intention* of the command. The words had once been spoken by Jesus as a concrete part of his call to repentance in view of the dawning new age and its radical demands and promises (see p 80). The Lord Jesus is now risen from the dead and dwells in and among his people by the Spirit. A new situation in redemptive history has come. Corresponding to this new situation Jesus' command is now addressed to believers, to those who have *already* tasted the powers of the age to come. It has lost some of its vivid sharpness and aims now to shed a helping light upon the path that the new man in Christ must follow.[38] As Jesus' love command once announced the demand of the inbreaking Kingdom of God and thus summoned men to faith, so now it is addressed to those 'who have been transferred into the Kingdom of his beloved Son' (Col 1:13) and who accordingly live by faith.

4. The Use of the Old Testament in Explicating and Motivating the Paraenetic Command of Enemy Love

a. Explication. We shall restrict our attention here to the command of enemy love as it is motivated and elucidated in Rom 12:17–20. It is striking that in all of Rom 12:1–13:7 Old Testament citations occur only in the section on enemy love (12:17–20),[39] and here with an amazing frequency – five different Old Testament references in four verses! They may be tabularized as follows.

Rom	LXX	Mas
12:17b προνοούμενοι καλὰ ἐνώπιον πάντων ἀνθρώπων	Prov 3:4 καὶ προνοοῦ καλὰ ἐνώπιον κυρίου καὶ ἀνθρώπων	Prov 3:4 וּמְצָא־חֵן וְשֵׂכֶל טוֹב בְּעֵינֵי אֱלֹהִים וְאָדָם
12:18 εἰρηνεύοντες	Ps 33:15 ζήτησον εἰρήνην	Ps 34:15 בַּקֵּשׁ שָׁלוֹם
12:19a μὴ ἑαυτοὺς ἐκδικοῦντες	Lev 19:18 οὐκ ἐκδικᾶταί σου ἡ χείρ	Lev 19:18 לִי נָקָם וְשָׁלֵם
12:19b Ἐμοὶ ἐκδίκησις ἐγὼ ἀνταποδώσω	Dt 32:35 ἐν ἡμέρᾳ ἐκδικήσεως ἀνταποδώσω	Dt 32:35 לִי נָקָא וְשָׁלֵם
12:20 ἀλλὰ ἐὰν πεινᾷ ὁ ἐχθρός σου ψώμιζε αὐτὸν ἐὰν διψᾷ πότιζε αὐτὸν τοῦτο γὰρ ποιῶν ἄνθρακας πυρὸς σωρεύσεις ἐπὶ τὴν κεφαλὴν αὐτοῦ.	Prov 25:21f ἐὰν πεινᾷ ὁ ἐχθρός σου τρέφε αὐτὸν ἐὰν διψᾷ πότιζε αὐτὸν τοῦτο γὰρ ποιῶν ἄνθρακας πυρὸς σωρεύσεις ἐπὶ τὴν κεφαλὴν αὐτοῦ ὁ δὲ κύριος ἀνταποδώσει σοι ἀγαθά.	Prov 25:21f אִם־רָעֵב שֹׂנַאֲךָ הַאֲכִילֵהוּ לָחֶם וְאִם־ צָמֵא הַשְׁקֵהוּ מָיִם: כִּי גֶחָלִים אַתָּה חֹתֶה עַל־רֹאשׁוֹ וַיהוָה יְשַׁלֶּם־לָךְ:

How are we to account for this concentration of Old Testament quotes and allusions precisely in this context?

As we argued in Chapter 1 (pp 14f) Paul is *not* rendering here verbatim a fixed Jewish code. The following observations point to Paul's compositional freedom. (1) 12:17a is found in other contexts in the tradition (I Thess 5:15; I Pt 3:9); (2) 12:17b is quoted elsewhere by Paul in its longer Old Testament form (II Cor 8:21); (3) the phrases 'if possible' and 'so far as it depends on you' in 12:18 depart from the absolute form of the terse traditional paraenesis and sound more occasional; (4) the insertion of the word 'beloved' (12:19) is probably Paul's own personal touch; (5) when Heb 10:30 is compared with Rom 12:19b it appears that 'says the Lord' is Paul's own insertion here as in I Cor 14:21. Thus we cannot attribute the concentration of Old Testament quotes here to a mechanical rendering of an already existing Jewish code.

This, of course, is not to deny that Paul was indeed using traditional Jewish material rather than simply relying directly on the Old Testament. We have shown that 12:17a was already shaped in the Hellenistic – Jewish paraenetic material as Paul took it over (p 64). Also 12:19 is an element of the Jewish tradition rather than going back directly to the Old Testament as its parallels in Heb 10:30 and Targum Onk.[40] show. They agree against the Mas and LXX.

In general, the frequency of Old Testament material in the early Christian paraenetic tradition can be accounted for on three grounds. (1) The tradition was born on Jewish soil and shaped by Jews. They lived out of the Old Testament and in a thought world formed by the Old Testament. When they became Christians all this was not overthrown. What did not conflict with the teachings of their Lord was gathered around and subordinated to his sayings, a critical procedure which Jesus himself had begun. (2) Corresponding to the conviction that 'all the promises of God are Yes in Christ' (II Cor 1:20), was the conviction that 'whatever was written beforehand was written for our instruction' (Rom 15:4; cf I Cor 9:10). This opened the way for a broad-scale typological use of the Old Testament in the early church[41] (cf Rom 5; I Cor 10) by which a theological and redemptive-historical continuity between the Old Testament and the present eschatological situation could be established. (3) One motive for the use of Old Testament material on Hellenistic soil which Michel suggests,[42] is to confront the charismatically oriented Christians with a sober, historical dimension of revelation.

These three grounds may account for the paraenetic use of Old Testament material *in general* by the early church, but they do not yet account for why precisely here in the context of enemy love and nowhere else in Rom 12:1-13:7 the Old Testament quotes are concentrated. It is not inconceivable that this is due simply to Paul's random selection from the traditional material available. But perhaps it is not accidental that also in I Pt the longest Old Testament quote is an expansion and ground of the command of enemy love (3:9-12; see p 127). In light of this, perhaps we should hazard a conjecture why Old Testament references were so attracted to the command of enemy love in the early Christian paraenesis.

The command of enemy love – to bless those who persecute you – is the hardest command made upon the new community. It is hard, not only because it demands an end to selfishness, but also because it seems unjust. The enemy who scorns God, who blasphemes the risen Lord, who abuses God's people without reason, does not deserve blessing. More than that, dozens of instances could be cited from the Old Testament to contradict such a non-resistance stance. For Paul, however, to follow Jesus did not mean the abolishing of the Old Testament but rather its establishment (Rom 3:31). When viewed from Christ, who lifts the veil from the 'reading of Moses' (II Cor 3:14), the Old Testament is seen to be 'written for our instruction'; it is παράκλησις (Rom 15:4; cf 4:23; I Cor 9:10; II Tim 3:16). Therefore, to lend weight to this hardest of all commands and to deflect criticism which might be brought against it from the Old Testament, the command was expanded and applied by the use of the very material by which it was threatened. In this way the tension in Jesus' own treatment of the Old Testament is preserved: on the one hand, the command of enemy love stands over the Old Testament material determining what is taken over and then providing the key to the proper interpretation of it, and on the other hand, the love command is the summation of the Old Testament (Mk 12:28-31 par; implied in Rom 12:14,17-20; stated in Rom 13:8-10; Gal 5:14, Ja 2:8-10) and is explicated by it.

In the previous section (pp 111f) we noted that the new situation in redemptive history occasioned a change in the use of Jesus' command of enemy love. This insight may also shed some light on our present problem. In Jesus' situation his command of enemy love was not intended primarily as a guide for how to get along in the world; it was in a real sense a summons to abandon all efforts to get along in this world and to ready oneself for an impending new world. In the formation of the paraenetic tradition, the early church, now aware of the new situation that came with Jesus' resurrection, could not ignore this world and the need to live in it for an indefinite period of time.[43] Jesus' command became, therefore, a guide to help the Christian orient himself in this new situation which included a continued historical existence. Thus while not losing its eschatological sharpness and its function as criterion, Jesus' command of enemy love was drawn into the sphere of wisdom teaching in the traditional sense of offering guidelines for getting along in the world. For this reason, we may suppose, other Old Testament wisdom teaching was connected to the love command in the paraenetic tradition (Rom 12:17b,20).[44] Jesus' command was explicated, and thus made more useful, more workable, by the use of related and selected Old Testament wisdom sayings.[45]

b. Motivation. The Old Testament citations in the paraenetic tradition do not merely explicate Jesus' command of enemy love, they also ground it. Rom 12:19-20[46] is not just a description, it is also an argument. The structure of the passage may become clear if we print it in the following schematic fashion:

(−) 19a Do not avenge yourselves, beloved,
    19b but give place to wrath;
        19c *because* it is written: Vengeance is mine, I will repay,
            says the Lord.

(+) 20a But if your enemy hungers, feed him;
    20b if he thirsts, give him drink;
        20c *because* by doing this you will heap coals of fire
            on his head.

The ἀλλά at the beginning of v 20 shows that v 20ab is the positive counterpart of v 19ab. What v 19ab expresses *passively* with reference to the renunciation of vengeance, v 20ab expresses *actively* with reference to the doing of good. Both commands are grounded by a following γάρ -clause. This parallel structure suggests very strongly that heaping coals of fire on the head is referring to the same eschatological vengeance as v 19c: 'Vengeance is mine, I will repay.'[47] In support of this view we may observe with Spicq that, 'In the Old Testament, live coals are invariably a symbol of divine anger (II Sam 22:9,13 = Ps 18:9,13), of punishment for the wicked (Ps 140:11), or of an evil passion (Sir 8:10; 11:32; Prov 6:27-29; cf Job 31:12). It would be very strange if St. Paul were to use the phrase in a favorable sense.'[48] Further, the word 'fire' in Paul's vocabulary always refers to eschatological judgement.[49] In II Thess 1:6-8 it is united to ἀνταποδοῦναι and ἐκδίκησιν, the same words we have in Rom 12:19c.

In spite of these reasons for understanding 'coals of fire' as eschatological judgment in parallelism with God's 'paying back' in v 19c, many commentators still prefer the interpretation in which 'coals of fire' signify the burning pangs of shame and contrition. Cranfield gives a typical example of the argumentation for this view: 'That as far as Paul's meaning is concerned, this latter interpretation is to be preferred is abundantly clear; for it is congruous with the context in Romans while the former interpretation is quite incompatible with it.'[50] More recently Käsemann goes in the same direction, appealing to Morenz's idea that behind Rom 12:20 there is an Egyptian rite of repentance 'in which we have to do with a forced change of mind.'[51] He gives no other arguments.

It may be that the majority of scholars with Cranfield and Käsemann are correct in their interpretation of Rom 12:19f. I cannot offer a different interpretation which is free from problems. Nevertheless the arguments for seeing the coals of fire as eschatological judgment are weighty enough to justify *seeking* an interpretation which takes these into account and yet does not damage the command of enemy love. I offer the following observations as such a *search*, not as a dogmatic statement or as a certified conclusion. It is hoped that the line of thought developed will prove valuable in understanding Paul's ethics even if it does not solve the problem of Rom 12:19f.

It is evident in the commentaries that the main argument against viewing 'coals of fire'[52] as eschatological judgment is that this would seem to contradict the context of the love command. Whether this is the case is, therefore, our main question. Rom 12:19 is usually considered compatible with the context and with Paul's theology in general. Supposedly it grounds the love command merely by reminding the church that all vengeance is God's business; we are not in any way to be occupied with it. We are to be about the business of loving and to leave judging to God. Verse 20, on the other hand, appears to make wrath the aim of 'loving' action: give water so the coals will fall! But is v 19 really saying anything different from v 20? Paul did not just negatively say, 'Don't avenge yourselves!' He went farther and said positively, 'Give a place to wrath,' or, as Bauer translates it, 'Give the wrath (of God) an opportunity to work out its purpose.'[53] And Paul grounded this appeal not just in the sovereignty of God to avenge as he pleases but also in the specific promise, $\dot{\alpha}\nu\tau\alpha\pi o\delta\dot{\omega}\sigma\omega$: 'I will pay back!' (cf II Thess 1:6). It seems to me that there is nothing essentially different between being kind so that fiery coals will fall and behaving so that the wrath of God will have an opportunity to work out its fiery purpose. Therefore the difficulty we face is not restricted to v 20; both verses seem to ground kind actions with an ulterior motive which really desires the destruction of the enemy.[54]

Preisker spares no words in excoriating Paul's apparent relapse into Judaism:

It is a completely foreign tone when Paul in Rom 12:20 grounds the command of enemy love with Prov 25:22 . . . Here a position often taken in Judaism has struck the Christian attitude at its heart. No longer does the boundless, God-given power of the obligation of an I to a Thou compel one to love, but rather a shrewd mind and petty revenge dictate an attitude which is supposed to look like love but is anything but love. Obviously a wholly other spirit has penetrated into Christian love.[55]

But Paul has posted a clear warning signal against understanding his words in this way. At the head of the whole paragraph on enemy love stands: 'Bless those who persecute you' (Rom 12:14a). With his usual down-to-earth wisdom C. H. Dodd remarks: 'To bless is to wish well and to turn the wish into a prayer.'[56] This command excludes every motive that would desire our neighbor's destruction. It is impossible to desire a person's damnation and to bless him in this sense. If this word of the Lord in v 14 governs the thought of the passage, then vv 19 and 20 probably were not intended by Paul to mean: do good deeds to your enemy with the hope of bringing wrath down on him. How else can these words be legitimately understood?

Preisker sees the proper motive of love in 'the boundless, God given power of the obligation of an I to a Thou.' What is this 'power' (*Gewalt*)? It must be the power of the new man in Christ who is living out of faith. In what does he have faith? In the God who raised Jesus from the dead (Rom 4:24) and will thus give life to his mortal body also (Rom 8:11). That is, the preaching of the gospel through which the new man of faith comes into being (Rom 10:17) is not just a recital of *past* events but a promise: it is the power of God *unto salvation* for everyone who has faith (Rom 1:16, cf I Cor 15:2). We are saved *in hope* (Rom 8:24) of full redemption (cf Rom 5:10). Paul says in Col 1:4f that it is this *hope* 'which we hear in the word of truth, the gospel' which grounds the Christian's *love*.[57] The fulfilment of the command of enemy love hangs on the surety of the Christian's hope. Therefore, in accordance with what we said earlier about the Spirit's leading in and through the body of Christ, it is entirely fitting, indeed indispensable, that the paraenesis be grounded in part by references to God's future action (cf I Pt 3:9-12) in which the Christian hopes.

God's action on the day of salvation in which the Christian hopes will involve the revelation of this wrath.[58] 'For he will render to every man according to his works: to those who by patience in good work seek glory and honor and immortality he will give eternal life; but to those who are selfishly ambitious and who disobey the truth but obey wickedness he will give wrath and fury' (Rom 2:6-8). The argumentation of Rom 12:19,20 suggests that the Christian can love his enemy only if he is sure that the future will bring wrath upon those enemies whom he loves. Why?

If God *never* brings vengeance on those who persist in disobeying the truth, or destruction on the enemies of the cross (Phil 3:18f), but rather continues to grant his people suffering (Phil 1:29) while his enemies prosper and are blessed (Rom 12:14), then he is an unfaithful God whose covenant is worthless. For he would be saying in effect that it is a matter of complete indifference whether one trusts in him or not. He would be discounting the greatness and worthiness of his own name[59] by admitting that faith and blasphemy are for him as good as equal. Or even worse, he would be awarding blasphemy the greater portion. If this were true, the hope of the gospel which hangs on God's faithfulness, would be shattered. And if the hope of the gospel is shattered, then the ground of enemy love, indeed of all Christian ethics, is lost. Therefore, there is a very real sense in which the Christian's love of his enemy is grounded in his certainty that God will take vengeance on those who *persist* in the state of enmity toward God's people.

But Rom 12:20 ('For, doing this *you* will heap coals of fire on his head') seems to lay the stress on the fact that precisely the Christian's love for the enemy is what brings judgment on him. If the interpretation which I am developing is to be plausible we must suppose that Paul intended the unexpressed conditional clause: '*If* the enemy is not moved to repentance by your love.' So Paul would be saying, 'If the one, who in spite of his enmity received love, nevertheless remains an enemy he will not escape the wrath of God.'[60] Rom 12:19f thus reminds the Christian that, if his enemies spurn his kindness, their guilt will be compounded. Similarly in Phil 1:28 Paul says of the Philippians' fearlessness before their opponents, 'This is a sign to them of destruction but of your salvation and this is from God.' And of his own apostolic ministry, the goal of which was to win men (I Cor 9:19ff), Paul says, 'To one it is the fragrance from death to death, to the other a fragrance from life to life' (II Cor 2:16). And, finally, the same is said of God's own love: 'Do you not know that God's kindness is meant to lead you to repentance? But by your hard and unrepentant heart you are storing up for yourself wrath on the day of wrath and of the revelation of the righteous judgment of God' (Rom 2:4f).[61] This 'storing up of wrath' is essentially the same as 'heaping up coals of fire.'

How is it then a motivation to love when Paul tells the Christian that his love, like the apostolic preaching and the love of God, makes the plight of the enemy worse if it meets an unrepentant heart? We have already concluded on the basis of Rom 12:14 that Paul does not mean that the aim of the Christian should be the destruction of his enemy. Rather, I would suggest that the two γάρ clauses (Rom 12:19c, 20c) are intended to give assurance that God is not unrighteous: 'God will render to every man according to his works' (Rom 2:6). Rom 12:20c does not present the conscious aim of the believer, but states the framework of justice in which enemy love becomes possible and good – a framework founded on God's own righteousness (Rom 2:4,5). To be aware of this framework will motivate to genuine enemy love just as much as God's consciousness of his own righteousness moves him to kindness.

With this complete confidence in the righteousness of God the Christian is freed to love his enemy. He is freed not only from the fear of death and of all threats to his ego, but he is now also freed from the insidious tendency in every man to keep an account of wrongs (I Cor 13:6) in the name of justice. The assurance that God will take vengeance justly on the evil of unrepentant animosity removes the last hindrance to enemy love. (Cf I Pt 2:23: 'Although he suffered, he did not threaten but submitted to the one who judges justly.')

The motivation we have been developing here from Rom 12:19f is subordinate to, but not inconsistent with, the overarching ground of enemy love which is expressed in Rom 12:1 – 'the mercies of God' (see Section II.B.1). The mercies of God hold out to the believer the hope of full redemption in the future (Rom 8:24; 5:10); and the transforming power of God's mercy in the present is a power flowing from this future redemption. The newness of the believer, appropriated already by faith, is an anticipation of his future consummated newness. The new man, the man of faith, is thus sustained by hope. *Therefore*, it is fitting that the paraenetic command of enemy love be grounded by promises of God's covenant-keeping faithfulness such as Rom 12:19-20.

We may note, finally, that the foundation for Rom 12:19f had been laid already in Jesus' teaching. As Schlatter points out, the problem of injustice rising out of the command not to resist evil received a solution in Jesus' teaching not unlike the solution it received in the early Christian paraenesis: 'In the new word of Jesus [Mt 5:39] the first word [Mt 5:22], which assigned to Gehenna one who debases his brother, lives on, and with that the objection is settled which Josephus had already made, namely that patience gives birth to injustice.'[62] Jesus also said that the rejection of his call to repentance and the failure to give heed to his mighty works exacerbated the guilt of his hearers and made them all the more liable to judgment (Mt 11:20-22 par;[63] cf Mt 18:23-25).[64] We need not hazard any historical, traditional connections in order to see that the development of the early Christian paraenesis is here not in *essential* disagreement with the teaching of Jesus.

C. I Peter

1. The General Structure of Kerygma and Paraenesis

There are several conceptual and structural differences between the paraenesis of I Pt and the paraenesis of Rom. *First,* the Petrine concept of new birth (1:3,23) is found nowhere in Rom nor anywhere else in Paul. 'In I Pt regeneration is God's act on man (1:3). It is effected by the resurrection of Jesus (1:3) or by the word of God (1:23), i.e. the gospel (cf v 25). The result of man's regeneration is a living hope (1:3).'[65] The concept, whether stemming originally from the mystery religions[66] or not, was widely known in the Christian tradition (cf Jn 3:3-8; Tit 3:5; I Jn 3:9;

5:8; Ja 1:18) and had a distinct and unique Christian meaning.[67] It has a peculiarly eschatological character: the Christians 'have been born anew' (1:23), they 'have purified their souls' (1:22) but this new condition is not static or complete. The metaphor is carried farther: 'as newborn babes' the Christians are now to 'grow up unto salvation' (2:2); salvation is consistently future (1:5,9) and the newborn babe is characterized essentially by joyful (1:8) and confident (1:21) hope (1:3,13). This leads to the *second* difference between I Pt and Rom.

The significance of hope for the paraenetic admonition is stressed more heavily by I Pt. The concept of hope dominates that of faith. This does not mean that faith is neglected; it means that faith is considered primarily from the standpoint of hope: Christians are 'guarded by God's power through *faith* for a salvation ready to be revealed at the last time ... As the outcome of your *faith* you obtain the salvation of your souls' (1:5,9; cf 1:13; 5:9). Faith and hope are almost identified and this hopeful faith then functions to ground the paraenesis (cf Διὸ, 1:13).

A *third* difference is cited by Lohse: 'Especially characteristic of the paraenesis of our letter is the way in which it is bound together with the kerygma which like the paraenesis was taken up from the tradition. Here the imperative is not, as with Paul, deduced from a preceding, unfolded indicative; rather the paraenesis stands first and is grounded in the added reference to the will and act of God.'[68] This structural feature of I Pt's paraenesis is most evident in 2:21-25 and 3:18 where the preceding admonitions are grounded in references to Christ's death.

These three differences between the paraenesis of I Pt and that of Rom are superficial and do not reveal the similarities and unity between the two which are more striking and more essential. *First,* Lohse's distinction cannot be pressed. In I Pt, the kerygma also *precedes* the paraenesis: following 1:3-12 comes the paraenetic appeal of 1:13ff; and the appeal of 2:1ff is grounded in the preceding indicative (1:23-25). Nor does the indicative in Paul always precede the imperative: Rom 6:14 grounds the foregoing admonitions and I Thess 5:8 is an indicative in the midst of imperatives. There is no fixed scheme in I Pt or in Paul. What matters is that in both the paraenesis is rooted in the accomplished work of Christ, as Lohse agrees.[69]

Second, there is a different accent in I Pt's treatment of hope and faith, but to focus on this accent would be to miss the forest for the trees.[70] We discussed earlier the importance of hope in Paul's motivation of the paraenesis (pp 117f, cf Rom 8:24; Col 1:4). In I Pt faith is not *merely* a forward-looking confidence in the 'grace being brought to you' (1:13); it also looks backward to the resurrection (1:3,21) and death

(1:19; 2:24; 3:18) of Christ. In fact it is best to say that faith is in *God* (1:21) who is known as 'the one who raised Christ from the dead' (1:21) and the one who 'keeps us for a salvation ready to be revealed at the last time' (1:5). This is essentially the same as Paul: we 'believe in him who raised from the dead Jesus our Lord' (Rom 4:24): 'The one who raised Christ Jesus from the dead will give life to your mortal bodies also' (Rom 8:11). The shift of accent onto hope in I Pt is probably due to the afflictions[71] of the recipients: they needed to be reminded of the bright prospect of the future salvation.

Third, the fact that Paul does not use the concept 'new birth' is a terminological, not an essential, difference. New birth has its essential counterpart in the Pauline concepts of the 'new creation' (Gal 6:15; II Cor 5:17), the 'new man' (Col 3:10) and related ideas. Just as in I Pt 1:3 Christians are 'born *anew* . . . through the resurrection of Jesus Christ from the dead,' so in Rom 6:4 it is because Christ was raised from the dead that 'we too might walk in *newness* of life.' The new reality is in both cases the work of God (I Pt 1:3; II Cor 5:18; Rom 6:17,13). In both it is an eschatological reality: those who have *already* been born anew must *still* put away all malice and grow up unto salvation (I Pt 2:1,2); those who have *already* died with Christ and *already* walk in newness of life must *still* reckon themselves dead to sin and alive to God (Rom 6:11). In neither case is the newness a mere state; it is at the same time a summons, for it is effected by the word of God, the gospel (I Pt 1:23,25; Rom 1:16; II Cor 5:18,20).

Fourth, both Rom and I Pt ground the paraenetic commands in the *mercies of God* shown in the death and resurrection of Christ. Instead of the word οἰκτιρμῶν (Rom 12:1), I Pt uses ἔλεος (1:3) and χρηστός (2:3). Paul says: 'I appeal to you, brothers, through the *mercies* of God' (Rom 12:1); I Pt appeals 'because you have tasted the *kindness* of God' (2:3). We saw from Rom 5:5-8 (pp 103f) that the 'mercies of God,' on the basis of which a man is called to love his enemy (Rom 12:14,17ff), consist primarily in the love of God shown in the death of Christ for sinners. The same ground of love is prominent in I Pt: servants are to be submissive to their masters and bear unjust suffering patiently, 'for unto this you were called *because* Christ too suffered on behalf of you, leaving for you a pattern that you might follow in his footsteps' (2:21). Christ's suffering is ultimately the ground for the paraenesis not because it was exemplary but because it was substitutionary (ὑπὲρ ὑμῶν). Such unusual behavior can be demanded of servants because 'Christ himself bore our sins in his body on the tree that we might die to sin and live to righteousness' (2:24; a similar argument appears in 3:17f).

Fifth, there are verbal parallels between I Pt and Rom which reveal an acquaintance with common tradition.[72] We may cite two which are taken from Rom 12.

Rom	I Pt
12:1 θυσίαν ζῶσαν ἁγίαν εὐάρεστον τῷ θεῷ	2:5 πνευματικὰς θυσίας εὐπροσδέκτους θεῷ
12:2 μὴ συσχηματίζεσθε τῷ αἰῶνι τουτῷ	1:14 μὴ συσχηματιζόμενοι ταῖς πρότερον

From these observations it is evident that the general structure of kerygma and paraenesis in Pt is *essentially* the same as the structure we find in Rom. All the paraenetic admonitions are grounded in the 'kindness' (= mercies) of the Lord *revealed* in the central events of redemptive history: the death (I Pt 1:19; 2:24; 3:18) and resurrection (1:3) of Christ, and *appropriated* in daily life by faith (1:5,9; 5:9). This structural similarity along with the verbal parallels suggests that we are dealing here with a structural motif already present in the early oral paraenetic tradition.[73]

2. The Ground of the Command of Enemy Love in I Pt

Turning from general considerations we focus now on the specific command of enemy love (I Pt 3:9) with the question: How is it grounded or motivated? The pertinent context is I Pt 3:9-12.

> Do not return evil for evil,
> or reviling for reviling,
> but bless,
> because unto this you were called
> in order that you might inherit a blessing.
> For he who would love life
> and see good days,
> let him keep his tongue from evil
> and his lips from speaking guile;
> let him turn away from evil and do good;
> let him seek peace and pursue it.
> For the eyes of the Lord are upon the righteous,
> and his ears are open to their prayer.
> But the face of the Lord is against those that do evil.

The Old Testament quotation brought in to elucidate and support the command of enemy love comes from Ps 33:13-17a (LXX).

I Pt	LXX	Mas
3:10-12	Ps 33:13-17a	Ps 34:13-17a

I Pt 3:10-12

ὁ γὰρ
θέλων ζωὴν ἀγαπᾶν καὶ
ἰδεῖν ἡμέραν ἀγαθὰς
παυσάτω τὴν γλῶσσαν
ἀπὸ κακοῦ
καὶ χείλη τοῦ
μὴ λαλῆσαι δόλον,
ἐκκλινάτω δὲ ἀπὸ κακοῦ
καὶ ποιησάτω ἀγαθόν,
ζητησάτω εἰρήνην
καὶ διωξάτω αὐτήν.
ὅτι ὀφθαλμοὶ κυρίου
ἐπὶ δικαίους
καὶ ὦτα αὐτοῦ εἰς δέησιν
αὐτῶν,
πρόσωπον δὲ κυρίου
ἐπὶ ποιοῦντας κακά.

LXX Ps 33:13-17a

τίς ἐστιν ἄνθρωπος ὁ
θέλων ζωὴν ἀγαπῶν
ἡμέρας ἰδεῖν ἀγαθάς;
παῦσον τὴν γλῶσσάν
σου ἀπὸ κακοῦ
καὶ χείλη σου τοῦ
μὴ λαλῆσαι δόλον.
ἔκκλινον ἀπὸ κακοῦ
καὶ ποίησον ἀγαθόν,
ζήτησον εἰρήνην
καὶ δίωξον αὐτήν.
ὀφθαλμοὶ κυρίου
ἐπὶ δικαίους,
καὶ ὦτα αὐτοῦ εἰς δέησιν
αὐτῶν.
πρόσωπον δὲ κυρίου
ἐπὶ ποιοῦντας κακά.

Mas Ps 34:13-17a

מִי־הָאִישׁ הֶחָפֵץ חַיִּים
אֹהֵב יָמִים לִרְאוֹת טוֹב:
נְצֹר לְשׁוֹנְךָ מֵרָע
וּשְׂפָתֶיךָ מִדַּבֵּר מִרְמָה:
סוּר מֵרָע וַעֲשֵׂה־טוֹב
בַּקֵּשׁ שָׁלוֹם וְרָדְפֵהוּ:
עֵינֵי יְהוָה אֶל־צַדִּיקִים
וְאָזְנָיו אֶל־שַׁוְעָתָם:
פְּנֵי יְהוָה בְּעֹשֵׂי רָע

According to 3:9b, we are to bless those who revile us ὅτι εἰς τοῦτο
ἐκλήθητε ἵνα εὐλογίαν κληρονομήσητε. The primary exegetical question
here is: What does the τοῦτο refer to? Does it refer (A) to what precedes,
namely, blessing one's revilers; or (B) to what follows in the ἵνα -clause,
namely, the hope of inheriting a blessing? The sense of 'A' would be: Bless
those who revile you because you have been called to do this in order that
as a consequence you might inherit a blessing. The sense of 'B' would be:
Bless those who revile you because you know that through God's call[74] a
blessing awaits you. 'A' makes the inheritance of the blessing conditional
upon loving one's enemy. 'B' makes the surety of the inheritance the
motive of loving one's enemy. Thus 'A' seems to conflict with the general
structure of the kerygma and paraenesis determined above, according to
which the imperatives are grounded in the finished work of God in Christ
and the surety of the coming salvation.

It is precisely this apparent theological conflict which leads most
commentators to favor interpretation 'B'.[75] Kelly sums up the three
additional arguments for 'B'. (1) According to 'A' there is an awkward
parenthesis: 'Bless those who revile you (for unto this you were called) in
order that you might inherit a blessing.' (2) I Pt 4:6 offers a parallel which
shows that τοῦτο in this construction can look forward:[76] εἰς τοῦτο γὰρ
καὶ νεκροῖς εὐηγγελίσθη ἵνα κριθῶσι . . . (3) 'Freely you have received,

freely give' is better in tune with the spirit of the passage. A fourth argument could be that interpretation 'A' fails to take account of the possibility that ἵνα could imply result instead of purpose. Are these arguments compelling?

With regard to the *first* argument it may be said that there need be no parenthesis at all. The sentence makes good sense if the ἵνα clause is subordinate to ἐκλήθητε: 'Bless those who revile you because you were called to do this and the purpose or aim of this call to love your enemy is that you might be blessed.' The *second* argument shows that interpretation 'B' is grammatically *possible,* but I Pt 2:21 provides a more striking parallel than 4:6 and points in the opposite direction.[77] Slaves should endure suffering patiently εἰς τοῦτο γὰρ ἐκλήθητε ... Here we have almost the identical wording (γάρ instead of ὅτι) of 3:9b and the τοῦτο certainly refers backward. The *third* argument that interpretation 'B' is better in tune with the passage is, so far as I can see, not true if one focuses on 3:10-12 (see below). To the *fourth* argument, that ἵνα can have the force of result as well as purpose, we can only say that the context must determine which sense is appropriate. To this, therefore, we should now turn.

The decisive thing in favor of interpretation 'A' is the way Ps 34:13-17 (LXX 33) has been used in this context. Besides replacing the original second person of the LXX with third person, there has been added the γάρ of 3:10 and the ὅτι of v 12. The γάρ introduces the entire Old Testament quote as an expansion and restatement of the argumentation in 3:9. Because the Old Testament is authoritative, its confirmation of what has been said in v 9 functions as a ground (γάρ). The argumentation of the Old Testament passage is precisely that of interpretation 'A', not 'B'. The sense is: '*If* someone desires to love life and to see good days,[78] *then* his tongue must cease from evil.' In the words of v 9: '*if* you desire to inherit a blessing, *then* you must bless those who revile you.' That this is the writer's intention is made clear by the redactional ὅτι of 3:12;[79] one must cease from evil and *do good* precisely because (ὅτι) the Lord is for the righteous and against those who *do evil*. In the words of v 9: one must bless those who revile him *because* his inheritance from the Lord depends on it.[80] In view of this conscious redactional treatment of Ps 34 as a support for the argumentation of 3:9, interpretation 'A' (that τοῦτο refers back to enemy love) has far more in its favor from the immediate context than does interpretation 'B' (that τοῦτο refers forward to inheriting the blessing).

The implication that without obedience to the paraenetic commands one will not inherit the future blessing and that salvation is, therefore, somehow conditional upon obedience is not limited to I Pt 3:9-12. In 1:17 the Christians are admonished to conduct themselves in fear during the time of their (earthly) exile *because* the one they call upon as Father is the one who judges each impartially according to his works. The writer apparently sees no conflict between pointing the Christians forward toward the future of God's judgment and backward, as he does in 1:18f, to their redemption through 'the precious blood of Christ.' Another example of I Pt's future-oriented paraenetic motivation is found in 4:13; 'Insofar as you share the sufferings of Christ, rejoice *in order that* (ἵνα) you might rejoice in gladness at the revelation of his glory' (cf Rom 8:17). The sequence of thought is the same as 3:9: here the Christian is to rejoice in suffering so that he might be able to rejoice in Christ's future glory; in 3:9 he is to bless those who revile him in order that he might inherit a blessing. Finally, we may cite two proverbial sayings from I Pt 5 which contain Old Testament wisdom and reflect the sayings of Jesus: 'All of you clothe yourselves with lowliness toward each other *because* (redactional ὅτι again) God resists the proud but gives grace to the lowly' (5:5b = Prov 3:34 LXX; cf Mt 23:12). 'Humble yourselves therefore under the mighty hand of God *in order that* (ἵνα) in the proper season he might exalt you' (5:6; cf Job 22:29; Mt 23:12; Lk 14:11; 18:14). We see therefore, that the interpretation 'A' of 3:9b, which sees enemy love as a condition for inheriting the blessing, is not an isolated instance in I Pt. How can this line of evidence be brought into harmony with our earlier conclusion that the paraenetic imperatives and their fulfilment are grounded in the renewing mercy of God which is expressed in Christ's death and resurrection and is appropriated in daily life by faith?

To answer this question we must give closer attention to I Pt 1:3–9. Three statements are made here concerning faith. *First,* we are guarded by the power of God through faith for salvation (1:5), i.e., for an incorruptible inheritance (1:4). *Second,* faith which has been proved and found genuine will participate in the glory of Christ's revelation (1:6f), i.e., in the coming salvation (1:5). *Third,* as the end of our faith we receive the salvation of our souls (1:9). In other words the power of God brings us to salvation through, or by means of, tested faith. Wherein does this testing (ποικίλοις πειρασμοῖς 1:6) consist? In 4:12 the πειρασμός which the Christians can expect (μὴ ξενίζεσθε; cf εἰ δέον, 1:6) is a 'fiery test' (πυρώσει;[81] cf διὰ πυρός, 1:7) which according to the following verses consists in sharing the sufferings of Christ (4:13), specifically, being reproached (ὀνειδίζεσθε 4:14) for his name (χριστιανός 4:16). If one rejoices in this suffering (4:13) and unashamedly gives glory to God (4:16), then he will participate in the revelation of Christ's glory (4:13). In other words, as in 1:6f participation in the glorious revelation of Christ depends on a proved faith, so in 4:12f participation in the glorious revelation of Christ depends on a certain kind of response to reproach from non-Christians, namely, a response of joy, boldness and concern for God's glory. This is none other than the response of *faith* (see 1:8, 'you believe and *rejoice*' [cf Rom 15:13]). The δοκίμιον τῆς πίστεως (1:7) which alone participates in the glory of Christ's revelation is nothing less than the faith which proves itself by the way it responds to its enemies.

The implication for the text on enemy love (3:9) is already evident. There are three points of contact between I Pt 3:9 and the two texts we have just discussed (1:3-9 and 4:12-16). *First*, the eschatological goal in each is the same: in 1:3-9 it is called an *inheritance* (1:4), salvation (1:5,9) and the revelation of Jesus Christ (1:7); in 4:13 it is called the revelation of his glory; and in 3:9 it is called *inheriting* a blessing.[82] *Second*, in 1:6f the writer speaks of a faith which must prove itself through being tested. In 4:13-16 this testing consists in the reproach of non-Christians and faith proves itself by its unusual response of joy, boldness and a concern for God's glory. Similarly in 3:9 the testing consists in being reviled by hostile neighbors and (we may assume) faith proves itself by blessing instead of reviling in return. *Third*, the approvedness of faith, the response of joy amid reproach and the response of blessing amid reviling are in each case that through which the Christian finally reaches salvation (cf the ἵνα in 1:7, 3:9 and 4:13);

Our conclusion, therefore, is that, while enemy love is that without which one cannot inherit the blessing in 3:9, this in no way means that the writer is here calling for the heroic ethical strength of a man to earn his inheritance. It means rather that he is calling for the response of *faith*. There can be no talk of the Christian earning his inheritance,[83] for faith is not a human power, but a reliance upon *God's* power which guards us for salvation (1:5). The prospect of inheriting a glorious[84] (4:13; 1:4) blessing should motivate us to put our confidence in him (1:21) who can make us new (1:3,23), thus enabling us to respond to persecution with love (3:9) and so guarding us for the salvation to come. Nor should we ever lose sight of the fact that, while in I Pt salvation is future, nevertheless the epistle stresses over and over the present reality of new life in which the Christian already shares.[85]

3. Implications for the Oral Paraenetic Tradition

The way the command of enemy love is grounded in I Pt 3:9ff corresponds to the book's accent on hope (see p 120). Insofar as this accent is probably a reflection of the situation into which the epistle was sent (see especially 5:9f), so the corresponding ground of enemy love in 3:9b has occasional (redactional) rather than traditional character.[86] Nevertheless, there is reason to think that a good deal of the *terminology* as well as, possibly, the *structure* of the argument was already at the author's disposal in the tradition.

First, we have already noted (see note 82) that while 'blessing' and 'inheriting' (I Pt 3:9) are common eschatological elements of the Old Testament and Jewish tradition, the combination of the two concepts as we have it here is not common in that tradition and yet occurs again in Heb 12:17. It is probably then a part of the early Christian tradition and not the formulation of the author. *Second,* the idea of being 'called' to bless those who revile you (3:9) is present also in 2:21 where one is 'called' to suffer meekly 'in Christ's footsteps'. This may be the author's own adaptation of a traditional idea of being 'called into the fellowship of God's Son' (I Cor 1:9) which is a call to 'suffering' (Phil 3:10) and 'holiness' (I Thess 4:7) and 'peace' (Col 3:15; I Cor 7:15). That $\kappa\alpha\lambda\acute{\epsilon}\omega$ had a fairly technical sense in the early Christian tradition need not be doubted.[87] That this was in the early tradition a call not only to God's Kingdom and glory but also to loving service and suffering is likely in view of the essential parallels between I Pt 2:21 and 3:9 and the other New Testament epistles. *Third,* we saw in Chapter 1 (pp 13f) that Ps 34 which is quoted here in I Pt 3:10-12 was both a constituent of the early Christian paraenetic tradition itself[88] as well as contributing its particular terminology to the tradition ('do good,' 'pursue peace,' etc., I Pt 3:11). Therefore the raw material with which the command of enemy love is grounded in I Pt 3:9-12 is primarily traditional.

Is it possible that also the *structure* of the argument here was a feature of the paraenetic tradition on enemy love? We will not be able to reach certainty here but a comparison with the structure of Rom 12:19f suggests a positive answer. In the *first* place, both Rom 12f and I Pt employ their longest Old Testament quotes to ground and elucidate the command of enemy love (see p 113). *Second,* in both texts the argument of the Old Testament quote has reference to the future, although the content of the argument is different in both. *Third,* in both cases the Old Testament citations are of the proverbial wisdom variety.[89] We have already discussed the theological reason for the use of the Old Testament (specifically proverbial wisdom) in these contexts (see pp 113f). On the basis of these general similarities it is not unlikely that the structure of the arguments in Rom 12:19f and I Pt 3:10-12 had a common type in the early Christian paraenetic tradition. And it is fair to say that the way the command of enemy love is motivated in I Pt and in Paul is not due entirely to the peculiarity of the author but also reflects the general early Christian understanding embodied in the paraenetic tradition.

In discussing *Jesus'* understanding of the relation between his love
command and the Kingdom of God, I concluded (p 79), on the one
hand, that Jesus' love command must be obeyed if one is to enter into
the Kingdom of God and, on the other hand, that apart from the powers
of that Kingdom the obedience of the love command is impossible.
Only that person will enter the Kingdom whose living has already
reflected the life and power of the Kingdom. That is, in order to participate in the future consummation of redemption a man must be transformed even in his behavior by the 'mysterious' redeeming power of
God already at work through Jesus. Obedience to the command of
enemy love is both a condition for entrance into the Kingdom and a
gift of the King. I Pt presents the same basic pattern when it maintains on the one hand that the Christian's inheritance depends on his
loving his enemy (3:9), yet, on the other hand, that it is God's power
which guards us through faith for this inheritance (1:4f). Here we
have an indication that the early church preserved not merely the isolated sayings of Jesus such as the words of Jesus behind the tradition
in I Pt 3:9, but also took over the *theological structure* contained in
Jesus' message.

III. The Content of the Command of Enemy Love

We are concerned in this section with the question: Wherein does obedience
to the command of enemy love consist? Just as in Chapter 3, far less space
will be given to this question than to the preceding question on motivation.
The reason here is the same as there (p 69): the motivation or ground of
the command of enemy love, as I have described it, is such that, when a
man truly experiences it, the perception of what he ought to do happens
naturally, just as a 'new man' naturally leads a new life. I do not mean that
a man is left alone with his conscience and with no external guidance (see
pp 106-10),[90] but rather that in the New Testament paraenesis the
essential thing is the renewing of the mind so that one can prove 'naturally'
what is good (Rom 12:2). It is appropriate, therefore, that our stress should
fall on the ground of the command of enemy love rather than on its content. There follow, accordingly, some brief observations on the general
features of enemy love and a discussion of the command of enemy love in
relation to the general norm of love and to the institutions of society.

A. General Features of Enemy Love

Nowhere in the New Testament outside the synoptics do we find Jesus'
command; 'Love your enemies!' As we argued in Chapter 2 (p 56), this
command would have had a discomforting sharpness in Jesus' situation
where nationalistic feelings ran high and scribes discussed, 'Who is my
neighbor?' For the early church, however, neither nationalistic allegiance
nor scribal exegesis formed the immediate backdrop of the love command.

The question the early church faced was: How shall we act toward the unbeliever, the hostile townspeople, the ridiculing old friends (cf I Pt 4:4)? 'Love your enemies' would not strike home here like it did in Jesus' situation. Therefore the command was paraphrased and the 'enemies' were specified: persecutors, revilers, those who do evil to you, etc.

When it came to specifying how the Christian should behave toward these 'enemies,' the paraenesis said very little. There is no comparison to the large amount of elaboration which love for the brotherhood received. We find a few negative and positive commands: Do not repay evil for evil or reviling for reviling; Bless those who revile you and curse you, don't curse them; Do good to them; Seek peace; Do not avenge yourselves; Give food and water to your needy enemies. Many pages could be used to draw out the implications of these for daily life but that is properly the role of the sermon. Here we may simply observe four things.

First, enemy love is ready and willing to meet the *physical* needs of the enemy. 'If your enemy is hungry, feed him; if he is thirsty, give him drink' (Rom 12:20). Enemy love is disposed to do good to the enemy (I Thess 5:15) and therefore is not content to let him suffer when it has the power to help. Wherein the 'good' of the enemy consists is perceived by the 'renewed mind' of the believer in the concrete encounter with him and this will include the good of his body and mind.[91]

Second, enemy love desires and seeks the *spiritual* welfare of the enemy. The most common positive admonition concerning the enemy is that the Christian 'bless' him (Rom 12:14; I Pt 3:9; I Cor 4:12). Enemy love desires that the enemy be blessed and *not cursed* (Rom 12:14). This desire would be sheer hypocrisy if it were not dominated by a longing for the enemy's participation in the 'fullness of Christ's blessing' (Rom 15:29; cf I Pt 2:12). Enemy love is, therefore, at its heart, a desire and activity aimed at the conversion of one's unbelieving neighbor.[92] Being free from all, it makes itself the servant of all in order to win the more (I Cor 9:19). In this the Christian lacks no zeal: he is aflame with the Spirit and constant in prayer (Rom 12:11,12).

Third, enemy love in no way implies that one finds evil less abhorrent: 'Let love be genuine: hate the evil (ἀποστυγοῦντες τὸ πονηρόν) and hold fast to the good' (Rom 12:9). The existence and seriousness of evil is the very reason there is such a thing as an enemy. And this evil which is the source of enmity is hated by enemy love. Hate is not directed at the person but at his 'works': 'This you have, you hate the works of the Nicolaitans which I also hate,' says Jesus to the church at Ephesus (Rev 2:6). If there is no intense hatred of evil, then there will be no intense love for one's enemy because the good which love desires for the enemy is primarily the removal of the cause of enmity which is the evil of unbelief. Thus if one is ignorant of or insensible to real evil in the world and in his enemy (and in himself!) then he will not know how to love his enemy because he will scarcely perceive his enmity. 'Genuine love' hangs on 'abhorring evil and holding to the good' (Rom 12:9).

The *fourth* point is implied in what I have said already: since enemy love is not merely deeds but is also 'blessing' and ἀνυπόκριτος (Rom 12:9), one cannot achieve it except by becoming a new kind of person. If enemy love involves blessing then there is no possibility that enemy love can mean doing what you do not want to. It is impossible to bless the enemy, i.e., wish (= want) him well, and at the same time not want to. You cannot desire his welfare and not desire it. Either your heart desires his good and blesses him or it does not. But we do not immediately determine the desires of our heart. They spring out like fruit on a tree, either good or bad. Therefore, genuine enemy love involves first and foremost getting a heart that bears the fruit of blessing and not cursing. This was in fact what the first part of this chapter was all about.

B. Love and the Command of Enemy Love and the Institutions of Society

It is outside the scope of this work to deal fully with the general theme of love in the New Testament paraenesis. Nor can we develop from the standpoint of our question a New Testament social ethic. It is inevitable, therefore, that in this section questions will be raised that we cannot stop to answer. Nevertheless if we seek to determine the relationships between the general norm of love,[93] the institution and the specific command of enemy love, the proper application and limitation of this command will become more clear.

The Christian is to do *everything* ἐν ἀγάπη (I Cor 16:14). Love is the *way* (ὁδός) of his life (I Cor 12:31). It is most fully defined in I Cor 13 with no reference to the object to which it is directed but rather with a description of the Christian as he is to feel and act in all relationships.

This means that not only day-to-day personal relationships are governed by love, but also the relationships within institutions. For example, in I Thess 5:13 Paul beseeches the church to 'esteem very highly' their leaders in the church because of their work (διὰ τὸ ἔργον αὐτῶν), and it is to be done ἐν ἀγάπη. It is instructive to reflect for a moment that, according to Paul, esteem can be shown to the church leaders both 'in love' and 'on account of their work.' We are accustomed to thinking that doing something 'in love' excludes doing it because of a person's position or achievement. Paul, however, apparently understood love in such a way that the person who acted in love did not disregard rank or position. Love, as that which forms the Christian's whole life, does not mean he responds the same way to every man. Rather, love takes on shape appropriate to the rank or position of the other person. Love does not ignore, but takes into account 'the work' of the other and gives him his due.

In I Cor 16:16, Paul describes this due, which we owe those who labor (κοπιάω, I Cor 16:16; I Thess 5:12) in the service of the saints, in terms of *subjection*: ὑποτάσσησθε τοῖς τοιούτοις.[94] That is, subjection is urged (I Cor 16:15) for certain relationships *within* the church[95] as it is in the *Haustafeln* for certain relationships *outside* the church (e.g., to the state or to the non-Christian slave owner). But there is little doubt that I Cor 16:15f was seen by Paul in the light of the immediately preceding πάντα ὑμῶν ἐν ἀγάπῃ γινέσθω. Thus from I Thess 5:13 and I Cor 16:14-16 (as well as I Cor 12:31-13:13) we may say that Paul understood love as the attitude which should shape the relationships of subjection within the church.

If this is so, then there can be no objection in principle to understanding every command for subjection in the *Haustafeln* as a call for *love* to take a particular form in given relationships. For whether love is an over-arching principle which embraces relationships of subjection does not depend on whether the objects of love are Christian or not. It depends on whether acting 'in love' and 'in subjection' are *separate* and *distinct* ways of acting or whether walking 'in love' can include walking 'in subjection.' The preceding paragraphs have suggested the latter to be the case: love does subsume subjection as a particular form which love assumes. As Schrage remarks, 'All relationships and orders of the world become for the Christian the sphere and framework of loving conduct . . . . Probably even respect for the orders is itself to be an expression of love.'[96]

Therefore love must be understood in a very broad way. It cannot, for example, be defined so that it necessarily includes non-resistance; because subjecting oneself to the state, which 'does not carry the sword in vain' (Rom 13:1,4), may very well involve one in resistance. As L. Goppelt says, 'Nowhere is the demonstration of love, whose sign is non-resistance, made the authoritative guideline for behavior in the orders, as is the case in the relationship to the neighbor. One can only say that Christians even in the orders of society should act completely out of love, insofar as one understands love to be the free offer of help to men which wills their life (Rom 13:8-10).'[97] Goppelt distinguishes here between a *Liebeserweis* characterized by non-resistance and a *Handeln aus Liebe* characterized more generally as a free act of service which desires life for others. Some such distinction as this is needed to account for the data. For besides the wide understanding of love which we have worked out so far, there is the command of enemy love which is characterized, negatively, by not

resisting evil (I Thess 5:15; Rom 12:17; I Pt 3:9) and, positively, by returning good for evil (I Thess 5:15), by blessing those who persecute (Rom
12:14) or revile (I Pt 3:9; I Cor 4:12) you, and by giving food and water to
your enemy (Rom 12:20). This is certainly an expression of love[98] but it
is an expression which does not remain entirely in harmony with the
motif of 'subjection' in the paraenetic tradition. Conflict is inevitable
because a person whose action is based alone on a command to be subject
aims not to do good to another, but to obey.[99] He may be commanded by
the subjecting power to punish or kill. So long as he is subjecting himself
to that power he will do it; this may easily lead one into conflict with the
command of enemy love.

Therefore, it is evident that the *love* in which all things are to be done
(I Cor 16:16; 12:31ff) is not to be identified with the *enemy love* which is
the central object of our study. The command of enemy love does not stand
over the other individual commands in the tradition as a unifying norm; it
stands beside them, indeed, in tension with some of them. Enemy love is
just one manifestation of the over-arching way of love.

For the sake of precision it must be stressed that in the New Testament paraenesis the command of enemy love is not made the norm of
behavior in the institutions of the *Haustafel.* It has its own sphere of
application, namely, the daily encounter with one's hostile neighbor. We
may illustrate this with a chart. Within the structure of I Pt 2:13–3:12
various institutions of society are discussed in turn, three of which have
their parallel in Rom 12 and 13.

	I Pt	*Rom*
State	2:13–17	13:1–7
Servants	2:18–25	–
Wives–husbands	3:1–7	–
Brotherhood	3:8	12:9–13, 15–16
Neighborhood	3:9–12	12:14,17–21

In the first three of these institutions the command is 'be subject'; in the
last two the command is for brotherly love and enemy love respectively.[100]
The command of enemy love (which blesses its persecutors) is never made
the norm for behavior in an institution where the command ὑποτάσσεσθε
is given.

But this division between the orders does not solve the conflict between
the subjection and non-resistance motifs. Our sister in the Lord may also be
our wife; our employee may also be our neighbor or fellow church member.
Besides this overlapping of social orders there is, as we noticed earlier,
within the church itself an 'order' of 'subjection'. There is no synthesis of

these two commands worked out in the New Testament paraenesis. The question is never explicitly posed: What should I do when the command to feed my enemy conflicts with the command to be subject to the state? Nor was it the intention of the New Testament paraenesis to answer with a command every such question. Rather it admonished: 'be transformed by the renewal of your mind *so that you can prove what is the will of God*' (Rom 12:2).

As we said at the beginning, to try to answer all the questions raised by these remarks is beyond the scope of this work.[101] We may round out this section by recalling that a similar tension existed in Jesus' own ministry. Alongside the command 'Love your enemies!' (Mt 5:44 par) stood the command 'Render to Caesar the things that are Caesar's!' (Mk 12:17). The tension between the two commands is a reflex of the basic eschatological tension of the 'already' and 'not yet' of the Kingdom of God which stamped Jesus' whole ministry (p 97) and is preserved in the New Testament paraenesis. The presence of the *new age* demands a radically new kind of behavior which draws its strength from the hidden, saving reign of God and is thus a sign of it – hence the demand for enemy love (cf Chapter 3, Sections II. C and D). The continuing reality of the *present historical age* demands a recognition of and alignment with the fact that God is the sovereign of history who ordains its institutions for its good – hence the demand for subjection. As long as the church is still 'in the flesh' (Gal 2:20) as long as she walks by faith and not by sight (II Cor 5:7) the tension between enemy love and subjection within human institutions will remain. The over-arching way of love along which one is *always* to walk is therefore not determined merely by the commandments of the paraenesis but depends also upon the renewed mind of faith (Rom 12:2).

5

THE GOSPEL TRADITION OF JESUS' COMMAND OF ENEMY LOVE AND ITS USE IN MATTHEW AND LUKE

I. The Gospel Tradition of Jesus' Command of Enemy Love before the Gospels

By 'gospel tradition' I mean that stream of tradition, the written form of which we have in our synoptic gospels. That this stream of tradition, which flows from the spring of Jesus' words and deeds, is not identical with the 'paraenetic tradition,' which is also rooted in the words of Jesus, is one of the central theses of this study. This thesis has been propounded by L. Goppelt in an article entitled 'Jesus und die "Haustafel"-Tradition.' He concludes: 'Our analysis has shown that there are . . . *two traditions,* which bear the differing stamps of their own main intention. The gospel tradition intends to witness to the sayings of Jesus primarily as proclamation within his own situation,[1] that is, as a summons to repentance in view of the coming Kingdom; the paraenetic tradition passes the sayings on from the exalted Lord to his community as helpful examples for behavior. Therefore they are not usually designated here as the words of Jesus' (p 103).

In Chapter 4 our treatment of Jesus' command of enemy love in the paraenetic tradition confirmed the latter part of Goppelt's conclusion. We turn now to consider the gospel tradition of Jesus' command of enemy love, its form, *Sitz im Leben,* and relation to the paraenetic tradition.

A. Determining the Vorlage

In Chapter 2, pp 49–63, I tried to determine as precisely as possible what the teaching of Jesus was behind Mt 5:38–48/Lk 6:27–36. As a means to that end I tried to show which elements in these texts are probably to be assigned to an earlier level of the tradition. The rigorous work to determine the *Vorlage* of Mt and Lk has, therefore, already been done and this present section will be a *summary of the results of that work.* Instead of repeating the arguments for my conclusions I will merely give the page numbers from Chapter 2 where they are found.

Lührmann has shown that there is a 'gemeinsame Grundstruktur von Bergpredigt und Feldrede' (see chart, pp 49f). Both Mt and Lk found their material on enemy love already imbedded in a collection of sayings. It is impossible, however, to maintain with certainty that Mt and Lk had as their *Vorlage* the same form of this basic collection. There are differences between Mt and Lk which cannot adequately be explained as alterations of Lk's form by Mt or of Mt's form by Lk. It is thus necessary, with a large group of scholars (see Chapter 2, note 93), to postulate two distinct forms of the collection of sayings behind the Sermon on the Mount and the Sermon on the Plain.[2] This means that neither Mt nor Lk can be assumed *a priori* to preserve the form of the material which was originally gathered together into the traditional collection behind Mt 5:38-48/Lk 6:27-36. There is here no fixed text of Q against which Mt and Lk can be contrasted. This makes a reliable determination of redactional elements almost impossible. Nevertheless we can make some definite statements about what the two *Vorlagen* had in common; and, on the basis of the context and the peculiar habits of the evangelists, learned elsewhere, we may venture some probable statements about the redaction of these *Vorlagen*.

In general we may say with a fair degree of certainty that the *Vorlagen* of Mt (5:38-48) and Lk (6:27-36) had the following common elements:[3] the command, 'Love your enemies!' (Mt 5:44a/Lk 6:27a; see p 56); the command, 'Pray for your abusers!' (Mt 5:44b/Lk 6:27d; see p 57); the commands about turning the other cheek, giving up your shirt, walking the extra mile, and giving to the one who asks (Mt 5:39b-42/Lk 6:29-30; see p 58); the rhetorical questions (Mt 5:46,47/Lk 6:32-34; see pp 59f); the promise of sonship (Mt 5:45/Lk 6:35b; see pp 61f); the command to be like God (Mt 5:48/Lk 6:36; see p 63). Possibly the commands to do good to those who hate you and to bless those who curse you (Lk 6:27b,c; see p 57) should also be included here.

It cannot be established with so much certainty, however, which of the variations within these common individual elements are to be attributed to the evangelists and which go back to an intermediate altered form of the common collection of sayings. First of all the antithetical form of Mt 5:38 and 43 cannot with certainty be attributed to Mt's redaction (see pp 51-5). But on the other hand, the arguments for its originality are also not totally convincing. We have chosen to leave the question open.[4] For the rest of the material we may simply list the possible redactional elements.

One could attribute to *Lk*: ὑπέρ (Lk 6:27b; see Chapter 2, note 123); the elimination of the legal technicalities from Mt 5:39b-42 including δεξίαν (Mt 5:39b), κριθῆναι (Mt 5:40), and all of Mt 5:41 (Lk 6:29,30; see p 58); the replacement of 'tax collectors' and 'gentiles' (Mt 5:46,47)

with 'sinners' (Lk 6:32-34; see p 59); the substitution of the abstract
χρηστός (Lk 6:35; see p 62) for the concrete 'he causes the sun to rise . . .
and gives rain . . .' (Mt 5:45).[5] The examination of Lk's usage of these
terms outside this context reveals that ἁμαρτωλός (Mt - 5 times; Mk - 6
times; Lk - 17 times) is with greater probability due to Lk's own work.

One could attribute to *Mt*: διωκόντων (Mt 5:44b; see p 56); περισσόν
(Mt 5:47; see p 59); τέλειος (Mt 5:48; see p 63); τελῶναι and ἐθνικοί
(Mt 5:46f; see p 59).[6] The examination of Mt's usage of these words outside this context reveals that their presence here could well be his own
work.[7]

In spite of these terminological variations between Mt and Lk the
argumentation in both is basically the same. The main point in each is that
one should love his enemies (Mt 5:44a/Lk 6:27a). This command is
expanded with illustrations (Mt 5:39-42,44b; Lk 6:27b-31,35a), and a
positive and negative argument are given why one should act this way.
Positively, loving one's enemies means becoming a son of God because
God loves his enemies (Mt 5:45/Lk 6:35b,c). Negatively, failing to love
one's enemies means getting no reward because that is the way the tax
collectors/gentiles/sinners act (Mt 5:46,47/Lk 6:32-34). Essentially the
same conclusion is then drawn in both gospels: since acting like your
Father means the reward of sonship and failing to be like him means no
reward at all, therefore be (perfect-merciful) like your Father (Mt 5:48/
Lk 6:36)! It is thus evident that this basic argument was already found in
the gospel tradition and constituted the basic structure of the *Vorlage* in
Mt's Sermon on the Mount and Lk's Sermon on the Plain.

B. Determining the Sitz im Leben of the Vorlage

The basic elements of Mt 5:38-48/Lk 6:27-36 (as described in the preceding
section) go back to a common collection of sayings on enemy love. This
collection is very probably of Palestinian origin as we see from the Jewish
situation preserved in the reference to the blow on the *right* cheek (Mt
5:39),[8] and in the reference to one who conscripts you to go with him a
mile (Mt 5:41),[9] and in the Semitic turns of phrase and poetic forms
(see p 58).

Knowledge of the collection was not, however, restricted to Palestine.
There is good evidence (e.g., p 156) that the formal hellenizing tendencies
evident in Lk's version were not first accomplished by him. A fairly widespread dissemination of the gospel tradition throughout the early church
is one of the conclusions of the following discussion.

To the question of the *Sitz im Leben* of this collection of sayings, i.e.,
for what purpose the sayings were gathered in this way, Dibelius gives the

following answer: they were gathered for hortatory purposes.[10] That is, these words of Jesus were apparently put into a unit for the paraenetic purpose of giving ethical instructions to Christians. If this is correct, the unit is a part of what Jeremias calls 'eine urchristliche Didache,' the theme of which is 'the way Christians lead their lives in distinction from their Jewish contemporaries.'[11]

However, when we compare this traditional collection of sayings on enemy love (which we shall now call the 'gospel tradition') with the paraenetic tradition on enemy love which we discovered behind Rom 12: 14–20; I Thess 5:15; and I Pt 3:9–12, the question arises: If the gospel tradition was formed and preserved simply for ethical instruction of the church, why does it differ so markedly from the paraenetic tradition which was formed and preserved for the same reason?

This marked difference is brought out clearly by C. H. Dodd. He cites the following distinctions between the paraenetic tradition of Rom 12:10– 16 and the gospel tradition of Mt 5:39–42. 'The sayings of the Gospels have an incomparably greater liveliness and pregnancy than the maxims in the catechesis . . . These two sets of precepts are not conceived on the same level. The precepts in Romans are perfectly straightforward, general maxims which you could transfer directly to the field of conduct.' Not so the gospel commands: 'These precepts are simply not suitable as the precepts in Romans are for use as a plain guide to conduct, if you take them literally as they stand. Evidently they were not intended for such use.'[12]

Floyd Filson formulates the difference between the paraenetic and gospel traditions as follows. 'During the early decades of the church, when teaching was a spiritual gift, the teacher used scripture and tradition about Jesus; but he was always concerned primarily to drive home a challenge and make the material apply to the situation at hand. This element of interpretation, application and direct challenge is not included in our Gospels, which are remarkably restrained records.'[13] To these distinctions may be added the fact that the paraenesis is addressed explicitly to baptized believers, but in the gospel tradition the hearers are ostensibly Jesus' own contemporaries. These observations call into question the assumption that the sayings of Jesus lying behind Mt 5:38–48/Lk 6:27–36 were collected and used *as such* for ethical instruction in the church.[14]

The differences between the gospel tradition on enemy love and the paraenetic tradition on enemy love must not, however, be stressed to the exclusion of the intimate relation between the two. If the results of our investigation into the traditional background of the early Christian paraenesis on enemy love (Chapter 2) are correct, it is impossible to maintain that this paraenesis was formed in isolation from the gospel tradition of Jesus' sayings.[15] Rather, these sayings on enemy love were paraphrased, interpreted and applied. They constituted the criterion according to which other paraenetic elements were taken up into the tradition (see p 64). That is, the marked difference between the gospel tradition on enemy love and the paraenetic tradition is not to be explained by the fact that those who shaped the paraenetic tradition were ignorant of or indifferent toward the gospel tradition of Jesus' sayings.[16] The difference must be accounted for in another way.

Thus, as we have seen, *two factors* determine the relation between the gospel tradition on enemy love and the paraenetic tradition on enemy love. One factor is the gulf that separates the two traditions in form and conception. The other factor is that the paraenetic tradition is built around the sayings of Jesus, paraphrasing, expanding, interpreting and applying them. The first factor suggests a distinct separation between the gospel tradition and paraenetic tradition; the second factor suggests an intimate relation between the two. Any explanation of the historical relationship between these two traditions must account for both sides of this picture. The difficulty of finding such an explanation is shown by the fact that C. K. Barrett,[17] writing in 1968, and E. P. Sanders,[18] writing in 1969, have left the question open.

Let us try, however, to find at least a tentative explanation. C. H. Dodd makes a helpful distinction when he maintains that 'the catechetical instruction of the early Church . . . provided *an occasion* for preserving the sayings [of Jesus] rather than the *means* by which they were preserved.'[19] In other words the need for ethical teaching in the church was one (not the only) motivation for the preserving of Jesus' sayings on enemy love; but this does not mean that these sayings were identical with that ethical teaching; nor does it mean that Jesus' sayings were transmitted in a hortatory context. As Dodd continues: the catechetical instruction 'does not appear to be the main channel through which the tradition [of Jesus' sayings] came down, but presupposes an *independent* tradition upon which it could draw and by which it was influenced while it also exerted a reciprocal influence.'[20]

This general understanding of how the gospel tradition on enemy love and the paraenetic tradition are related stresses the *independence* of the gospel tradition and the *use* of it to form the paraenetic tradition. It thus takes into account the two factors mentioned above. This position has been best described and most ardently defended by the Scandinavians Harald Riesenfeld and Birger Gerhardsson, who have stressed the fact that the most probable historical analogy for the transmission process of the gospel tradition is the rabbinical model. 'The Gospel tradition is not to be regarded as a section within the tradition, but as a focus. We may make a comparison, though we do so fully aware of the dangers of using such a terminology, and say that this central corpus is the mishnah to which the rest of the Apostles' preaching, teaching and "legislation" is the talmud.'[21] So long as the uniqueness of Jesus and his community[22] are kept in view to balance the picture, I believe this is a fundamentally true insight into the relation between gospel tradition and paraenetic tradition in the early church.

Thus the *Sitz im Leben* of the collection of Jesus' sayings on enemy love cannot be equated with the *Sitz im Leben* of the paraenetic tradition on enemy love. As a foundation and source for the paraenesis it is one step removed from the actual event of ethical instruction. As such it stands ready to serve the church in other ways. As Paul Hoffmann has suggested, for example, these sayings may have been used during the decades following Jesus' death in the tense situation between Jews and Romans in Palestine in order to call the insurgent Jews to repentance, i.e. to gather in the 'sons of peace'.[23] The important point is that the motivation and means for the collection and transmission of Jesus' sayings should not be identified with any one of the *uses* made of these sayings.[24] Apparently the tradition of Jesus' words and deeds was the soil out of which the separate and distinct paraenetic tradition grew. Whether or not Riesenfeld is entirely right in calling the gospel tradition 'holy word', he does seem to be right in saying that 'in its verbal form and in its *Sitz im Leben* in the community it was *sui generis.* '[25]

II. The Gospel Tradition of Jesus' Command of Enemy Love in the Gospels

A. *The Approach and Methodology*

It is one of the main aims of this study to discover the way in which Jesus' love command was passed on and used in the different streams (paraenetic and gospel) and levels of the tradition in the early church. I have just examined the gospel tradition of this command prior to the writing of our gospels. In an earlier chapter I discussed the use of this command in the paraenetic tradition. We now come to the last level in the transmission (and interpretative) process in the New Testament: the use of the tradition of Jesus' command by Mt and Lk.

Since my concern is ultimately with Jesus' love command in the synoptics I will first pose the question: In taking over the tradition on enemy love and incorporating it into their own larger framework, what attitude did Mt and Lk manifest toward the historicity of that tradition? That is, what interest do they show in the way this teaching was originally given by

Jesus and how is this interest affected by their desire to address their own situation? I must stress that in posing this first question, I am *not* asking whether the evangelists did in fact preserve the historical words of Jesus (we have discussed this in Chapter 2, Section VII), rather I am asking whether the evangelists *intended* to preserve as historical teaching what they perceived to be such. I am interested here in the evangelists' *attitudes* toward the tradition at their disposal – with how much freedom and to what end do they use it?

Then in order to penetrate to the heart of Mt's and Lk's understanding of Jesus' love command, I pose two questions which seem to me to be theologically and practically the most important: Wherein does obedience to the command of enemy love consist? and, How is this obedience to be grounded or motivated? To approach Mt's and Lk's redaction in this way has the advantage of maintaining consistency with the previous chapter, for there the same questions were asked in discussing the use of the love command in the paraenetic tradition. Thus a comparison and contrast of the ways Jesus' love command is used in the two streams of tradition is made easier. (Note: I will not try to exhaust the answers Mt and Lk give to these two questions. I will only trace out some of the particular features characteristic of each evangelist).

But we also encounter a disadvantage in dealing with the redaction of the pericope on enemy love, no matter what specific question we pose. The disadvantage is that the influence of the evangelists on this pericope can be established with high probability only in a very few instances (see pp 135f). How are we to overcome this barrier to finding Mt's and Lk's understanding of the material in this pericope? My attempt at an answer may be summed up in the following three reflections on the redaction-critical method.

(1) It is by no means certain that what distinguishes an author from others is that which he regards as most important. Thus to focus on an author's distinctives may be historically legitimate, heuristically helpful and in the long run theologically fruitful, but it also runs the risk of overlooking or underemphasizing what is most important to an author, only because this is what he has in common with the tradition he takes over. None of us would like to have our theology described only in terms of those elements which distinguish us from the traditions out of which we come. Therefore, I think it proper and fruitful to ask in this section not *merely* about the evangelist's distinctives, but also about his understanding of Jesus' command of enemy love apart from any consideration of distinctiveness.

(2) To argue that we cannot know what Mt or Lk intended to say except

where obvious redactional features are evident is in my judgment hermeneutically untenable:[26] it imputes to the evangelist an immense amount of nonchalance in his writing. To be sure one must take into consideration that Lk more so than Mt seems to be a mere *'Tradent'* with little interest in interpreting some of what he takes over. One is thus admonished to caution in over-interpreting Lk's own theology. Nevertheless, it is more courteous and reasonable, I think, to assume that the meaning of a gospel pericope in its present context is what the evangelist intended to communicate, if there are no redactional clues to the contrary.

(3) This does not mean that we abandon the task of synoptic comparison and literary analysis. We pursue this wherever possible in order to discover the evangelist's explicit and distinctive literary habits, topical interests, and theological ideas. These then function in two ways: (a) they serve as a corrective in the over-all picture of the evangelist's theology which we have gained from a judicious consideration of each pericope in its present context (not just from the redactional elements); (b) they offer pointers as to how we should approach a pericope in which significant redactional elements are imperceptible.

Thus our treatment of Mt's and Lk's understanding of the tradition on enemy love will be governed (a) by the initial assumption that the meaning of each pericope in its present context is the evangelist's meaning, and (b) by an effort to subject this assumption to scrutiny through an investigation of the evangelist's obvious redactional work where this is possible. In view of the minimal sure redactional elements in Mt 5:38–48 and Lk 6:27–36 I will try to find formal or essential points of contact between these texts and others where redaction is more obvious. If these points of contact represent a genuine link in the redactor's intention, then the more obviously redactional texts may shed light on the evangelist's understanding of the pericope on enemy love.

B. Mt's Use of the Gospel Tradition of Jesus' Command of Enemy Love

1. What is Mt's Attitude to the Earthly Teaching of Jesus?[27]
(a) Mt reveals by his composition that he is concerned to set forth the essential features of Jesus' earthly ministry. The two summary reports of Jesus' Galilean ministry (4:23; 9:35) which open and close Mt 5–9 show that Mt intends these chapters to depict 'an example of how Jesus came to "Israel", his "word" to the people (Chap 5–7 cf 5:1; 7:28f) and his "deed" (Chap 8–9).'[28] To be sure these chapters bear the mark of the evangelist and his contemporary concerns,[29] nevertheless his concern with the way it was in Jesus' lifetime is just as unmistakable.[30]

(b) The way in which the pericope on enemy love was taken over confirms this. Mt takes over the tradition on enemy love (5:38–48) without any effort to tone down the absoluteness of the individual commands. No qualifying phrases are added, the sharpness of the commands is nowhere blunted, their difficulty nowhere weakened. There is no discourse which attempts to explain to the reader how he is to use these radical demands as a guide for everyday behavior. Nowhere, for example, does Mt offer some practical advice on what to do about the nudity which results when you give up both your garments.[31] This unembellished non-casuistical rendering of the traditional pericope on enemy love, which in its absoluteness is so unsuitable for direct implementation in practice, is a clear indication that Mt's intention here is not first hortatory but historical. He intends to let Jesus speak as he had spoken decades earlier. Mt's desire to admonish his church is subordinate to his desire that the original demand of Jesus come to expression in his gospel.[32]

We have no reason to think, however, that Mt's historical concern was motivated by a detached interest in antiquity; on the contrary, the great commission with which Mt concludes his gospel shows that for him contemporary discipleship (or being a Christian[33]) consists in no less than keeping the commands of the *historical* Jesus ($\grave{\epsilon}\nu\epsilon\tau\epsilon\iota\lambda\acute{\alpha}\mu\eta\nu$, aorist, Mt 28:20) who *now* as resurrected Lord has all authority in heaven and on earth. Thus it is precisely as the *formerly* spoken words of Jesus that the tradition on enemy love has hortatory significance *now* for those who have been baptized. It is necessary to emphasize the backward-looking interest of Mt at this point in order to keep in proper perspective the heavy emphasis his ecclesiastical application of Jesus' sayings has received in recent study.[34]

2. Wherein Consists Obedience to Jesus' Command of Enemy Love?

Here we will focus our attention on two individual commands which are chosen because they aptly illustrate two contrasting dimensions of obedience to the command of enemy love which Mt emphasizes. The first is the command to pray for 'those who persecute you' (5:44).[35] The second is the implied command to greet even those who are not your brothers (5:47). Both commands as they now stand are unique to Mt; but they are not entirely his creation (see p 57 and Chapter 2, note 145). My interpretation of Mt's understanding of these two commands is not based primarily on the minor alterations in them which may be due to him, but rather, it is based on an attempt to see how these two commands fit into larger motifs in the Sermon on the Mount and in the gospel as a whole which are definitely Mt's concern.

'Pray for those who persecute you!' is parallel with 'Love your enemies!' (5:44) and gives a concrete illustration of what that involves in the church's experience. Nevertheless it is not a deed done to the enemy like giving him clothing or food or drink or visiting him when he is sick or in prison (cf 25:35f). Prayer is an act that turns not to the enemy but to God. As Mt stresses in the following context (Mt 6:5f) it is an act performed in private where nobody else can see. As such it is a way of love that cannot be motivated by a desire for the praise of men (6:5). If it exists, it exists in obedience to Jesus and in concern for the enemy. This illustration of Jesus' command to love stands in direct contradiction to those interpretations which claim that love is *only* possible in the concrete encounter between men.[36]

Not only has Mt brought into this context words on *how* one is to pray but also on *what* one is to pray. That the Lord's Prayer (6:9-13) should be read in close connection with the preceding commands of Mt 5 is shown by the essential relation between the commands and the petitions.[37] For example:

5:16	Live so that men give glory to your Father in heaven.	6:9	Pray that your Father's name be hallowed (by men).
5:23f	Be reconciled to your brother before you give an offering to God.	6:12	Pray for forgiveness as you have forgiven (your brother).
5:39	Do not resist evil.	6:13	Pray for deliverance from evil.

Thus if we ask: What in Mt's view should one pray for his persecutors, the Lord's Prayer is not to be excluded as a distant unrelated example of prayer. It forms the very heart of the Sermon on the Mount and is a proper source for Mt's understanding of the sermon's many imperatives.

Since the disciple is to pray, 'Let thy will be done on earth as in heaven,' and is also to pray for his enemy, we may assume that at least part of his prayer will be that his enemy do God's will. Moreover the thought that the prayer for one's enemy which Jesus commands should come short of an appeal that the enemy come to hallow God's name, would contradict the priorities of the Lord's Prayer and reduce the prayer for the enemy to humanistic well-wishing. It would cease to be an expression of love. Here I would disagree with the view that there is nothing in this pericope (Mt 5:43-48) about making the enemy into a friend.[38] To be sure, the emphasis falls on loving your enemy while he is an enemy, but it does not stop at that. The disciple's prayer that his enemy hallow God's name and do his will is in effect a prayer that he cease to be an enemy, since, as Mt especially stresses, the animosity of the enemy for whom we are praying is grounded

in his opposition to God's will.[39] That a man should pray for his enemy
and not request that the enmity between them be removed would be a
questionable manifestation of love, to say the least.

The implied command to greet even those who are not your brothers
(v 47) reveals another contrasting dimension of love. In 5:44 love calls
one to the religious act of prayer; here love calls one to an everyday
gesture of kindness.[40] There the enemy is defined as an active persecutor;
here he is only a passive outsider.[41] From this we see that the command to
love one's enemy refers to more than the dire circumstances of persecution.
The 'enemy' does not cease to exist when he ceases to persecute. He may
just simply be there on the street minding his own business. At this
moment, when the most natural thing to do would be to pass by on the
other side, Jesus summons the disciple to active kindness – to give a
greeting to his enemy.

With these two commands – to pray for those who persecute you and
to greet those who are not your brothers – we see illustrated two dimensions of obedience which Mt stresses. The command to greet accords with
Mt's concern that the commands of Jesus actually be obeyed in practice
for others to see. In Mt's view the command of Jesus cannot be reduced to
a call for a new disposition. He entitles, as it were, the imperatives in the
Sermon on the Mount with the command: 'Let your light so shine before
men that they might see your good works and glorify your Father in
heaven' (5:16). And in the final two paragraphs of the sermon the stress
on *doing* is the tone Mt wants to leave ringing in his readers' ears. To call
Jesus, Lord, and to prophesy, exorcize and do miracles in his name will
amount to nothing 'on that day' if one '*works* lawlessness' (7:23; cf 24:12);
i.e., if one does not '*do* the will of my father in heaven' (7:21). And,
finally, the one who hears 'these[42] my words' and does not *do* them is a
foolish man bound for destruction (7:26f). The command to love your
enemies is not merely a command to have a loving disposition: Mt emphasizes that it involves specific visible acts like greeting a neighbor.

The command to pray (5:44), however, does not aim at a visible act,
but it corresponds to another dimension of obedience which Mt also
stresses. We noted above that the prayer for one's enemies which Jesus
commands cannot be motivated by a desire for the praise of men (6:5f).
To pray for your enemy means, therefore, to be concerned not about
yourself but about your enemy. Since prayer for the enemy is not a
visible act before men, it is an act which must spring from a heart which
wills the enemy's well-being. It thus illustrates that dimension of obedience
which for Mt consists in a *change of heart*.

If Mt stresses that obedience to the love command consists in *doing*, he is not slack in emphasizing that obedience consists more basically in having a pure heart (5:8). Hearing without doing is foolish (7:26), but attempts at doing without being pure in heart are hopeless and result in becoming a ὑποκριτής.[43] To such ones Jesus commands: 'First cleanse the inside of the cup *in order that*[44] the outside of it might become clean' (23:26). With this sentence Mt makes explicit the priority of inner purity and its causal relation to outward goodness.[45] For he has learned from his tradition that 'out of the *heart* come evil thoughts, murders, adulteries, etc.' (15:19 = Mk 7:21f); that 'from the abundance of the *heart* the mouth speaks' (12:35 = Lk 6:45); and that 'a good *tree* cannot bear evil fruit neither can a bad tree bear good fruit' (Mt 7:18).[46] Thus, obeying the command of enemy love means more than mere doing, because as Mt shows (6:2ff) one can easily feign deeds of mercy in order to gain men's praise. It means also getting a pure heart because only from such a treasure can a man really bring forth love for his enemy.[47]

But this dimension of inward obedience is not exhausted with these observations. A heart is not reprehensible merely because it brings forth evil deeds. As the first two antitheses (Mt 5:21f; 27f) show the heart's evil is real ('. . . he has already commited adultery with her in his heart') and it is condemned ('Everyone who is angry . . . will be liable to judgment') even before it gives rise to any evil deed.

Thus the obedience Mt is calling for – and here he is in line with the message of Jesus which we saw in an earlier chapter – is an obedience which consists in a radical transformation of the deepest spring of man's being, even that depth over which he has no control.[48] This is ultimately the reason why Mt has preserved the tradition on enemy love even with its radical, impracticable commands: they are not intended to provide instructions for the gradual moral reformation of this world, not even with the aid of a new heart; rather, in accord with Jesus' intention, they are the continuing confrontation of another, perfect world – the Kingdom of heaven – with this world in order to expose the depth of this world's fallenness and to summon men to the perfection of *heart* and *action* which exists only in the Kingdom of heaven.

3. How is Jesus' Command of Enemy Love Motivated?

This question is not answered in Mt 5:38–48. If Mt reflected on this problem we will have to find points of contact between Mt 5:38–48 and the texts in which this reflection came to expression. In this way there emerges in Mt (a) a christological and (b) a theological ground for obedience to the command of enemy love.

(a) One of the most probable redactional elements of Mt 5:38–48 is the τέλειος of Mt 5:48 (against Lk's οἰκτίρμονες).[49] The only other place the word occurs in the synoptics is Mt 19:21 where it is very likely intentionally inserted by Mt. Are we justified in seeing here a point of contact between Mt 5:48 and Mt 19:21 which reflects a genuine link in the subject matter which accords with Mt's intention?[50]

In order to answer this question we must first determine the function of the command to be perfect in the context of Mt 5. Mt 5:48 has its main function in relation to the immediately preceding verses on enemy love. The command[51] to be like your heavenly Father follows naturally from the argument in 5:45 according to which sonship consists in being like your Father who makes the sun to rise on the evil and the good. Further, the emphatic (Matthean) ὑμεῖς of 5:48 is in direct contrast to the gentiles and tax collectors of 5:46f. Consequently it seems correct to refer the redactional οὖν[52] of 5:48 to the argumentation of 5:45–47: since being like your Father constitutes your sonship and merely being like the tax collectors and gentiles brings no reward, *therefore* be like your Father, be perfect. Since Mt sees 5:48 as the specific alternative of acting like tax collectors who love only those who love them, therefore he must conceive 'perfection' as consisting primarily in love which goes beyond this limit and includes the enemy (5:44).

One cannot, however, escape the impression that Mt 5:48 is the conclusion not merely of 5:43–47 but also of the whole complex of antitheses in Mt 5:21–48.[53] In accord with this impression is the fact that Mt's τέλειος is broader and thus more suitable to sum up all the antitheses than Lk's οἰκτίρμονες (6:36). Further, τέλειος expresses the positive answer to the question τί περισσὸν ποιεῖτε in 5:47, a question which Mt probably formulated under the influence of his περισσεύσῃ in 5:20. This would mean that the antitheses are introduced by a command for a righteousness which *exceeds* the scribes and Pharisees and are concluded by a command for a perfection which *exceeds* the tax collectors and gentiles.[54] Thus Mt not only stressed the connection between 5:48 and the immediately preceding pericope on enemy love but he also placed this pericope at the end of the antitheses so that 5:48 concludes the whole section and parallels its introduction (5:20). This leads us to the conclusion that for Mt the command to be τέλειος is a summation of all the radical commands of Jesus which, when obeyed, set a man off from the Pharisees on the one side and from the gentiles on the other, and finds its clearest expression in the love of one's enemies.[55]

Does τέλειος in Mt 19:21 have a similar meaning and function so that we can assume a link in Mt's mind between the teaching of Mt 5:43–48 and Mt 19:16-22? Let us take an overview of Mt's probable alterations of Mk.[56] Instead of addressing Jesus as *'good* teacher' and asking what he must do in order to inherit eternal life, the 'youth' (so designated only in Mt, vv 20,22) addresses Jesus simply as 'teacher' and asks what *good* he must do to have eternal life (19:16). This enables Jesus to respond not with Mk's offensive 'Why do you call me good?' (10:18) but with the question 'Why do you ask me concerning the good?' (Mt 19:17). Having taken the focus off Jesus' renunciation of goodness, Mt accordingly rephrases Mk's 'No one is good but one, God' (10:18) into 'One is good' (Mt 19:17). Then Mt converts Mk's simple 'You know the commandments' (10:19) into an interchange[57] between Jesus and the youth (19:17f) in which it is made explicit that precisely those[58] Old Testament commandments relating to human relationships (second table of decalogue) must be kept if one is to enter into eternal life. Reminiscent of 7:12 and 22:37, Mt inserts Lev 19:18 as the positive summary of these Old Testament commandments (19:19). After the youth claims to have kept all these, according to Mk Jesus informs him that he lacks one thing (10:21); according to Mt the youth himself asks, 'What do I still lack?' (19:20). With this change, Mt paves the way for Jesus to respond, 'If you desire to be perfect . . .' (19:21). This response is a formal parallel of the earlier one, 'If you desire to enter into life . . .' (19:17).

What function does Mt's reference to perfection have in this complex? If Mt agreed with the youth's claim that he had 'kept all these' (19:20), then $\tau\acute{\epsilon}\lambda\epsilon\iota o\varsigma$ would have to be construed as a higher level of morality or obedience than that required by the Old Testament commandments listed in 19:18f: now that you have achieved that Old Testament level there is one more step to take if you want to achieve perfection! Two considerations, however, exclude this interpretation of $\tau\acute{\epsilon}\lambda\epsilon\iota o\varsigma$. *First,* the youth's question, 'What do I still lack?' (19:20), refers to the attainment of eternal life, not to a higher perfection. If Jesus' answer is to correspond to the question, it must give only that which is required to enter eternal life.[59] Thus 'perfection' is not something *more* than what is needed to enter life. *Second*, it is apparent from 19:22-24 that what the youth refused to do did not merely keep him from perfection, but also blocked the way to eternal life. From these two considerations we may conclude that Mt did not think that the youth had in fact kept all the commandments listed in 19:18f, for Mt explicitly promises life to the one who keeps the commandments: 'If you desire to enter into life keep the commandments' (19:17). In support of this conclusion we may ask finally with St Jerome: 'If the commandment: "You will love your neighbor as yourself" had been carried into act, why then after hearing the words: "Go and sell your possessions and give the proceeds to the poor," did he depart sad because he had many possessions?'[60]

Thus τέλειος is not a higher level of obedience than that demanded in 19:18f. Rather it is a restatement in radical form of what Mt really intended when he added the love command to the list of Old Testament commandments in 19:19.[61] The love command of Lev 19:18 is not cited here in the same form as it was in Mt 5:43 where it was an antithesis to the command of enemy love. There it was casuistically limited ('and hate your enemies') and had to be abolished; here it appears in its unlimited form (as in 22:39; cf 7:12) and is thus the way to eternal life (19:17).[62] That the young man thought he had fulfilled this absolute command, even though he loved his possessions so much, shows that he completely misunderstood God's ultimate intention of the Old Testament commandments. In order to expose the root problem behind this misunderstanding, Mt lets Jesus confront the youth with the staggering demand for perfection – perfection which consists first in selling one's possessions and giving them to the poor, i.e. in obedience to the love command.

Our answer to the question raised above is, therefore, yes: τέλειος in Mt 19:21 has a meaning and function in its context similar to that of the τέλειος in Mt 5:48, so that we are justified in seeing here a genuine link between the subject matter of these two contexts which accords with Mt's intention. We may therefore hope that the context of Mt 19:21 will shed some light on our question: How is Jesus' command of enemy love (which is the clearest expression of τελειότης) motivated?

Except for the replacement of ὅσα ἔχεις (Mk 10:21) with σοῦ τὰ ὑπάρχοντα, Mt's condition for the attainment of perfection is the same as Mk's statement of the one thing the man lacks: 'Go, sell your possessions and give to the poor and you will have treasure in heaven, and come follow me' (19:21). The expression of perfection which is willing to renounce one's own rights and possessions for the sake of others we already saw in Mt 5:39–42: 'Give to him who asks from you and do not refuse him who would borrow from you.' That this behavior secures a treasure in heaven was also implied in Mt 5:46: 'If you love those who love you what reward do you have?' What we do not find in Mt 5:38–48 is a reference to following Jesus which in Mt 19:21 is an element of, or a means to, perfection: 'If you desire to be perfect . . . come follow me.' Bornkamm concludes rightly from this text: 'Fulfillment of the commands and perfection is no longer possible to realize except in following Jesus.'[63]

With this observation, the realization of the command of enemy love – the clearest expression of τελειότης – is inextricably united to discipleship. It would take us beyond the scope of this study to develop Mt's

conception of the burden and joy of discipleship.[64] It must suffice only
to point out briefly these two dimensions of discipleship in Mt's redaction.
The burden of discipleship is the burden of suffering which obedience to
Jesus brings.[65] Mt's interpretation of the saying '. . . every [disciple] is
like his teacher' (Lk 6:40) reads: 'If they called the master of the house
Beelzebul, how much more the members of his household!' (Mt 10:25).[66]
But the disciples are not left to bear the burden of discipleship alone. This
is brought out beautifully by Mt when he inserts the sayings on discipleship from Q (Lk 9:57-60) into the Markan order of miracle stories immediately before the account of the storm stilling (Mt 8:18-22, 23-27). As
Bornkamm has shown, the threatening storm, the cry of the disciples for
help, and the gracious and powerful response of Jesus in spite of their small
faith 'becomes . . . a typical situation of discipleship in general.'[67] Those
who follow Jesus cannot expect a life better than the master's; and the
master has no place to lay his head (Mt 8:19f). But if they are willing to
follow him into the boat, they see that he *does* have a place to lay his
head: 'the boat was being swamped with waves but he was asleep' (Mt
8:24). And if the disciples have faith in his saving presence they too can
rest in the storm.[68] The joy of discipleship is thus the assurance that Jesus
has all authority in heaven and on earth and that he is with the disciples
to the end of the age (Mt 28:18-20). In this assurance alone can the
burden of discipleship - the burden of the command of enemy love - be
borne.

(b) Besides developing the above christological[69] ground for the
realization of enemy love, Mt offers a theological ground.

The commands of Jesus in the Sermon on the Mount confront antag-
onists on two fronts.[70] On the one side they are directed against the
legalism (5:20ff) and hypocritical piety (6:1-6, 16-18) of the Pharisees.
On the other side they are opposed to the faithlessness (6:7f, 25-34) and
immorality (5:47) of the gentiles. We are concerned now with this second
front.

The reference to gentiles (ἔθνη) in Mt 6:32 ('For all these things the
gentiles seek') is given already in Q. The references, however, in 6:7 and
5:47 are unique to Mt. Moreover the word used in these two texts is not
ἔθνος as in 6:32 but ἐθνικός. The only other place this word is used in
the synoptics is another text unique to Mt (18:17), where it forms a
pair with tax collectors as it does here in 5:46f. This strongly suggests
that the reference to gentiles in 5:47 and 6:7 is due to Mt's own intention.
That these two references to the gentiles are to be grouped together with
the reference in 6:32 is seen from the close relation of 6:8 and 6:32. In

both texts the reason given (redactional γάρ in 6:32b) why one should distinguish himself from the gentiles is identical: οἶδεν γὰρ ὁ πατὴρ ὑμῶν . . . It appears fairly certain, therefore, that Mt consciously developed a second front (besides the Pharisees) in the Sermon on the Mount, namely against the gentiles. Hence we have found in accord with our method described earlier another point of contact between the command of enemy love and a broader Matthean motif. What does this motif disclose for our question concerning the motivation of the command of enemy love?

In each of the three texts concerning gentiles in the Sermon on the Mount the gentiles are to be *surpassed* by the disciples. In 5:47 their limited love must be surpassed by the disciples' love for their enemies. In 6:7 the gentiles' babbling and repetitive prayers must be surpassed by the disciples' prayer according to Jesus' teaching. In 6:32 in contrast to the gentiles' search for food, drink and clothing, the disciples must not be anxious about these things. The reasons given for the command in 6:7f and 6:31f are essentially the same: Do not be like them in their prayers 'for your Father knows what you have need of before you ask him' (6:8); do not be anxious like the gentiles, 'for your heavenly Father knows that you need all these things' (6:32).

Because the disciples are anxious about what they will eat and what they will wear, they are called ὀλιγόπιστοι (which, although it is here found in Q, cannot be considered unimportant for Mt in view of his wide use of it[71]). That is, they class themselves with the gentiles, for they act as if their Father were unable or unwilling to supply their needs. Similarly in 6:8 the gentiles think that by their many words they can coerce God to respond, thus showing that they lack faith in his gracious generosity. The disciples must not pray like this. In both of these instances the ground for the disciple's different behavior is the fact that he has a Father in heaven who knows all his needs and who, according to 7:11, is more than willing to give him what he asks.[72]

Given the inner unity between Mt 5:47 and the other two references to gentiles discussed above, we may conclude in accord with Mt's intention that God's fatherly care of the disciples is the ground for the command of enemy love which sets a man off from the gentiles. The command to love your enemy entails not defending yourself against physical attack (5:39) and giving away your clothing (5:40) and your money (5:42). But the only way a man can obey this command is not to be anxious about 'all these things which the gentiles seek' (6:32). The disciple can freely renounce these things for the sake of another person, precisely because he is not an ὀλιγόπιστος (6:30). He can dare to love like God (5:45) only because God is his loving heavenly Father in whom he trusts.[73]

Three brief observations reveal why it is consistent for Mt to ground the realization of enemy love both in discipleship to Jesus (christological) and in faith in the heavenly Father (theological). *First*, Mt especially stresses that it is precisely Jesus' disciples who do the will of his Father. When Jesus' mother and brothers desire to speak to him (Mt 12:46–50/Mk 3:31–35) Jesus points 'to his disciples' (against Mk's general 'those who sat about him,' 3:34) and calls *them* his mother and brothers (12:49). '*For* (redactional γάρ) whoever does the will of my father in heaven, this one is my brother and sister and mother' (12:50). To be a disciple of Jesus is the same as being aligned with the will of God.[74] *Second*, the context of Mt 11:27,28 shows that for Mt the call of Jesus: 'Come to *me* all who labor and are heavy laden . . .' is a call grounded in the truth that 'no one knows the *Father* except the Son and anyone to whom the Son wills to reveal him.' Thus for Mt true knowledge of God, and consequently faith in him as Father, happens only in fellowship with the Son, i.e. in discipleship. *Finally,* the unity of the christological and theological grounds for the Christian's loving behavior is evident in the fact that for Mt *Jesus* is Emmanuel 'which is interpreted: *God* with us' (1:23).

Excursus: The Antitheses and the Command of Enemy Love

Due to the uncertainty of the redactional origin of the fifth and sixth antitheses we will not devote a detailed exegesis to Mt 5:38f and 5:43f. Nevertheless we would be amiss to overlook completely the significance that the antitheses as a whole have for Mt and the relationship established by the antitheses between the command of enemy love and the law. Our theme in this section is *not* Mt's view of the relation between the love command and the law; for this reason my comments on this topic are confined to an excursus and will be in brief, summary form. For a more detailed treatment I would refer the reader to G. Barth's *Das Gesetzesverständnis des Evangelisten Matthäus* (especially pp 70–80, 'Die Bedeutung des Liebesgebotes') and W. Trilling's *Das wahre Israel* (especially pp 165–219, 'Die Tora des wahren Israel').

Whether or not the last two antitheses of Mt 5 are redactional, they belong to a pattern which for Mt is distinctive and important. Mt heads the section of antitheses with the demand for a righteousness that exceeds the righteousness of the scribes and Pharisees. Each successive 'But I say unto you . . .' thus exemplifies wherein this better righteousness consists. This better righteousness is placed antithetically over against the casuistical formulation of the law.[75]

We are thus encouraged by the context to understand the antitheses in the light of what was said of the law in 5:17–19,[76] namely that Jesus

has come to fulfil and not to abolish and that the whole law is still valid ·
In the light of 5:17 it cannot be said that Mt intends in the antitheses
to abolish the law. In the light of the antitheses, on the other hand, it
can only be said that Mt understands 5:18,19 (the continuing minute
validity of the law) in a metaphorical sense. Nevertheless the better
righteousness exemplified in the antitheses is not better in the sense of
being a stricter legalism which covers loopholes in the law. Jesus does
not fulfil the law by giving a more rigorous one. What Jesus demands in
the antitheses constitutes for Mt a better righteousness and a fulfilment
of the law, in that it is the accomplishment of that which the law
ultimately wanted but, in its casuistical form,[77] it could never
bring about. Necessarily, therefore, Jesus' demand was antithetical to
this expression of the law. To fulfil the law as the perfect will of God,
the law as a casuistical control of evil in society had to be abolished.

 ͜ · .sequently the command to love your enemies, which forms the
climax of the antitheses, is drawn into the discussion of the law which
is so dominant in Mt's gospel.[78] That this is redactionally no accident
can be shown by a brief glance at the way Mt brings the command
for love (not specifically enemy love) into connection with the law. In
19:19 Mt adds the command 'You shall love your neighbor as yourself'
(Lev 19:18) which climaxes the second table of the decalogue replacing
the tenth commandment against coveting. In 22:39, only Mt says of
the second command ('You shall love your neighbor as yourself') that
it is 'like' the first ('You shall love the Lord . . .' Dt 6:5); and only he
says of these two commandments that 'in these . . . hang the whole law
and the prophets' (22:40). In line with this, Mt renders the Golden Rule
with the interpretation: 'for this is the law and the prophets' (7:12). In
two places Mt inserts another 'love command' taken from the Old Testament to silence the criticism of the Pharisees. When they find fault with
his eating with tax collectors and sinners (9:10-13) and when they take
offence at his disciples for plucking grain to eat on a Sabbath (12:1-8),
Jesus responds with Hos 6:6: 'I desire mercy and not sacrifice.' If they
understood this, the Pharisees 'would not have condemned the guiltless'
(12:7), i.e. they would have interpreted the law differently. In the same
sense, only Mt shows Jesus criticizing the scribes and Pharisees for
neglecting 'the weightier matters of the law, justice and *mercy* and faith'
(23:23).[79] Finally, one of Mt's unique descriptions of the end-time is
that 'on account of the increase of ἀνομία the ἀγάπη of many will grow
cold' (24:12). On the basis of these texts the conclusion has been
drawn – correctly, I think – that for Mt the general love command is the
'Canon of the exposition of the whole Torah.'[80]

If a proper understanding of the love command yields a correct interpretation of the law, then it follows also that to obey the love command
would be to fulfil the law. Hence it is perfectly in accord with Mt's
intention when he places the command of enemy love – the most
radical expression of the love command in his gospel – at the climax of
the antitheses which in the light of 5:17 aim to fulfil the law.

C. Luke's Use of the Gospel Tradition of Jesus' Command of Enemy Love

1. What is Lk's Attitude to the Earthly Teaching of Jesus?[81]

Lk's attitude to the earthly teaching of Jesus is revealed (a) by the context of the Sermon on the Plain in which the tradition on enemy love is found, and (b) by the way this tradition itself was taken over.

(a) Hans Conzelmann drew attention to the fact that Lk, in order to set the stage for his Sermon on the Plain, reversed the Markan order of the preceding healing scene (Mk 3:7-12/Lk 6:17-19) and the appointment of the twelve (Mk 3:13-19/Lk 6:12-15).[82] Jesus is thus enabled to come down from the mountain of prayer (6:12) with the chosen twelve into the midst of 'great crowd of disciples and a great multitude of the people' (6:17) where he then gives his sermon. Hans-Werner Bartsch draws the following conclusion from Lk's redaction here: 'The mountain is the place of revelation to the disciples, the church, while the open area is the place of proclamation to the crowds.'[83] Bartsch therefore views Lk's sermon not as teaching for the disciples, i.e. as paraenesis or catechism, but rather as an eschatological[84] proclamation characteristic of early Christian missionary preaching. For the three elements of the missionary sermon in Acts – kerygma, scripture proof, call to repentance – he finds parallels in the beatitudes and woes (6:20-26), the unfolding of the love command (6:27-45), and the parable of the two builders (6:46-49). For Bartsch this confirms that the Sermon on the Plain 'intends not only to render a sermon of Jesus but also with this rendering to prove the continuity between the early Christian preaching and the preaching of Jesus.'[85]

Baumbach is not persuaded by this argument 'since on the one hand Luke stresses more strongly than Mt 5:1f that Jesus is talking to the disciples [6:20], and on the other hand verses 27-46 have such a clear ethical aim that they have little to do with an "eschatological sermon." Therefore the Sermon on the Plain should be viewed as addressed to the same circle of hearers as the Sermon on the Mount (Mt 5-7).'[86] However, on the basis of Lk's statement that those from as far away as the coastland of Tyre and Sidon came *to hear* Jesus (6:18 different from Mk), Baumbach admits 'that for Lk there is surely also a missionary intention to be taken account of.'[87] He settles for a designation somewhere in between paraenesis for the apostles and missionary preaching: 'Lk 6:20-49 would best be characterized as a Hellenistic Christian catechism, which is aimed more strongly at a wide circle of beginners in the faith than at a small circle of apostles.'[88]

Schürmann, however, will not allow that 'Anfänger im Glauben' are here being addressed. For him John's 'Taufansprache' already in 3:7–18 has reminded the readers of the instruction they received before baptism, and Jesus' baptism (3:21f) has called to mind each Christian's own baptism, and the stories from 4:1 – 6:11 have offered instruction and admonition in various areas of the Christian's life.[89] 'If any baptized person has with interest read Lk 3:1–6:1 in this way, he will understand that 6:12–49, the "Sermon of Jesus on the mountain," intends to offer to the baptized basic instruction in Christian living.'[90] But he specifies – and here he differs from Baumbach – that Lk 6:20–49 'does not intend to give a catechism for neophytes. The church as a whole is addressed, not neophytes but veterans who in later days must be reminded afresh of the event of baptism and the basic demands that spring from it.'[91] The Sermon on the Plain 'is the fundamental post-baptismal instruction to the baptized.'[92]

This would seem to be the precise opposite of Bartsch's view; but Schürmann too takes into account Lk's redactional introduction to the sermon in 6:17ff: 'Lk lets the Sermon on the Mount be directed to concentric circles of hearers: first on the crowd of his disciples (v17a, cf v 20), and then on "the great crowd of the people" (v 17b, cf 7:1) who are thought of as listening in and willing to hear (v 18, cf 7:1). With this description we can see the post-Easter circumstances shining through: in the crowd of disciples we see the church and in the crowd of people we see willing masses ripe for Christian mission.'[93] It seems to be Lk's intention therefore that 'The word of Jesus should resound through the church as living kerygma.'[94] It is not clear to me how Schürmann conceives the relation between post-baptismal instruction and kerygma addressed to non-Christians. But be that as it may, the fact that he and Baumbach cannot reduce Lk's aim to *either* church instruction *or* missionary proclamation points to the uniqueness of the gospel tradition and the characteristic use of it by the evangelist.

Schürmann is surely correct in seeing in 'the great crowd of disciples' (6:17) a picture of the whole church.[95] This must be set against Degenhardt's idea that Lk 'separates the μαθηταί from the λαός and thus understands the μαθηταί as a special group among the followers of Jesus.'[96] Degenhardt says the redactional aim in this is the 'transference of the instruction to the disciples onto the church officers of Luke's time.'[97] But this conception does not correspond to the setting of 6:12–20 in which there is indeed a 'special group' but it is not the disciples themselves but the twelve, whom Jesus chose from the disciples and named apostles (6:13).

Moreover the other 'followers of Jesus,' 'the great multitude of people' (6:17) from whom the disciples are distinguished, are not to be identified with the mass of ordinary Christians. To the *disciples* (against Mk's οἱ περὶ αὐτὸν σὺν τοῖς δώδεκα, 4:10) has been given the knowledge of the 'mysteries of the Kingdom of God,' but to *everyone else* (τοῖς δὲ λοιποῖς Lk 8:10) all is in parables 'in order that seeing they might not see' (Lk 8:9,10; cf 10:21-24). Therefore 'the great multitude of people' are not to be equated with Christians, and the 'disciples,' upon whom Jesus lifts his eyes and speaks his sermon (6:20), do not represent a special group within the church. They are simply a foreshadowing of Christians in general.[98]

But it is true also that Lk looks beyond the disciples (Christians), for he makes explicit that Jesus gave his sermon in the presence of a great multitude of the people who had come 'to *hear* him' (6:18) and that he completed '*all* of his sayings in the hearing of the people' (7:1). Moreover the pronouncement of woes in 6:24-26 fits more easily into a sermon directed to the people than it does into teaching for the disciples.[99] Thus Lk has given the Sermon on the Plain a setting similar to that in 20:45 where he introduces the warning against the scribes (from Mk 12:38-40) with his own words: 'And in the hearing of all the *people* he said to his *disciples* . . .' Or again in 12:1, Lk sets the stage for the warning against the leaven of the Pharisees (from Mk 8:15) with the words: 'After the thousands of the *multitude* had gathered . . . he began to say to his *disciples* . . .' It thus seems that Lk does not intend to divide the teachings of Jesus into that which is directed only at the disciples and that which is directed only at the crowds. Helmut Flender draws from this evidence the conclusion that for Lk: 'To be a disciple is not a once for all fixed right; rather it must be preserved ever anew in obedience. The border between disciples and people is not absolute, it is constituted ever anew in the hearing (or not hearing) of the word of Jesus. . . . In the spoken word of Jesus the division of the two groups occurs.'[100]

Lk reveals here that his composition is in line with the original proclamation of Jesus. Jesus' public call to repentance consisted in a demand for the kind of behavior that accompanies the repentant heart. The change of behavior he called for publicly was realized through discipleship. Therefore, there needed to be no esoteric ethical teaching. Ethical instruction for the disciple was a description of the fruits which befit repentance and was at the same time, therefore, a call to repentance. To this extent in Jesus' ministry, ethical instruction for the disciples and public proclamation overlapped. For this reason Lk is able to address the Christians of his day[101] while faithfully rendering the essential content and context of Jesus' own proclamation. That Lk's first concern was to give the teaching of Jesus in its typical original orientation is seen by the fact that no description of the function of the Sermon on the Plain within the church can account for all the features of its context in the gospel. This historical interest of Lk is confirmed when we focus on the way he took over the tradition on enemy love.

(b) Van Unnik gives a representative opinion when he says that Lk 'in seinem Wortlaut deutlich auf griechische Auffassung Rücksicht genommen hat, also hellenisiert.'[102] From our earlier reflections upon the possible redactional elements in Lk (see pp 135f) I would qualify this statement and say that it seems clear that there has been hellenization but it is not clear that Lk has done it. For example, van Unnik is especially concerned to show that Lk, in changing the rhetorical question τίνα μισθὸν ἔχετε (Mt 5:46) into ποία ὑμῖν χάρις ἐστίν (Lk 6:32-34), has taken a word from Greek ethics (χάρις) and with it severely criticized that ethic. 'In this whole context of reciprocity in human relationships the χάρις had a firm place among the Greeks. Therefore this word must have been added by Lk, because μισθός, which Mt had used (5:46), would have made no sense.'[103] But although Lk does show a preference for the word group this does not mean he supplied the word in this context, for as Wrege points out 'χάρις is in this context firmly anchored in the catechetical usage.'[104] It occurs in a closely related context in I Pt 2:20 and in Did 1:3 (ποία γὰρ χάρις). That either of these documents was dependent on Lk is unlikely. Therefore, contrary to van Unnik, it is not likely that χάρις is due to Lk's redaction but had found its way into the tradition before him.

I have cited this one example to show that the evident hellenization in Lk 6:27-36 is not necessarily Lk's work. Elsewhere in the text Greek influence is evident in the removal of the Jewish/Palestinian features of the 'right cheek' (Mt 5:39/Lk 6:29), the legal suit for one's shirt (κριθῆναι Mt 5:40/Lk 6:29) and the conscription of citizens to go one mile with a soldier[105] (Mt 5:41; absent in Lk). The use of 'sinners' (Lk 6:32-34) instead of 'gentiles' (Mt 5:47) or 'tax collectors' (Mt 5:46) may also have been for the sake of gentile readers. But none of these changes can with certainty be attributed to Lk; for, among other reasons, this would mean that the distinctive patterns and the Semitic poetic structure of the passage in its present form would have to be Lk's work.[106]

Two things are important to notice about the hellenizing redaction. *First*, in the changes that were made for the sake of Greek readers – whether by Lk or perhaps by an earlier translator out of the Aramaic – the tendency was never to weaken the radical demand of Jesus. On the contrary, as Bartsch points out in two instances: 'With regard to one's coat the issue is not being sued for a garment as in Mt 5:40 but more radically it says: whoever takes your coat do not demand it back (6:29).

And the admonition to give to the one who asks is sharpened with an addition: Give to *every one* who demands.'[107] Thus the redactional changes were not carried out in order to make the teachings of Jesus more feasible as practical ethics but were simply intended to make Jesus' original teaching more comprehensible in a new situation.

The *second* thing to notice is that even if Lk is not responsible for these changes, they did not conflict with his purposes. What we said of Mt's use of the tradition on enemy love holds true for Lk's use as well: he makes no efforts to tone down the absolute commands of Jesus found in the tradition, nor does he give casuistical expansions to make the commands more practicable in daily life. Evidently Lk's main aim is not primarily catechetical or paraenetic but historical[108] – not in a modern disinterested sense, but with the conviction that this particular history of Jesus is of paramount significance for his church. Thus the content of the pericope on enemy love (Lk 6:27–36) confirms what was intimated in the framework Lk gave to the entire Sermon on the Plain: Lk's desire to address his own situation relevantly did not lead him to abandon his first aim to render an account of what and how Jesus had taught decades earlier.

2. Wherein Consists Obedience to Jesus' Command of Enemy Love?

I will not try to exhaust Lk's conception of the content of the command of enemy love. My intention rather is to examine that aspect of the love command in Lk 6:27–36 which Lk chooses to develop at greater length in the rest of his gospel. In following this development I will try in accordance with the methodology described earlier to establish between the texts examined and the pericope on enemy love (Lk 6:27–36) points of contact which reveal a genuine link in Lk's intention and thus shed light on his understanding of this pericope even though its Lukan features are uncertain. Lest the treatment of just one line of development in Lk's understanding of the command of enemy love seem too one-sided, I will, at the end of this section, pose the question of other possible lines of development and their relation to the one here treated.

Over against its Matthean parallel, Lk 6:27–36 has a peculiar stress on the use of one's possessions. Mt 5:42a commands, 'Give to the one who asks. To this Lk 6:30b adds, 'From the one who takes your things do not *demand* them *back*.' The command to give is taken farther: let go what you have given or what has been taken; do not even try to get it back. The word for 'demand back' ($\dot{\alpha}\pi\alpha\iota\tau\epsilon\iota$) is unique to Lk's gospel in the New Testament (found only here and in 12:20). Further, Mt 5:42b commands, 'Do not turn away from the one who desires to borrow from you.' Lk 6:35 again goes farther: 'Loan, not *hoping* for anything *back*.' 'Even sinners loan in order to *receive back*' (6:34). The word for 'hoping back' (ἀπελπίζω) is a *hapax legomenon* in the New Testament (except for a poorly attested variant reading in Eph 4:19) and is used here contrary to contemporary usage.[109] The word for 'receive back' (ἀπολαμβάνω) has 5 of its 10 New Testament occurrences[110] in Lk. On the basis of these word statistics and the difference between Mt and Lk, it appears that we have here a peculiar Lukan stress[111] on the way one should use his possessions: never use your possessions to seek your own earthly aggrandizement. In letting your riches go, don't hope for more of the same in return. Do not just be liberal, but be liberal in such a way that your liberality is not calculated to bring you more earthly treasure. Is it possible to confirm this supposedly Lukan emphasis from the wider context?

This emphasis on freely letting one's possessions go with no desire to have them back comes as no surprise after the Lukan form of the beatitudes (6:20-23) and woes (6:24-26).

> It seems impossible to determine whether Lk or his source inserted the woes at this point so that they correspond to the four beatitudes so perfectly. According to Grundmann (*Lukas*, p 144) and Hirsch (cited by him) 'They were probably inserted before Luke.' Bultmann (*History*, p 111f), however, thinks that while they are not Lk's formulation, they were probably inserted by him since 6:27a 'is manifestly a transition which again leads us back to a source (Q) passage.' Another point in favor of an insertion by Lk would be the πλήν with which the woes begin (6:24), because this is a favorite word in Lk (once in Mk, 5 times in Mt, 15 in Lk). It is probably his own suturing word in 6:35 where he repeats the love command (see Chapter 2, note 114) and he probably uses it against his sources in 12:31/Mt 6:33; 22:21/Mk 14:20; 22:22/Mk 14:21. And as we shall see below there is not only essential but also formal connection between the woes and other more distant material unique to Lk. But we need not insist that the woes were here inserted by Lk in order to find in them a clear expression of one of his chief concerns in the gospel (Kümmel, *Introduction*, p 98; Rengstorf, *Lukas*, p 4). This concern would be no less Lk's if it were also the concern of one of his sources.

20a	Blessed are you poor	24a	But woe to you rich
b	for yours is the Kingdom of God	b	for you have back your consolation
21a	Blessed are you who hunger *now*	25a	Woe to you who are filled *now*
b	for you shall be satisfied	b	for you shall hunger

The poor[112] are blessed and the rich are condemned.[113] The condemnation of the rich (6:24) is due in essence to the fact that the use of their possessions does not correspond to Jesus' commands. He commands: care so little for riches that, when they are given or taken, you do not even hope to have them back (6:35). The rich on the other hand seek and find their comfort or 'consolation' precisely in their riches.

Here again a difference in emphasis between Lk and Mt is evident. Offering a substantial parallel to Lk 6:24f, ὅτι ἀπέχετε τὴν παράκλησιν ὑμῶν, is Mt's threefold repetition of ἀπέχουσιν[114] τὸν μισθὸν αὐτῶν (6:3,5,16). Mt warns against seeking reward in the praise of men by showing off one's alms, prayers and fasting. Lk warns against seeking consolation in riches by a refusal to give freely without hoping for repayment. When one does not heed the warning, he is given precisely what he seeks: the praise of men (in Mt) and the consolation of riches (in Lk) – but nothing more! The way both evangelists use this same kind of argument shows the unity and distinctiveness of their different emphases. They are one in their concern that men not seek their happiness and security in the things at their disposal in this world. But Mt's focus is on the misuse of Jewish religious practices while Lk's concern is with the misuse of riches[115] and for Lk this is a clear failure to obey the command of enemy love.

Comparing the word ἀπέχω from Lk 6:24 which we just discussed with the words ἀπαιτέω, ἀπολαμβάνω, and ἀπελπίζω from Lk 6:30,34f (see above) we see that both texts, the woes and the love command, not only address the same issue, the use of possessions, but they do so with a similar vocabulary as well. As we shall see again below it is characteristic of Lk to use compound verbs, the prepositional prefixes of which connote reciprocity. In each of these four verbs the ἀπό prefix connotes that the person acting is aiming to get something *back* for himself. This peculiarity of Lk's writings is probably not accidental but a conscious effort to combat what van Unnik calls the *Gegenseitigkeitsregel*[116] which still regulated the behavior of Lk's Greek contemporaries even though some Greek moralists opposed it.[117] It seems, therefore, that the aspect of the tradition on enemy love which Lk has chosen to develop is its denunciation of the rule of reciprocity in the use of one's possessions. Where else in his gospel can this development be seen?

If we follow Lk's use of the word group just mentioned we are led to the parable of the rich man and Lazarus (Lk 16:19-31).[118] In this parable which only Lk records we have a rich man who flaunts his wealth by the clothes he wears and by his daily feasts (16:19); and we have a poor and miserable beggar, hungry and full of sores (16:20f). The situation is like that of the good Samaritan (Lk 10:29-37) in that the poor, diseased man lies at the rich man's gate so that the rich man must pass him every day as he goes in and out. Like the priest and the Levite in that parable, so the rich man here passes by and ignores the need of his poor neighbor. The poor man dies and is carried to Abraham's bosom (16:22), the rich man dies and goes to be tormented in Hades (16:23). The rich man pleads to Abraham for mercy (16:24) and Abraham's response is important for our theme: 'Child, remember that you *received back* (ἀπέλαβες) your good things in your life and Lazarus likewise evil things; but now here he is consoled (παρακαλεῖται) but you are tormented.'

Why had the rich man not even given Lazarus the crumbs from his table? Because Lazarus was in no position to pay back any good thing. But the rich man's life was determined by what he could *receive back* in all his dealings. Abraham acknowledged how tragically successful in this the rich man was. But his success was disobedience to Jesus' command never to use your possessions with the desire to 'receive back' (Lk 6:30,34f). Therefore Jesus' 'woe' of Lk 6:24 applies to the rich man, and here the parallel is striking. 'Woe to you that are rich, for you have back your *consolation* (παράκλησιν).' The rich man had received back his good things, his consolation, 'in his life,' but now he has exchanged it for torment. But Lazarus has exchanged his evil things, his torment, for *consolation* (παρακαλεῖται). The emphatic '*now*' of 16:25 recalls the 'now' of 6:25,21: 'Woe to you who are filled *now*, for you shall hunger.' 'Blessed are you who hunger *now*, for you shall be satisfied.' Lk 16:19–31 puts in parable form what, according to Lk, Jesus proclaims to the people in the beatitudes and woes and command of enemy love.

> Like the beatitudes and woes and love command, the parable of the rich man and Lazarus is in Lk's view not merely instruction for the disciples but also a call to repentance (see p 155). Jesus is addressing 'the Pharisees who were lovers of money' (16:14f). The parable closes with a warning to the five brothers of the rich man, who were also sons of Abraham (cf 16:25), that they needed to repent: 'If someone goes to them from the dead they will *repent*' (16:30). The parable is a call to repentance in that it shows that a failure to bear the fruit worthy of repentance brings irrevocable (16:26) separation from the blessings of the heavenly banquet.[119] As Lk pointed out already in John's preaching, '°. uits worthy of repentance' (3:8) are this: 'He who has two coats let ⹂im share with him who has none; and he who has food let him do likewise' (3:11).[120]

I mentioned above that it is characteristic of Lk to use compound verbs, the prepositional prefixes of which connote reciprocity. Besides the verbs beginning with ἀπό, Lk also seems to favor verbs beginning with ἀντί. Taking into consideration all words in the synoptics and Acts formed with ἀντί (not the preposition itself) we find the following.[121] Of the 21 words with the ἀντί prefix which occur in the synoptics and Acts, 20 occur in

Lk/Acts, while only 4 occur in Mt and Mk. Of the 17 which do not occur in Mt and Mk, 10 are unique to Lk/Acts¹ in the whole New Testament. It is fair to say therefore that Lk shows a partiality for words compounded with ἀντί.

Three of these words cluster together in a text which is important for Lk's denunciation of the rule of reciprocity in the use of one's possessions (Lk 14:12–14).

> Jesus said also to the one who had invited him: 'Whenever you make a breakfast or a dinner, do not call your friends or your brothers or your relatives or your rich neighbors, lest they also *invite* you *back* (ἀντικαλέσωσιν) and you have a *repayment* (ἀνταπόδομα). But whenever you give a banquet, call the poor, crippled, lame and blind; and you will be blessed because they cannot *pay* you *back* (ἀνταποδοῦναι). You will be *paid back* at the resurrection of the just.

This command (again directed at a Pharisee, 14:1) goes beyond the command not to hope for repayment when you loan or give. It even goes beyond the parable of the good Samaritan in which we are admonished to help those in our path. Here we are not merely commanded to be indifferent to earthly repayment, but more, to actively avoid it. Here we are to go out of our way and reach out to help those in need. The danger is so great that our actions will be controlled by the rule of reciprocity that we should guard against the temptation by making it our aim to give only where repayment is impossible. With this obvious overstatement, which is similar to the requirement to hate your relatives (14:26), Lk drives home how radical the inversion of values must be in the person who hopes to participate in the resurrection of the just (14:14).

Thus in developing his denunciation of the rule of reciprocity in the use of possessions, Lk does not abandon that original absoluteness of Jesus' command which we saw in the pericope on enemy love (cf p 156). His emphasis on the theme shows how important he thinks it is for the church but he does not give church rules on the use of possessions.¹²² He intends to let the piercing voice of Jesus come through and stab the consciences of his readers; for it is not with external regulation that Lk is concerned, but with the heart. Lk was perhaps more aware than any of the other evangelists of how decisive is the sentence: 'Where your treasure is, there will your heart be also' (Lk 12:34). To be sure, Lk emphasizes that obedience to Jesus' command of enemy love consists in *concrete acts* of mercy (6:36) toward those who may naturally be repulsive to us. But prior to the act comes that change of heart by which riches become so insignificant to us that our act of mercy is never calculated to bring back our own material aggrandizement.

conversion
acts of mercy

To close this section we may now pose the question of other lines of development of the command of enemy love in Lk. The line that we have focused on – Lk's denunciation of the rule of reciprocity in the use of one's possessions (6:30,35,20f,24; 16:19-31; 14:12-14, etc) – has surprisingly little to do with *enemies*. In Lk the 'poor, crippled, lame, and blind' (14:13) are the prime objects of love, not because they bear animosity, but because they are naturally repulsive (16:20) and thus, like enemies, are hard to love. We could have focused on the parable of the good Samaritan (10:29-37) where a stripped and wounded man was also an 'enemy.'[123] This would have brought in the dimension of enmity which love overcomes. But I have not given attention to this parable, first, because it has received so much attention in contemporary research, and, second, because it is not formally connected with the pericope on enemy love, and, third, because the motif of loving national or political enemies is not one of Lk's chief interests.

In fact, for Lk the 'enemies' of the Christians are no longer primarily outside, but inside, the church. They are 'the cares and riches and pleasures of life' (8:14; cf 16:9; 12:15).[124] The emphasis on persecution that we find in Mt (5:10,11,12,44; 10:23; 23:34) is missing from Lk.[125] This accords with what has often been noted about his two-volume work: in his apologetic interests, Lk avoids calling attention to animosity between the Christians and Romans.[126] He is less interested in stressing that Christians love their enemies than he is in stressing that Christians do not make enemies in the first place. For this reason, apparently, Lk chose to develop the renunciation of reciprocity in using one's possessions, instead of developing a dimension of enemy love which calls attention to animosity.

3. How is Jesus' Command of Enemy Love Motivated?

What did Lk conceive to be the motivating power behind the obedience to Jesus' command? In the texts we have just discussed one aspect of Lk's conception is most obvious and at the same time most problematical from the theological standpoint, namely, the idea of reward in the age to come. To focus our attention anywhere but here would be to avoid a dimension of Lk's thinking which poses a problem for the average Bible reader who believes that he is justified by faith and not by works.

Let us recall now how Lk argues in the texts which we looked at above. The pericope on enemy love climaxes with the words: 'Love your enemy, do good, loan, not hoping for anything in return; and your reward will be great and you will be sons of the Highest' (6:35). The counterpart to future reward is future loss, and of this Lk warns in the preceding woes: 'Woe to you who are filled now, for you shall hunger' (6:25a).[127] The parable of the rich man and Lazarus combines a promise of future blessing and a warning of future destruction: 'Abraham said, "Child, remember that you received back your good things in your life and Lazarus likewise evil things, but now here he is consoled and you are tormented"' (16:25). And, finally, in 14:13f, Jesus warns his host: 'When you give a banquet invite the poor and crippled and lame and blind and you will be blessed because they cannot repay you; for it will be repaid to you in the resurrection of the just.' Each of these texts as it stands is unique to Lk's gospel and we may assume in the light of what follows that they correspond to his intention.

The thought of reward and its counterpart of perdition form not a minor but a major aspect of Lk's portrayal of Jesus' teaching. In the following table I have tried to list every instance where future blessing (+) or perdition (–) is joined together with an explicit or implied command of Jesus (or John the Baptist) in Lk's gospel. (S = no parallel in Mt or Mk; Mk = parallel in Mk; Q = parallel only in Mt).

Q–	3:9	Every tree that does not bear good fruit is cut down and thrown into the fire (cf 3:17).
Q+	6:20	Blessed are you poor for yours is the Kingdom of God.
Q+	6:21	Blessed are you who hunger now for you shall be satisfied.
Q+		Blessed are you who weep now for you shall laugh.
Q+	6:22f	Blessed are you when men hate you . . . Rejoice in that day and leap for joy because your reward is great in heaven.
S–	6:24f	But woe to you that are rich for you have back your consolation.
S–		Woe to you that are full now for you shall hunger.
S–		Woe to you who laugh now for you shall mourn (cf 6:26).
Q+	6:35	Love your enemies . . . and your reward will be great and you will be sons of the Most High (cf 6:32–34).
Q+	6:37f	Judge not and you will not be judged;
S+		condemn not and you will not be condemned;
S+		forgive and you will be forgiven;
S+		give and it will be given to you: good measure, pressed down, shaken together, running over, will be put into your lap.
Mk+		The measure you give will be the measure you get back.
Q+	6:46–49	The one who does my words has an unshakable house,
Q–		but the one who does not – his house will be destroyed.
Mk–	9:24	Whoever would save his life will lose it,
Mk+		and whoever loses his life for my sake he will save it.

Mk—	9:26	Whoever is ashamed of me and my words, of him will the Son of Man be ashamed when he comes in his glory (cf 12:8–10).
Q—	10:13f	Woe to you Chorazin . . . Bethsaida for if the mighty works done in you had been done in Tyre and Sidon they would have repented long ago . . . but it shall be more tolerable in the judgment for Tyre and Sidon than for you (cf 11:31f).
S+	10:25,28	Teacher, what shall I do to inherit eternal life? (Love God and neighbor:) do this and you shall live (cf 18:15ff).
Q+	11:4	Forgive us our sins for we ourselves forgive everyone who is indebted to us.
Q—	12:4f	I tell you, my friends, do not fear those who kill the body, and after that have no more that they can do. But I will warn you whom to fear; fear him who after he has killed has power to cast into hell.
S—	12:20f	Fool, this night your soul will be required back from you . . . So is everyone who lays up treasure for himself and is not rich toward God.
Q+	12:31	Seek the Kingdom and these things shall be yours as well (cf 12:6f,22ff).
S+	12:32	Fear not, little flock; it is your Father's good pleasure to give you the Kingdom.
S+	12:33	Sell your possessions and give alms; provide yourselves with purses that do not grow old, with a treasure in the heavens that does not fail. . . for where your treasure is there will your heart be also.
S+	12:37	Blessed are those servants whom the master finds awake when he comes, truly I say to you he will gird himself and have them sit at table and he will come and serve them.
Q—	12:45f	But if that servant says to himself: 'My master is delayed in coming,' and begins to beat the men-servants . . . the master of that servant will come on a day when he does not expect him . . . and will punish him and put him with the unfaithful.
S—	13:5	Unless you repent you will all likewise perish.
Q—	13:24,27f	Strive to enter by the narrow door, for many, I tell you, will seek to enter and will not be able . . . Depart from me all you workers of iniquity. There you will weep and gnash your teeth . . . (cf 14:24).

S– S+	14:11	Everyone who exalts himself will be humbled, and he who humbles himself will be exalted (cf 18:14).
S+	14:13f	When you give a feast, invite the poor . . . and you will be blessed because they cannot repay you; you will be repaid at the resurrection of the just.
Q–	14:34	Salt is good but if salt has lost its taste how shall its saltness be restored . . . men throw it away.
S+	16:9	Make friends for yourselves from unrighteous mammon in order that, when it fails, they might receive you into eternal habitations.
S–	16:11f	If you have not been faithful in unrighteous mammon, who will entrust to you the true riches? And if you have not been faithful in what is another's, who will give you that which is your own?
S–	16:25	Son, remember that you in your lifetime received your good things and Lazarus likewise evil things; but now he is comforted here and you are in anguish.
Mk–	17:2	It would be better for him if a millstone were hung around his neck and he were cast into the sea than that he should cause one of these little ones to sin.
Mk+	18:29f	Truly I say to you there is no man that has left house or wife . . . for the sake of the Kingdom of God who will not receive manifold more in this time, and in the age to come eternal life.
Q+ Q–	19:26	I tell you, to everyone who has, will more be given; but from him who has not, even what he has will be taken away (cf 8:18).
S–	19:27	But as for these enemies of mine, who did not want me to reign over them, bring them here and slay them before me.
Mk–	20:15f	What then will the owner of the vineyard do to them? He will come and destroy those tenants and give the vineyard to others.
Mk–	20:46f	Beware of the scribes who like to go about in long robes . . . they will receive the greater condemnation.
Mk+	21:17–19	You will be hated by all for my name's sake. But not a hair of your head will perish. By your endurance you will gain your lives.

I do not mean to imply a uniformity of argumentation in each of these texts, nor that each one is equally representative of Lk's specific conception of ethical motivation. I have gathered these texts together, rather, to dispel any notion that the argumentation which Lk develops with regard to the motivation of enemy love is an isolated phenomenon in his gospel. And I hope that this accumulation of sayings will cause us to consider seriously the legitimacy of the role of future blessing or punishment in motivating ethical behavior. It could be that the frequency with which this legitimacy is rejected or ignored today inside and outside the theological establishment is based less on exegesis than on presuppositions that do not accord with the New Testament. C. S. Lewis, the Oxford scholar of Medieval Literature, preached a sermon in 1941 in which he tried to expose the fallacy of the presupposition that hoping for our own future good is a bad thing. (He is not a New Testament scholar and his comments should be read for the basic insight, not for his critical use of the sources.)

> If you asked twenty good men today what they thought the highest of the virtues, nineteen of them would reply, Unselfishness. But if you asked almost any of the great Christians of old he would have replied, Love. You see what has happened? A negative term has been substituted for a positive, and this is of more than philological importance. The negative ideal of Unselfishness carries with it the suggestion not primarily of securing good things for others, but of going without them ourselves, as if our abstinence and not their happiness was the important point. I do not think this is the Christian virtue of Love. The New Testament has lots to say about self-denial, but not about self-denial as an end in itself. We are told to deny ourselves and to take up our crosses in order that we may follow Christ; and *nearly every description of what we shall ultimately find if we do so contains an appeal to desire.* If there lurks in most modern minds the notion that to desire our own good and earnestly to hope for the enjoyment of it is a bad thing, I submit that this notion has crept in from Kant and the Stoics and is no part of the Christian faith. Indeed, if we consider the *unblushing promises of reward and the staggering nature of the rewards promised in the Gospels,* it would seem that our Lord finds our desires, not too strong, but too weak. We are half-hearted creatures, fooling about with our drink and sex and ambition when infinite joy is offered us, like an ignorant child who wants to go on making mud pies in a slum because he cannot imagine what is meant by the offer of a holiday at the sea. We are far too easily pleased.[128]

In my opinion Lewis' insight is indispensable for understanding the way Lk intends to motivate the command of enemy love – or, more specifically, to motivate the use of one's possessions for the sake of the poor and rejected. Applied to Lk, the insight is this: Lk never asks a man to act against his own best interests. In fact he never tires of reminding his readers that obedience to Jesus, no matter what it costs, brings ultimate satisfaction – whether this be described as great reward (6:35) or laughter (6:21b) or consolation in Abraham's bosom (16:25) or participation in the resurrection of the just (14:14). The appeal to our desire for well-being penetrates the whole gospel. (That is, in fact, ultimately why the early Christians called it εὐαγγέλιον.) We should perhaps say in advance that the 'reward' for which we hope is not conceived as a *thing* one wants to have; rather it is to be a son of *God* (6:35), to find his favor (18:14), to have fellowship with him.[129]

With this general groundwork laid we may now move on to the specific question how Lk understood the motivation of enemy love. The clearest statement of motivation in the texts we treated in the preceding section is found in Lk 14:13f.

> Whenever you give a feast, invite the poor, the crippled, the lame and the blind, and you will be blessed, because they cannot pay you back, *for* it will be paid back to you in the resurrection of the just.

It is not uncommon to read comments like T. W. Manson's on Lk 14:14, 'The promise of reward for this kind of life is there as a fact. You do not live this way for the sake of reward. If you do you are not living in this way but in the old selfish way.'[130] But a great deal of caution is in order here, for at such crucial points our own theological bias may tend to silence the voice of the evangelist lest he disturb our system. Manson, I think, has over-simplified. He is saying in effect that the promise of reward is mentioned as the *result* of loving behavior but should not be the *aim* of such behavior. However, two texts which are related to our theme and are found only in Lk make this interpretation problematical.

First, Lk writes in 12:33,[131] 'Sell your possessions, and give alms, provide yourselves with purses that do not grow old, with a treasure in the heavens that does not fail.' The connection here between giving alms and having an eternal treasure in heaven is not mere *result* but *aim*: 'Make it your aim to have treasure in heaven and the way to do this is to sell your possessions and give alms.' Second, Lk concludes the parable of the unrighteous steward with the command: 'Make friends for yourselves by means of unrighteous mammon, in order that when it fails they may receive you into eternal habitations' (16:9).[132] Lk thus understands the parable as instruction for the disciples (16:1), i.e. the church, about the proper use of material possessions. He does not say that the *result* of the proper use of possessions is to receive eternal habitations; he says: Make it your *aim* to secure an eternal habitation by the use of your possessions.[133]

Thus if we are to think like Lk we must express ourselves differently from T. W. Manson about the relationship between obedience to the love command and future reward.

It seems to me that one of the most significant questions facing the non-theologian, Theophilus, as he read Lk's gospel was: Why are there some fifty promises of reward and warnings of perdition connected with the commands of Jesus in Lk's gospel if these are not to form part of my motivation? The idea that the concept of reward is only the accidental clothing of Jesus' commands which is inherited from Judaism and can therefore be stripped away with no indecency to these commands is untenable,[134] at least from Lk's point of view. The promises and warnings are too prevalent and too intentional for us to say that Lk considered them to be discardable clothing. If the promise of reward to motivate Christian love is theologically inadmissible, then Lk is on this issue an inadmissible theologian.

But let us pose the question to Lk again: How should the promise of reward in heaven function in motivating the command of enemy love? I see two mutually exclusive possibilities. According to the first possibility, Theophilus would view his attainment of the heavenly reward as unsure, and in order to make it sure he would strive to obey the commands. That is, he would feel the need to show himself deserving of the reward. According to Conzelmann[135] this is, in fact, how Lk 12:33 must be understood: 'Sell your possessions and give alms; provide yourselves with purses that do not grow old and with a treasure in heaven, which does not fail.' But he says Lk has unwittingly contradicted himself here because in 17:10[136] 'it is made quite clear that any claim, any reckoning as to one's desert is excluded.'[137] But as we noticed above, Lk 12:33 is not an isolated example but forms only one tributary of a stream running through the whole gospel. It is more probable therefore – at least more courteous to assume – that Lk did not unknowingly contradict himself in two of the main emphases of his gospel, but that he was aware of what he was saying in both cases and believed that between them existed an essential unity. This would mean that 12:33 should be understood in some other way than just described and this leads us to the second possibility of how the promise of reward might function in motivating the command of enemy love.

According to this second possibility Theophilus would take note of the 'mercy' of the heavenly Father (6:35b,36)[138] who 'delights' to give his children the Kingdom (12:32)[139] precisely when they know their own 'unworthiness' to be called sons (15:21; cf 17:10).[140] Appealing to this 'mercy' as a 'sinner' (18:13),[141] Theophilus will trust confidently that he is fully accepted[142] by God and will surely inherit 'eternal life' (10:25;

18:18; 18:30). In this assurance of how 'great' his 'reward' will truly be as a 'son of the Highest' (6:35)[143] he 'rejoices and leaps for joy' (6:23):[144] the unspeakable longings of his heart are satisfied in hope, so that he is *freed from all behavior which aims to secure his own happiness at the expense of another.* He acknowledges that the only way he, as a human being with his overwhelming thirst for fulfilment, can love people genuinely and not merely use them as means to his own worldly pleasure is for his thirst to be satisfied in God (6:21; cf 12:21).[145] In this way the promise of reward may function to motivate love without contradicting Lk's understanding of undeserved mercy (15:21f; 17:10; 18:13).

But Lk talks as if our loving behavior secures the promise (12:33; 16:9) and so in a sense it does. The man whose consolation is not in riches (6:24)[146] nor in human acclaim (20:46; cf 16:15; 14:7–11)[147] *can* only use his possessions and position to seek the consolation of others. No good tree bears bad fruit (6:43). If a man begins to store up possessions for himself it is a certain sign that he has ceased to be 'rich toward God' (12:21)[148] and that he has begun to seek his riches (cf 16:25) and his consolation (6:24) in this world – but upon such a man Jesus pronounces not beatitudes but woes. Since the only man who will finally enjoy the promise is the man who truly loves his enemy (i.e. in Lk: the man in need who cannot pay back, p 162), therefore it is appropriate for Lk to say that to behave like this is to provide yourself with a treasure in heaven that does not fail (12:33). The reader understands that in loving his enemy he is doing that without which he will not have eternal life and he is thus motivated to take his behavior very seriously. But he also knows that such love is only possible if his hope of sonship is sure and he is thus motivated to realize the full assurance of faith in God's undeserved mercy (15:21f; 17:10; 18:13). Without this unconditional surety, his efforts at loving behavior would become abortive attempts to show himself worthy of sonship – which Lk says is impossible (17:10).

If we ask why Lk so often couples Jesus' command of 'enemy' love (along with many other commands) with warnings and promises about our eternal destiny the most basic answer seems to be that Lk saw the church in constant need of such reminders. As we saw earlier (p 162) the real danger facing the Christians of Lk's day was, in his opinion, the 'cares and riches and pleasures of life' which threaten to choke the Christian so that he does not come to maturity (8:14, cf notes 115,124). But the only way riches and pleasures can choke a man is to lead him to the absurd conclusion that they are more to be desired than all the wealth in the Kingdom of God. When this happens genuine love ceases, because the goal of riches and pleasures will become so important that other persons will be insignificant except as stepping stones to that goal. Lk's repeated warnings of destruction (cf 6:49) and promises of 'true riches' (16:11) aim to preserve the church from this absurd shortsightedness and to open the vision of the church onto the inestimable worth of eternal life at home with the Father. Only from this vantage point will the church truly know how and be able to love her enemies.

I should admit in closing that Lk did not make all the connections explicit which I have. Only in one place did he explicitly relate the undeserved mercy of God to the motivation of the command of enemy love: 'Be merciful as your Father is merciful' (6:36). For the most part he portrayed the mercy of the Father, on the one hand, and commanded love in view of future reward, on the other hand, without drawing the two together. That these two aspects of Lk's gospel do in fact cohere becomes evident only upon theological reflection of the sort I have tried to record here. Such reflection is justifiable here, I think, on the same grounds as it was in interpreting Jesus' message (see 'The Validity of Systematizing,' pp 67f).

It is perhaps no accident that the absence of an explicit systematic connection between these two aspects of Lk's gospel has its parallel (as we saw earlier, pp 79, 85) in the message of Jesus. He offered his unconditional and merciful forgiving-fellowship to sinners, on the one hand, and made radical demands in view of the coming Kingdom of God, on the other hand, without explicitly drawing the two together. And yet, as we saw there, it was the power of the Kingdom that was experienced through Jesus which enabled the fulfilment of his radical commands. That this theological coherence was only implicit in Jesus' message and is still only implicit in Lk's gospel may serve as a confirmation of our earlier conclusion (p 157) that Lk's first concern as an evangelist was to render the teaching of Jesus in its typical original orientation and through *this* means to address his contemporary readers with the gospel.

CONCLUSION

The study took its starting point from the observation that there are close parallels between the command of enemy love in the paraenesis of the New Testament epistles (cf Rom 12:14,17-20; I Thess 5:15; I Pt 3:9; I Cor 4:12) and the command of enemy love in the synoptics (Mt 5:38-48 and Lk 6:27-36). These parallels called for an explanation; so Leonhard Goppelt suggested that I test his hypothesis, that the paraenetic command of enemy love and the command of enemy love in the synoptics both rest on the words of Jesus. It was hoped that such an investigation would shed some more light on the use of tradition by the early church, and specifically on its use of the tradition of Jesus' sayings.

From this starting point the study developed as an analysis of the history of Jesus' command of enemy love in the tradition of the early church, with a conscious emphasis on the *meaning* of this command at the various levels of the tradition. The two fundamental problems to be solved by the study (taken as a whole, rather than in its individual parts) were these: First, if both the paraenetic and synoptic commands of enemy love somehow rest on Jesus' own command, why are there distinct differences in form and use? Second, in view of the differences can there be an essential unity or continuity between Jesus' command and the later formulations and uses?

In order to make sure that the initial question (Do the synoptic and paraenetic commands of enemy love both rest on the command of Jesus?) was legitimate, Chapter 1 was devoted to demonstrating three things: (1) that there was such a thing as an oral paraenetic tradition current among the earliest Christian churches; (2) that the command of enemy love in the New Testament paraenesis was a part of this tradition and owed its similarities in Rom and I Pt to their use of this common tradition; (3) as nearly as possible, what form the command of enemy love had in the paraenetic tradition. (See the fuller summary statements on pp 17f.)

After this, the natural question to pose was: Where did this command of enemy love in the paraenetic tradition come from? Chapter 2 was devoted to answering this question. I concluded there that, as far as the *raw material* used to expand the central command of enemy love is concerned, the paraenetic tradition drew upon both Old Testament and Jewish Hellenistic sources. (See the tabulation of this material on pp 63f.) But it did not do so without distinction, so that the raw material taken over does not merely reflect the character of the sources. It was chosen for its suitableness to serve *Christian* purposes and was altered by the context into which it was put (cf p 64). The kernel of this raw material, however, was *Jesus' command* of enemy love. This became evident, first, from the formal similarities between Jesus' command and the paraenetic command (cf Rom 12:14 and Lk 6:28), and, second, from the results of the history-of-religions survey, namely, that what sets the church off from its environment is that which it has in common with Jesus (cf p 64). The remaining chapters have confirmed the conclusion drawn at the end of Chapter 2: the interpreted, paraphrased and applied command of Jesus forms the center of the paraenetic teaching on enemy love, and the peculiar character of his command constituted the unique criterion according to which the non-Christian paraenetic elements were taken up into the early Christian paraenetic tradition.[1]

The initial hypothesis, that the commands of enemy love in the New Testament paraenesis and in the synoptics both rest on the words of Jesus, was thus confirmed. But why then the marked differences between the commands? The answer which has emerged from our study is that the paraenetic tradition and the gospel tradition (see definition, p 134) formed two distinct streams in the early church and had different intentions and settings. I can do no better than to quote Goppelt again to summarize my conclusion on this point.[2] 'Unsere Analyse ergab, dass hier über alle durch die lokale und zeitliche Verkündigungssituation bedingten Unterschiede hinaus *zwei Traditionen* vorliegen, die auf Grund ihrer Hauptintention je verschieden geprägt sind. Die Evangelienüberlieferung will die Logien primär als Verkündigung in der Situation Jesu, d.h. als Umkehrruf auf das kommende Reich hin, bezeugen [see my pp 79f]; die paränetische Tradition gibt sie vom erhöhten Herrn her seiner Gemeinde als beispielhafte Verhaltenshilfen weiter [see my pp 111, 114].' (I have tried to assess the historical relationship between these two streams of tradition on pp 136-9.) This then is the general structure of the tradition which our study uncovered.

In accord with this structure I investigated the *meaning* of Jesus' love command in three spheres: in his own earthly ministry (Chapter 3), in the early Christian paraenetic tradition as it came to be deposited in the

New Testament epistles (Chapter 4), and in the gospel tradition as it was employed by Mt and Lk.[3] Instead of recording the individual conclusions in each of these spheres, I shall mention four features of the interpretation of Jesus' love command which all of these areas have in common, and thereby try to answer the question of continuity or unity between the meaning of *Jesus'* command of enemy love and the various formulations and uses it later received.

First, the fundamental motivation of Jesus' command of enemy love, or that which enables its realization in life, is in all three spheres the prevenient mercy of God, manifest in Jesus. In *Jesus'* ministry this mercy is the mysterious presence of the Kingdom of God manifest in Jesus' forgiving-fellowship with sinners. For the *paraenesis* this mercy is seen in the gospel of Jesus' death and resurrection. For *Mt,* the mercy of God is seen in Jesus' call to discipleship, which is a call to trust the almighty Lord who stills the waves and who has all authority in heaven and on earth and who promises eternal fellowship to his disciples. For such a disciple, God is a merciful heavenly Father who knows what his children need before they ask him. For *Lk,* the mercy of God is shown in Jesus' acceptance of sinners. In this, God is revealed as the Father who 'delights to give his children the Kingdom' precisely when they know their own unworthiness to be called sons.

The *second* feature common to all three spheres is that one's final eschatological blessing is in some sense dependent upon one's obedience to the command of enemy love. The prevenient mercy of God does not exclude this conditional character of the love command, but rather lets the perfect demand of God stand unweakened, and grants the enablement needed to obey. Corresponding to this feature, there is in each of the three spheres additional motivation not only on the basis of the past and present mercy of God but also on the basis of future blessing. In other words, since it is only along the path of obedience that one arrives at the final realization of one's hopes, therefore the greatness of that hope is properly held out as a motivation for obedience.

As a concrete expression of *Jesus'* call to repentance in view of the coming Kingdom, the command of enemy love must be obeyed if one is to enjoy the blessings of that Kingdom. In the *paraenesis,* the Christians are called to return blessing for reviling in order that they might inherit a blessing (cf I Pt 3:9). In *Mt* 'Not every one who says to me, Lord, Lord, will enter into the Kingdom of Heaven, but he who does the will of my Father in Heaven,' that is, he who 'hears these my words and does them' (7:21,24). In *Lk* we are told, 'Make friends for yourselves by means of unrighteous mammon so that when it fails they may receive you into eternal habitations' (16:9) or, in other words, 'Sell your possessions, give alms, provide yourselves with . . . a treasure in the heavens that does not fail' (12:33). It was my conclusion that all of these appeals for obedience in view of future blessing are properly understood only when they are seen as integral constituents of the fundamental ground of enemy love in the already experienced mercy of God.

The *third* feature common to the understanding of the command of enemy love in Jesus' teaching, the paraenesis and the synoptics is that the content of the command of enemy love is determined by the tension of the eschatological situation which Jesus has brought. The inbreaking of the powers and blessings and demands of the age to come has created a situation of ambiguity and stress for the person who knows himself both grasped by this new inbreaking power and yet bound 'in the flesh' in this age. He is called, as it were, to live in two worlds whose rules are not the same.

For *Jesus,* the command of enemy love in one sense abolishes the *lex talionis* as the remnant of the old aeon of sin and suppression. But in another sense Jesus affirms the institutions essential to historical existence in this age. Obedience to the command of enemy love, which is the oppo-site of the *lex talionis,* is, therefore, only as absolute and unambiguous as is participation now in the age to come. In the *paraenesis*, the command of enemy love is not the over-arching norm, but is rather, one command in tension with others under the norm of love. It stands beside the subjection motif just as Jesus' love command stands beside his affirmation of the historical institutions. They cannot be brought into full harmony any more than those who have been 'transferred into the Kingdom of God's beloved Son' can feel in harmony with this world. *Mt,* with his program of antitheses prefaced by the affirmation of the law's enduring validity, brings out more vividly the tension already mentioned in Jesus' own teaching. While *Lk* maintains the eschatological tension in the motivation of the command of enemy love, this is not evident, so far as I can see, in his treatment of its content. This may be due as much to the particular content which he has emphasized (use of possessions) as to his peculiar conception of redemptive history.

The ambiguity of Christian existence leads to the *fourth* common feature, namely, the necessity for a renewed mind which can prove the perfect will of God. *Jesus* called for a transformation so radical that it left nothing in a man untouched (cf pp 77f). The *paraenesis* summons the Christian to realize the newness which he has been given 'through the resurrection of Jesus Christ from the dead' (I Pt 1:3). *Mt* stresses the need for a pure heart and a cup that is first clean on the inside so that the outside may become clean as well (Mt 23:26). And *Lk* seems to simply let his tradition speak without any peculiar stress of his own: 'No good tree bears bad fruit, nor again does a bad tree bear good fruit . . . The good man out of the treasure of his heart produces good, the evil man out of the evil treasure of his heart produces evil' (6:43,45). The tacit appeal of the command of enemy love is, therefore: Become a good tree! Whether it is described as the radical transformation of 'metanoia,' or as a 'new birth,' or 'new creation,' or as becoming pure in heart, or becoming a good tree, the reality intended is essentially the same, and it is the ground and goal of the command of enemy love. For the fruit of this tree abounds through Jesus Christ to the glory and praise of God (Phil 1:11; Jn 15:8; Mt 5:16; I Pt 2:12).

NOTES

Introduction

1 Schlier suggests ('Eigenart', p 340), 'Actually one should avoid the use of "paraenesis" as a designation for New Testament admonitions' because the related Greek word occurs only two times in the New Testament (Acts 27: 9,22). 'Properly (*sachgemäss*) one would have to say "paraclesis".' Hence the title of his student's excellent book: *Paraklese und Eschatologie bei Paulus* (which contains a concise report of the recent research in New Testament paraenesis, p 6) by Anton Grabner-Haider. See also Schlink, 'Gesetz,' p 326. I appreciate this desire to be *sachgemäss* but have chosen to retain throughout the work the word 'paraenesis' for two reasons: first, and most practically, because the word has imbedded itself in the literature of New Testament studies; second, and more basically, the word 'paraenesis' communicates distinct ideas about the form of a given text and its intention. Dibelius (*Jakobus,* pp 19–23) gave five characteristics of the literary form, paraenesis: '(1) eclecticism, (2) the absence of context, (3) catchword connections, (4) repetition of the same motif in different places, (5) the admonitions do not fall within the bounds of one particular situation.' In any given instance these characteristics may have to be qualified, but that there are such formally distinct units in the New Testament epistles (for example, I Thess 5:15–22 and Rom 12:9–21) is significant for understanding the traditional background of the epistles. Paraclesis does not focus on this formal side of the admonitions and therefore is not as suitable for our purpose as paraenesis.

2 'Command of enemy love' is a somewhat clumsy English rendering of the German *Gebot der Feindesliebe.* The phrase always means: 'command that one love one's enemies.' I take the freedom to use the phrase because otherwise I would constantly have to use ponderous subordinate clauses to define 'command'. It should be noted at the beginning that where I shorten this phrase simply to 'love command' I always mean 'the command of *enemy* love' unless the context indicates otherwise.

3 In place of a formal report on the present state of research, the literature pertinent to my topic will be assessed at those points within the work where it substantially relates to a particular issue. An extended bibliography on works on love in general is found in Spicq, *Agape* III, pp 247ff. William Klassen ('Love Your Enemy,' pp 155–7) gives a good history of the research specifically on enemy love including several works not available to me.

4 Furnish, *Love,* p 18.
5 Furnish, *Love,* p 19.
6 Furnish, *Love,* p 19.
7 Methodologically the work is thus closely related to David Dungan's *Sayings* which, however, treats only sayings of Jesus which are *explicitly* cited in Paul as words of the Lord.
8 Furnish, *Love,* p 19.
9 For a further definition and discussion of this, see Chapter 5, pp 134ff.
10 For a closer designation of this term, see Chapter 1.
11 The 'how' of this transmission is indeed disputed and will be discussed in Chapter 5.
12 Schlatter, *Jesus,* p 50.

Chapter 1. In Search of the Paraenetic Tradition of a Command of Enemy Love

1 On the Haustafeln in the New Testament see Schrage, *NTS* 21/1, pp 1–21; Goppelt, 'Haustafel'; *Petrusbrief,* pp 163–79.
2 Schelkle, *Petrusbriefe,* p 93f; Kelly, *Peter,* p 135f; Selwyn, *I Peter,* p 189: 'The whole passage, verses 8 and 9, is a beautiful summary of the ethical and spiritual qualities required of members of the Church in their relations one with another and in their attitude to their non-Christian and often hostile neighbors.'
3 Beare, *I Peter,* p 134. The efforts of E. G. Selwyn 'establish more clearly than ever the literary dependence of I Peter upon several if not all of the epistles of the Pauline corpus . . .' (p 195).
4 Dodd, *Gospel,* pp 19f. 'I do not suppose that in such passages we have anything like a direct reproduction of an existing document, or even verbal quotation of an established form transmitted by word of mouth . . . Different writers develop and elaborate the common pattern of the tradition at different points and in characteristically different ways.'
5 Daube, appended note in Selwyn, *I Peter,* pp 481, 486. As will be evident from the following pages, I do not think these imperative participles imply necessarily a fixed *written* code behind the New Testament paraenesis. C. H. Talbert (*NTS* 16, p 93) cites C. H. Dodd, W. D. Davies and A. M. Hunter as those who have approved of Daube's contention. E. Lohse (*ZNW* 45, p 75) has taken Daube's research farther and confirmed his findings from Jesus Sirach and the Wisdom of Solomon. From Daube's *Rabbinic Judaism* (pp 90–105) I have assembled the following summary of his view. 'There is a post-Biblical form of legislation where the action enjoined, allowed or prohibited is expressed by a participle' (p 90). 'If we want to give it a name we should call it, not imperatival participle or participial imperative, but rather advisory, didactic participle, or perhaps best, the participle stating the direct practice' (p 92). 'How can a statement of fact ["Women singing dirges but not wailing"] impose a duty or grant a privilege? The answer is that the teacher or lawgiver employing this form addresses an elite among whom the right thing, provided only it is known, is done – or at least is supposed to be done – as a matter of course. There is no need for exhortation or warning . . . No doubt the form gradually became stereotyped and more and more similar in import to other forms of legislation' (p 94). 'There are at least three points showing that the participle never

acquired full imperative force in all connections . . . First, the participle never occurs in a specific demand on a specific occasion . . . Secondly, even in rules the participle is never employed where a basic absolute unquestionable principle is to be enunciated . . .' Thirdly, the participle 'is too impersonal, too cold' for personal advice (p 96). 'It occurs not a single time in the Old Testament. Nor, apparently is it to be found in any of the non-Jewish Semitic systems. Yet in the earlier part of the Talmudic literature, in Mishnah, Tosephta and Baraitha it is more frequent than any other form' (p 90). 'The distinctive feature of the situation in that period was that . . . direct revelation no longer took place. It is this setting in life which accounts for the form under notice, the participles as a means of injunction, permission or prohibition. More precisely the form reflects the rabbinic view of the secondary, derivative, less absolute nature of post-Biblical rules' (p 91).

In the New Testament paraenesis 'the most probable explanation of these strange participles . . . is that they are literally taken over from the Hebrew . . . They appear not in basic injunctions like the prohibition of murder, but in directions as to the proper behavior of members of the new Christian society . . . Everything points to the existence of early Christian codes of duties in Hebrew, from which the participles of the correct practice crept into the Greek of the epistles' (pp 102f).

6 This is confirmed by our investigation (Chapter 2, pp 37–9) of the traditional origin of the phrase μὴ ἀποδιδόντες κακὸν ἀντὶ κακοῦ.

7 Selwyn (*I Peter,* p 413) says of I Pt 3:8f, I Thess 5:13–22 and Rom 12:9–19, 'A more probable explanation than literary dependence is surely that behind all three there lies a common catechetical material.' So Carrington, *Catechism,* p 88. Lohse (*ZNW* 45, p 75) also sees I Pt 3:8–12 as 'parä-netisches Traditionsgut' but cautions against Selwyn's effort to reconstruct a five-fold catechism, 'weil man sich dabei zu leicht auf das Gebiet von nicht beweisbaren Hypothesen begibt. Die formgeschichtliche Untersuchung der paränetischen Stücke wird darum noch behütsamer geführt werden müssen, und das Urteil ist in Einzelnen zurückhaltender und vorsichtiger zu fällen. Können wir in den Synoptikern mit grosser Wahrscheinlichkeit bis in Versteile hinein Markus oder das Logiengut als Vorlage des Matthäus und Lukas ermitteln, so reichen die Beziehungen, die zwischen der paränetischen Teilen der Briefe aufzuweisen sind, nicht aus, um etwa schriftliche Quellen als gemeinsame Vorlage herauszuschälen' (p 72). In addition Kelly (*Peter,* p 135) and Schelkle (*Petrusbriefe,* p 95) see I Pt 3:8f as composed of traditional catechetical material. From the standpoint of Rom, Michel (*Römer,* p 305) finds in Rom 12:14ff 'feste katechetische Überlieferung,' and Cranfield (*Rom* 12–13, p 54) remarks, 'The close similarity between [Rom 12] verse 17a, I Thess 5:15, I Pt 3:9 suggests that we have here the fixed formulation of the catechetical tradition.'

8 Since I Thess and Rom are both written by Paul it is pointless to ask (as we did with I Pt and Rom) whether there is literary dependence of Rom on I Thess. We may assume that whatever is the traditional source of Rom 12:17 is also the source behind I Thess 5:15.

9 Talbert, *NTS* 16, p 86.

10 Dibelius, *Thessalonicher,* p 31. He had expressed himself more cautiously

earlier: 'Allerlei Ermahnungen, offenbar ohne besondere Veranlassung' (p 31).

11 Frame (*Thessalonians,* p 199) maintains that vv 14 and 15 'suggest that, though the exhortation is general and characteristic of Paul, a specific situation, namely, that of the friction between workers and idlers within and chiefly the persecutions from without at the hands of Gentiles directly and Jews indirectly, had stirred up a spirit of impatience destined to express itself, if it had not done so already, in revenge.'

12 Oepke, 'Thessalonicher,' p 178 'Die eingeschobene Aufforderung [5:14] zu allgemeiner brüderlicher Seelsorge erinnert noch einmal an die schon 4:11f gerügten Mängel.' Best (*Thessalonians,* p 230) agrees cautiously.

13 Should it be admitted with Kümmel (*Introduction,* pp 188f) that II Thess was written by Paul shortly after I Thess, then the references to the 'idle' in II Thess 3:6,7,11 would confirm the conclusion I have drawn from I Thess alone.

14 The remaining two imperatives of I Thess 5:14 do not help us in deciding their traditional or occasional origin. Ἀντέχεσθε is found nowhere else in the New Testament with the meaning 'to help' (Bauer, *Lexicon,* p 72; the only other uses are Tit 1:9; Mt 6:24 par). Μακροθυμεῖτε occurs only in I Cor 13:4 where it has no object and is not a command.

15 The traditional character of these verses in Phil is brought out in 4:9 where Paul sums up: 'What you have learned (ἐμάθετε) and received (παρελάβετε) . . . these things do.'

16 Outside Paul only: Mt 8:4 par; 9:30; 18:10; 24:4 par; Mk 4:24 par; Heb 3:12; 12:25, II Jn 8. In Paul: I Cor 1:26; 3:10; 8:9; 10:12; 16:10; Gal 5:15; Eph 5:15; Col 4:17. Paul, however, ordinarily uses βλέπω instead of ὁράω.

17 So Bornemann (*Thessalonicherbriefe,* p 228). The intention of the command is 'dass die Gemeindevorsteher darüber wachen sollen.'

18 So Lünemann (*Thessalonicher,* p 148). Reasons: (1) the leaders are not free from feelings of revenge; (2) the accomplishment of the commandment belongs to the area of individual life so that it is seldom possible to hinder revenge in another. Best (*Thessalonians,* p 229) gives five arguments for this view.

19 Dobschütz, *Thessalonicher-Briefe,* p 222 'Es ist doch klar, dass bei ὁρᾶτε nicht andere gemeint sind als bei διώκετε, und dies richtet sich doch an alle.'

20 Compare Col 3:13, χαριζόμενοι ἑαυτοῖς ἐάν τις πρός τινα ἔχῃ μομφήν.

21 The parallel in Gal 6:10 shows, however, the general applicability of the thought expressed here: ἐργαζώμεθα τὸ ἀγαθὸν πρὸς πάντας μάλιστα δὲ πρὸς τοὺς οἰκείους τῆς πίστεως.

22 Dibelius, *Jakobus,* p 21.

23 Michel (*Römer,* p 308) thinks Paul has transformed the meaning of this quote from Prov 3:4 LXX so that the Semitic ἐνώπιον πάντων ἀνθρώπων in accordance with the context now means: 'dass die Gemeinde sich darüber Gedanken machen soll, wie sie Gutes (als Gegensatz zum Bösen) allen Menschen zuteil werden lassen kann.' This would bring 12:17b into essential harmony with I Thess 5:15b, but given the lack of systematization in Rom 12:14-21, I do not think the context justifies the conclusion that this Old Testament quote no longer has its original sense. Moreover in II Cor

8:21, Paul uses the same quote with the meaning to take thought for what is good in the eyes of others. This concern for living respectably before outsiders is also part of Paul's thought elsewhere (I Thess 4:12; Col 4:5; I Cor 10:32f) and of Peter's (I Pt 2:12). Daube (in Selwyn, *I Peter*, p 478) translates: 'Provide things honest in the sight of all men.'

24 Selwyn (*I Peter*, p 413) sees the influence of Ps 33:15 LXX in I Thess 5:15 (διώκετε) and 5:21f (εἴδους πονηροῦ) and in Rom 12:9,18. 'Ps 34 was so admirably adapted to the instruction of catechumens as its use in I Pet 2:3,4 exemplifies, that it may well have been used at a very early stage, as it stood, in the teaching of the primitive church, or made the basis of shorter paraenetic forms.'

25 See Lk 6:33,35; Rom 13:3; I Pt 2:15,20; 3:6, 17; 2:14; 3:13; 4:19; III Jn 11.

26 Heb 12:14; Rom 14:19; 12:18; I Thess 5:13; Mk 9:50; Mt 5:9.

27 See note 23.

28 Michel, *Römer*, p 307.

Chapter 2. The Origin of the Command of Enemy Love in the New Testament Paraenetic Tradition

1 'Toward the end of the first century B.C. the Stoic philosophy through many devotees penetrated to Alexandria and surely also through individuals to Palestine, which at the time of Christ had taken up many elements of hellenistic culture. The so-called *via maris*, the main trade route, which connected Damascus and Ptolemais, cut straight through Galilee with all its pagan travellers.' (Barth, *Stoa*, p 243.)

2 Leopold Schmidt (*Ethik*, p 366) characterizes the personal ethics of the Greek classical era in this way: 'Even today we recognize that a state must strive to be sought out as an ally and to be feared as an enemy; when the Greeks made the same demand on the individual the reason was largely a social condition in which the preservation of many interests was left to the voluntary activity of the individual. Another cause was the . . . basic inadequacy of the national-Hellenic ethic, an inadequacy which manifested itself in the possibility of being outlawed and cursed. There was lacking a clear consciousness of the relationship of man to man as such.'

H. Bolkestein (*Wohltätigkeit*, p 170) concludes his section on 'Die Motive des Wohltuns' of the Greeks in the Hellenic period: 'The mainsprings of the εὖ ποιεῖν have been shown to be the following: the *joy* which the giver gets from his act, the *honor* which he expects, and the *reward* or advantage which he counts on. That these are the mainsprings which are actually decisive is to be assumed from an expression of Isocrates in which he states his conviction: ἐγὼ μὲν οὖν ἡδονῆς ἢ κέρδους ἢ τιμῆς ἕνεκά φημι πάντας πάντα πράττειν.

3 Pohlenz, 'Stoa', p 538.

4 'In Christian times Epicureanism was anathema because it taught that man is mortal, that the cosmos is a result of accident, that there is no providential god, and that the criterion of the good life is pleasure' (*Oxford Classical Dictionary*, p 390).

5 Bonhoeffer, *Epiktet*, p 72.

6 Sevenster, *Seneca*, p 9.

7   Sevenster, *Seneca,* p 14. Augustine and Jerome knew of the correspondence so that it was in existence before 392. But 'in view of the fact that Lactantius was obviously ignorant of such a correspondence, when in 325 he wrote that Seneca would have been a true Christian if he had had someone to guide him, it is probable that these letters date from between 325 and 392.' From the sample which Sevenster quotes one can see its 'empty phraseology, its meaninglessness, insignificance, and insipid and exaggerated flattery' (p 13).

8   All quotations of Epictetus and Seneca are taken from the *Loeb Classical Library.*

9   The same anecdote is found again in *De Constantia* 14.3.

10 Or again the calculating concern not to get entangled in useless and harmful affairs is seen in the following excerpt from *De Ira* II.34.5: 'Animosity, if abandoned by one side, forthwith dies. It takes two to make a fight. But if anger shall be rife on both sides, if the conflict comes, he is the better man who first withdraws; the vanquished is the one who wins. If someone strikes you, step back; for by striking back you will give him both the opportunity and the excuse to repeat his blow; when you later wish to extricate yourself, it will be impossible.' Or again *De Beneficiis* VII.28.3: 'You must pardon if you would win pardon.'

11 Compare also *De Constantia* 2.1,3: 'For Cato himself I bade you have no concern, for no wise man can receive either injury or insult . . . Think you that what the people did to such a man could have been an injury, even if they tore from him his praetorship or his toga? even if they bespattered his sacred head with filth from their mouths? The wise man is safe and no injury or insult can touch him.' *De Constantia* 3.3: 'The invulnerable thing is not that which is not struck, but that which is not hurt; by this mark I will show you the wise man.'

12 Sevenster, *Seneca,* p 183. Likewise Bultmann ('Nächstenliebe,' p 236): 'Und zwar ist hier die Liebesforderung durch den Humanitätsgedanken begründet, durch das Ideal des Menschen, der sich auch durch widerfahrenes Unrecht nicht aus der Harmonie seines seelischen Gleichgewichts bringen lässt, durch das Ideal der Charakterstärke und menschlichen Würde.'

13 Bonhoeffer, *Epiktet,* p 335.

14 Similarly in *Discourses* IV.5.32: 'But if the right kind of moral purpose and that alone is good, and if the wrong kind of moral purpose and that alone is bad, where is there any longer room for contention, where for reviling? About what? About the things that mean nothing to us? Against whom? Against the ignorant, against the unfortunate, against those who have been deceived in the most important values?' However in *Encheiridion* 33.9 Epictetus speaks from a different standpoint: 'If someone brings you word that So-and-so is speaking ill of you, do not defend yourself against what has been said, but answer, "Yes indeed, for he did not know the rest of the faults that attach to me; if he had these would not have been the only ones he mentioned".'

15 Or again in *Encheiridion* 1: 'If you think only what is your own to be your own, and what is not your own to be, as it really is, not your own, then no one will ever be able to exert compulsion upon you, no one will hinder

you, you will blame no one, will find fault with no one, will do absolutely nothing against your will, you will have no personal enemy, no one will harm you, for neither is there any harm that can touch you.'

16 *Encheiridion* 20: 'Bear in mind that it is not the man who reviles or strikes you that insults you, but it is your judgment that these men are insulting you . . . So make it your first endeavor not to be carried away by the external impression, for if once you gain time and delay, you will more easily become master of yourself.' See also *Discourses* IV.5.28.

17 The stone metaphor is used of the Cynic in *Discourses* III.22.100–103. In *Discourses* III.22.90–92 the charm and ready wit of the Cynic is essential and the example given seems to extol the cleverness of the repartee at the expense of the interlocutor.

18 Bonhoeffer, *Epiktet*, p 380.

19 Bonhoeffer, *Epiktet*, p 381.

20 I shall discuss the origin of Rom 12:17a; I Thess 5:15a and I Pt 3:9 as a development from Prov 17:3 when I examine Joseph and Asenath below. We may note in advance that this development may have been suggested by similarly worded Old Testament texts: Prov 20:22; 24:29; Gen 44:4. Cf also 1QS 10:17f.

21 For a discussion of how this psalm influenced the New Testament tradition see Chapter 1, pp 13f.

22 Quell, *TDNT* I, pp 21–35.

23 Michel, *TDNT* IV, pp 685–8.

24 Schmauch, *Matthäus*, p 43.

25 See also Job 31:29f; II Kg 6:21–23.

26 *TDNT* VI, pp 314f; Jeremias, *Theology,* p 213; Strack–Billerbeck I, p 353; Seitz, *NTS* 16, p 48.

27 The גֵּר may be circumcised if he wishes (Ex 12:45ff). He participates if he desires in the sacrificial cult (Lev 22:18; 17:8). He is subject to the death penalty like the Israelite (Lev 20:2). He can be 'cut off' from the people like an Israelite (Lev 17:9,10). He is classed with the poor Israelites who are to be provided for by leavings in the field (Lev 19:10). An Israelite who becomes too poor to support himself is to be supported by his brother 'as a stranger (גֵּר) and a sojourner (חָי).' As such, no interest or profit is to be taken from him (Lev 25:35ff). The sojourner may become rich and have Israelite hired servants (Lev 25:47ff).

28 We may make brief mention here of the *lex talionis* found in Ex 21:24; Lev 24:10; and Dt 19:21. This is not a license for personal retaliation but a legal clause based on the principle of just retribution. Nor is there necessarily a personal or national enemy involved.

29 Similarly Josh 6:15; 8:1,18; 10:8,11,14,30,32,42; 11:8; 13:6; 23:5.

30 Another instance where David treats his enemies with kindness is in the accession narrative where he spares Saul's life so that Saul says, 'You have dealt well with me, while I have dealt wickedly with you . . . For if a man finds his enemy will he let him go away safely?' (I Sam 24:17–18 cf 25:26, 33). This, however, was not David's only response toward those who hated him. His final charge to his son was that his enemies Joab and Shimei should be brought down with blood to Sheol (I Kg 2:5–9).

31 For God's hate of evildoers see Ps 5:4–6; 11:5; 31:6; Prov 3:32; 6:16ff; Hos 9:15.

32 Montefiore, *Rabbinic Literature,* p 63: 'If one were to take the Old Testament as a whole, I am not so sure that one can honestly say that its general teaching is very definite on the love of enemies, even of Israelites.'

33 It would not even be correct to say that the Christians gave up the principle: hate what God hates (Ps 139:21). But there seems to be a shift of emphasis from the person to the works: 'Yet this you have: you hate the *works* of the Nicolaitans, which I also hate' (Rev 2:6).

34 All English quotations from the Apocrypha and Pseudepigrapha are taken from R. H. Charles, *Apocrypha and Pseudepigrapha.*

35 Eissfeldt, *Introduction,* p 584. Rost (*Einleitung,* p 46) agrees with this date but says it could as well have been composed in Egypt.

36 Rost (*Einleitung,* pp 75f) sets the *terminus ad quem* of the composition of Aristeas at 63 B.C. since the 'letter' presupposes that the island of Pharos is populated, but Caesar had removed the population by this date. Most scholars place the composition at the beginning of the first century B.C. in Alexandria. Cf Denis, *Introduction,* pp 109f.

37 Presupposing the existence of II Macc, the *terminus a quo* of its composition is the middle of the first century B.C. Some have dated it as late as A.D. 117. Eissfeldt makes no decision. Rost thinks the existence of the temple is assumed and therefore puts the composition in the first half of the first century A.D. All agree it was written in either Antioch or Alexandria.

38 Charles, *Pseudepigrapha,* p 664.

39 Unlike the Ethiopian Book of Enoch, Slavonic Enoch was originally written in Greek which is shown in 30:13 by an acrostic of the name Adam possible only in Greek. Individual parts may have existed previously in Hebrew (Rost, *Einleitung,* p 83), but it is generally agreed that the book stems from the Greek-speaking diaspora Judaism probably in Alexandria (Denis, *Introduction,* p 29; Rost, *Einleitung* p 84; Eissfeldt, *Introduction,* p 623; Plöger, *RGG* III, columns 224f; Michl, *Sac Mun* I, column 216). Concerning the date of composition there is also general agreement: 'Da Sirach, der äthiopische Henoch und die Weisheit Salomos schon vor dem Verfasser vorlagen, der Tempel aber noch da steht (51:59, 61, 62, 68), ist wohl die erste Hälfte des 1.Jh.n.Chr. für die Entstehung anzusetzen' (Rost, p 84). Concerning the matter of Christian interpolations or authorship there is not so much agreement. S. Pines (*Encycl Jud* VI, pp 798f) denies that the shorter version of Slavonic Enoch which has come down to us has any certain echoes of Christian doctrine. Plöger (*RGG* III, column 224) says the Christian church received the book 'wenn auch christliche Interpolationen ausgeprägten Stiles unmittelbar nicht zu erkennen sind.' The more commonly held view is that Slavonic Enoch in its present form is a Christian production (Rost, *Einleitung,* p 84; Eissfeldt, *Introduction,* p 623; Michl, *Sac Mun* I, column 216). Denis (*Introduction,* p 29) writes: 'Oeuvre d'un Juif d'Egypte du I^{r}s. ap. J.C., il développe la doctrine syncrétiste de la diaspora alexandrine, ou bien l'auteur est peut-être plutôt un chrétien d'origine juive.'

40 It is generally agreed that the work was originally written in Greek (Denis, *Introduction,* p 46) and is the product of Egyptian Jewry (Philonenko, *Encycl Jud* X, column 223; Kuhn, 'Lord's Supper,' p 74; Burchard, *Joseph und Aseneth,* p 142). The date of composition has been set at the end of

the first century B.C. (Burchard, p 151) and at the end of the first century A.D. (Philonenko, p 223). Denis (p 47) leans toward the later date. Earlier scholarship saw Joseph and Aseneth as a Christian product (Brooks, *Joseph and Aseneth,* p xi) or saw it as a Jewish book reworked by Christians (Bousett, *Religion,* p 24; Schürer, *Geschichte,* p 401, note 126; Batiffol, *Proseuchē Aseneth,* pp 7f). More recently Kuhn (p 74), Denis (p 46) and Philonenko (p 223) have denied the existence of Christian interpolations in the short recension of Joseph and Aseneth.

41 The Greek quotations are taken from Philonenko, *Joseph et Aseneth.* The translations are my own.

42 Lührmann, *ZThK* 69, p 427: 'Die Aufhebung der talio, die die fünfte Antithese bei Mt formuliert, arbeitet also mit einer bereits jüdischen Tradition.'

43 Best (*Thessalonians,* p 233) does call attention to it in this connection.

44 Burchard, *Joseph und Aseneth,* p 100.

45 Thomas, 'Aktuelles,' p 96. See p 49.

46 Burchard (*Joseph und Aseneth,* p 100) cites the use of the phrase in I Thess 5:15; Rom 12:17; and I Pt 3:9 and comments: 'es ist an allen drei Stellen bloss negativer Vordersatz zu einer Positiven . . . Hier wird ein jüdisch-hellenistischer Satz übernommen und im Fortgang verchristlicht.' Similarly Thomas, 'Aktuelles,' p 96, note 60: 'Durch Paulus oder die vorpaulinische Gemeinde wurde sie ein negatives Gegenstück zum Liebesgebot und Grundregel für das Verhalten gegenüber nicht Christen (Rom 12:17ff).'

47 Burchard, *Joseph und Aseneth,* p 100: 'Es ist kaum denkbar, dass eine christliche Ethik nur aus solchen Sätzen bestände, denen eigentlich christliches ganz fehlt und die bezeichnenderweise auch alle Verbote sind, wodurch sich diese Ethik bei aller Ähnlichkeit schon formal wenigstens von der ntl. unterscheidet.' There is a possible exception to this statement. But at the point of the exception another non-Christian feature appears: a concern for personal advantage. When Levi refuses to let Benjamin kill Pharaoh's son he says: 'We want to heal him from this wound and if he stays alive he will be our friend and Pharaoh his father will be our father' (23:4).

48 Barth, *Stoa,* p 237: 'Am stärksten ist die stoische Ader bei Philo in seiner Ethik. Diese wandelt überall auf stoischen Wegen nach stoischen Zielen.'

49 In *De Agricultura* 110 he says the winner of a reviling contest is worse than the loser.

50 There are now at least nine manuscripts of the original Hebrew of the Book of Jubilees, two from Cave I, two from Cave II and five from Cave IV. Fragments from an Aramaic Testament of Levi and a Hebrew Testament of Naphtali have been found in Cave I. Cf J. T. Milik, *RB* 62, pp 398–406.

51 The quotations are taken from Dupont-Sommer, *Essene Writings.*

52 See the Damascus Document 6:20–21 for a further exposition of this love of the brotherhood.

53 For a further exposition of divine predestination see the Hymn Scroll 15.

54 The early Christian teachers would probably have disputed that such a development from these psalms was necessary or proper. Both Paul (Rom 11:9,10 = Ps 69:22,23) and Luke (Acts 1:20 = Ps 69:25) are able to see in the imprecatory psalms the decrees of God rather than the mere vindictive-

ness of an individual. Cf Murray, *Romans* II, p 74; Dabney, *Discussions* I, pp 706–21; Martin, 'Imprecations'.

55 It is generally agreed that the date of composition is right around 100 B.C. Rost (*Einleitung*, p 100), Eissfeldt (*Introduction*, pp 607f) and Dupont-Sommer (p 298f) argue successfully that this book derives from the Qumran (Essene) Community. Also Davenport (*Jubilees*, p 16) argues that 'the conjunction of the use of the Jubilee calendar there, the hostility of the Qumran Community toward the Temple hierarchy, and the similarity of views in the Temple Scroll and Jubilees as to the future Temple make it a highly probable location.' The date generally accepted for the final redaction of Jubilees is about A.D. 100.

56 In Abraham's farewell address (20:2) R. H. Charles' (*Pseudepigrapha*, p 92) translation reads: 'and love each his neighbor and act on this manner among all *men*.' However in a footnote Charles notes that 'men' (*sab'ē*) is an emendation from the original 'war' (*ṣab'ē*).

57 Jervell, 'Interpolator,' p 31.

58 Jervell, 'Interpolator,' p 30: 'Fest steht nur, dass die Testamente auch christliche Auffassungen darbieten.'

59 Denis, *Introduction*, pp 58f.

60 Charles, *Pseudepigrapha*, pp 290, 288, 282.

61 De Jonge, *Testaments*, pp 117, 125. Even if De Jonge is right, the Testaments are not useless for our purpose for, since he says that the author used traditional Jewish material, the task would then be the isolating of Jewish material instead of the isolating of Christian interpolations.

62 De Jonge, *Studies*, pp 209f.

63 Rost, *Einleitung*, p 104.

64 Dupont-Sommer, *Essene Writings*, p 305. Similarly Eissfeldt, *Introduction*, p 635.

65 Philonenko, *Interpolations*, p 59: 'Les Testaments des Douze Patriarches nous ont été transmis avec une remarquable fidélité et, tels que nous les connaissons par la tradition grecque, ils sont libres de toute interpolation chrétienne de quelque importance.'

66 Woude, *Messianischen Vorstellungen.*

67 De Jonge, *Studies*, pp 191–246.

68 Becker, *Zwölf*, p 373.

69 Becker, *Zwölf*, p 383. He refers to Jubilees 20 and 36 to show that a comman to love in a farewell address is not unusual in the Jewish literature. See our discussion of the passages above, p. 42.

70 Becker, *Zwölf*, p 393.

71 Becker, *Zwölf*, p 388.

72 Becker, *Zwölf*, p 395.

73 Becker, *Zwölf*, p 397.

74 Becker, *Zwölf*, p 394.

75 Becker, *Zwölf*, p 397. Conversely evil is repaid immediately in Levi 6:7 and Gad 5:9–11. Walter Harrelson ('Patient Love,' p 34) disagrees with Becker's effort to distinguish the teaching on love in the Testaments from the teaching on love in the New Testament: 'Our author has, I believe, stated with extraordinary originality and power some of the fundamental dimensions of "Christian" love in his document from a time two centuries earlier than the

establishment of Christian communities in his locality.' Similarly Thomas, 'Aktuelles,' p 95.

76 In his more recent work De Jonge confesses that only a beginning has been made on investigations into the *ethical* teaching of the Testaments and its relation to Qumran and Christian tradition; 'much more will have to be done' (*Studies,* p 246).

77 Cf Rost, *Einleitung,* p 50; Eissfeldt, *Introduction,* p 597.

78 Contrast how the argument from the imitation of God is used when good deeds within the congregation are being considered (4:7–10; cf 28:1–7):

> Make yourself beloved in the congregation;
> bow your head low to a great man.
> Incline your ear to the poor,
> and answer him peaceably and gently.
> Deliver him who is wronged from the hand of the wrongdoer,
> and do not be fainthearted in judging a case.
> Be like a father to orphans,
> and instead of a husband to their mother;
> you will then be like a son of the Most High.

79 All quotations are taken from the *Loeb Classical Library* edition of his works. Schlatter carries on a running discussion with Josephus in his commentary on Mt. Therefore many pertinent quotations are given in his treatment of Mt 5:38–48 (*Matthäus,* pp 184–98).

80 In *Against Apion* II.145f, Josephus defends the law against the criticisms of Apollonius Molon and Lysimachus by claiming it is designed to promote, among other things, 'humanity towards the world at large' (πρὸς τὴν καθόλου φιλανθρωπίαν).

81 Strack–Billerbeck I, p 354. Montefiore (*Gospels,* p 84) gives no support for his contention: 'Neighbor (*rea*) had gradually or largely lost its meaning of fellow Israelite. When a rabbi taught his pupils about the love of neighbor being the chief injunction of the whole law, he had not the antithesis of Jew and foreigner in his mind. He meant fellow being, brother man in a general sense.'

82 Strack–Billerbeck I, p 354.

83 Michel, 'Nächstenliebe,' p 63.

84 Montefiore, *Rabbinic Literature,* p 68: 'The truth is that the Rabbis are not entirely of one mind on the matter of loving or hating the non-Jew. It would be unjust to sum up the matter by saying that the Rabbis generally taught that it is right or permissible to hate the gentiles; on the other hand it would be hardly less unfair to say that the Rabbis taught that the love which was to be shown to the Jewish "neighbor" was to be extended equally to all men, whatever their race or nationality or creed. One can hardly quote any unequivocal utterance from the Rabbis which goes as far as this.' Pp 50–111 of his work offer a very large amount of rabbinic material pertaining to enemy love.

85 *Pesahim* 113b, cited by Seitz, 'Enemies,' p 48. Also Strack–Billerbeck I, p 368.

86 Strack–Billerbeck I, p 369.

87 Around A.D. 90 R. Eliezer disputed with Jehoshua that all the gentiles without exception are forgotten by God and bound for Sheol (T. Sanhedrin 13:2).

Around 150, R. Shimeon interpreted Ez 34:31 to mean that the Israelites are called men and the nations are only cattle (Jebamoth 60b). Around 260, R. Shemuel said that, if all the nations came together and wanted to sell all they possessed and keep the commandments of the Torah, God would turn them away with a curse (Num. Rabba 2.138b). Cited from Strack–Billerbeck I, pp 359f.

88 According to Strack–Billerbeck I, pp 354, 358, only since the second century A.D. do there appear rabbinic instances of commands to love men in general: 'Ben Azzai (um 110) dürfte der erste Lehrer der alten Synagoge sein, der für das Verhalten gegen Nichtisraeliten dieselbe Norm aufstellt wie für das Verhalten gegen einen israelitischen Volksgenossen.' For other rabbinic references see Banks, *Jesus and the Law*, pp 198–201, and Nissen, *Gott und der Nächste*, pp 308–28.

89 In *Redaktion*, p 53, and in *ZThK* 69, pp 414f.

90 Lührmann's criticism of Wrege's *Bergpredigt* (which traces the two sermons back to individual independent traditions) strikes home: 'Wrege geht nirgends auf die doch auffällige gemeinsame Grundstruktur von Bergpredigt und Feldrede ein' (*ZThK* 69 pp 422f). As far as Lk 6:27–36 par Mt is concerned the following scholars deny that Mt and Lk use a common source: Schmauch, *Matthäus*, pp 135, 144; Rengstorf, *Lukas*, p 89, 'Wir werden auch hier besser nicht mit einer gemeinsamen Quelle, sondern mit zwei verwandten, von einander abhängigen Spruchüberlieferungen rechnen'; Schlatter, *Matthäus*, p 198, 'Die Ableitung des von Matthäus gegeben Textes aus Lukas oder aus einem beiden bekannten Vorgänger scheitert . . . an der selbständigen sprachlichen Fassung der einzelnen Sätze . . .'

91 Schulz (*Q*, p 121) appears to think simply in terms of a common document Q that Mt and Lk used when dealing with the material on enemy love. So also Grundmann, *Lukas*, pp 139f.

92 This will become clear in the individual analyses below.

93 Those who postulate different forms of Q behind Mt and Lk in our context include: Lührmann, *ZThK* 69, pp 415ff, 420; Neuhäusler, *Anspruch*, p 45; Knox, *Sources* II, p 34; Glover, *NTS* 5, p 14; Beare, *Records*, p 60.

94 I do not think Schlatter's remarks are too old-fashioned to be useful here: 'Von Vermutungen hielt ich mich möglichst frei und verzichtete darum auch auf die Widerlegung von solchen. Ich halte dieses nicht für ein fruchtbares Geschäft. Denn Konjekturen werden nicht dadurch widerlegt, dass man andere macht. Sie versinken dann, wenn eingesehen ist, dass die Beobachtung fruchtbarer ist als die Konjektur . . . Ich heisse "Wissenschaft" die Beobachtung des Vorhandenen, nicht den Versuch, sich vorzustellen, was nicht sichtbar ist. Vielleicht entsteht daraus eine Einrede gegen den Wert einer solchen Darstellung, da die ratende Vermutung anrege und unterhalte, während die Beobachtung eine schwierige, harte Arbeit sei. Richtig ist freilich, dass Spiel leichter als Arbeit ist. Das Evangelium ist aber missverstanden, wenn aus ihm ein Spielzeug wird" (*Matthäus*, p xi).

95 Bultmann, *History*, pp 134ff; Schürmann, *Lukasevangelium*, p 346; Goppelt, *Christologie*, p 29; Flender, *Botschaft*, p 61, note 165; Lohse, 'Ich aber sage euch,' p 189. More thoroughly on the issue of the antitheses is R. Guelich, *NTS* 22/4, pp 444–57. He concludes that 'The third, fifth and sixth Antitheses were redactional, that the fourth Antithesis was traditional,

and that at least the antitheses of the first and second Antitheses were traditional' (p 455).

96 Jeremias, *Theology*, pp 251ff.

97 Bultmann, *History*, p 135.

98 The imperatives of vv 24f, 29f, 37, and 39f are not reckoned as part of the basic antithetical formulations.

99 I am not sure why Jeremias concludes 'in the first, fourth and sixth antitheses the O.T. quotation has been expanded by an addition' (*Theology*, p 253). The fourth antithesis does not add a non-Old Testament phrase as do the first and sixth. It is made up entirely of Old Testament material. Cf Num 30:2f; Dt 23:22f; Ps 50:14.

100 With regard to form, one other observation may be made. One might think that the third antithesis (5:31f) is molded on the pattern of the first two since the antithetical half of each is strikingly similar: ἐγὼ δὲ λέγω ὑμῖν ὅτι πᾶς ὁ plus participle. But precisely at this point where the antithetical halves are almost identical, the thesis halves reveal the strongest differences (5:31 is reduced to the mere Ἐρρέθη δὲ). Why?

101 Bultmann, *History*, pp 135f.

102 Bultmann cites Dobschütz (*ZNW* 27, p 342) who in fact does conclude that Mt 5:21f and 27f are the only original formulations (*History*, p 136).

103 The first (5:21f) has a non-Old Testament addition upon which the antithesis is based; the second (5:27f) has no addition to the Old Testament quote. The point of the second is that the lustful glance *is* adultery; the point of the first is not that anger *is* murder, but that both are equally liable to judgement.

104 Lührmann, *ZThK* 69, p 413. He uses this, however, as part of his argument that *none* of the antitheses is original.

105 Bultmann, *History*, p 135; Goppelt, *Christologie*, pp 28f. Jack Suggs (*Wisdom*, p 110) calls this standard argument into question.

106 Jeremias, *Theology*, p 252.

107 Hoffmann, *BL* 10, p 265: 'Erst Mt fasste nämlich mit dem Leitwort, "Widersteht nicht dem Bösen" die Spruchreihe 5:39b–42 zusammen.' He argues that 5:42, however, 'hat mit dem Widerstand dem Bösen gegenüber nichts zu tun.' Moreover 'diese matthäische Regel erfasst die Intention Jesu nur zum geringen Teil' (p 268). It is not clear to me, however, why the discrepancy between 5:42 and 5:39a is not an argument against Mt's creation of this 'title' for surely he could have created something more suitable, or simply left it out.

108 To argue that the command circulated in another context from which Mt took it is to prefer speculation from silence to the data we have.

109 Nor does πονηρός ever appear as that which is to be tolerated; it is always to be hated (Rom 12:9); driven out (I Cor 5:13); abstained from (I Thess 5:22); overcome (I Jn 2:13f). This pervasive attitude toward πονηρός in the New Testament makes it even less likely that the command 'Do not resist πονηρῷ' was invented by Mt.

110 So Percy, *Botschaft*, pp 148ff; T. W. Manson, *Sayings*, p 159; H. Hübner, *Gesetz*, p 231. That the form ἠκούσατε ὅτι ἐρρέθη – ἐγὼ δὲ λέγω ὑμῖν goes back to Jesus is not to be doubted 'because this has neither Jewish nor early Christian parallels' (Jeremias, *Theology*, p 251). The attempts of Morton Smith (*Tannaitic Parallels*, pp 27–30) and David Daube *Rabbinic Judaism*,

pp 56–60) to explain the antithetical form as a copy of rabbinic forms are criticized effectively by Jack Suggs (*Wisdom*, pp 112f).

111   The difficulty of ever gaining a consensus on this issue is stated clearly by Trilling, *Christusverkündigung*, p 102: 'Die Fragen werden heute unterschiedlich beurteilt, und eine Einigung ist wohl kaum zu erwarten.'

112   For the sake of convenience I will designate the form of Q which Lk used as Q-l and the form which Mt used as Q-m. For our purposes here it is not important to distinguish Matthean redaction from that of Q-m or Lukan redaction from that of Q-l.

113   Only the broad outlines of the redactional possibilities are discussed here. See under 'Analysis of the Individual Sayings' (pp 56ff) for the detailed redactional considerations.

114   So Bultmann (*History*, p 96) argues that, because of Lk's reordering of the sayings, he had to add v 35a in order to make the promise of v 35b depend on loving one's enemies.

115   This is essentially the reconstruction Schürmann (*Lukasevangelium*, p 358) suggests.

116   Percy, *Botschaft*, p 149: 'Vor allem ist zu beachten, dass schon die Mahnung, seine Feinde zu lieben, in Lk 6:27 wegen seines paradoxen allen üblichen Auffassungen widerstreitenden Charakters als Hintergrund den Gedanken der gegenseitigen Liebe der Freunde und Gesinnungsgenossen zu fordern scheint, es ist deshalb bezeichnend, dass dieses Gebot bei seiner Wiederholung in Lk 6:35, als Antithese zu dem in v 32–34 geschilderten unter den Menschen üblichen Verhalten dargestellt wird; nur hätte dies schon bei v 27 geschehen sollen.'

117   Jeremias, *Theology*, p 252; Gaechter, *Matthäus*, p 169. Seitz (*NTS* 16, pp 42, 45) claims that both Lk 6:27 and Mt 5:44 stem from a synagogue setting on a Sabbath immediately following the reading of the Torah, namely Lev 19:18. Jesus said to those who had been listening to the Torah: 'But to you who give heed (to this command, Love your neighbor) I am now saying (that it means also) Love your enemies.' Against this argument, however, is the present tense of ἀκούουσιν in Lk 6:27 and the fact that Lk 6:27 does not stress the contrast between *Jesus'* words and some other words, but rather it stresses the contrast between *you* who hear (emphatic position of ὑμῖν and absence of ἐγώ) and those who don't hear. Hasler (*AMĒN*, p 59) and Schulz (*Q*, p 127) see the forms in Mt and Lk both as redactional variations of the λέγω δὲ ὑμῖν of Q.

118   Lührmann, *ZThK* 69, p 415. The discrepancy between Mt 5:11 (διώκειν) and Lk 6:22 (μίσεω) is taken up again in Mt 5:44 and Lk 6:27. The 'peacemakers' of Mt 5:9a are those who obey the love command of Mt 5:44 because εἰρήνη is the opposite of ἔχθρα. Ἐλεήμονες of Mt 5:7 corresponds to οἰκτίρμων of Lk 6:36. Schürmann, *Lukasevangelium*, p 346: 'Das μίσεω von Lk 6:22a wird v 27 wieder aufgenommen; das καταρᾶσθαι und ἐπηρεάζειν v 28b führt inhaltlich das ὀνειδίζειν und ἐκβάλλειν τὸ ὄνομα von v 22b fort. Auch μισθός v 22b und Mt 5:46 könnte ein ursprünglich näheres Beisammen dieser Verse verraten.'

119   Lührmann, *ZThK* 69, p 415.

120   R. Guelich (*NTS* 22/4, p 449) favors this second set of arguments: 'It would seem more reasonable that each [i.e. Mt and Lk] used a common, composite

tradition and that Matthew separated the two units.' But his argument at the
bottom of p 449 which makes this 'seem unavoidable' is in my judgment too
imaginary to be persuasive.

121   Besides those listed in note 110, see also Davies, *Setting*, p 431.

122   H. Hübner (*Gesetz*, p 235) concludes his discussion of the antitheses saying,
'dass sich in der *antithetischen Form* von Mt 5 die *antithetische Verkündigung
Jesu widerspiegelt.*' R. Banks (*Jesus and the Law*, p 186), who thinks it is
'questionable whether the antithetical character of these particular sayings
goes back to Jesus himself,' insists that the Matthean form 'condensed the
impression which the teaching and attitude of Jesus conveyed, and that
formally it was not altogether without foundation in the manner in which
his own message was at times presented.'

123   Compare Mt's peculiar use of διώκειν in 5:10,11,12; 10:23. The word is
especially suited to the experience of the early church (Rom 12:14; I Cor
4:12; II Cor 4:9; Gal 5:11; 6:12; II Tim 3:12; Rev 12:13), although it
occurs nowhere in the paraenesis in connection with prayer as it does here.
According to Schulz (*Q*, p 128) Mt replaced ἐπηρεαζόντων since Lk doesn't
avoid διώκειν (cf Lk 21:12/Mt 24:17) but Lk replaced ὑπέρ with his more
frequent περί.

124   Bultmann, *History*, p 79.

125   Seitz, *NTS* 16, p 52.

126   Lührmann (*ZThK* 69, p 416) reasons like this: Lk's command to 'do good
to those who hate you' (6:27b) can be constructed from the words in
6:22,26 and his command to 'bless those who curse you' (6:28a) has a
parallel in Rom 12:14 which shows 'that Paul knew these lines as a free
saying.' These reasons do not seem to me to be convincing.

127   The reason for rejecting Mt 5:44b is this: the rhetorical questions (Mt 5:46f)
could never have stood alone but were attached from the time of their formation to the command of Mt 5:44. But the only correspondence between
the rhetorical questions and the commands is the reference to love. 'Das
lässt den Schluss zu, dass sie zu einer Fassung des Gebotes hinzutraten, die
nur die erste Zeile "Liebet eure Feinde!" enthielt' (Lührmann, *ZThK* 69,
pp 425f). Against this argument we can set Schürmann's (*Lukasevangelium*,
p 354) sharp observation that Mt's ἀσπάσησθε (5:47) may well be a
'Gräzisierung' of Lk's εὐλογεῖτε (6:28a) which has been dropped by Mt in
5:44 and which would then be original.

128   Schulz, *Q*, p 130.

129   Nor does Jesus ever at any time explicitly qualify this command and call for
hate or revenge. See further on love of enemies Mt 18:21; Lk 10:29–37;
14:12–14 (23:34).

130   Schmauch (*Matthäus*, p 146) goes too far when he says, 'Hier zum ersten
Male in der Geschichte des Gebetes wird eine Fürbitte gefordert für Menschen,
die den Beter deshalb angehen, weil auch sie Menschen, von Gott geschaffen
sind.' Becker (*Zwölf*, p 391) observes that 'Joseph bittet Testament Benjamin
3:6 seinen Vater, auch bei Gott um Vergebung für die feindlichen Bruder
einzutreten.' In Ps 109:4,5 we read: 'In return for my love they accuse me,
even *as I make prayer* for them. So they reward me evil for good, and
hatred for my love.'

131   In I Tim 2:1 prayers are to be made for *all* men. The two well-known

examples of prayer for one's enemies are Jesus' prayer on the cross (Lk 23:
34, but a textual problem here) and Stephen's prayer while being stoned
(Acts 7:60).

132 ἀγαθὸν ποιεῖν (or ἀγαθοποιεῖν) occurs in Rom 13:3; Eph 6:8; I Pt 2:14,
15,20; 3:6,16,17; 4:19; III Jn 11. Two variations which *do* have (prepositional)
objects are ἐργαζώμεθα τὸ ἀγαθόν (Gal 6:10; cf Rom 2:10) and τὸ
ἀγαθὸν διώκετε (I Thess 5:15).

133 So Barrett, *Romans*, p 241; Althaus, *Römer*, p 116; Cranfield, *Rom 12-13*,
p 49; Dodd, *Romans*, p 200; Ridderbos, *Jesus*, p 50; Schmidt, *Römer*, p 214.

134 Lührmann, *ZThK* 16, p 417; T. W. Manson, *Sayings*, p 159. It might be
questioned, though, whether the nature of the case (striking on the cheek)
might not demand the singular form even in a context where the plural is
dominant.

135 Although, as Schürmann (*Lukasevangelium*, p 348) points out, Lk did not
have to omit Mt 5:41 for the sake of his readers (cf only Lk 23:26), there
is nevertheless reason to think that he did so: (1) he (or Q-1) shows a tendency to eliminate legal technicalities (see below); (2) the poetic form of
vv 29,30 allows no place for Mt 5:41.

136 So Rengstorf, *Lukas*, p 90; Jeremias, *Theology*, p 239; Schulz, *Q*, p 122
(who, however, assigns Mt 5:41 to Mt's redaction). Grundmann (*Matthäus*,
p 170) and Gaechter (*Matthäus*, p 188) consider Lk's simpler form to be
original. With regard to the discrepancy between Mt 5:42b δανίσασθαι and
Lk 6:30b αἴροντος, Mt is probably more original because: (1) the occurrence
of δανείζω in Lk 6:34,35 seems to indicate Lk read Mt's form of
5:42b; (2) ἀπὸ τοῦ αἴροντος provides a formal parallel with 6:29b
and smoothes the contrast between the content of 6:29 and 30. So Lührmann,
ZThK 16, p 418, and Schürmann, *Lukasevangelium*, p 349.

137 T. W. Manson, *Sayings*, p 50; Taylor, *Formation*, p 96, appealing to B. S.
Easton's *Christ in the Gospels*, 1930; Grundmann, *Lukas*, p 146. For the
translation into Aramaic see C. F. Burney, *Poetry*, p 169.

138 In Mt 5:39b,41 the sentences begin with ὅστις and are each followed by a
positive imperative. Alternating with these two commands are the two
dative participles (5:40, 42a) followed by positive aorist imperatives. As an
example of Semitic influence Schlatter points to the redundancy of αὐτῷ
after τῷ θέλοντι in 5:40: But against the primacy of Mt's poetic form
Schulz (*Q*, p 121) shows the Matthean character of ὅστις (with 5:39,40
compare 12:50; 13:12; 19:29; 21:33; 23:12; 27:55).

139 Lührmann, *ZThK* 16, p 418: 'Wie die Q Fassung inhaltlich ausgesehen
hat lässt sich also für Lk 6:29/Mt 5:39b,40 nicht mehr ausmachen.'

140 Mt 5:42/Lk 6:30 may not originally have belonged to the preceding
verses since they do not deal directly with the disciple's response to force
used against him. There seems to be no reason to doubt the original unity
of Mt 5:39b-41/Lk 6:29.

141 Dodd, *Gospel*, p 52. He compares Mt 5:39-42 with the paraenesis in Rom
12 and concludes: 'The sayings in the Gospels have an incomparably
greater liveliness and pregnancy than the maxims in the catechesis . . .
These two sets of precepts are not conceived on the same level.' See also
Moule, *JTS* NS 3, pp 75-9, for examples in the epistles of 'unadorned'
versions of Jesus' picturesque sayings.

142 Bultmann, *History*, p 105; Braun, *Radikalismus* II, p 92, note 1: 'Um dieser andringlichen Radikalität willen wird man Mt 5:39b–41 unbedingt als für Jesus typisch bezeichnen und ihm selber zuschreiben müssen.'

143 Van Unnik, *NovTest* 8, p 299: 'In vs 32 und 33 ist das Subjekt ein Mensch der etwas empfängt und dann zurückgibt; hier ist es ein Mann, der selbst anfängt etwas zu geben in der Hoffnung etwas zurück zu bekommen.'

144 So Lührmann, *ZThK* 69, p 420. Schürmann (*Lukasevangelium*, p 354) uses the same evidence to draw precisely the opposite conclusion: since Lk did not find or did not preserve δανίσασθαι in Lk 6:30 he could *not* have introduced it in 6:34. This kind of contradiction between scholars reveals the haziness of the criteria by which such stylistic judgments are made.

145 According to Schulz (*Q*, p 129) ἀγαθοποιεῖν is secondary to ἀσπάζεσθαι and Lk accordingly replaces Mt's τοὺς ἀδελφοὺς ὑμῶν with τοὺς ἀγαθοποι-οῦντας ὑμᾶς. That ἀσπάσησθε belongs to Mt's redaction is doubtful because he takes over neither of Mk's two instances of ἀσπάζεσθαι (Mk 9:15; 15:18).

146 So Neuhäusler, *Anspruch*, p 46; Lührmann, *ZThK* 16, p 420; Schulz, *Q*, p 129, who gives three reasons: (1) χάρις occurs 8 times in Lk's *Sondergut* and 17 in Acts; (2) ποία is redactional in 5:19; (3) εἶναι with the dative is expressly Lukan. However, on the other side it must be mentioned that: (1) χάρις *in this sense* is used only once in all of Lk–Acts (Lk 17:9); (2) Lk did not eliminate μισθός because he wants to avoid it (see μισθός 6:35b which is probably redactional); (3) χάρις in this kind of context already has an anchor in the early Christian paraenetic tradition before Lk (cf I Pt 2:19f).

147 Grundmann, *Matthäus*, p 179, note 146; Schmauch, *Matthäus*, p 148; Wrege, *Bergpredigt*, p 89: 'Ursprünglich steht χάρις in diesem Zusammenhang durchaus nicht im Gegensatz zu μισθός: vielmehr bedeutet sie zunächst das gleiche, nämlich "geschuldeter Dank", "Belohnung".' This sense is current not only in Christian and Jewish literature (I Tim 1:12; II Tim 1:3; Heb 12:28; Sirach 12:1; Wisdom 3:14; Ignatius to Polycarp 2:1), but also, as van Unnik (*NovTest* 8, pp 295f) shows, in Greek ethics.

148 Lk does not avoid taking over from Q a similar use of ἔθνη in 12:30; nor does he avoid the use of τελῶναι as a parallel with ἁμαρτωλοί (5:30; 7:34; 15:1). Thus the taking over of τελῶναι and ἐθνικοί in the present context would not have contradicted Lk's usage.

149 According to Lk's own usage, ἁμαρτωλός can mean the class of people outside Israel who do not give strict attention to the law. Wrege, *Bergpredigt*, p 91: 'Der Sünder ist hier also der Gottlose, der die Weisung Gottes ("Gesetz") nicht kennt oder anerkennt.'

150 Cf Mt's use of περισσεύειν: Mt 13:12/Mk 4:25; Mt 25:29/Lk 19:26; Mt 14:20/Mk 6:43. Wrege, *Bergpredigt*, p 90.

151 Lührmann, *ZThK* 69, p 426.

152 Cf only Mk 2:17 par. Schlatter, *Matthäus*, p 194: 'Der sittliche Unterschied zwischen den Menschen: ἀγαθοί und πονηροί, δίκαιοι und ἄδικοι ... bleibt bejaht. Das ist das feste Band der Einheit, das Jesus mit dem Pharisäer verband.'

153 The word ἐθνικός occurs only four other times in the New Testament: Mt 6:7; 18:17; III Jn 7; Gal 2:14 (ἐθνικῶς). 'There is no question here of national distinction, but of the inner mark of a representative of the ἔθνη,' *TDNT* II, p 372.

154   N. Perrin (*Rediscovering*, p 148) concludes concerning these verses and their
        immediate context (Mt 5:44–48), 'That Jesus challenged his followers in
        these terms is not to be doubted, indeed is never doubted' [sic].

155   See Mt 5:12/Lk 6:23; Mt 6:33; Mk 10:30/Mt 19:29/Lk 18:30; Mt 25:31–
        46; Lk 20:28.

156   So Schmauch, *Matthäus*, p 149: The reward is 'einzugehen in das Himmel-
        reich.' Schniewind, *Matthäus*, p 73: 'Der Lohn besteht einfach darin, dass
        Gott uns bei seinen ewigen Gericht annimmt (Mt 25:34ff; 20:8ff), da zeigt es
        sich, dass es sich gelohnt hat, Gott zu folgen.'

157   See discussion of this parable on p 84.

158   Kümmel, *Theologie*, p 49: 'Hier ist ganz deutlich *die Erfahrung der* Liebe
        Gottes in der Begegnung mit Jesus die Voraussetzung und Ermöglichung
        des Gehorsams gegen die durch Jesus verkündete Forderung Gottes.'

159   Similarly Jeremias, *Theology*, p 217: 'Experience of the boundless goodness
        of God, his unwearying patience with the wicked and unrighteous is the
        source from which love of one's enemies flows.' Also Goppelt, *Christologie*,
        p 39: The Sermon on the Mount 'wird realisierbar, wenn Gott, wie Matthäus
        besonders betont, für die Menschen zum Vater wird . . .' The reciprocity
        characterizing the commands of Lk 6:37f must also be seen from this
        vantage point.

160   The non-Pauline character of 'Kingdom of God', plus the phrase that the
        warnings had been given before, plus the περὶ πάντων τούτων in I Thess
        4:6 when only *one* thing is being considered, indicate that such a warning
        was probably a common part of the tradition and not merely a thought of
        Paul. So Schlier, *Galater*, p 255. Other warnings: Rom 8:4–7; 11:22; Eph
        5:5; Heb 13:4; Rev 21:7,8.

161   The redactional ὅτι at the beginning of I Pt 3:12 shows that the author intends
        for the favor and disfavor of the Lord to motivate 'doing good' and 'seeking
        peace'. See the discussion of this text below, pp 123f.

162   That either Mt's γένησθε or Lk's ἔσεσθε is redactional is doubtful since the
        discrepancy between the two is exactly reversed in Mt 5:48/Lk 6:36. Schulz
        (*Q*, p 128) thinks Lk's καὶ ἔσεσθε is secondary, being patterned on the
        preceding καὶ ἔσται. The scales may be tipped in favor of the originality of
        Mt's πατρός since ὕψιστος as a divine proper name is peculiar to Lk in the
        New Testament (Lk 1:32,35,76; 6:35; Acts 7:48) and πατρός fits the idea
        of sonship better. However, Lührmann (*ZThK* 69, p 421) is justifiably
        cautious: 'Die Gottesprädikationen sind bei beiden Evangelisten als redak-
        tionell verdächtig, so dass ein Rückschluss auf die Q-Formulierung hier
        nicht möglich ist.'

163   Schulz, *Q*, p 128. Lührmann, *ZThK* 69, p 421.

164   The Rabbis spoke often of the obligation of sons to act like the Lord. Qid
        36a Bar: 'You are sons of the Lord your God (Dt 14:1). When you behave
        like children, you will be called children. But when you do not behave like
        children you will not be called children. Those are the words of R. Jehuda
        (around A.D. 150). R. Meir (around A.D. 150) said: in either case you will
        be called children.' Cf Strack–Billerbeck I, pp 371–6.

165   See p 21 above for a discussion of this quote in its context.

166   Bultmann (*Jesus*, p 111) leaves the question of authenticity open: 'One
        can scarcely still determine whether and how Jesus used such words.'

167 Compare L. Goppelt, *Christologie*, p 212: 'Jesu Begründung ist weder ein rationaler Schluss aus der Naturbeobachtung noch ein Ausdruck schlichter "Volksfrömmigkeit" sondern der Reflex seines eschatologischen Heilswirkens: Jesu schenkt den "Sündern" vor den Gerechten seine helfende Gemeinschaft (Mk 2:17; Mt 11:19; 21:28–31; Lk 15).'

168 Cf also I Jn 3:1–3; 4:7–9; and I Pt 1:15.

169 Schürmann's objection (*Lukasevangelium*, p 357) that Lk 6:36 is not the close of 6:27ff, 'da es darin nicht um "Barmherzigkeit" sondern um Feindes-liebe ging,' seems overplayed, since it is surely as merciful to love one's enemies as it is not to judge (Lk 6:37). Lk 6:35 has just said in effect: You become sons if you act like God. It is very natural then to close with a command of divine imitation.

170 Mt's command is harder and thus less likely to have been secondarily con-structed. Bultmann, *Jesus*, pp 83f: 'Probably the first wording is older and Luke changed it in order to make a connection with the following words.' M. Black (*Aramaic Approach*, p 181) sees behind τέλειος the Semitic sh^{e}lim which creates a word play with the Semitic greeting sh^{e}lam in Mt 5:47. This word play would certify not only the originality of Mt's form but also its connection to the preceding unit. He refers also to the Pseudo Jonathan Targum of Lev 22:28, 'as your Father is merciful (raḥam) in heaven, so be ye merciful on earth,' and claims that under the influence of this Targumic saying Mt's original form was altered. Jeremias (*Theology*, p 212) refers to the same parallel and draws the opposite conclusion, that it confirms the originality of Lk's form. Beare (*Records*, p 60) argues that Lk changed Mt's τέλειος because his gentile readers would not have under-stood its original Semitic meaning.

171 So Schulz, *Q*, p 130. Lührmann (*ZThK* 69, p 421) makes an observation similar to Bultmann's (preceding note) but draws the opposite conclusion: 'Lk 6:36 ist bei Lk die Überleitung zu 6:37ff während Mt 5:48 als Abschlusswendung fungiert, also einer erst von Mt geschaffener Einheit, weshalb Lk 6:36 vermutlich der Q Fassung entspricht.'

172 Such direction was not superfluous in Jesus' environment as Sirach 12:1–6 shows. We read the commandments:

δὸς τῷ εὐσεβεῖ καὶ μὴ ἀντιλάβῃ τοῦ ἁμαρτωλοῦ
εὖ ποιήσον ταπεινῷ καὶ μὴ δῶς ἀσεβεῖ
ὅτι καὶ ὁ ὕψιστος ἐμίσησεν ἁμαρτωλοὺς
καὶ τοῖς ἀσεβέσω ἀποδώσει ἐκδίκησω.

Jesus turns the tables completely: he reverses both the commands and the ground. This is a terrible abuse of the concept of imitation which Jesus rejects as does the church after him (Rom 12:19, μὴ ἑαυτοὺς ἐκδικοῦντες). The underlined words form remarkable parallels with the synoptic material in Mt 5:42–48/Lk 6:27–36.

173 The additional Old Testament material used in the paraenetic tradition to elucidate the command of enemy love (see Rom 12:19,20; I Pt 3:9–12) will be discussed in Chapter 4.

174 It is no argument against this being a saying of Jesus to say that Jesus is not *explicitly* cited as in I Cor 9:14 and 7:10 and that the wording is only approximate. For, as Selby (*Paul*, p 306) points out, the wording precisely in these two texts is less close to their synoptic parallels (Mt 10:10; Mk 10:11f)

than the wording in Rom 12:14 is to Lk 6:28. For a suggested explanation why the words of Jesus are cited explicitly in I Cor, See Goppelt, 'Haustafel,' pp 103f.

175 Selwyn (*I Peter*, p 176) says I Pt 2:19f 'is surely dependent on the verba Christi.' Van Unnik's (*NovTest* 8, p 296) objection is not convincing.

176 William Klassen, following Hans Haas (*Idee und Ideal der Feindesliebe*), rightly rejects the idea that enemy love distinguishes Jesus' teachings as unique: 'This study by Hans Haas (1927) gives such a plethora of evidence in refutation of that claim, that the focus of any comparative study must now be on the motivation, the scope, and the grounding of this commandment, rather than any supposition that the imperative "love your enemy" is unique to Christianity' ('Love Your Enemy,' p 156).

177 A more detailed discussion of what this peculiar character is and whether the early Christian paraenesis was faithful to it appears in the following two chapters.

178 Without intending to equate the views of the following scholars we may nevertheless cite them as representative of those who see the teaching of the historical Jesus playing a major role in shaping the paraenesis of the early church: Feine, *Paulus*, pp 319, 328ff; *Jesus Christus*, p 69; Juncker, *Ethik* I, p 192; Moe, *Paulus*, p 131; Scott, *Christianity*, p 14; Schniewind, 'Botschaft,' pp 22–35; C. H. Dodd, 'Ennomos' p 107; *History*, p 65; Davies, *Paul*, p 140; Hunter, *Predecessors*, pp 11f, 49; Goppelt, *KuD* 4, p 224; Selby, *Paul*, p 298; Fannon, *Scripture* 16, p 55; Ridderbos, *Paulus*, p 194; Dungan, *Sayings*, p 149; *Interpretation* 28/1, pp 98–101; B. Fjärstedt, *Synoptic Tradition*, pp 35, 173; J. W. Fraser, *Jesus and Paul*, pp 90–9.

179 We shall discuss this problem further in Chapter 5. Here we may simply list some of those who have come to a different conclusion: Schweitzer, *Paul*, pp 42f; Weiss, *Urchristentum*, pp 431f; Heitmüller, 'Paulus und Jesus,' p 130; Bultmann, *Theology* I, pp 35, 43, 188; 'Bedeutung' pp 188ff; Schoeps, *Paul* p 57; Wilckens, *ThLZ* 89, p 519; Schrage, *Einzelgebote*, pp 239ff; Schmithals, *ZNW* 53, p 142; Neuhäusler, *LZ* 1/2, p 106; Boman, *Jesus-Überlieferung*, pp 66ff; Flender, *Botschaft*, pp 75, 90; Bornkamm, *Paulus*, p 122; Kuhn, *ZThK* 67, p 320.

Chapter 3. Jesus' Command of Enemy Love in the Larger Context of his Message

1 Jeremias, *Theology*, p 37. See also R. T. France, *Jesus and the OT*, p 22.

2 Perrin, *Rediscovering*, p 39.

3 A. Schlatter, 'Theology of the NT and Dogmatics,' p 138. Schlatter makes a good case for the belief that the historical task is not complete until the interrelations and connections of Jesus' various statements are found. 'We fail to do them justice if we simply note each one separately . . . Jesus will be comprehensible to us in proportion as these connections are perceived.'

4 Machoveč, *Jesus*, pp 129f. Similarly T. W. Manson, *Teaching*, p 286: 'To divorce the moral teaching of Jesus from his teaching as a whole is thus to make it practically useless; it is also to make it theoretically unintelligible.'

5 Thus this section is *not* a *Forschungsbericht*. The wider spectrum of the literature will be cited in the notes in the course of the chapter.

6 Perhaps with the exception of Lührmann whose article is not primarily a theological statement.

7 Until 1970 Machoveč was Professor of Philosophy in the Karls University in Prague.

8 I am not implying that all of our presuppositions are the same: Machoveč starts as an atheist, I do not. The important point of agreement is the conviction that all interpretations of Jesus' love command are arbitrary when 'they are torn out of the context of the synoptic tradition.'

9 Machoveč, *Jesus,* p 96. The page numbers in the text refer to this book.

10 Braun, *Jesus,* p 54. The page numbers in the text refer to this book.

11 'Jesus does not see God as one before whom you can deserve something but rather as the process in which the evil and hopeless man receives a future and a hope' (p 170).

12 'God is not the ground of this self-acceptance; he is rather the event which is here coming to pass' (p 169). '*God* shows mercy in that *men* assume the role of the physician who is there for those who are sick' (p 167).

13 Niederwimmer, *Jesus,* p 58. The page numbers in the text refer to this book.

14 Lührmann, 'Liebet eure Feinde,' *ZThK* 69, p 412, footnote 1.

15 Lührmann, *ZThK* 69, p 438. It is not clear to me whether this conclusion stems from an inadequate textual basis for exegesis ('Wir haben offenbar geformte Spitzensätze vor uns, deren Kontext im Reden Jesu nicht mitüberliefert ist,' p 432), or from a modern view of meaning as open-ended ('es [das Liebesgebot] bleibt frei und geht nicht auf in seiner Inter-pretation,' p 438).

16 Bultmann, *Theology* I, p 2. The page numbers in the text refer to this book.

17 On this matter there is no essential difference between Bultmann and his student Günther Bornkamm, who asserts with a bit more color: 'The claims of Jesus carry in themselves "the last things" without having to borrow validity and urgency from the blaze of the fire in apocalyptic scenes. They themselves lead to the boundaries of the world but do not paint a picture of its end' (*Jesus,* p 109).

18 Bultmann, *Jesus,* p 38.

19 Bultmann, *Jesus,* p 38. So also Bornkamm (*Jesus,* p 108): 'Jesus' message of the Kingdom of Heaven and his preaching of the will of God become completely one. Both show forth the pure and unveiled will of God. Both witness to his reign and both are the judgments upon a life which exists solely on an earthly diet and its supposed realities and standards.'

20 Similarly Schnackenburg, *Gottes Herrschaft,* p 72: 'Die sittliche Haltung die Jesus verlangt . . . lässt sich nur im Zusammenhang einer Basileia Botschaft begreifen.' So also Batdorf, *JBR* 27, p 216.

21 Goppelt, *Christologie,* p 36.

22 On Jesus' use of the concept of reward see chiefly Pesch, *Lohngedanke* (literature, pp 147ff); also Michel, *ZSTh* 9, pp 47–54; Bornkamm, 'Lohngedanke.'

23 Ridderbos (*Kingdom,* p 250) denies that this conditional element is here and sees good works *only* as a manifestation of sonship. Our interpretation has the advantage of taking seriously the ὅπως γένησθε while not ruling out Ridderbos' theological concern, as will be shown below.

24 This assertation is not at first glance obvious for it seems to wed a Jewish

wisdom saying (Mt 5:45, see Chapter 2, note 164) to the eschatological message of Jesus – a marriage not without problems. Hans Windisch (*Bergpredigt,* pp 5–24) has stressed the distinction between Jesus' 'Weisheitslehre' and his 'eschatologische Heils- und Gerichtsverkündigung' and cautioned against sacrificing the one to the other or seeking a modernizing synthesis. More recently Heinz Schürmann ('Liebesdienst,' p 219) has warned against sacrificing the 'theologische' to the 'eschatologischer Motivation' in Jesus' ethical demands: 'Without doubt both series of sayings interpenetrate each other; the message of the nearing Kingdom and the revelation of God as Lord and Father . . . Nevertheless one must resist the attempt to dissolve this lively tension in favor of one series or the other.' We may note first that the seeking of a synthesis here need not be 'modern' for Mt surely sought one when he sandwiched the promise of sonship (which in 5:45 is part of a wisdom saying) between two eschatological promises of the Kingdom of God (Mt 5:9 between 3 and 10). That this synthesis was essentially present in Jesus' preaching need not be doubted: it is 'our Father in heaven' who sends the rain, feeds the birds, answers prayer, to whom we pray 'Thy Kingdom come.' God does not cease to be the gracious sovereign over creation and history just because the consummation of his Kingdom is yet future. Jesus' 'theocentric' and 'eschatological' ethics find a synthesis in the fact that it is precisely the heavenly Father whose Kingdom is coming, indeed has come. The 'Gegenwartseschatologie' is nothing less than 'the finger of God' (Lk 11:20): Jesus' eschatology is theocentric (which poses the christological question most sharply; cf. Lk 17:21). It is thus unthinkable that one's relation to the God of creation (Mt 5:45) as son is not essentially connected to one's entrance into or rejection from *his* Kingdom.

25   O. Bayer (*EvTh* 35/4, p 313), commenting on Mt 5:44f, equates the two: 'Aus Teilhabern jener Welt, die als Bruderliebe durch Feindeshass besteht, sollen sie zu "Söhnen des himmleschen Vaters" werden, d.h. zur nahen und Vertrauen schaffenden Herrschaft Gottes gehören.'

26   I do not mean that Mt offers the original *form* of the beatitudes. I mean rather that his conscious enclosure of 5:4–9 between two promises of the Kingdom of heaven (5:3,10) is an interpretation of the meaning of the Kingdom which corresponds essentially to Jesus' intention. Cf Goppelt, *TDNT* VI, p 18; Schniewind, *Matthäus,* pp 41, 49.

27   So Schmauch, *Matthäus,* p 149; Schniewind, *Matthäus,* p 73. See Chapter 2, note 156.

28   L. Goppelt, *Christologie,* p 49. We are not to think this principle or reward foreign to Jesus, for it appears throughout the synoptics; nor should we think that it contradicts the sovereign prevenient work of God in salvation. Schürmann ('Liebesdienst,' p 211) cites the following texts as representatives of this principle in Jesus' message for the motivation of loving service: Mt 5:7,23f;6:14f;18:35;25:40,45;Mk 9:35;10:21;11:25;Lk 6:37;12:33, 57ff;16:1–8. Against Braun's rejection of this principle in Jesus' message he says (p 225, note 32), 'Dass die Bindung des göttlichen Vergebens an das menschliche Vergeben spätjudisch und für Jesus "untypisch" sei (H. Braun, *Radicalismus,* II, p 87, Anm. 4), kann angesichts der angeführten Stellen nur ein Vorurteil behaupten.' Cf also Kümmel, *Theologie,* p 41.

29 Schniewind, *Markus*, p 134.

30 Lohmeyer (*Markus*, p 213) rejects the suggestion that Mk 10:23–27 is a later formulation around a genuine saying of Jesus (Bultmann), and he argues for its unity with the preceding Mk 10:17–22. So also Taylor, *Mark*, p 430: 'The account of the conversation 10:23–27 is not an independent narrative. There can be little doubt that the story rests on authentic tradition, ultimately that of an eyewitness, for it is lifelike and contains teaching on wealth that transcends that of Judaism.'

31 Lohmeyer, *Markus*, pp 214f: 'Der Fall des Reichen ist also nur besonders schwierig, aber grundsätzlich besteht für alle eine ähnliche Schwierigkeit . . . Das Wort "gerettet werden" meint ohne Zweifel das Gleiche wie das "Eingehen in das Gottesreich".' Likewise on both points Schniewind, *Markus*, pp 134f.

32 Bultmann (*History*, p 163) calls the authenticity of this saying into question – but without reason. That the long list of relatives in Lk 14:26 is an expansion of a shorter list may be granted. But that this severe saying (*hate* father and mother) should be created by the church is unlikely. It fits in well with Jesus' radical call to discipleship. So Grundmann, *Lukas*, p 302. Mt's 'love less' (10:37) is a proper interpretation of 'hate' in this context, cf Michel, *TDNT* IV, p 690, note 24.

33 Lk 18:9–14 (the parable of the Pharisee and the tax collector) is unique to Lk. Its Palestinian origin is evident from the 'sprachlichem Charakter der Erzählung.' 'Kein anderes Gleichnis bei Lukas enthält so viele semitisierende Asyndeta wie dieses' (Grundmann, *Lukas*, p 349). Cf Jeremias, *Gleichnisse*, p 139; Black, *Aramaic Approach*, pp 59f. Mt 6:1ff belongs to the same sphere of thought: self-exaltation in religion separates one from God.

34 Against the stream of opinions that Mt 11:25–27/Lk 10:21,22 is a construction of the Hellenistic church, Manson (*Sayings*, p 79) says 'The passage is full of Semitic turns of phrase, and certainly Palestinian in origin. There is no good reason for doubting its authenticity.' Similarly Knox, *Hellenistic Elements*, p 7; Jeremias, *Theology*, pp 56–61. For our purpose it is only important that wisdom can be a stumbling block which separates a man from Jesus and God.

35 See discussion of this text on p 86.

36 Of Mk 8:35 Taylor (*Mark*, p 382) says, 'Few sayings of Jesus are so well attested as this, for the saying stood in Q (Lk 17:33/Mt 10:39) and is found also in Jn 12:25.' Cf Manson, *Sayings*, p 145.

37 This assertion rests less on specific sayings of Jesus than it does on the over-all tendency of his ministry. His call to repentance, his radical commands, his conflict with the religious leaders and consequent death all show that Jesus knew that men do not naturally love the Kingdom of God more than they love this world.

38 Schniewind (*Markus*, p 135) comments on Mk 10:17: 'Gott schafft die neue Welt, er schafft, in Jesu Wort, den neuen Menschen.' Pesch, *Lohngedanke*, p 129: 'Sogar die Umkehr selbst wäre ohne göttliche Hilfe nicht möglich, denn sie setzt ausser dem Bussruf auch die Hilfe Gottes voraus . . . Auch Umkehr und Glaube kommen von Gott her, sind Gnade.'

39 Büchsel, *Theologie*, p 30: 'Jesu Urteil über die Leistungsfähigkeit des Menschen ist also genau dasselbe wie die des Paulus und der kirchlichen

Erbsündenlehre, wenn Jesus auch dies Urteil nicht zu einer Lehre vom
Menschen (oder vom Gesetz) ausgebaut noch als solche vorgetragen hat.'
So Schlatter, *Jesus,* p 53.

40 Wendland, *Eschatologie,* p 130: 'Die Leistung ist, wie treffend gesagt
worden ist, nicht Voraussetzung, sondern Wirkung der Gabe Gottes.'
Soiron, *Bergpredigt,* p 465: The Sermon on the Mount sets conditions for
entering the Kingdom but also offers the confidence 'dass Gott selbst
durch seine Gnade diese Bedingungen zu schaffen bereit ist.' Similarly
Liechtenhahn, *Gebot,* p 37; Schnackenburg, *Gottes Herrschaft,* p 73;
Sittliche Botschaft, p 63; Grundmann, *Matthäus,* p 173; Percy, *Botschaft,*
p 115: 'Der Gott Jesu fordert alles, weil er zuerst selbst alles gibt.' Cf
Augustine, *Confessions,* p 197.

41 It is not crucial to our point whether, as Jeremias supposes (*Gleichnisse,*
p 192), these words were originally spoken to the opponents of Jesus or to
his disciples. The point remains the same: totally loyal service results in
no merit for the servant.

42 Even if this verse is a Matthean formulation (Grundmann, *Matthäus* p 140)
on the basis of 5:13-15, it is a formulation which is in line with other
sayings of Jesus: Mt 7:17 (good tree – good fruit); Mt 6:3 (seek no
glory from men); Mk 10:21,27 (God makes discipleship possible). The
saying in Mt 5:16 means 'dass niemand auf den Gedanken kommen kann,
diese Werke seien die eigenen Taten der Christen: sie sind vielmehr offen-
sichtlich nur von Gott gewirkt und weisen unmittelbar auf ihn als ihren
Ursprung' (Schniewind, *Matthäus,* p 52).

43 Percy, *Botschaft,* p 114: 'Das Primäre ist aber bei Jesus das Reich Gottes als
eine Gabe an die dafür Empfänglichen; erst die Annahme dieser Gabe
ermöglicht den Gehorsam gegen die Forderungen Gottes. *Allerdings wird dies
nicht ausdrücklich gesagt.'* So Ridderbos, *Kingdom,* pp 186,251.

44 Ladd, *Jesus,* p 294: 'The righteousness of the Kingdom can be experienced
only by the man who has submitted to the reign of God which has been
manifested in Jesus, and who has therefore experienced the *powers* of God's
Kingdom.' Wilder, *Eschatology and Ethics,* p 160: Jesus demands a righteousness which is 'the righteousness of those living in the days of the new covenant
and *empowered* and qualified by the reconciliation and redemption of that
age.' Similarly Wendland, *Ethik,* p 28; cf also Dibelius, *Jesus,* p 98 ('die jetzt
schon wirkenden Kräfte des Reiches').

45 The 'consistent eschatology' of A. Schweitzer (*Leidensgeheimnis; Leben-
Jesu Forschung*) and J. Weiss (*Reich Gottes*) excluded any present aspect
of the Kingdom of God from Jesus' preaching. Besides those who still hold
this kind of view (e.g., M. Werner, *Die Entstehung des christlichen Dogmas*),
those who interpret Jesus' message existentially also show their indebtedness
to consistent eschatology, for here the *eschaton* is consistently future but it
is existentially interpreted so as to confront man in the Now with the demand
for decision for God against the world. For such a view consult R. Bultmann,
Theology I, pp 13-32; E. Grässer, *Parusieverzögerung;* R. H. Fuller, *Mission
and Achievement,* pp 20-49; G. Bornkamm, *Jesus,* pp 82-7.

46 At the other end of the spectrum from the consistent eschatology is the
realized eschatology of C. H. Dodd (*Parables*) which can find no future
element in Jesus' preaching of the Kingdom (cf also E. Stauffer, *Jesus:*

Gestalt, pp 117–20). There has been however increasing recognition that the one-sidedness of both consistent and realized eschatology does not do justice to Jesus' preaching and work. Rather than excluding the expectation of a coming Kingdom, the presence of the Kingdom grounded it. 'In diesem hochgemüteten Wissen der Erfüllungszeit würzelt letztlich auch die "Naherwartung" das Wissen, dass Gott, der mit seinem letzten grossen Werk begonnen hat, dieses nun auch "bald" zu Ende führen wird' (Schürmann, 'Liebesdienst,' p 226, note 39). Others who recognize a tension of the already and not yet in Jesus' preaching of the Kingdom include G. Delling (*Zeitverständnis*); O. Cullmann (*Christ and Time*); R. Morgenthaler (*Kommendes Reich*); W. G. Kümmel (*Promise*); G. Ladd, *Jesus.*

47 Bultmann (*Theology* I, p 20) although he starts from a completely different standpoint, also says, 'Fulfilment of God's will is the condition for participation in the salvation of his reign' (God's will is 'the demand for love,' p 18), and stresses that ' "condition" in that statement must not be taken in the external sense of an arbitrarily set task, in place of which some other could have been set.'

48 The actual verb $\mu\epsilon\tau\alpha\nu o\epsilon\omega$ is found in Jesus' mouth in the synoptics on only two occasions in an imperative sense: Mt 4:17/Mk 1:15; Lk 13:3f. The other occasions of its use by Jesus are indicative: Mt 11:21/Lk 10:13; Mt 12:41; Lk 11:32; 15:7,10; 16:30, 17:3. Flender (*Botschaft,* p 58) doubts that Jesus used the word. For our purposes it does not matter if the word was on his lips. That he called for the transformation which is called $\mu\epsilon\tau\acute{\alpha}\nu o\iota\alpha$ is clear (cf p 78). The whole proclamation of Jesus with its categorical demands ... is a proclamation of $\mu\epsilon\tau\acute{\alpha}\nu o\iota\alpha$ even when the term is not used' (Behm, *TDNT* IV, p 1002).

49 The Lord's Prayer, especially Mt 6:13, constitutes one such call.

50 Schnackenburg, *Gottes Herrschaft,* p 70: 'Umkehr im Sinne Jesu ist ... eine tiefgreifende Wandlung des Herzens, ein Zurückfinden zu Gott, ein völliges Sich-Ausliefern an seine Barmherzigkeit, ein dankbarer Neubeginn.'

51 My emphasis here falls on the 'certainty and seriousness' of the coming day, not on its *nearness* in contrast, for example, to Wilder's emphasis (*Eschatology and Ethics,* p 133): 'The *nearness* of the Kingdom of Heaven, viewed both as promise and menace is the dominant sanction for righteousness' (my italics). For one who reckons with the inevitability of judgment both of the dead (Mt 11:20–24; 12:41f) and of the living (Mt 25:31f) and who reckons realistically with the uncertainty of earthly life (Mt 6:27; Lk 12:20f), the indefinite nearness of the Kingdom of God will not place man in a more urgent situation than the indefinite nearness of death. Barrett ('Stephen and the Son of Man,' p 35f) makes a similar observation in another context: 'for the individual Christian death was truly an *eschaton* (though not *the eschaton* ...) marked by what we may term a private and personal parousia of the Son of Man [cf Acts 7:56]. That which was to happen in a universal sense at the last day, happened in individual terms [at death].' The coming of the Son of Man in glory to judge and the coming of death are *for the ethical sanction* the same event. As far as ethical motivation is concerned the Kingdom always comes within one generation. Cf on the relation of the nearness of the Kingdom and Jesus' demands, Kümmel, *Theologie,* p. 43; Schnackenburg, *Sittliche Botschaft,* p 63; Grant, *JR* 22, p 367.

52 'Gott, der dem Menschen im Aufruf zur Liebe versprochen wird, begegnet ihm in der konkreten Gestalt, eines Liebe verschenkenden Menschen. Insofern müsste man sagen: Jesu Person gehört zu seiner Verkündigung unabdingbar dazu' (Luz, 'Erwägungen,' p 130).

53 In the following discussion I do not mean to imply that it was Jesus' custom verbally to pronounce forgiveness upon the 'sinners' with whom he fellowshipped. The forgiveness referred to is grounded in the meaning of tablefellowship itself. See below.

54 Augstein's (*Jesus*, p 159) protest here is not based on historical reasoning: 'Im ersten, dem Markus-Evangelium, tafelt Jesus nicht mit Heiden und Huren [but cf Mk 2:15–17]. Auch isst und trinkt er dort nicht derart, dass die Leute, wie bei dem offenbar sinnenfreudigen Matthäus, sagen: "Siehe, wie ist der Mensch ein Fresser und ein Weinsäufer, der Zöllner und der Sünder Gesselle!" Der richtige Jesus war das offenbar gar nicht, was die Evangelisten später in ihn hinein gedichtet haben . . .' Cf Braun, *Jesus*, pp 73f: 'Das gegen Jesus verwendete Schimpfwort, er sei ein Freund von Zöllnern und Sündern (Mt 11:19) stellt es ausser Frage: Jesus hatte Umgang mit den religiös Deklassierten.'

55 Cf Jeremias (*Theology*, p 109) on the relation of Mt 11:6 to the preceding verses.

56 As the context of Is 61:1–3, as well as the rest of the prophetic literature and the psalms, shows, the significance of 'the poor' is not exhausted by financial condition. In the Old Testament עָנִי comes to mean the one who in his real affliction and need appeals to the help of Yahweh and is the object of his special care. It comes to mean even 'humble' or 'pious' (cf Ps 18:27, ταπεινός). Cf *TDNT* VI, p 888; Ridderbos, *Kingdom*, pp 188–92.

57 Those whom Jesus designated 'poor' included the tax collectors, harlots, 'the disreputable, the 'ammē hā-'āreṣ, the uneducated, the ignorant, whose *religious* ignorance and *moral* behavior stood in the way of their access to salvation, according to the convictions of the time' (Jeremias, *Theology*, p 112).

58 ἁμαρτωλοί were not only those who led a flagrantly immoral life but also those who followed certain dishonorable vocations. Beyond this the term included all those who either out of ignorance or unwillingness did not subject themselves to the Pharisaic ordinances (*TDNT* I, p 328). Both the tax collectors (Lk 19:7) and harlots (Lk 7:37) were called sinners. In our discussion of Jesus' table-fellowship we will use the word in its most inclusive sense.

59 Jeremias, *Theology*, p 115. Cf Michel, *TDNT* VIII, p 105, note 152.

60 Bultmann (*History*, p 18) sees Mk 2:17 as an independent saying of which the second half is a secondary explanation of the first (p 92). The first half, he admits, may have been taken up by Jesus from the secular wisdom of his day 'and used to defend his own way of going to work' (p 105). Lohmeyer (*Markus*, p 58) says that the right question is not 'secondary or genuine saying?' but, Does Mk 2:17 correspond in language and essence to Jesus' whole proclamation? He answers affirmatively, as does Taylor (*Mark*, p 207). In the light of Mk 1:38 and 6:20, ἦλθον and δίκαιος do not point to the later church perspective. If the originality of v 17 is granted, the question may be asked: In what other context could it be materially more at home than in connection with Jesus' eating with sinners?

61 Schlatter, *Matthäus,* p 304: 'Durch die Gewährung der Tischgemeinschaft handelt Jesus als der Vergebende. Was beim Täufer das Bad war, das die Unreinheit wegnimmt, das war bei Jesus das gemeinsame Mahl. Die Vergebung stiftete die Gemeinschaft, wie die Anrechnung der Schuld die Gemeinschaft aufhebt. Indem Jesus die Verschuldeten an seinem Mahl teilnehmen liess, hob er jede Trennung zwischen sich und ihnen auf.' However, Jesus' presence at table with sinners does *not* mean automatic renewal on the part of the guests any more than mere water baptism accomplishes repentance. Jesus also eats with Pharisees (Lk 7:30ff). The forgiving fellowship Jesus offers must be personally accepted.

62 Also against the unity is Wellhausen. See his argument in Jüngel, *Paulus und Jesus,* p 160, note 1.

63 Even though Linnemann will not *identify* the Pharisees with the elder brother, she does admit: 'Gewiss spielt Jesus in der Figur des ältesten Bruders auf die Pharisäer an' (*Gleichnisse,* p 86). Cf especially 15:29.

64 Similarly Gutbrod, *TDNT* IV, p 1060: 'The publicans and sinners are with Jesus and he extends to them his fellowship even to the point of eating with them. This means that the lost sheep and the lost coin are found, that the prodigal son comes home again . . . If the sinner is received into pardoning fellowship with Jesus he is at home in the father's house.'

65 Linnemann (*Gleichnisse,* p 154, note 24) cites Schlatter and Schniewind as proponents of this interpretation. Her own objection (p 86) that the Pharisees' complaint was not that of the elder brother does not seem to me to carry much weight. Jüngel's (*Paulus und Jesus,* p 162) view of the parable as a language event (following E. Fuchs), in which 'die Gottesherrschaft als die sich ereignende Liebe zur Sprache kommt,' rightly brings out the power of Jesus' word, but does not go far enough to do justice to the second half of the parable and the Lukan setting. In attempting to avoid a 'Sicher-Stellung' (p 139) of the parable, the concrete intention of the parable seems to get lost in generalization.

66 Jeremias, *Theology,* pp 117f.

67 Schniewind, *Markus,* p 24, cf p 42.

68 'In der Verklammerung des Kommens des Königtums Gottes mit der Verkündigung und dem Handeln Jesu (in Mt 11:5f) ergibt sich eine Schau der Reichsgottesbotschaft die weder in der Apokalyptik noch in Qumran noch bei den Rabbinen eine vergleichbare Aussage besitzt' (Grundmann, *Matthäus,* p 304). Therefore Braun (*Radikalismus* II, p 51), Bultmann (*History,* p 151; *Theology* II, p 7), Schniewind (*Matthäus,* p 141), and Jeremias (*Theology,* pp 103f) regard the saying as original. '*Even now the consummation of the world is dawning'* (Jeremias, p 105).

69 The problem must be faced, however, that not all were changed by Jesus' personal fellowship (Lk 7:37ff, the Pharisee) and not all accepted Jesus' personal call to discipleship (Mk 10:17ff, the rich young man). Why? The divine prevenient grace referred to in Mk 10:27 finds explicit expression in Jn 6:44,65: 'No one can come to me unless the Father who sent me draws him . . . No one can come to me unless it is granted him by the Father.' Similarly in Mt 11:25 it is the Father who reveals and hides the mystery of Jesus' work according to his gracious will. This does not diminish the necessity of Jesus' concrete personal work in granting forgiveness, but it

does mean that one cannot adequately explain Jesus' ministry apart from the transcendent work of God. Machoveč's explanation of Jesus as one who swept men into discipleship because he lived and embodied the program he preached (*Jesus*, pp 93,103) does not adequately account for *why* some were 'mitgerissen' and others were not.

70 Schlatter, *Christus*, p 201. 'Jesus schenkt die der totalen Gehorsamsforderung entsprechende totale Vergebung ohne Bedingung einer menschlichen Leistung (Lk 19:1–7) *und doch so dass sie nie ohne die totale Umkehr des Menschen real wird*' (Goppelt, *Christentum*, p 53).

71 Schlatter, *Matthäus*, p 307.

72 On Mt 5:38–42 Soiron (*Bergpredigt*, p 294) says 'Es zu erfüllen gelingt nicht dem Menschen, der sich auf die Kräfte seiner Natur verlässt. Es fliesst eben aus der Gemeinschaft mit Jesus und lässt sich nur dort verwirklichen, wo sich die Menschen Gemeinschaft in Jesus gefunden haben. Kümmel, *Theologie*, p 49, on Mt 18:23ff: 'hier ist ganz deutlich die Erfahrung der Liebe Gottes *in der Begegnung mit Jesus* die Voraussetzung und Ermöglichung des Gehorsams gegen die durch Jesus verkündete Forderung Gottes.' Similarly Büchsel, *Theologie*, p 30; Dibelius, *Jesus*, p 101; Ladd, *Jesus*, p 294; Liechtenhahn, *Gebot*, p 37; Neuhäusler, *LZ* 1/2, pp 91–102; Wendland, *Eschatologie*, p 131.

73 See Section I. B. above, 'The Validity of Systematizing,' pp 67f.

74 Dibelius, *Jesus*, p 102: 'Von diesen Forderungen gilt es: sie sollen wörtlich erfüllt werden, wo die Erfüllung nicht als Aberwitz, nicht als asketische Leistung, sondern als *Zeichen des Gottesreiches* zu Wirken vermag' (my italics). Preisker (*Ethos*, p 49) comments similarly: 'dass die Bergpredigt nicht nur die Schwelle vom Alten ins Neue Testament, sondern Willens- und *Lebenszeichen des neuen Reiches*, "nicht von dieser Welt" ist' (my italics). Cf also Goppelt, *Christologie*, p 39.

75 Wendland, *Ethik*, p 26 (my italics).

76 We do not need to go into a detailed history-of-traditions analysis of these sayings and those immediately following. On p 86 above the authenticity of Mk 10:43,44 and Lk 14:11 has been discussed and these sayings here follow the same essential line. Thus by the 'criterion of coherence' (cf Perrin, *Rediscovering*, p 43) we may reasonably apply the *sense* of these sayings to Jesus.

77 Beyer, *TDNT* II, p 85.

78 Schlatter, *Christus*, p 204: 'Im Verkehr mit den Jüngern war es Jesu Ziel, sie dahin zu bringen, dass sie auf das bedacht seien, was Gottes ist, im Gegensatz zu dem, was des Menschen ist. "Gebt Gott, was Gottes ist"; aus diesem Begehren erwuchs sein ganzer Bussruf. Als "Gerechtigkeit" wertete er in der Bergpredigt dass, was die Jünger für Gott tun; dem gab er aber die reine Art der vollendeten Liebe, die einzig Gott vor Augen hatte. Für den Dienst an den Menschen, zu dem die Jünger als das Licht der Welt und das Salz der Erde verpflichtet sind, bleibt es *das letzte Ziel. dass die Menschen ihretwegen ihren Vater preisen.* Jesus richtete ihren Blick nicht nur auf die Bedürftigkeit derer, die an ihren Dienst gewiesen waren, auch nicht nur auf den Wert der Gabe, die sie ihnen boten, sondern legte das ganze Gewicht des Vaternamens in ihren Dienst hinein' (my italics).

79 With all the other 'I have come' sayings of Jesus, Bultmann (*History*, pp 152–

5) rejects the authenticity of these words from Q. Against Bultmann see
Grundmann, *Lukas*, p 269. It is unlikely that the early Christians looking
back from their present understanding of Jesus' victory would have put into
his mouth: 'I have not come to bring peace, but a sword' (Mt 10:34). We
have no evidence from the epistles that the early Christians created such
vivid, sharp sayings. They were rather a problem for the church (see Lk's
softening). To see that the whole of Jesus' ministry is marked by division
(cf Mt 6:24,32; 8:22; 10:37, etc) and that this division happened precisely
at the point where Jesus revealed the Father (Mt 11:25-27 par) is as important as the authenticity of these particular sayings.

80   In this regard we may notice that it is no accident that Mt connected the
      Golden Rule (7:12) to the preceding saying on the Father's generosity
      with the word οὖν. This follows from an essential fact in Jesus' message. We
      are called to fulfil the love command precisely *because* the Father is
      generous and will give us the necessary resources. This understanding of
      Mt's perceptive redaction is preferable to Furnish's comment (following
      G. Barth) that the only way to understand οὖν in 7:12 is as the intro-
      duction to a paragraph summarizing all the commandments in 5:21 – 7:11
      (*Love*, p 57). Of thirteen instances of οὖν in the Sermon on the Mount
      (5:19,23,48; 6:2,8,9,22,23,31,34; 7:11,12,24) none is used to introduce
      summaries and all but five introduce imperatives which follow logically
      from immediately preceding indicatives.

81   On the 'hardness of heart' in Jesus' message see below, pp 89ff.

82   So also Lohse, 'Ich aber sage euch,' p 200: 'Tatsächlich wird in der dritten,
      fünften und sechsten Antithese eine Aufhebung im Gesetz enthaltener
      Bestimmung ausgesprochen.' Wendland, *Eschatologie,* p 122: 'Nun setzt
      aber Jesus seine Antithesen in derselben Form den Geboten des Gesetzes
      entgegen.' So Goppelt, *Christologie,* pp 194f. The alternative view is that
      Jesus is here opposing *not* the old Testament regulation but a Jewish
      misuse of it. So Bultmann, *Existence,* p 204: 'His criticism was not directed
      against what was in the Old Testament as such, but against the practice of
      justice by the scribes.' Similarly: Spicq, *Agape* I, p 6; Schweizer, *NTS* 16/3,
      p 215 (who ascribes this view to Mt). This latter interpretation, which goes
      against the natural sense of the words, fails to take account of the real
      tension that doubtlessly existed between Jesus and the statutory aspect of
      the Old Testament (see below, especially Mk 10:2ff, p89). So Guelich,
      Annul, p 192. Should it be the case that the fifth antithesis is Mt's con-
      struction (see pp 51–5), the following treatment should nevertheless show
      that it coincides essentially with Jesus' intention.

83   Jesus' position with regard to the law is regularly summed up in four state-
      ments (cf Wendland, *Ethik*, pp 9–12; Jeremias, *Theology*. pp 204–8). (1)
      He acknowledged the validity of the law and the oral tradition (Lk 10:26;
      Mk 1:21,44; Mt 23:1ff). (2) He criticized the traditions where they contra-
      dicted the will of God (Mk 2:18–3:6; 7:5,13). (3) He 'radicalized' Old
      Testament commandments (Mt 5:21f; 27f). (4) He abolished Old Testament
      commandments (Mk10:5; Mt 5:32,34,38f). Our main concern here will be
      with the last of these statements since it is most closely connected to the
      command of enemy love. The discussion should, however, offer an expla-
      nation of the apparent contradictions in these four statements.

84 It is doubtful that Mk 7:9-13 represents the 'polemical equipment of the church' which was only later put in the mouth of Jesus (suggested by Bultmann, *History*, p 49). The controversy over the 'Corban' was not an issue for Mk's readers (he had to explain the term's meaning! 7:11) and could originate only in the area of the Temple. But if the saying has its home so close to the soil of Jesus, 'there can be no reasonable doubt that the words were spoken by Jesus and illustrate his attitude to the oral law' (Taylor, *Mark*, p 339).

85 Quoted by Flender, *Botschaft*, p 54, from Jeremias' *Jesus*, pp 68f.

86 Bultmann (*History*, p 27) says of this pericope: 'The debate here certainly derives from the Church; it is set out in a unified way, though use is made of material from the polemics of the Church. The awkwardness of the construction shows its artificiality.' But then on p 49 he writes, 'It is probable that the way in which Mk 10:2-9 sets one quotation of scripture against the other actually goes back to Jesus. For, so far as I know, this was unheard of among the Rabbis.' In line with this second observation Jeremias (*Theology*, p 224) defends the genuineness of the debate 'because Jesus ventures to set himself up against the *Torah.*' Cf Taylor, *Mark*, p 415. Banks (*Jesus and the Law*, p 159) concludes that the versions of this pericope in Mt and Mk 'preserve the fundamental tenor of Christ's attitude to the law.'

87 Against Ridderbos, *Kingdom*, pp 325f: 'We find a very positive appreciation of justice, of the ordinances that have been from the beginning *or that have been instituted on account of sin.* Jesus does not abolish or devaluate all of this' (my italics).

88 Gutbrod, *TDNT* IV, p 1064: 'The law as it is presupposes the sin of man as a given factor which cannot be altered. With relationship to Jesus and membership of the $\beta\alpha\sigma\iota\lambda\epsilon\dot{\iota}\alpha$ $\tau o\hat{\upsilon}$ $\theta\epsilon o\hat{\upsilon}$, however, there is restored the order of creation which does not accept sin as a given factor.' An attempt to explain Jesus' new radical command as a call for extraordinary moral effort in the short time before the world ends, is contradicted by Jesus' own argument: he does not show any sign that the institution of marriage is now insignificant (nor can this be deduced from Lk 14:26), which we would expect if the end were determining his thought; rather, he appeals to the original will of the creator with the aim of making marriage what it ought to be.

89 Similarly Goppelt, 'Haustafel,' p 100. Jesus' concern with the heart, with the 'inside of the cup,' is a motif running throughout the gospel and tallies with the whole picture of his ministry which we have been developing. See, e.g., Mt 5:8,28; 6:21; 9:4; 12:34; 13:15; 15:8,19; 18:35; 22:37; 23:25-28; 24:48.

90 Against Bultmann, (*History*, p 135) and R. Guelich (*NTS* 22/4, p 455) who do not see an abrogation of the thesis in Mt 5:33 but rather a 'surpassing' or 'transcending' of it. Their position can only be sustained by arguing (as Guelich does, p 454) that 5:33b ('render to the Lord your oaths') 'was secondary to the original complex.' For if it is not secondary then the command 'Do not swear at all' (5:34a) does in fact abrogate verse 33. In my opinion Guelich has introduced unnecessary complexity into the text seeing 'awkwardness' (p 451) and tension (p 452) where a more sympa-

thetic reading need not see any. I see nothing awkward in the following: 'You have been told: negatively, never fail to keep your oath, and positively, always keep your oaths to God. But I tell you be done with oaths entirely.' (Similarly Dietzfelbinger, *Antithesen*, p 32.) Insofar as 5:33 presupposes the rightness of oath-taking to that degree is 5:34 an abrogation and not a mere surpassing as in 5:21f and 5:27f. The authenticity of the basic antithesis in Mt 5:33–37 is defended by J. Jeremias (*Theology*, pp 220, 251ff) and R. Guelich (*NTS* 22/4) while C. Dietzfelbinger (*Antithesen*, pp 32, 35), M. J. Suggs ('Antitheses') and I. Broer (*BZ* 19/1, pp 50–63) deny that Jesus spoke these words in an antithetical way. The arguments brought against originality are to a large extent valid only if one assumes (as Suggs and Dietzfelbinger apparently do) that a redactional or traditional origin is to be *assumed* until strong arguments are produced that make it impossible. Against this tendency see O. Cullmann, 'Out of Season Remarks,' p 274.

91   Guelich (*NTS* 22/4, p 454) refers to Mt 5:37b ('but what is more than these is from evil') as 'clearly redactional.' For support he cites G. Strecker (*Weg*, p 133). Strecker gives one sentence: 'Die zweite Satzhälfte wird durch περισσόν (vgl 5:47) und πονηρός (vgl 5:39 u.ö.) für Matthäus sprachlich ausgewiesen.' This is scarcely a 'demonstration.' In the one other place where περισσόν may be redactional (5:47 reflecting the περισσεύσῃ of 5:20), the usage is precisely the opposite from here. There: more is righteous; here: more is evil. Nor is it clear that πονηρός signals Matthean redaction. Of its 26 occurrences in Mt only 4 are clearly redactional over against Mk and/or Lk (9:4; 13:9; 15:19; 22:10) and 9 come from Q (5:11, 45; 6:23; 7:11; 12:35; 12:39, 45; 16:4; 25:26). The remaining 11 instances have no parallel. Moreover the closest analogy to Mt 5:37b is Mt 12:35 which is traditional (par Lk 6:45), not redactional. It seems to me that a stronger argument against the originality of 5:37b will be needed especially in view of the more significant *substantial* connections between the *idea* of 5:37b and other teachings of Jesus. (Cf The 'criterion of coherence' developed by Perrin, *Rediscovering*, p 43.)

92   Schlatter, *Matthäus*, p 184.

93   Schlatter, *Matthäus*, p 184. Cf Goppelt, *Christologie*, p 32: over against Jesus' demand for wholeness (Mt 5:48) 'reden die Antithese den Menschen an, der sich mit Hilfe der alttestamentlichen Weisungen in der unvermeidlichen Koexistenz mit dem Bösen einrichtet.'

94   Gutbrod, *TDNT* IV, p 1064: 'This is implied . . . especially clearly in [Mt 5] vv 38ff where the Law limits unrestrained vengeance but Jesus frees his disciples from the whole spirit of revenge. Inasmuch as the Law presupposes the sin of man it is set aside by Jesus, since he establishes the obedience of love which foregoes itself and its own rights and relies wholly and utterly on God.'

95   Liechtenhahn, *Gebot*, p 31: 'Das Gesetz schränkt die Vergeltungssucht, die zur natürlichen Herzenshärtigkeit gehört, auf den Grundsatz Auge um Auge, Zahn um Zahn, d.h. Gleiches mit Gleichem ein, Gott aber will gar nichts von ihr wissen.'

96   Von Rad, *Theology* II: 'The content of the passage [Ez 36:22ff] shows it to be closely parallel, feature by feature, to Jeremiah's pericope on the new covenant (Jer 31:31ff) . . . The fact that the word covenant is not

here mentioned means nothing – there are other passages where he did
designate the saving event as covenant (Ez 34:25; 37:26)' (p 235).
'Ezekiel's ideas are so much his own that it is unlikely that his pericope
about Israel's spiritual renewal was taken directly from Jer 31:31ff. It is
therefore all the more significant that the climax of his forecasts in
Ez 36:25ff should correspond almost exactly to Jeremiah' (p 270). 'In
this matter Jeremiah and Ezekiel were, of course, far from being lone
voices crying in the wilderness' (p 267). For example, a similar idea
occurs in Dt. While Dt is looking back toward the old covenant and Jer
is looking forward toward the new, nevertheless, the new covenant was not
materially different from the old so that 'Here his view of the fulfilment of
the Sinai covenant is exactly the same as Deuteronomy's. The new thing
lies in the human sphere, in *a change in the hearts of men'* (p 270, my
italics). Cf especially Dt 5:26a; 11:16.

97   Cf Goppelt, *Jesus, Paul and Judaism*, p 73. Discussing Mk 10:2-9, he
remarks, 'Jesus' injunction against divorce will not become an actual
possibility until the "hardness of heart" is removed. As the prophets
predicted, this would not occur until the era of salvation (Ez 36:26).
Consequently Jesus' commands would be meaningless if he himself did not
produce that renewal of the heart promised for the time of salvation.'

98   L. Schottroff (*Gewaltverzicht*, pp 197f, 216) raises strong objection
against the way R. Bultmann, H. Braun and D. Lührmann in their treatments of the command of enemy love allow the emphasis to fall on 'dem
Geschehen beim Liebenden,' his overcoming of selfishness and self-
righteousness etc. Her objection is basically 'das die Selbstliebe und die
Haltung des natürlichen Menschen für den Text gar kein Thema sind'
(p 198). Schottroff has a good point in her emphasis on the *act* of love
and the change of the enemy (p 215) but I think she overstates her case.
There is a concern in the text with the one who loves – he is to become
a son of God and be τέλειος. Moreover the full meaning of a command
cannot be determined merely by restricting oneself to a single pericope.
One must, as I am here attempting, relate these commands to the wider
context of Jesus' message – which Schottroff does not do. See below
pp 98f and Chapter 5, note 38, for a fuller treatment of Schottroff's
views.

99   Strack–Billerbeck I, p 353, postulate that Mt 5:43 is a popular maxim
among the Jews in Jesus' day. Jeremias (*Gleichnisse*, p 201) agrees but
translates the maxim, 'You shall love your fellow-Israelite, only your
enemy you do not have to love.' So also Gaechter, *Matthäus*, p 192.
O. J. Seitz (*NTS* 16, p 51) sees it from a political standpoint as a
'partisan rallying cry.' Braun (*Radikalismus* II, p 58) and Grundmann
(*Matthäus*, p 177) see the verse as Mt's conscious reference to Qumran;
so also a long list of scholars in Braun, *ThR* 28, p 113. Strecker (*Weg*,
p 25) and Guelich (*Annul*, p 195) reject Qumran reference. Guelich
(*Annul*, p 198), Goppelt (*Christologie*, p 32) and Hoffmann (*BL* 10,
p 270) see Mt 5:43b as 'the compositional element of Mt in order to place
the limited nature of the Old Testament love command (5:43a) and its
casuistic consequences (5:43b) clearly in antithesis to that of Jesus'
demand' (Guelich). Similarly Schlatter (*Matthäus*, p 191), Percy (*Botschaft*,

p 155) and Schniewind (*Matthäus*, p 70) who, however, attribute the interpretation to Jesus.

100 *Jewish War* III.10. Referring to the Jews' attack on Ascalon: 'This is an ancient city 520 furlongs from Jerusalem, but the hatred with which the Jews had always regarded it made the distance . . . seem less.' Tacitus (*Histories* V.5) also writes, 'The Jews are extremely loyal toward one another, and always ready to show compassion, but toward every other people they feel only hate and enmity.'

101 Strack–Billerbeck II, pp 515ff. Cf Jeremias, *Gleichnisse*, p 200.

102 Peter Noll (*Jesus*, p 17) has stated this 'destructive' function of Jesus' love command well: 'Das Gebot der Feindesliebe mag als Radikalisierung des Gebotes der Nächstenliebe von Jesus gemeint gewesen sein; durch die Universalisierung wird aber das Gebot der Nächstenliebe zugleich begrenzt, relativiert und teilweise aufgehoben. Die Identifikation mit Familie, Freundenkreis, Vaterland, Kulturkreis uzw. wird fragwürdig. Die Norm der Feindesliebe hat zunächst desintegrierende, "zersetzende" Funktion. Ihr Adressat muss sich von der Gruppe und den Trieben, die ihn an sie binden, distanzieren; er wird sich sofort den Vorwurf eines Verräters zuziehen, weil er auch der gegnerischen Gruppe Verständnis entgegenzubringen bemüht sein muss.'

103 Burchard, 'Das doppelte Liebesgebot,' p 61. Page numbers in the text refer to this work.

104 A. Hultgren, *CBQ* 36/3, p 373, and others cited by him in footnote 2 argue for a form of the double command in Q because of the agreements of Mt and Lk against Mk.

105 A. Nissen's investigation, *Gott und der Nächste*, has confirmed this, pp 237–44, 415f.

106 A. Nissen (*Gott und der Nächste*, p 416) after an enormous analysis of the substance of the Jewish double love commands concludes, 'Doppelgebote als Summe der Tora sind mithin unmöglich, ein Doppelgebot der Liebe ist, wäre es mehr als eine Koppelung zweier grosser Gebote, nicht jüdisch.' He goes on then to ask suggestively (pointing in a different direction from Burchard), 'Sollte aber Jesu Doppelgebot der Liebe Summe und Mass des Gotteswillens gewesen sein – was bedeutet es dann, wenn es heisst: Jesus war Jude?'

107 Burchard ('Das doppelte Liebesgebot,' p 59) says: The double command is 'bei Markus ausgesprochenermassen Teil des jüdischen Erbes, das zu übernehmen notwendige, aber nicht hinreichende Bedingung ist.' Lohmeyer (*Markus*, p 259), on the other hand, maintains that the scribe's summation of what Jesus said (12:32–33) breaks out beyond the 'jüdischen Erbe.' 'Nur in solchem Verständnis, dass schon von dem gegebenen jüdischen Grundlagen sich zu lösen anschickt, scheint auch das letzte Wort Jesu gerechtfertigt.'

108 Michel, 'Nächstenliebe,' p 69: 'Es ist fraglich, ob das Wort des Schriftgelehrten Mk 12:33 ganz der Meinung Jesu entspricht.'

109 Similarly A. Nissen, *Gott und der Nächste*, p 502.

110 Nissen, *Gott und der Nächste*, p 241: 'Eine Verknüpfung von Dt 6,5 und Lev 19,18 ist übrigens in der gesamten antik-jüdischen Literatur zumindest bis ins Mittelalter nirgendwo belegt!'

111 Bornkamm, 'Doppelgebot,' p 38. Burchard's quote from Philo (p 56) is too distant. Furthermore his insistence that the 'first' and 'second' in Jesus' answer in Mk's version could not belong to a Palestinian situation may be pressing the details too hard. With Burchard, denying that Jesus used the double command, is Braun, *Jesus*, pp 114, 163. For the authenticity of the double command: Lohmeyer, *Markus*, pp 260f; Taylor, *Mark*, pp 485ff; Michel, 'Nächstenliebe,' p 57; Ernst, *ThGl* 60, p 6: 'Was für Jesus kennzeichnend ist, das ist die bewusste Konzentration des gesamten sittlichen Verhaltens auf dieses Eine, Ganze und damit dann auch die betonte Identifikation von Gottesliebe und Nächstenliebe.' Schnackenburg, 'Mitmenschlichkeit,' p 81: 'Diese unlösliche Verbindung und Verklammerung der beiden grundlegenden Forderungen ist zweifellos eine entscheidende und in dieser entschiedenen Weise originale Tat Jesu.'

112 Bultmann, *History*, p 178: '... artificially blended into its context by Luke.' Against this, Rengstorf (*Lukas*, p 139) maintains that 'Gespräch und Gleichnis ... der Sonderüberlieferung des dritten Evangeliums zugehört.' Braun (*Jesus*, p 130) says of its authenticity, 'Die Beispielerzählung vom barmherzigen Samariter ... stammt von Jesus selber oder ist, als Gemeindebildung, völlig von seinem und nicht von jüdischreligiösem Denken bestimmt.'

113 R. Fuller ('Das Doppelgebot der Liebe') has undertaken a careful attempt to reconstruct the earliest form of the double love command in the Christian tradition (pp 317–24) and then, with the application of the criteria of dissimilarity and consistency, to determine its genuineness (pp 324–9). His conclusion is that the double love command was probably a genuine part of Jesus' wisdom teaching (p 329).

114 Schniewind, *Matthäus*, p 70; Jeremias, *Gleichnisse*, p 203; Greeven, *TDNT* IV, pp 316f.

115 Goppelt, *Christologie*, p 194: 'Die fünfte Antithese der Bergpredigt hebt *die Grundlage jeder staatlichen Ordnung*, das Strafrecht, auf' (my italics).

116 Soiron, *Bergpredigt*, p 283: 'Wehrlosigkeit als Prinzip des weltlichen Lebens ist gottlose Zerstörung der von Gott gnädig erhaltene Ordnung der Welt.'

117 A detailed survey of the various attempts to solve this problem is found in Soiron, *Bergpredigt*, pp 1–90, or Thielicke, *Ethics* I, pp 333–63. Other shorter surveys include Wendland, *Ethik*, pp 17–20; Grundmann, *Matthäus*, pp 181–9; Goppelt, *Christologie*, pp 33–36; W. S. Kissenger, *The Sermon on the Mount*. Due to the thorough and numerous treatments available we shall only mention the options here.

118 The solution to this paradoxical attitude to the law should not be attempted by bringing in the cultic–ethic distinction. 'Denn Jesu Konservatismus bezieht sich auf Kultisches (Mk 1:44) und seine Gesetzesaufhebung geht auch auf Ethisches (10:1ff). Er scheint das Gesetz ganz zu bejahen und ganz zu verneinen' (Schniewind, *Markus*, p 97).

119 Starting from the generally accepted view that Mt's ἕως ἂν πάντα γένηται is redactional, Schulz (*Q*, p 114) argues that Mt's ἕως ἂν παρέλθῃ ὁ οὐρανός ... is more original than Lk's Εὐκοπώτερον δέ ἐστιν τὸν οὐρανὸν ... παρελθεῖν because Mt would not have constructed such an awkward sentence; therefore, the first ἕως ἂν he found in the tradition. Moreover Lk

16:17 is structured exactly like Lk 18:25 and could be influenced by this text. Bultmann, 'Sermon,' p 204: 'Even if the famous sayings that he has not come to abolish the law and that not a letter of the law shall perish (Mt 5:17–19) are words that were subsequently put into his mouth by the church, they still correctly convey his total attitude . . .' This is not to say that Jesus shared the Jewish view that the Mosaic law is eternal (Bar 4:1; Tobit 1:6; IV Ezra 9:37; Apoc Bar 77:15). For a detailed excursus of Mt 5:18/Lk 16:17 see Guelich, *Annul,* pp 294ff; Trilling, *Geschichtlichkeit* p 87; Banks, *Jesus and the Law,* pp 213–20.

120 Instead of dealing here with the important controversy over the tribute to Caesar (Mk 12:17) I merely cite the excellent treatment by Goppelt, 'Kaisersteuer,' *Christologie,* pp 208–20. In the same work ('Das Problem der Bergpredigt,' p 40) he sums up: 'That means: The person who follows the new demand of Jesus, that is, the person who believes and whose conduct springs from this belief, "renders to God the things that are God's" namely, everything. Therefore he has the freedom "to render to Caesar the things that are Caesar's." *So whoever has found the freedom not to resist* [Mt 5:38] *can also* in this freedom *resist wrong* for the sake of order and his neighbor. He will resist in a different way from the man who, full of anxiety and greed, wants to make his life secure. The person who is freed by faith does not hate; he suffers under the necessity that he must resist. Even this new way of resisting is a behavior that accords with the Sermon on the Mount.' See also Piper, 'Deciding What We Deserve.'

121 Hoffmann, *Studien zur Theologie der Logienquelle,* p 76.

122 Hengel, *War Jesus Revolutionär?* p 22.

123 See note 98 and Chapter 5, note 38.

124 Schottroff's observation (p 220) that these commands are found in the paraenesis near political texts (Rom 13:1–7; I Pet 2:13ff) is not helpful because no essential connection between them is shown.

125 Cf Mk 11:15–18; compare Mt 5:22 and 23:17.

Chapter 4. The Use and Meaning of Jesus' Command of Enemy Love in the Early Christian Paraenesis

1 There may well have been written notes which certain bearers of the tradition used (II Tim 4:13?) but the formal variations in the various traditional elements in the New Testament (cf Chapter 1) argue against the widespread use of common writings. Sanders (*Tendencies,* p 296) cites a letter from B. Gerhardsson in which he suggests that written notes gradually replaced the oral tradition.

2 Carrington, *Catechism*; Selwyn, *I Peter,* Essay II. See below, p 102.

3 Dibelius, *ThR* NS 3, pp 212f.

4 Dibelius, *From Tradition to Gospel,* p 239.

5 Following his lead and going farther are the works of Karl Weidinger (*Haustafeln,* 1928); Anton Vögtle (*Tugend- und Lasterkataloge,* 1936); Siegfried Wibbing (*Tugend- und Lasterkataloge,* 1959); Ehrhard Kamlah (*Form der katalogischen Paränese,* 1964); and Albrecht Dihle (*Die goldene Regel,* 1962). In Britain, A. M. Hunter (*Predecessors,* p 53) uses the same words Dibelius does to describe the relation of Paul's ethics and his theology.

6 Schrage, *Einzelgebote*, pp 15ff.
7 In the introduction to the 1966 printing of Seeberg's *Der Katechismus der Urchristenheit*, p xxvii.
8 Carrington (*Catechism*, p 31) outlines the content of this catechism under five recurrent headings: (1) new creation/birth; (2) wherefore putting off all evil; (3) submit yourselves; (4) watch and pray; (5) resist the devil.

	Col	Eph	I Pt (A)	I Pt (B)	Ja	Heb
(1)	3:9f	4:22f	1:22,25	–	1:18f	–
(2)	3:8	4:25	2:1	–	1:21	12:1
(3)	3:18	5:21	2:13	5:5	4:7	12:9
(4)	4:2	6:18	4:7	5:8	–	13:17
(5)	4:12	6:11	–	5:9	4:7	–

9 Dodd, *Gospel*, p 25. He cites four specifically Christian sanctions which govern the paraenetic material: (1) Christian eschatology (p 30), (2) the body of Christ (p 34); (3) the imitation of Christ (p 41); and (4) the primacy of love (p 42).
10 Davies, *Paul*, p 136. He is opposing A. M. Hunter's view here, which rests on Dibelius'.
11 Paul was not only *the* great theologian of the early church; he was also one of the chief bearers and formers of the traditions (cf II Thess 2:15; 3:6; I Cor 11:2,23; 15:3; I Thess 2:13; Phil 4:9). On the question of tradition in the New Testament, especially in Paul, see: J. P. Brown, *NTS* 10, pp 27–38; Cerfaux, *Catholica* 9, pp 94–104; Cullmann, *Tradition*; Dungan, *Sayings*; P. Fannon, *Scripture* 16, pp 47–56; Filson, *JBL* 60, pp 317–29; Gerhardsson, *Memory*, pp 193–336; *Tradition*; Goppelt, *KuD* 4, pp 213–33; Hanson, *Tradition*; Hunter, *Predecessors*; Riesenfeld, *Gospel Tradition*, pp 1–31; Wegenast, *Verständnis*; Fraser, *Jesus and Paul*; Fjärstedt, *Synoptic Tradition*.
12 Note the parallel between the love command in I Thess 5:15 and Paul's prayer in 3:12. From this, one can conclude that it is the Lord who enables and effects the realization of the love command. This corresponds to the fact that the Thessalonians received the *gospel* eagerly (1:4) and that through their faith this 'word of God' is 'at work in them' (2:13). In other words it is through their faith in the gospel that the Lord effects in them an abundance of love 'to each other and to all' (3:12; 5:15).
13 Cranfield (*Rom 12–13*, p 49), Dodd (*Romans*, p 198) and others (e.g. Kühl and Lagrange) see a division between 12:9–13 and 14–21. Michel (*Römer*, p 301) rejects such a division because 'V 14 gehört zu dem Gedankenkreis von V 17–21. V. 15–16 dagegen lassen sich auch auf das Verhältnis der Gemeindeglieder untereinander beziehen.' Cranfield, however, refers v 15 to outsiders and Daube (*Rabbinic Judaism*, p 345) refers both v 15 and v 16 to outsiders. But it is not usually noticed that v 12, 'be patient in tribulation,' has reference to one's response to outsiders. The division is there but it is not at all strict.
14 Just where the boundaries of the individual pieces of the tradition behind Rom 12 and 13 are to be drawn is debatable. Rom 13:8–10 and 11–14 may well belong to the foregoing in a traditional connection but such precision is not important for our purposes here.

15 Wendland, *Ethik,* p 60: 'Die ganze Paränese von Röm 12 und 13 wird mit dem Hinweis auf die Barmherzigkeit Gottes eingeleitet und begründet (12:1); in diesem Zusammenhang folgt dann auch die . . . Auslegung des Liebesgebotes.' So Sanday and Headlam, *Romans,* p 351; Furnish, *Love,* p 103; Michel, *Römer,* p 288: 'Schon dem Stil nach fällt Rom 12:1–2 besonders auf; die beiden Verse sind offenbar als eine Art *Überschrift* und Bestimmung des christlichen Lebens gedacht.'

16 The recurrence of the thematic word 'good' (12:2,9,17,21; 13:3,4) and its counterpart 'evil' (12:9,17; 13:3,10) supports the unity of the paraenesis under 12:2, 'prove what is good.'

17 For the theological significance of Paul's use of παρακαλέω see Schlier, *Besinnung* II, pp 340–4. He concludes: 'Gottes Erbarmen in der Milde und Sanftmut Christi durch die Liebe des Geistes ist es, das in dem mahnenden Zuruf des Apostels spricht und ihn zur eindringlichen Bitte und drängenden Ermunterung eines Vaters oder Bruders werden lässt.' But see Carl Bjerkelund's history-of-religions analysis of the *parakalô* sentences (*Parakalô,* p 190): 'Die Bedeutung der p. Sätze liegt nicht auf der theologischen sondern auf der Ebene der persönlichen, brüderlichen Begegnung.'

18 Against Barrett, *Romans,* p 279 and Sanday and Headlam, *Romans,* p 415, who limit 'the love of the Spirit' to mean brotherly love worked by the Spirit, Paul would probably not press the distinction here since it is through the Spirit's love of us (or God's love of us through him) that any genuine brotherly love can arise in our hearts (see Gal 5:22; cf II Cor 3:17 and Gal 5:13).

19 That the reference to 'our Lord Jesus Christ' in 15:30 has in view the *mercy* shown in his saving deeds is suggested (1) by the close similarity in form to 12:1, (2) by Paul's similar appeals elsewhere (cf II Cor 10:1, 'I appeal to you through the meekness and gentleness of Christ'; cf Phil 1:1f), (3) by the fact that from the subject matter it is fitting to ground an appeal for help (by prayer, 15:30) in help that has been received, namely, through Christ.

20 Michel, *Römer,* p 292.

21 Selwyn (*I Peter,* p 407) sees 12:9a as the heading for the rest of the chapter: 'Love's Sincerity'. Michel (*Römer,* p 288) sees ἀγάπη as 'das Stichwort, das den ganzen Abschnitt 12:9–21 beherrscht.'

22 The words λατρεία and λειτουργία appear to be synonymous in the LXX, both almost always translating the cultic עֲבֹדָה . Cf Phil 2:17 where θυσία (cf Rom 12:1) and λειτουργία are combined.

23 So Bultmann, *Theology* I, p 335.

24 See Schrage, *Einzelgebote,* p 72, note 7, for literature on the relation of the Holy Spirit and ethics.

25 See especially Bultmann, *ZNW* 23; also in Rengstorf, *Paulusbild,* pp 179ff; H. Windisch, *ZNW* 23; Schlier, *Galater,* pp 194ff; Oepke, *Galater,* Exkursus.

26 Grabner-Haider (*Paraklese,* pp 33–44) points in this direction: on the basis of I Thess 2:2–3, 9–14; II Cor 5:19–20; Rom 1:11–14, etc., he concludes: 'Paraklese ist eine Weise des Evangeliums' (pp 39f). 'Im Wort des Apostels ist der Kyrios selbst am Werk' (p 36). 'Es ist Gott selber der zur Versöhnung aufruft in der Weise der Paraklese' (p 38). This raises the question: How do the work of the Kyrios in the word of the apostle, on the one hand, and the work of the Spirit (of the Kyrios) 'in the believer,' on the other hand, relate to each other?

27 See Schlier in note 17.

28 Conzelmann, *Korinther*, p 131: 'Die Art, wie er diesen Satz einführt, lässt annehmen, dass er in Korinth bekannt war und gebraucht wurde, vgl. die Wiederholung 10:23.' Paul does not deny the validity of the slogan – only its misuse.

29 At the head of the list of χαρίσματα in Rom 12:6 Paul puts 'prophecy' and says that one possesses the gift of prophecy κατὰ τὴν χάριν τὴν δοθεῖσαν. To this degree its origin parallels Paul's apostolic office (cf Rom 12:3). Like the apostle, the prophet is 'appointed by God' (I Cor 12:27). In I Cor 14:1 prophecy is one of the πνευματικά; thus one who prophesies speaks ἐν πνεύματι θεοῦ (cf I Cor 12:3). The purpose of this speaking by the Spirit of God is, according to I Cor 14:3, to address men with παράκλησις (as well as οἰκοδομή and παραμυθία). Therefore, the Spirit speaks words of admonition to the members of the body not only through the gospel and paraenesis of the apostle (as we showed above) but also through its gifted members.

30 While W. D. Davies (*Paul*, p 226) may go too far in labeling the Spirit as 'a kind of Torah,' yet I think he has seen something very important for understanding Paul: 'The obedience of the Christian man is loyalty to the promptings of the Spirit, but since this Spirit derives his character from a person and is rooted in the words, life, death and resurrection of Christ, it is also for Paul a kind of Torah.'

31 I have found C. H. Dodd consistently perceptive in this whole area. To quote him at length concerning the supposed tension between ethical imperatives and spiritual guidance: 'The apparent tension between the two ways of regarding Christian behavior is lessened if we no longer think (as too much modern interpretation of Paul has thought) of the Christian πνευματικός as a solitary individual taking his stand upon the guidance he receives from the Spirit as "inner light" over against the tradition and authority of the community, and think of him rather as one who lives and moves within the Body which the Spirit inhabits. The Body is constituted by the act and the word of Christ, proclaimed in the Gospel and witnessed by his apostles. Each member by virtue of the κοινωνία τοῦ πνεύματος is offered the guidance and help of the Spirit to understand the law of Christ, to apply it, to discern its relevance to fresh situations, and finally to fulfil it; but he is not promised (at least by Paul) independent knowledge of the law of God, unrelated to the teaching which Jesus delivered to his people' ('Ennomos,' p 109).

32 Another text showing the same thing is Rom 6:17: 'You were once slaves of sin but have become obedient from the heart to the *standard* of teaching to which you were committed.' The parallel to this verse in 6:22 reads: 'You have been set free from sin and have become slaves of *God*.' Thus to be a slave of God and to be obedient to the tradition are in Paul's mind not conflicting ways of Christian existence. They are rather two parts of the same work of God. It is God who speaks in the tradition and it is God who takes us personally captive so that we obey the tradition 'from the heart,' that is, freely with joy.

33 Col 1:28: 'We proclaim Christ, admonishing every man and teaching every man in all wisdom in order that we might present every man mature in Christ.'

34 C. H. Dodd's comments bring out beautifully how the concrete words of

Christ (which he calls the law of Christ) function practically in our experience to shape our minds: 'The law of Christ works by setting up a process within us which is itself ethical activity. His precepts stir the imagination, arouse the conscience, challenge thought, and give an impetus to the will, issuing in action. Insofar as we respond, holding the commandments steadily in view, reflecting upon them, and yet treating them not merely as objects for contemplation, but as spurs to action, there gradually comes to be built up in us a certain outlook on life, a bias of mind, a standard of moral judgment. The precepts cannot be directly transferred from the written page to action. They must become through reflection and through effort, increasingly a part of our total outlook on life, of the total bias of our minds. Then they will find expression in action appropriate to the changing situations in which we find ourselves. That is what I take to be the meaning of the "law written on the heart" ' (*Gospel*, p 77).

35   I Cor 7:10; 9:14; 11:23ff; I Thess 4:15. That Paul gives imperatives explicitly from the Lord only in I Cor 7:10 and 9:14 does not necessarily mean he knew no more commands of the Lord. The explicit citation in I Cor may result from the specific need of that church. L. Goppelt ('Haustafel,' p 104) suggests that they were so cited, 'um die Äusserungen des Pneuma wieder der Orientierung an dem irdischen Jesus (I Kor 12,3) zu unterwerfen – nicht deshalb weil sich vielleicht Gegner auf ihn berufen.' This last phrase is directed against the hypothesis developed in Robinson and Köster, *Trajectories*, pp 158–204. Nor should the fact that only four dominical sayings are cited lead to the conclusion that Paul knew no more, because this lack of citation is present in Acts and I Jn whose authors we know were acquainted with the gospel tradition. In fact, as Goppelt points out ('Haustafel,' p 104). 'Logien in der Evangelienform fehlen nicht nur bei Paulus sondern in der gesamten frühchristlichen Briefliteratur bis zum 2. Klemensbrief so gut wie durchweg . . .' Why this is so we will attempt to answer in Chapter 5. Cf Neugebauer, *ZNW* 53.

36   Goppelt, *Theologie* II, p 367.

37   Schlatter, *Apostel,* pp 389–97.

38   Goppelt, 'Haustafel,' p 103: 'Die Evangelienüberlieferung will die Logien primär als Verkündigung in der Situation Jesu [rightly so in the case of our command], d.h. als Umkehrruf auf das kommende Reich hin, bezeugen; die paränetische Tradition gibt sie vom erhöhten Herrn her seiner Gemeinde als beispielhafte Verhaltenshilfen weiter.'

39   In the rest of Rom 13, Old Testament citations occur only in the context of the command of neighbor love (13:9).

40   Strack–Billerbeck III, p 300.

41   See especially Goppelt, *Typos.*

42   Michel, *Römer,* p 289.

43   I am not saying that the formation of the paraenesis was only begun *after* the expectation of the near-parousia and thus represented a de-eschatologizing process. See Schrage's criticism of this idea (*Einzelgebote*, pp 13–26) and the literature there. The paraenetic tradition was already well formed before I Thess (20 years after Jesus' death and resurrection) and we tried in Chapter 3 to show that a kind of 'de-eschatologizing' was already begun by Jesus himself; i.e., he did not disregard life in this age entirely but rather placed his

followers into the tension of having to live for him in two worlds, two ages at once.

44   I owe this insight to L. Goppelt (*Theologie* II, p 371). who observes that Jesus' command of enemy love in the paraenetic tradition 'wird Orientierungshilfe fur den Vollzug eschatologischer Existenz in der Geschichte und daher mit geschichtserfahrener Spruchweisheit verbunden, aber so, dass es Auswahlkriterium bleibt.'

45   Cf p 30 above on the takeover of Prov 25:21f.

46   M. Dahood, *CBQ* 17; E. Smothers, *CBQ* 6; J. Steele, *ET* 44; J. Young, *The Expositor* 3rd series 2; F. Zyro, *ThStKr* 18; W. Klassen, *NTS* 9; K. Stendahl, *HTR* 55; others in Michel, *Römer*, p 311, note 1.

47   It should not be objected that such an eschatological conception could not have been intended by the ancient wise man. More than once we find proverbial material taken up into a new eschatological situation and thus given a new dimension of meaning. See I Pt 4:18 = Prov 11:31 LXX; I Pt 3:10–12 = Ps 34:12–16. K. Stendahl (*HTR* 55) argues for an eschatological interpretation of Rom 12:19–21 not unlike the one I am suggesting, but some of his inferences are unacceptable: e.g., the assertion that 'Neither Qumran nor Paul speaks about love for the enemies. The issue is rather how to act when all attempts to avoid conflict with the enemies of God and of his Church have failed (vv. 17f)' (p 354). He even says of Jesus' love command in Mt 5:44 'that there is no intimation that such an attitude is envisaged as a means to cause repentance or toward overcoming enmity' (p 355). But both Jesus (Mt 5:44; Lk 6:28) and Paul (Rom 12:14; 9:3; 10:1) admonish believers to bless and pray for religious outsiders (i.e. God's enemies). To what is this blessing and prayer directed if not their conversion? See below, Chapter 5, note 38.

48   Spicq, *Agape* II, p 208.

49   *TDNT* VI, p 944.

50   Cranfield, *Romans 12,13*, p 57. So also Nieder, *Motive*, p 71; Sevenster, *Seneca*, p 184; Althaus, *Römer*, p 117.

51   Käsemann, *Römer*, p 333; Morenz, 'Feurige Kohlen,' pp 187–92.

52   Michel, *Römer*, p 311, gives an array of analogies outside the New Testament. These present the *possibilities* for the meaning of 'coals of fire' but none can be shown to have determined Paul's intention here. We are dependent on the context. I Pt 2:15 and 3:16, where good behavior puts an opponent to shame, are related to Rom 12:20 only if one assumes this meaning for 12:20; there are no close language similarities. At any rate the command of enemy love in I Pt 3:9 is supported by an Old Testament quote whose meaning includes eschatological judgment (3:12 = Ps 33:16 LXX) not pangs of shame.

53   Bauer, *Lexicon*, p 831. Cf Michel, *Römer*, p 301: '"Anlass" oder "Gelegenheit geben", "Platz machen" oder "das Feld vor jemandem räumen"'.

54   Such an attitude would correspond with that of the 'perfect' Qumran sectary who must hate the men of the Pit (IQS 1:10; 9:21) and yet do them good:

> To no man will I render the reward of evil,
> with goodness will I pursue each one;
> for judgment of all the living is with God,

and He it is who will repay to each man his reward.
I will not envy from a spirit of wickedness
and my soul shall not covet the riches of violence.
As for the multitude of the men of the Pit,
I will not lay hands on them till the Day of Vengeance;
But I will not withdraw my anger far from perverse men,
I will not be content till He begins the Judgment. (1QS 10:18–20)

55 Preisker, *Ethos,* p 184.
56 Dodd, *Romans,* p 200. Similarly Schelkle, *Petrusbriefe,* p 94: εὐλογεῖν
'bedeutet in der LXX und im Neuen Testament segnen, indem man Gottes
Gnade auf jemand herabruft.'
57 See especially A. Grabner-Haider, *Paraklese,* p 90, for the development of
the *future* ground of Paul's paraklesis. So also Lohse, *Kolosser,* p 47.
58 In the Old Testament the demonstration of God's righteousness, his 'saving
acts in history' (von Rad, *Theology* I, p 372), always involved the destruction
of the enemies of his people. It was a part of the salvation and thus a part of
his righteousness (Ps 9:8,16; 72:4).

> For thy name's sake, O Lord, preserve my life!
> In thy righteousness (בְּצִדְקָתְךָ) bring me out of trouble!
> And in thy steadfast love (וּבְחַסְדְּךָ) cut off my enemies,
> and destroy all my adversaries (Ps 143:11f).

It is because Paul saw wrath and salvation as one eschatological event that
the revelation of wrath in Rom 1:18 is a ground (γάρ) for the revelation
of God's righteousness in salvation (Rom 1:16f). The appearance of one is
evidence for the presence of the other. So Barrett, *Romans,* p 34.
59 From Ps 143:11 (cited in previous note) and from Dan 9:16–19 etc., we see
that for God to be righteous and to act for his own name's sake are the same.
60 Schlatter, *Gerechtigkeit,* p 349; so also Lang, *TDNT* VI, p 945.
61 A similar understanding of the incarnation is found in Jn 3:17–21. 'God did
not send the Son into the world in order to judge the world . . . This is the
judgment: that the light has come into the world and men loved darkness
more than light for their deeds were evil.'
62 Schlatter, *Matthäus,* p 187.
63 Bultmann's (*History,* p 112) judgment that here we have 'a community formulation since the sayings look back on Jesus' activity as something
already completed and presuppose the failure of the Christian preaching in Capernaum.'
is rightly disputed by Grundmann (*Lukas,* p 211): 'Diese Worte tragen
prophetischen Charakter und haben apokalyptischen Einschlag; sie können,
da die Überlieferung durch sie nicht entscheidend bestimmt ist, auf Jesus
Selbst zurückgehen.' Why would the church invent a saying about a city
(Chorazin) that plays no role in the tradition at all? 'Wir erfahren also
über die Wirksamkeit Jesu Genaueres als sonst' (Schniewind, *Matthäus,*
p 147).
64 One could note further in the parable of the tares (Mt 13:24–30) how the
farmer forbade his servants from gathering out the tares of the *enemy*
because at the harvest time the reapers (= divine judgment) would gather
and burn them. See too the purpose clauses in Mt 23:35/Lk 11:50 and cf
Hummel, *Matthäusevangelium,* p 88.

65 Büchsel, *TDNT* I, p 673.

66 See concise discussions of the religious history of the concept in Selwyn, *I Peter*, pp 305–9; Schelkle, *Petrusbriefe*, pp 28–31; Büchsel and Rengstorf, *TDNT* I, pp 665–70; and the literature mentioned in these.

67 Büchsel, *TDNT* I, p 674: 'There is a profound gulf between the religion of the Mysteries, in which man is deified by magical rites, and this religion of faith (2:6; 1:5,9,21; 5:9), of hope (1:3; 3:15) and of the fear of God (1:17; 2:18; 3:2,15).' Schelkle, *Petrusbriefe*, p 31: 'Den Mysterien steht er so fern, dass er das Wort nicht unmittelbar und absichtlich von dort entlehnt hat.'

68 Lohse, *ZNW* 45, p 85.

69 Lohse, *ZNW* 45, p 87: 'So findet die Paränese ihre eigentliche Verankerung, indem sie auf das Kerygma zurückgeführt wird.'

70 The importance of faith for I Pt can hardly be overstressed. The genuineness of *faith* is more precious than gold (1:7) because only through *faith* does God's power come into play to guard us for salvation (1:5,9). Only he who has *faith* in Christ will not be put to shame (2:6). It is by *faith* that we are to resist our adversary the devil (5:9), and it is only because faith unleashes the power of God that a mere man can withstand that 'roaring lion.'

71 The πειρασμοί (1:6; 4:12) which the Christians are enduring are not apparently an organized, official persecution. The words διωγμός and θλῖψις do not occur. They are bearing the reproach of their former companions (2:12; 4:4). 'Wohl ist die Öffentlichkeit schon missgünstig oder feindselig. Die Behörden aber scheinen bislang höchstens vereinzelt einzugreifen. Allenfalls mag da und dort die Polizei Untersuchungen und Verhöre, auch Verhaftungen vornehmen. Aber noch gibt es kein allgemeines, rechtliches Verbot der christlichen Religion und kein Gesetz der Verfolgung. Vielmehr hat der Brief zur Stadt und den Behörden noch das Vertrauen, dass sie das Recht wahren werden (2:14; 3:15f)' (Schelkle, *Petrusbriefe*, p 8). Similarly Selwyn, *I Peter*, pp 52–6: 'The qualifying words εἰ δέον ἐστί make it plain that these trials were of a local and haphazard kind' (p 53). Also Goppelt, *Apostolic Times*, pp 109ff, who points out that according to 5:9 the current suffering is typical for 'your brotherhood throughout the world.'

72 Since Selwyn's *I Peter* appeared it has been increasingly recognized that the extensive formal and substantial parallels in the New Testament epistles are due not to literary interdependence but to mutual dependence on common tradition. We came to a similar conclusion in Chapter 1 (pp 5–8).

73 See note 8.

74 For God's call see I Pt 1:15; 2:9; 5:10.

75 Bigg, *Peter*, p 156: Kelly, *Peter*, p 137; Selwyn, *I Peter*, p 190; Schelkle, *Petrusbriefe*, p 94; Reicke, *Peter*, p 105.

76 Robertson (*Grammar*, p 699) cites I Pt 3:9 along with Acts 9:21; Rom 14:9; II Cor 2:9; I Jn 3:8 as examples of texts in which εἰς τοῦτο is followed by a ἵνα clause in apposition.

77 So Schenk, *Segen*, p 62: 'Vom eschatologischen Ziel der Berufung spricht nicht unsere Stelle, sondern 5:10.'

78 Schelkle, *Petrusbriefe*, p 95: 'Im Brief sind Leben und gute Tage eschatologisch verstanden vom ewigen Leben.' So also Schenk, *Segen*, p 63. See I Pt 4:18 = Prov 11:31 (LXX) for a similar eschatologizing of an Old Testament quotation.

79 Lohse, *ZNW* 45, p 86: 'Durch die Einfügung eines ὅτι in v 12 . . . ist die theologische Begründung, die im Psalm den vorangegangenen Imperativen unverbunden folgte, unterstrichen worden.'

80 Windisch, *Katholischen Briefe*, p 69: 'Die Motivierung würde einem Logion εὐλογεῖτε ἵνα εὐλογηθῆτε entsprechen.' Furnish, *Love*, p 168, agrees that εἰς τοῦτο looks backward, in opposition to Kelly, but he does not discuss the significance of the ἵνα clause.

81 Πυρώσει should not be taken to refer to severe persecution or conflagration (such as that which devours Babylon, Rev 18:9,18), but to the testings of faith brought on by hostile countrymen. The suffering is typical for 'your brotherhood throughout the world' (5:9). Cf note 71.

82 Schenk, *Segen*, p 63: ' "Segen erben" (= Heb 12:17) ist eine Formulierung zur Besuchung der künftigen Heilsvollendung, die ihre beiden Elemente aus der alttestamentlichen und früh jüdischen Tradition hat (eschatologischer "Segen", z.B. 4 Esra 5:41; Syr.Bar. 55:8; Hen. 45:4f; eschatologisches "Erben", z.B. 4 Esra 7:9,16; 8:58). Sie ist aber in dieser Verbindung dort anscheinend nicht belegt.'

83 It should be noted that the idea of 'inheritance' is inimical to any thought of earning, as John Calvin pointed out long ago: 'And hence in those very passages in which the Holy Spirit promises eternal glory as the reward of works, by expressly calling it an inheritance, he demonstrates that it comes to us from some other quarter' (*Institutes* III.13.2).

84 Merkel, Georgi and Baltzer, *Meditationen*, p 233: 'Auf die Frage wie das Güte doch zum Ziel kommt, antwortet das Henochbuch damit, dass der göttliche Ausgleich in Jenseits erfolgt, wo die Gerechten über ihre Peiniger triumphieren werden (Hen. 94-105). In I Petr. dagegen folgt aus der Erwartung des verheissenen Segens der Aufruf zu segnen. Weil der Gegenstand der Hoffnung so herrlich ist, lebt der Glaubende nicht aus der Verdammung der Bösen sondern er weiss sich aufgerufen dem Bösen durch Frieden zu wehren.'

85 'We *have been* born anew' (1:3,23); 'You *were* ransomed' (1:18); '*Having* purified your souls . . .' (1:22); 'You *are* a royal priesthood, a holy nation' (2:9); 'He *bore* our sins in his body on the tree' (2:24); 'Christ *died* for sins *once for all*' (3:18).

86 Schenk, *Segen*, p 62: 'Die antithetische Mahnung zum Verzicht auf Vergeltung V 9a . . . ist wohl hinsichtlich der Begrifflichkeit wie hinsichtlich der antithetischen Formung, geprägte urchristliche Paränese. Die darauffolgende doppelte theologische Motivierung dieser Mahnung (V 9b) ist die besondere Stilisierung dieses Briefverfassers.'

87 Schmidt, *TDNT* III, p 489.

88 Selwyn, *I Peter*, p 414: 'Ps xxxiv was so admirably adapted to the instruction of catechumens, as its use in I Pet ii.3,4 exemplifies, that it may well have been used at a very early stage, as it stood, in the preaching of the primitive Church, or made the basis of shorter paraenetic forms.'

89 Selwyn (*I Peter*, p 190) quotes Kirkpatrick in agreement that in Ps 34 'Thought and style are those of the book of Proverbs.' So Weiser, *Psalmen*, p 200: 'Sein Verfasser hat . . . die Neigung seine Erfahrungen in allgemeingültige Wahrheiten umzuprägen unter Anlehnung an die Formen der Spruchweisheit, die von V 12 ab sein Gedicht beherrschen.'

90   It must be remembered that I included in the motivation of enemy love the
     use of concrete individual commands as the Spirit's means of leading his
     people. Thus I am not saying that no external guidance is needed for the
     Christian at all as Bultmann ('Nächstenliebe,' p 235) implies: 'Nirgends ist
     ein Was des Handelns angegeben . . . Es bleibt also die Frage: Was soll ich
     tun? dem Einzelnen, nämlich seinem jeweiligen Verständnis seiner jeweiligen
     Verbundenheit mit den Du überlassen.'

91   I do not mean that the good is determined only in the concrete encounter
     between men. The 'new man' will also *reflect* on what is good in view of
     the New Testament paraenetic admonitions, and will develop out of his
     faith and his view of the world, attitudes and principles by which he can
     live daily *and* according to which he can seek to influence his society.

92   The notion that genuine love involves a respect for another person's
     unbelief and a consequent renunciation of any desire or activity aimed at
     his change is utterly foreign to the New Testament and totally unintelli-
     gible in view of the ultimate realities involved!

93   On the norm of love in relation to other norms in the Pauline paraenesis,
     see especially Schrage, *Einzelgebote,* pp 249–71.

94   Similarly see Phil 2:29; I Tim 5:17; Heb 13:17.

95   Goppelt, *Christologie,* p 126: When we look at the situation of the church
     in Paul's letters it is evident, 'dass es auch in ihr ein Noch-Nicht gibt. Sie
     existiert als die Schar der Glaubenden "im Fleische" (vgl Gal 2:20). Daher
     ist innerhalb der Gemeinde neben dem "Dienen", das der Basileia des
     Kyrios entspricht (I Cor 12:5; Mk 10:43) auch noch ein Ordnen und sich
     unterordnen nötig.' So also Schrage, *Einzelgebote,* p 264.

96   Schrage, *Einzelgebote,* pp 260f. He points out further that the μὴ πικραίνεσθε
     and μὴ ἐρεθίζετε of Col 3:19,20, where Paul is discussing husbands–wives and
     children–parents, are a way of commanding love (cf I Cor 13:5). Col 3:18f
     combine love, and subjection together in the marriage relation. Lohse,
     Kolosser, p 226: 'Die Forderung μὴ πικραίνεσθε ist Ausdruck des Liebes-
     gebotes.'

97   Goppelt, *Christologie,* pp 130ff, cf p 121. I think Schrage (*NTS* 21/1, p 13)
     is unfair to Goppelt when he says, 'Nichts berechtigt nun aber dabei zu der
     Annahme, das ἐπὶ πᾶσιν δὲ τούτοις τὴν ἀγάπην von Kol 3:14 gelte nur im
     Raum der Gemeinde und nicht für das Verhalten im den Strukturen der Welt.
     Ich kann darum L. Goppelt an diesem Punkt nur widersprechen, wenn er
     erklärt, nirgends werde der Liebeserweis zur massgeblichen Richtschnur des
     Handelns in den Ständen gemacht . . .' Schrage has misquoted Goppelt who
     carefully said that *non-resistant love* is not the guideline for society's
     institutions. Goppelt says very plainly that 'die Christen auch in den Ständen
     durchweg aus Liebe handeln sollen.' I think Goppelt would agree when
     Schrage says, with H. D. Wendland ('Sozialethik,' p 76), 'da nach den Haus-
     tafeln die Liebe auch in die profane Strukturen der Gesellschaft eindringt,
     die mitmenschlichen Beziehungen dadurch ihrer Eigengesetzlichkeit entrissen
     und zum Ort liebenden Dienstes und Daseins für den anderen werden'
     (*NTS* 21/1, p 14).

98   'Doing good' to one's neighbor (I Thess 5:15; Gal 6:10) is what one does
     when one 'does no wrong to his neighbor'; and this according to Rom 13:10
     is love.

99 Delling (*TDNT* VIII) makes the following observations on the meaning of ὑποτάσσομαι: 'Ὑποτάσσομαι does not mean so much "to obey" – though this may result from self-subordination – or to do the will of someone, but rather "to love or surrender one's own rights or will" ' (p 40). 'In the New Testament the verb does not immediately carry with it the thought of obedience . . . To obey or to have to obey, with no emphasis, is a sign of subjection or subordination. The latter is decisive as regards the content of the word' (p 41). 'In ὑποτάσσεσθαι the supremacy of the ὑπερέχων is acknowledged to be legitimate' (p 43). While Delling takes the emphasis off obedience he does not, so far as I can tell, remove obedience as a *necessary* part of the concept, for if subjection involves *surrendering your own will* and acknowledging the *legitimacy* of the superior, then obedience must result. This is evident too if we note that it would make little sense to Paul for a Christian to say: I am subordinate to you but I will not obey you. Obedience is a necessary part of ὑποτάσσεσθαι (assuming one's superior is making any demands) even if this is not his primary focus. Similarly Schroeder, *Haustafeln*, p 121.

100 So Kelly, *I Peter*, p 136; Selwyn, *I Peter*, p 189.

101 On the general problem area see especially Goppelt, *Christologie*, pp 102,136, 190–206, 208–19 and the literature there mentioned.

Chapter 5. The Gospel Tradition of Jesus' Command of Enemy Love and its Use in Matthew and Luke

1 For a development of this view of the gospel tradition, see Roloff, *Kerygma*.

2 It is possible, as Jeremias (*Bergpredigt*, p 17) observes, that many of the variations in the Sermon on the Mount and the Sermon on the Plain are due to different translations of one Aramaic tradition. Were this the case, our remarks on the difficulty of determining what is redactional and what is traditional would still hold because we do not know at what level in the tradition the Aramaic was translated. That is, we do not know how much alteration may have occurred between translation and the final redaction.

3 What arrangement these elements were in depends on the answer one gives to the question of the originality of Mt's antithesis (p 51ff).

4 It does not follow from this uncertainty that the antitheses will have no redactional significance.

5 Whether one accepts as primary Lk's 'ungrateful and evil' (6:36) or Mt's 'evil and good . . . just and unjust' (5:45) will depend again on whether one thinks the sixth antithesis is original in which Mt's 'good and evil' is paralleled by 'neighbor and enemy.'

6 Note that this would mean that neither Mt nor Lk gives the original *Vorlage* at this point.

7 Compare Mt 5:44b with 5:10ff; 5:47 with 5:20; and 5:48 with 19:21.

8 Cf Jeremias, *Bergpredigt*, p 26: 'Der Schlag auf die rechte Wange, der Schlag mit dem Handrücken, ist noch heute im Orient der entehrende Schlag.'

9 See note 105. Each of these Jewish elements has been changed or omitted in the Hellenistically oriented Lukan text.

10 Dibelius, *From Tradition to Gospel*, p 246.

11 Jeremias, *Bergpredigt*, pp 21f.

12 Dodd, *Gospel,* pp 52f. Similarly Brown (*NTS* 10, p 46) who sees the use of Q behind the New Testament epistles: 'If we agree that the epistles (or the catechism) drew from Q, it is clear they used it very selectively. They chose the abstract formula rather than the image: or if they take the image, they treat it merely literally . . .'

13 Filson, *JBL* 60, p 328. Even though this statement does not take explicit cognizance of the interpretive element in the gospel records, it still brings out a valid distinction, because the interpretation in the gospel records is performed on a different level than that of the paraenetic tradition. All is couched in terms of the history of Jesus.

14 Coming at the problem from the sociological side, Gerd Theissen (*ZThK* 70) writes: 'Ethischer Radikalismus macht die Worte Jesu absolut untauglich zur Regelung alltäglichen Verhaltens. Um so mehr stellt sich das Problem: Wer hat solche Worte 30 Jahre und länger mündlich tradiert? Wer hat sie ernst genommen? Wer hat sie ernst nehmen können?' (p 248). He is dealing specifically with commands like Lk 14:26 (hate relatives) rather than the command of enemy love, but he seems to draw generalizing conclusions. The answer he gives to the question he just asked is: 'wandernde Charismatiker, die Apostel, Propheten und Missionaren,' as we see e.g. in Did XI. 5f (p 253). 'Der ethische Radikalismus der Wortüberlieferung ist Wanderradikalismus. Er lässt sich nur unter extremen Lebensbedingungen praktizieren und tradieren' (p 252). It seems to me unjustified to conclude that *only* those homeless wandering preachers who literally followed Jesus' commands could have handed down these commands. Theissen acknowledges that we owe the preservation of these commands to the gospels where they remain within 'Darstellungen des Lebens Jesu, die ausnahmslos auf eine vergangene Epoche zurückschauen' (p 270). Is it not possible that the historical interest which motivated the evangelists to preserve these impractical commands was also present at an earlier stage, so that the apostles may have preserved the sayings from the first at least partly out of such an interest? The picture of Peter, for example, before (Mk 2:19) and after (I Cor 9:5) the resurrection is not one of a man who followed the radical commands literally, but he was surely involved in their transmission (Acts 2:42; 6:4, cf Gerhardsson, *Memory,* pp 240f).

15 One work in this area which draws the same general conclusion is David Dungan's *Sayings;* see especially pp 144–150. See Larsson, *Vorbild,* p 27: 'Für uns genügt hervorzuheben, dass wir dank der neueren Forschungsresultate auf diesem Gebiet berechtigter sind als vorher, anzunehmen, dass Paulus bedeutungsvolle Elemente des Materials kannte und verwendete, das nun unsere Evangelien enthalten.' For exemplary study see Riesenfeld, 'Schätzesammeln,' pp 47–58: 'Der unabkömmliche Schluss-satz ist, dass die Evangelientradition in ihren noch nicht fixierten Formen schon früh den lokalen Gemeinden bekannt war und bei ihnen vorausgesetzt werden konnte' (p 50).

16 It would be beyond the scope of this study to enter into the detailed discussion of the general problem: Jesus and Paul. This discussion has, however, been the larger background against which I have carried on my own investigation. I hope that my observations will shed some more light on the whole question of Paul's relation to the historical Jesus and

specifically to the gospel tradition. For a list of those who think the teaching of Jesus played a major role in shaping the paraenetic tradition of the early church, see Chapter 2, note 178. For the opposite view, see note 179 of the same chapter.

17 Barrett, *Gospel Tradition*, p 12: 'It is still true that we are confronted in primitive Christianity with two traditions [in Paul and in the Gospels] . . . and we have so far been able neither to identify them, nor to explain the relation between them.'

18 Sanders, *Tendencies,* p 296: 'Just what the method of transmission in Christianity was remains an open question.' More recently B. Fjärstedt still writes concerning the period of oral tradition between Jesus and Mark, 'We have the bud and the full blossom, so to speak, but cannot find out what happened in between' (*Synoptic Tradition*, pp 14, 38).

19 Dodd, 'Catechism,' p 116 (my italics).

20 Dodd, 'Catechism,' p 116 (my italics). Similarly Filson, *JBL* 60, p 328.

21 Gerhardsson, *Memory,* p 295.

22 Gerhardsson, in his subsequent work, *Tradition,* emphasized the singularity of Jesus as a teacher without contemporary analogy (p 41); and he stressed that 'the early church regarded its work on the Word as a *charismatic* work . . . It would of course be a grave mistake if we were to regard the work carried out on the Word by the first Christians as a purely intellectual activity of the modern secularized academic type. But we should be almost equally mistaken if we were to underestimate the rational mechanisms which were obviously operative in the activity of the early Church' (p 46).

23 Hoffmann, 'Anfänge der Theologie,' pp 149f. The opposite of Hoffmann's view of Q may be found in Bammel, *NTS* 18, p 105: 'Q is not interested in the world outside the community, for it lacks all missionary features and certainly social impetus and political activity.'

24 Gerhardsson, *Memory,* p 335; 'We must distinguish in principle between this *transmission* in the strict meaning of the word, and the many *uses* to which the transmitted oral texts were put.' I. H. Marshall (*Luke*, p 48) writes: 'The epistles of John are free from the type of historical material found in the Gospel of John. This is a compelling indication that the two types of material were deliberately kept separate . . . It would seem legitimate to conclude that the Gospel tradition was a distinct stream in the early church with its own special channel of transmission.' Cf similarly Goppelt, *Apostolic Times,* pp 154ff; 'Haustafel,' p 104. In *Jesus of Nazareth* G. N. Stanton argues successfully 'that the early church was interested in the past of Jesus' (p 186) and 'that the church referred to the past of Jesus as part of its preaching, especially its missionary preaching' (p 188). His concern is to show that 'there is no dichotomy between the gospel tradition's concern with the life and character of Jesus and their use in preaching' (p 183), and that 'the resurrection faith of the church did not obscure the past of Jesus. On the contrary the resurrection acted as a catalyst which encouraged the retention of traditions which told about the past of Jesus . . .' (p 191). While I find his argument persuasive, I see some ambiguity in his presentation of the *Sitz im Leben* of the gospel tradition. Although stressing (with Dibelius) the primacy of missionary preaching as the *Sitz im Leben* of the gospel tradition, he does admit that 'many parts

of the traditions could have been used effectively in a variety of settings in the early church' (p 181). This seems to suggest, as I have, that there was a gospel tradition preserved distinct from the various forms of teaching and preaching in which it was *used*. Yet Stanton does not discuss the existence of such a stream of tradition. It is unclear to me therefore how he conceives the handing down of the gospel tradition.

25 Riesenfeld, *The Gospel Tradition*, p 23. See W. D. Davies' critique of the Scandinavian approach in 'Reflections,' pp 14–34. He doubts that the tradition was so fixed as Gerhardsson's 'Holy Word' implies (p 19) but agrees that the gospel tradition 'must be understood in the light of Pharisaic usage in dealing with oral tradition' (p 16).

26 Cf Schütz, *Der leidende Christus*, p 19: 'Die redaktionsgeschichtliche Forschung hat . . . die Freiheit der Evangelisten bei der Aktualisierung übernommener Tradition deutlich gemacht. So kann von einer Aktualisierung der Tradition durch den Evangelisten auf seine theologische Intention geschlossen werden. Für den Exegeten kann eine solche Tradition jedoch auch dann für das Anliegen der Evangelisten transparent werden, wenn sich keine redaktionellen Eingriffe feststellen lassen. Tradition kann in sich aktuell sein, so dass sie ohne Veränderungen übernommen werden kann.' Similarly Marshall, *Luke*, pp 19f.

27 The primary concern here is with what *Mt perceived* to be the historical teaching of Jesus, not with what contemporary critical scholarship has determined it to have actually been. See 'Approach and Methodology,' pp 139–41.

28 Walker, *Heilsgeschichte*, p 34. Similarly Ziener, 'Synoptische Frage,' p 176; Eichholz, *Bergpredigt*, p 16; Jeremias, *Bergpredigt*, p 16.

29 See for example E. Schweizer, *NTS* 16/3, pp 224ff; Held, *Wundergeschichten*, pp 234ff.

30 I view the following comment by Perrin (*Rediscovering*, p 16), therefore, as far too one-sided: 'So far as we can tell today there is no single pericope anywhere in the gospels, the present purpose of which is to preserve a historical reminiscence of the earthly Jesus, although there may be some which do in fact come near to doing so because a reminiscence, especially of an aspect of teaching, such as a parable, could be used to serve the purpose of the Church or the evangelist.' Against this view is the better-balanced one of L. Goppelt: 'Matthäus hat einerseits die Sachzusammenhänge gesehen, in denen die Gebote Jesu gegeben wurden und in denen sie allein sinnvoll sind. Er stellt die Bergpredigt zunächst nicht wie im Sinne der klassischen Formgeschichte oft behauptet wurde, als Gemeindekatechismus zusammen, sondern bewusst *berichtend* als Zusammenfassung der öffentlichen Predigt Jesu' (*Christologie*, p 41).

31 Manson, *Teaching*, p 51: 'In either case [Mt or Lk] the issue would be nudism, a sufficient indication that it is a certain spirit that is being commended to our notice not a regulation that is to be slavishly carried out.' So Rengstorf, *Lukas*, p 89.

32 We do not mean to say here that Mt always renders the tradition of Jesus' words without casuistical alteration. Mt 5:32/Lk 16:18 and Mt 19:9/Mk 10:11, for example, show the contrary. Cf Strecker, *Weg*, p 132: 'In Form einer Ausnahmeregel hat Mt den Gemeindebedürfnissen Rechnung getragen

und den ursprünglichen Radikalismus zugunsten eines praktikablen Gesetzes aufgegeben.' For other examples in Strecker, see pp 134ff, 180ff, 222ff.

33 Cf Trilling, *Wahre Israel*, p 31: 'So gilt für Matthäus die Gleichung Jünger = Christ, zum Jünger machen = zum Christ machen.'

34 Strecker, *Weg*, p 134: 'Dass ein Grossteil der Reden des Evangeliums unmittelbar den Gemeindeverhältnissen angepasst ist, so dass er geradezu als Gemeindeordnung bezeichnet werden kann . . . ist bekannt und braucht an dieser Stelle nicht ausgeführt zu werden.' Trilling, *Wahre Israel*, p 213: 'Der tradierte Stoff wird so umgestaltet, das seine Aussage transparent und unmittelbar auf die Situation der Kirche anwendbar wird.'

35 Mt's διωκόντων may well be his own (against Lk's ἐπηρεαζόντων 6:28) in view of the three-fold use of διώκω in 5:10–12 against Lk. This would mean that Mt is not mechanically taking over this command, but is conscious of its intention which he makes clear by equating the object of prayer precisely with those who persecute on account of Jesus (5:11).

36 Bultmann, *Jesus*, p 80: 'Es gibt also keinen Gehorsam gegen Gott im luftleeren Raume, keinen Gehorsam losgelöst von der konkreten Situation, in der ich als Mensch unter Menschen stehe, *keinen Gehorsam, der sich direkt auf Gott richtet*' (my italics). See similarly Bornkamm, *Jesus*, p 111. On the other side see Schnackenburg, 'Mitmenschlichkeit,' p 83, who, in opposition to H. Braun, states: 'Wer nur nach Mitmenschlichkeit strebt braucht nicht nach der Bergpredigt zu greifen, sie ist nur dem verständlich der an Gott glaubt und sich ihm konfrontiert.'

37 The Lord's Prayer is the center and heart of the Sermon on the Mount because it offers that without which all of the commands of the Sermon would be lifeless. If the Father's will could be done without dependence on the Father in prayer, there would be no need for the prayer: 'Let thy will be done!' Thus the prayer should be related to each command as the heart is related to all the parts of a living body. Besides the parallels noted above, we may cite further:

6:33 Seek first the Kingdom.	6:10 Pray that the Kingdom come.
7:21 Only the one who does the will of the Father will enter the Kingdom.	6:10 Pray that the Father might let his will be done.
6:25 Don't be anxious about what you shall eat.	6:11 Pray that the Father give you your daily bread.
7:15 Beware of false prophets who come to you in sheep's clothing.	6:13 Pray that you not be led into temptation.

38 Furnish, *Love*, p 67: 'There is nothing here about "making the enemy into a friend".' He gives literature on both sides in note 139. L. Schottroff ('Gewaltverzicht,' p 215) has argued forcefully that 'Die Feindesliebeforderung ist Appell zu einer missionarischen Haltung gegenüber den Verfolgern . . . Dieser Anspruch dürfte den Feinden durchaus nicht gefallen haben . . . Feindesliebe ist Inhalt christlicher Verkündigung, aber auch missionarisches *Mittel*. . . . "Besiege das Böse durch das Gute" (Rom 12, 21) trifft die Feindesliebeforderung voll. Es geht um einen Sieg über die

Feinde, nicht um "Selbstauslieferung ans Böse" [cf I Pt 3:1] ... Der Feind soll gewonnen werden, er soll überzeugt werden, ein anderes Leben zu führen und an der christlichen Hoffnung Anteil zu haben.'

39 Mt's δ ιωκόντων (5:44b) parallels his threefold use of δ ιώκω in 5:10–12 where it is a persecution of the disciples for Jesus'/righteousness' sake. Thus he stresses that those for whom we are to pray are precisely those who oppose us and God most violently.

40 While it is true that the greeting in the Orient had a greater significance than for us (Strack–Billerbeck I, p 380), and certain Rabbis laid great stress on greeting all men (Klostermann, *Matthäusevangelium*, p 51), nevertheless we probably should not see in the greeting here an eschatological blessing such as Lk 10:5 (Schmauch, *Matthäus*, p 150). This is forbidden by the sentence: 'The gentiles do the same.'

41 The term 'brother' in 5:47 probably means nothing more than the member of a mutual admiration society since, on the one hand, it is parallel with 'those who love you' (v 46) and, on the other hand, the gentiles are said to do the same, namely to greet their brothers (which means that 'brothers' cannot mean simply disciples or Israelites).

42 With the addition of τούτους (7:24,26; contrast Lk 6:47,49), Mt focuses attention on the words just spoken in the Sermon on the Mount.

43 Occurs in Lk 3 times; Mk once; Mt 10 times, only 2 of which are already given in Mk or Q (7:5; 15:7); cf 6:2,5,16; 22:8; 23:13,14,15; 24:51.

44 The differences between Lk 11:39–41 and Mt 23:25–26 are so great that we cannot say certainly that they were using a common source. It is not possible therefore to determine how much of Mt 23:26 is due to Mt's redaction. In view of Mt's tendency to make logical connections explicit (see note 52), Strecker (*Weg*, p 31) may be right when he claims: 'Jedenfalls wird das interpretierende ἵνα (gegen Lk 11:41; vgl. 26:4,16 u.ö.) matthäisch sein.'

45 Mt 23:25 refers to *ceremonial* purity and thus grants to the 'hypocrites' that they have cleansed the outside. When 23:26 then has external purity for its aim (ἵνα) this can only refer to ethical behavior in general. So Strecker, *Weg*, p 32.

46 Mt 7:18 is unique to Mt, but was possibly taken over by him from the tradition.

47 Insofar as forgiveness is a necessary element of enemy love, the heart is the source of this love; for, as Mt 18:35 says, true forgiveness must come 'from your heart.'

48 Thielicke, *Ethics* I, p 355. Discussing the inadequacy of the view which sees the Sermon on the Mount as advocating merely a new disposition he insists rightly that the demands probe much deeper: 'Now it is precisely here, in this innermost part over which I have no control, that I am called into question. This can only mean that what is innermost is imputed to me; I am responsible for it and must acknowledge it as "mine".'

49 Even if τέλειος in Mt 5:48 is original, 19:21 shows that it took on a special significance for Mt. See p 63.

50 See my methodological reflections on p 141.

51 Ἐσεσθε is an imperative future; Dana and Mantey, *Grammar*, p 192. This usage corresponds to that of 5:21,27,33,43. An indicative statement

introduced by 'therefore' would, moreover, in this context make no sense.

52 Mt tends to make logical connections explicit. Cf Mt 7:12/Lk 6:31; Mt 8:34/Mk 5:17. Of the 13 instances of οὖν in the Sermon on the Mount (5:19,23,48; 6:2,8,9,22,31,34; 7:11,12,24), eight introduce imperatives which follow logically from immediately preceding indicatives.

53 Trilling, *Wahre Israel*, p 195: '5:48 greift auf 5:20 zurück und schliesst die Antithesen ab.'

54 The appeal to tax collectors and gentiles is in a sense inconsistent with the theme of surpassing the most rigid law keepers (scribes and Pharisees, 5:20). Nevertheless the motif of doing *more* is obvious in both texts as in 6:7,32. The inconsistency is probably due to Mt's intention to juxtapose Jesus' command to both a legalistic and libertine front (see pp 149f). Moreover, the argument of the rhetorical questions (5:46f) would collapse if tax collectors and gentiles were replaced by scribes and Pharisees.

55 G. Barth, *Gesetzesverständnis*, p 91: τέλειος is 'das Mehr, das die Täter der Lehre Jesu von anderen unterscheidet, es ist das Merkmal der Gemeinde.'

56 That Mt is probably dependent on Mk is shown from the following. (1) The story occurs in the same series of events in Mt and Mk: departure to Judea Mt 19:1/Mk 10:1; on divorce and celibacy Mt 19:3–12/Mk 10:2–12; Jesus blesses the children Mt 19:13–15/Mk 10:13–16; the rich young man Mt 19:16–22/Mk 10:17–22; on riches and the rewards of discipleship Mt 19:23–30/Mk 10:23–31. (2) The basic line of conversation is the same in both gospels. (3) The alterations by Mt can be explained from his redactional interests.

57 Cf Held, *Wundergeschichten*, p 224, where he shows 'wie sehr der Evangelist Matthäus in der Form des Gespräches denkt und schreibt.'

58 I take this to be the intention behind having the youth ask, 'Which?' (Mt 19:18).

59 This and the following argument are found in G. Barth, *Gesetzesverständnis*, pp 89f.

60 St Jerome, *Commentarium in Evangelium Matthaei*, PL 26:142, quoted in Spicq, *Agape* I, p 24. Spicq also quotes a similar interpretation from the Gospel according to the Hebrews (according to the Latin pseudo-Origen, PG 13:1393–94): 'and the Lord said to him: "How sayest thou: I have kept the law and the prophets? For it is written in the law: Thou shalt love thy neighbor as thyself, and lo, many of thy brethren, sons of Abraham, are clad in filth, dying for hunger, and thine house is full of many good things, and nought at all goeth out of it unto them."'

61 Similarly Trilling, *Wahre Israel*, p 193; Stonehouse, *Origins*, p 98: Bornkamm, 'Enderwartung,' p 26; Barth, 'Gesetzesverständnis,' p 93. Banks (*Jesus and the Law*, p 163) concludes to the contrary, that 'what Jesus requires here is something altogether new, more a surpassing of the Law than a radicalization.' But his arguments do not take into account the possibility that the young man's conviction that he had 'kept all these' may not have been true.

62 I disagree with Guelich (*Annul*) at this point because he says the love command is inserted here (Mt 19:19) for the same reason as in Mt 5:43, namely to represent the Old Testament commandments 'in terms of their *legal implications*' (p 101) which are then 'countered by Jesus'

radical demand' (p 100). But as Goppelt (*Christologie*, p 32) says, 'In Mt 19:17-21 nennt Jesus dem reichen Jüngling gegenüber die Gebote der zweiten Tafel des Dekalogs samt dem Liebesgebot nicht, wie in den Antithesen als rechtlich begrenzte Bestimmungen, sondern als apodiktische Gebote.' For this reason Jesus does *not* 'counter' the commandments but says 'If you would enter into life keep the commandments!' (19:17). Thus it is inappropriate to say that in *this text* Jesus demanded 'a conduct which exceeded by far the Law's requirements' (Guelich, p 93). What Jesus does 'counter' and does 'exceed' is the young man's idea of his own obedience to the will of God. Perhaps we can paraphrase Jesus' response following the pattern of Mt 12:7 (cf 9:13): 'If you knew what this really means: "Love your neighbor as yourself," you would not have excused yourself so easily, saying, "I have kept this commandment" even though you love your riches more than the poor. I will show you what God wills: perfection. Therefore sell your goods, give to the poor and follow me.'

63 Bornkamm, 'Enderwartung.' p 26. Cf G. Barth, *Gesetzesverständnis*, p 93: 'Die Vollkommenheit besteht in der Nachfolge.'

64 Cf Strecker, *Weg*, pp 191ff, 230ff, Trilling, *Wahre Israel*, pp 28ff; Bornkamm, 'Enderwartung' pp 26ff; G. Barth, *Gesetzesverständnis*, pp 88-116; Held, *Wundergeschichten*, pp 171ff, 189ff.

65 Cf 'for my sake,' 'for my name's sake': Mt 5:11; 10:18,22,39 (16:25; 19:29; 24:9 taken from Mk).

66 Other texts where Mt stresses the suffering of the disciples: 5:10ff; 10:17ff; 16:24ff; 23:32ff.

67 Bornkamm, 'Sturmstillung,' p 52. Cf Mt's insertion of ἠκολούθησαν (8:23) and the cry of the disciples: κύριε σῶσον (8:25).

68 Mt develops the same motif in 14:28-33: Peter wants to come to Jesus; he sees the waves and fears; he calls to Jesus for help; Jesus saves him and rebukes his 'little faith.'

69 See G. Barth, *Gesetzesverständnis*, pp 117ff for the relation of Christology and ethic in Mt. 'Die Annahme erscheint daher berechtigt, dass überhaupt die Christologie der Grund ist, der Mt zu der obengezeigten Auslegung des Gesetzes durch Liebesgebot und Nachfolge geführt hat.'

70 Trilling, *Wahre Israel*, p 115: 'Im Matthäus geht es eben um die rechte Gottesverehrung überhaupt; sie kann gegen pharisäische Scheinheiligkeit wie auch gegen heidnische Unsitte abgegrenzt werden.'

71 Bornkamm, 'Sturmstillung,' p 52: 'Es findet sich ausser Lk 12:18 nur bei ihm . . . und zwar immer zur Bezeichnung eines schwachen Glaubens, der in Sturm (8:26; 14:31) und Sorge (6:30; 16:8) erlahmt und damit sich als Scheinglaube erweist (17:20), der dem Ansturm dämonischer Gewalten nicht gewachsen ist.'

72 Similarly in 10:20 the reason the disciples are *not to be anxious* about how to speak is that 'the spirit of your *Father* (against Lk's 'Holy Spirit') is speaking in you.' In 10:29 it is your *Father* (against Lk's 'God') who is concerned even for the sparrows. Therefore (redactional οὖν 10:31) you should *not fear* since you are of more value than the sparrows. Cf 18:14.

73 Similarly Goppelt, *Christologie*, p 39: the commands of the Sermon on the Mount 'werden realisierbar, wenn Gott, wie Matthäus besonders betont, für die Menschen zum Vater wird . . .' Also Jeremias, *Theology*, p 217. It is

probably no accident that Mt connected the Golden Rule (7:12) to the preceding saying on the Father's generosity with οὖν. This accords with Mt's conception of God's fatherhood and ethics. We are called to fulfil the love command precisely *because* the Father is generous and will give us the necessary resources. It is thus unnecessary, with Furnish (*Love*, p 57), to ascribe to Mt's οὖν a mere summary function.

74 Trilling, *Wahre Israel*, p 30: 'Nur von [Jüngern] kann gesagt werden, dass sie den Willen Gottes tun. Doch auch das Umgekehrte gilt: ein Jünger ist (nur) der, der den Willen des Vaters tut' (cf p 189). See also Barth, 'Gesetzesverständnis,' p 95.

75 Goppelt, *Christologie*, p 31: 'Die Antithesen kennzeichnen die vom Alten Testament herkommenden Weisungen Gottes als von Menschen zu vollstreckenden Rechtssätze, die das Zusammenleben der Menschen ermöglichen wenn das Böse eine nicht zu beseitigende, nur einzuschränkende Gegebenheit ist.' Guelich, *Annul*, p 200: The premises designate 'neither the Old Testament law as such nor the specific scribal interpretation of the law, but rather the legal ramifications of the law's demands.' Bornkamm, 'Enderwartung,' p 22: 'Ihr [die Antithesenreihe] durchgängiges Motiv ist der Durchstoss durch ein in formale Rechtssätze verkehrtes Gesetz, hinter dessen Ordnung das ungehorsame Herz des Menschen sich in Ordnung wähnt . . .'

76 Trilling, *Christusverkündigung*, p 100: 'Nur dann wenn man die Antithesen zusammen und jede einzelne in dem durch 5:17–19 bereiteten Verständnis auslegt, handelt man entsprechend der Intention des Evangelisten.'

77 For a concise description of the distinction between apodictic and casuistic law, see Mendenhall, *Law and Covenant*, pp 6–11.

78 This is one of the clearest distinctions between Mt's use of the sayings on enemy love and Lk's use of them: for Lk the problem of the law is, by comparison, of minor significance; Kümmel, *Introduction*, p 105.

79 Strecker (*Weg*, p 136) considers (with Haenchen, *ZThK* 48, p 49) that Mt's form is primary to Lk 11:42, but thinks (with Bornkamm, 'Enderwartung,' pp 23f) that it is to be understood within Mt's own larger conception.

80 Bornkamm, 'Doppelgebot,' p 45. So also G. Barth, *Gesetzesverständnis*, p 74; and E. Schweizer, *NTS* 16/3, p 216: 'The commandment to love one's neighbor is for Mt the key that opens the new understanding of the law.' Cf Strecker, *Weg*, pp 136,147.

81 Again the primary concern here is with what *Lk perceived* to be the historical teaching of Jesus, not with what contemporary critical scholarship has determined it to have actually been. See 'Approach and Methodology,' p 140.

82 Conzelmann, *Luke*, p 45.

83 Bartsch, *Wachet*, p 67. See also *ThZ* 16, pp 5–18.

84 Bartsch, *Wachet*, p 75: 'Als wesentliches Ergebnis des Vergleichs der Feldrede mit der Bergpredigt, dass die eschatologische Ausrichtung das Wesensmerkmal der Feldrede ist, demgegenüber die Bergpredigt bereits stärker von der Paränese bestimmt ist, ohne die eschatologische Ausrichtung damit zu verlieren.'

85 Bartsch, *Wachet*, p 76.

86 Baumbach, *Bösen*, p 126.

87 Baumbach, *Bösen,* p 127.

88 Baumbach, *Bösen,* p 127.

89 Schürmann, *BZ* NS10, p 57.

90 Schürmann, *BZ* NS10, p 58.

91 Schürmann, *BZ* NS10, p 58.

92 Schürmann, *BZ* NS10, p 80.

93 Schürmann, *BZ* NS10, pp 60f.

94 Schürmann, *BZ* NS10, p 60.

95 Schürmann, *BZ* NS10, p 59: 'Lukas sieht in ihn das Vor- und Urbild der christlichen Gemeinde.'

96 Degenhardt, *Lukas,* p 215.

97 Degenhardt, *Lukas,* p 215.

98 Schürmann (*BZ* NS10, p 59) observes that only one other place besides 6:17 does the group of disciples swell to a 'multitude,' namely at the triumphal entry into Jerusalem (19:37): 'man möchte wiederum meinen zeichenhaftprophetisch.' Thus in these two places Lk probably envisions proleptically the involvement of the whole church.

99 The fact that the beatitudes and woes (6:20–26) as well as the final parable (cf 6:46) are in the second person form of direct address (different from Mt) also shows that we have here public proclamation.

100 Flender, *Heil,* pp 28f. He points out further that in Lk the same saying can be addressed once to the disciples (8:16) and once to the people (11:33).

101 Since we are not concerned primarily with the whole Sermon on the Plain we cannot discuss the question how all the elements of Lk's composition are relevant for his situation. Schürmann (*BZ* NS10, pp 61f) has attempted to answer this question in some detail. He divides the main section of the sermon into two halves: 'Unverkennbar handelt . . . 6:27–45 in unreflektiert positiver Darlegung (V 27–38) und in reflektierter Abhebung (V 39–45) vom neuen Gebot Jesu.' He describes the situation behind the second half as follows: 'Es gibt in den Gemeinden bzw. in ihren Umkreis Lehrer, die sich als Führer anbieten (V 39) und die oben (V 27–38) dargelegte Lehre des einzigen Lehrers hinaus wollen (vgl V 40); die mehr fordern als Jesus das tat, und die von diesem "Mehr" her sich Kritik am christlichen Gemeindeleben erlauben, dabei aber Jesu Liebesgebot selbst nicht leben (V 41) und deren "Reden" (V 45) schlechten Früchten (V 43f) gleichen.' He cites the commentaries of Zahn, Schlatter, Rengstorf and Grundmann as those who similarly see in 6:39–45 an address to the 'Lehrstand' in Lk's church.

102 Van Unnik, *NovTest* 8, p 298.

103 Van Unnik, *NovTest* 8, p 299.

104 Wrege, *Bergpredigt,* p 89.

105 Although the custom was not unique to Palestine (Epictetus, *Discourses* IV.1.79: 'You ought to treat your whole body like a poor loaded-down donkey . . . and if it be commandeered and a soldier lay hold of it, let it go, do not resist nor grumble.'), it would have been especially onerous there (cf Mt 27:32) because of the hated foreign occupation. To the Greeks it may not have been the burden it was to the Jews.

106 Cf Taylor, *Formation,* p 96 'We can hardly trace the Semitic parallelism to the hand of the Gentile Evangelist.' See also note 137 of Chapter 2. The

'distinctive pattern' referred to can be seen in Lk 6:29-30: the sequence
dative participle – present positive imperative – ἀπό and participle –
negative imperative in 6:29 is duplicated in the following verse. For Mt's
different form principle see note 138 of Chapter 2.

107 Bartsch, *Wachet*, p 69. Note: Mt's order of χιτῶνα and ἱμάτιον is reversed in
Lk 6:29 apparently to show that a theft is in view (so that the outer
garment is grabbed first) instead of a legal claim of the shirt. In addition,
instead of Mt's command to loan (5:42b), Lk has the command not to
demand back what has been taken from you (6:30b).

108 I would agree therefore with the conclusion reached by J. Roloff (*Kerygma*,
p 270) that we must be more careful than the classical form critics in
determining 'aktualisierende Tendenzen' in the gospel tradition and 'dass
historisierende Motive innerhalb des von uns überschaubaren Gestaltungs-
und Tradierungsprozesses der Jesusgeschichten von den Anfängen an eine
weit grössere Rolle gespielt haben, als vielfach angenommen worden ist.'
Similarly, G. Stanton, *Jesus of Nazareth*, p 171.

109 The normal meaning of ἀπελπίζω is 'to give up hope' or 'to despair' of
something. Thus it is used in Josephus (*Wars* 4, 397; 5, 354); Eth. Enoch
103:10; Is 29:19 (LXX); I Clement 59:3 et al. W. Bauer (*Lexicon*, p 83)
argues that the word here in Lk 6:35, 'because of the contrast with παρ'
ὧν ἐλπίζετε λαβεῖν vs. 34, demands the meaning . . . *expecting nothing in
return.*' The variant reading μηδένα ἀπελπίζοντες ('despairing of no one,' ℵ
W X* et al) is rejected by the editorial committee of the BSGNT because
the reading 'which introduces into the context an alien motive, appears to
have arisen in transcription, the result of dittography' (Metzger, *Textual
Commentary*, p 141). Perhaps Lk's unique usage of ἀπελπίζω is influenced
by its close association with three other words compounded with the ἀπό
prefix which connote receiving something back: ἀπέχετε, 6:24; ἀπαιτεί, 6:30;
ἀπολάβωσιν, 6:34.

110 Lk 15:27; 16:25; 18:30; 23:41; Mk 7:33; Rom 1:27; Gal 4:5; Col 3:24;
II Jn 8.

111 Even if some or all of these differences from Mt were pre-Lukan (which is
very hard to determine) we will see that they fit into a motif of reciprocity
which Lk is especially concerned to combat.

112 That Lk is thinking of those who are poor in this world's goods will be
shown from the remainder of our discussion. But that he was referring
merely to the external circumstances is not likely (see notes 56, 57 of
Chapter 3).

113 That 'woe' has this meaning is shown by Lk 10:13f (woe to Chorazin) and
Lk 17:1f (woe to the one by whom temptations come); both meet destruction.

114 The occurrence of ἀπέχω in Lk 6:24b and Mt 6:3,5,16 is an even more
striking parallel because the word has the meaning 'receive back' only here
in the synoptics. Elsewhere it means 'be at a distance.'

115 Cf Degenhardt, *Lukas*, p 185: 'Der Gegensatz zur pharisäischen Haltung ist
für ihn und seine Gemeinde nicht mehr aktuell; im Vordergrund steht
stattdessen "der Gegensatz des Glaubens zur Besitzgebundenheit".' Cf
Grundmann, *Lukas*, p 140; Rengstorf, *Lukas*, p 4.

116 Van Unnik, *NovTest* 8, pp 293f. Having cited texts from Dio Chrysostomus,

Epictetus, and Lucian, he concludes, 'Dass man auch in der ntl. Zeit die alte Praxis handhabte; dass man auch damals bestimmten Leuten Freundlichkeit bewies, i.c. reich bewirtete, um von ihnen etwas zurück zu empfangen.'

117 Bolkestein (*Wohltätigkeit*, pp 471f) tries to show (from Seneca and Plutarch) how the *Gegenseitigkeitsregel* was overcome.

118 The parable has no parallel in the other synoptics but Jeremias shows that the parable is not Lk's formation (*Gleichnisse*, p 182). It contains two historical presents (ὁρᾷ, v 23; λέγει, v 29) but of the 90 historical presents in the Markan material which Lk takes over only one is preserved. Moreover the story has a long prehistory and has its parallels in the rabbinic tradition. Since we have no synoptic parallel we cannot determine where Lk may have altered the tradition. It is possible that the vocabulary with which we are concerned was Lk's way of providing a link between this parable and other sayings on riches in his gospel.

119 Jeremias, *Gleichnisse*, p 183: in the bosom of Abraham 'ist Bezeichnung des Ehrenplatzes beim himmlischen Gastmahl zur Rechten (vgl. Joh 13:23) des Hausvaters Abraham.'

120 See also the story of Zacchaeus (Lk 19:1-10): 'Behold, Lord, the half of my goods I give to the poor . . .' 'Today salvation has come to this house.'

121 The reference work consulted was Moulton and Geden, *Concordance*.

122 Nor is the selling of possessions in Acts 2:44f; 4:32-37 meant as a pattern to be imposed on the church of Lk's day (Conzelmann, *Luke*, p 233). Mary the mother of John Mark still possessed her house (Acts 12:12) and Peter says to Ananias of the piece of property he had sold: 'While it remained unsold, did it not remain your own? And after it was sold was it not in your authority?' However the free sacrifice of many in the early Jerusalem community for those in need must have seemed to Lk an exemplary, concrete fulfilment of Jesus' commands (cf Lk 12:33).

123 The implication of 10:30 is that the robbed man is a Jew. The lesson in love comes from a Samaritan and, as Jeremias (*Gleichnisse*, p 202) points out, in the time of Jesus 'es beherrschte beiderseits unversöhnlicher Hass.'

124 Rengstorf, *Lukas*, p 4: 'Jesu Kampf gilt bei Lukas vor allem der allgemein menschlichen Gefährdung durch den Mammon.'

125 He refers twice (11:49 Q; 21:12) to persecutions of Christians by the Jews. Note also that the reference to (Roman) conscription in Mt 5:41 is missing in Lk. Only in Lk does Jesus pray for his (Roman) executioners (23:34; note textual uncertainty). Lk apparently weakens the original, 'I have not come to bring peace but a sword' (Mt 10:34), and uses *'division'* instead of 'sword' (Lk 12:51).

126 It is the Jews who bear the primary blame for Jesus' death (Lk 20:20,26; 23:2,5,18f,23,25) and Pilate and Herod are shown struggling for justice (23:13-16; contrast 23:25 with Mk 15:15 and Mt 27:26). In Acts there are no serious clashes between Christians and Romans (in 16:19ff and 19:23 the trouble is started by personal property interests but ends with Paul's vindication) and it is stressed that the Romans can find no fault in this new religion worthy of imprisonment (13:7,12; 16:39; 18:15-17; 19:35-41; 23:29; 25:25; 26:32; 28:30f). Cf Bruce, *Acts,* p 23; Kümmel, *Introduction,* p 114.

127 See p 158 for the Lukan character of the woes.

128 Lewis, *The Weight of Glory*, pp 1f (my italics).

129 Bornkamm, 'Lohngedanke,' p 78: 'Der Schatz im Himmel ist die Gottesherrschaft selbst.' Cf Lk 12:33ff.

130 Manson, *Sayings*, p 280.

131 Riesenfeld ('Schätzesammeln,' p 47) argues that, since the texts on anxiety
(Lk 12:22–32/Mt 6:25–33) and treasure in heaven (Lk 12:33f/Mt 6:19–21)
are juxtaposed in Mt and Lk, therefore Mt and Lk probably found the two
texts already joined in their sources. But this does not establish that they
had identical *Vorlagen*: why are Mt and Lk so similar in the pericope on
anxiety and yet so different in the pericope on treasure in heaven? Manson
would assign Mt 6:19–20 to M and Lk 12:32f to Q (*Sayings*, pp 114,172).
Grundmann (*Lukas*, p 262) on the other hand (following Schlatter) would
see Lk 6:32f as originally attached to the parable of the rich fool (Lk 12:
13–21) and thus belonging to S-Lk. It seems to me that the situation is
such that we cannot with certainty determine what Lk himself has added
or changed. What is plain is that in saying 'Provide yourselves with a
treasure in the heavens,' he departs from the Matthean parallel.

132 Jeremias (*Gleichnisse*, p 43) points out the break between 16:1–8 and
16:9 and the turn the meaning takes in 16:9. There is disagreement however
whether the interpretative saying of v 9 was added by Lk (Bultmann,
History, p 176) or whether it is 'die Stimme eines urchristlichen Predigers
. . . , der bemüht ist, dem Gleichnis eine Lektion für seine Gemeinde zu
entnehmen' (Jeremias, *Gleichnisse*, p 43). Compare I Tim 6:17–19: 'As
for the rich in this world, charge them not to be haughty, nor to set their
hopes on uncertain riches but on God who richly furnishes us with everything to enjoy. They are to do good, to be rich in good deeds, liberal and
generous, thus laying up for themselves a good foundation for the future,
so that they may take hold of life which is life indeed.' Cf also Heb 10:34;
I Cor 9:24: 'Run *in order that* you may obtain.'

133 There is no contradiction between this statement and Lk's emphasis that
we are to give or loan not *hoping* for anything *back* (6:34f; 14:13f)
because it is clear in each text that he means we are not to calculate in
order to get back the riches of *this age*. He never implies that we should
not hope for 'repayment' (14:14) in the age to come.

134 Bultmann (*History*, p 103) for example, says of Lk 14:12–14, 'The saying
is much more akin to the grudging spirit of the last chapter of Eth. Enoch
than to the preaching of Jesus.' Cf also Josephus, *Bellum* 2.157. In his
Theology (p 15), Bultmann says that Jesus appealed to the motive of
recompense and that this is a self-contradiction in his preaching. Bultmann's
attempted solution of this contradiction applies to the general problem of
reward in the gospels and will thus be instructive to cite here with a short
critique: 'The motive of reward is only a primitive expression of the idea
that in what a man does his own real being is at stake – that self which he
not already is, but is to become. *To achieve that self is the legitimate
motive of ethical dealing and his true obedience,* in which he becomes
aware of the paradoxical truth that in order to arrive at himself he must
surrender to the demand of God – or, in other words, that in such surrender
he wins himself' (my italics).

Bultmann is so hesitant to allow man to have an objective motive outside himself like the reward of *God*, that he makes *man* the center and man's becoming himself the only legitimate ethical motivation. Man cannot be motivated by a hope for *God* but he may be motivated by the hope for a complete *self!* It is wrong to surrender yourself in order to win *God* but perfectly fine to surrender yourself in order to win *self*. Bultmann still lets a man act for a reward which is future, but that this reward should be *God* is 'primitive'; it must rather be *myself!* In all this, Bultmann has left behind the New Testament in which God in all his transcendent glory stands at the center, not man. Lk stresses the glory of God more than the other synoptics: cf 2:9,14,20; 5:25f; 7:16; 9:26; 13:13; 17:15,18; 18:43; 19:38; 23:47.

135 Conzelmann, *Luke*, p 234.

136 'So you also when you have done all that is commanded you, say, "We are unworthy servants; we have only done what was our duty"' (unique to Lk).

137 Conzelmann, *Luke*, p 234.

138 '. . . he is kind to the ungrateful and evil. Be *merciful* therefore as your Father is merciful' (unique to Lk).

139 'Fear not, little flock, it is your Father's *good pleasure* to give you the Kingdom' (unique to Lk).

140 'And the son said to him, "Father, I have sinned against heaven and before you; I am *no longer worthy* to be called your son"' (unique to Lk).

141 'But the tax collector standing afar off would not even lift up his eyes to heaven but beat his breast, saying, "God be merciful to me a *sinner!*" I tell you this man went down to his house justified' (unique to Lk).

142 This would be the essential meaning of δεδικαιωμένος in 18:14. Jeremias (*Gleichnisse*, p 140) cites IV Ezra 12:7 where we find the parallel: 'If I have *found favor* in thy sight, if I am justified with thee . . .'

143 'Your *reward* will be *great* and you will be sons of the Highest.'

144 '*Rejoice* in that day and *leap for joy* for behold your reward is great in heaven.'

145 'Blessed are you who hunger, for you shall be satisfied.' That this 'eschatological satisfaction' is experienced already in this age is shown by (1) the presence of the Kingdom (6:20) and (2) the great rejoicing of the disciples (6:23).

146 'Woe to you who are rich, for you have received your consolation.'

147 'Beware of the scribes who like to go around in long robes and love salutations in the market places and the best seats in the synagogues and the places of honor at the feasts.'

148 The man is a 'fool . . . who lays up treasure for himself and is not rich toward God.'

Conclusion

1 This function of Jesus' command of enemy love should not be misunderstood as an academic or bookish procedure as if the church made detailed comparisons between Jesus' saying and the sources available to them. Rather, we should probably think of the consciousness of the early Christians being shaped and molded by their new faith in the gospel of Christ

and its ethical implications expressed in the words of Jesus. These words then, as practical expressions of the gospel, functioned naturally to determine what might suitably be used to expand and apply them in the building of the paraenetic tradition.

2 The quote is taken from Goppelt's last published essay before his death: 'Jesus und die "Haustafel" -Tradition,' p 103. For a translation of the quote see p 134.

3 Here in the conclusion I will not attempt to distinguish between the interpretation of Jesus' command of enemy love in the written paraenesis of the New Testament and its interpretation in the oral paraenetic tradition, nor will I attempt to discuss the interpretation of Jesus' command in the (oral?) gospel tradition prior to and independent of its deposit in Mt and Lk. I tried to keep these levels of the tradition in view in the body of the work. But it has been my general conclusion that our knowledge of the *context* of the love command in these dark periods is so meager and uncertain that it would be presumptuous to assert what the *meaning* of Jesus' command was for these anonymous guardians of the tradition. On the basis of common features in the synoptics and in the epistles it may be possible to make assumptions about the underlying oral traditions. See, for example, pp 126ff.

BIBLIOGRAPHY

From all the works cited in the text only certain well-known reference works have been omitted from the bibliography. Some works are included which were not cited but are considered pertinent to the subject. The abbreviations used in the footnotes for the various works cited are a sufficient guide for finding the works here in the bibliography.

Althaus, P., *Der Brief an die Römer*, NTD 6, 3rd edn, Göttingen 1963.
Aschermann, P. H., *Die paränetischen Formen der 12 Patriarchen und ihr Nachwirken in der frühchristlichen Mahnung*, Dissertation, Berlin 1955.
Augstein, R., *Jesus Menschensohn*, Gütersloh 1972.
Augustine, *The Confessions of St Augustine*, translated by E. B. Pusey, New York 1962.
Bach, E., *Die Feindesliebe nach dem natürlichen und dem übernatürlichen Gesetz*, Kempten 1913.
Balcomb, R. E., *The Written Sources of Paul's Knowledge of Jesus*, Dissertation, Boston 1951.
Bammel, E., 'The Baptist in the Early Christian Tradition,' *NTS* 18, October 1971, pp 95–128.
Banks, R., *Jesus and the Law in the Synoptic Tradition*, SNTS Monograph Series 28, Cambridge 1975.
Barrett, C. K., *The Epistle to the Romans*, London 1957.
Barrett, C. K., *The New Testament Background: Selected Documents*, New York 1961.
Barrett, C. K., 'Stephen and the Son of Man,' in: *Apophoreta: Festschrift für Ernst Haenchen*, W. Schneimelcher (ed.), BZNW 30, Berlin 1964.
Barrett, C. K., *Jesus and the Gospel Tradition*, Philadelphia 1968.
Barth, G., 'Das Gesetzesverständnis des Evangelisten Matthäus,' in: *Überlieferung und Auslegung im Matthäusevangelium*, G. Bornkamm, G. Barth and H. J. Held, 6th edn, Neukirchen-Vluyn 1970, pp 54–154.
Barth, P., *Dia Stoa*, 5th edn, Stuttgart 1941.
Bartsch, H-W., 'Feld-Rede und Bergpredigt: Redaktionsarbeit in Luk. 6,' *ThZ* 16, 1960, pp 5–18.
Bartsch, H-W., *Wachet aber zu jeder Zeit (Entwurf einer Auslegung des Lukasevangeliums)*, Hamburg 1963.
Batdorf, E. W., 'How Shall We Interpret the Sermon on the Mount?' *JBR* 27, 1959, pp 211–17.
Batiffol, P., *Proseuchē Aseneth, Studia Patristica*, Paris 1889.
Bauer, W., *A Greek-English Lexicon of the New Testament*, Cambridge 1957.

Bauer, W., 'Das Gebot der Feindesliebe und die alten Christen,' in: *Aufsätze und kleine Schriften,* G. Strecker (ed.), Tübingen 1967, pp 235–52.

Baumbach, G., *Das Verständnis des Bösen in den synoptischen Evangelien,* Berlin 1963.

Bayer, O. 'Sprachbewegung und Weltveränderung, Ein systematischer Versuch als Auslegung von Mt 5:43–48,' *EvTh* 35/4, 1975, pp 309–21.

Beare, F. W., *The First Epistle of Peter,* 2nd edn, Oxford 1958.

Beare, F. W., *The Earliest Records of Jesus,* Oxford 1964.

Becker, J., *Untersuchungen zur Entstehungsgeschichte der Testamente der Zwölf Patriarchen,* Leiden 1970.

Berger, K., *Die Gesetzespredigt Jesu,* Neukirchen-Vluyn 1972.

Best, *The 1st and 2nd Epistles to the Thessalonians,* BNTC, London, 1972.

Bigg, C., *Epistles of St Peter and St Jude,* ICC, Edinburgh 1901.

Bjerkelund, C. J., *Parakalô: Form, Funktion und Sinn der Parakalô-Sätze in den paulinischen Briefen,* Bibliotheca Theologica Norwegica, Oslo 1967.

Black, M., *An Aramaic Approach to the Gospels and Acts,* 3rd edn, Oxford 1967.

Bolkestein, H., *Wohltätigkeit und Armenpflege im vorchristlichen Altertum,* Utrecht 1939.

Boman, T., *Jesus-Überlieferung im Lichte der neueren Volkskunde,* Göttingen 1967.

Bonhoeffer, A., *Epiktet und das Neue Testament,* Giessen 1911.

Bornemann, W., *Die Thessalonicherbriefe,* MK, Göttingen 1894.

Bornkamm, G., *Jesus of Nazareth,* New York E.T. 1960.

Bornkamm, G., 'Das Doppelgebot der Liebe,' in: *Geschichte und Glaube,* Part 1 (*Gesammelte Aufsätze* III), München 1968, pp 37–45.

Bornkamm, G., *Paulus,* Stuttgart, 1969.

Bornkamm, G., 'Der Lohngedanke im Neuen Testament,' in: *Studien zu Antike und Urchristentum* (*Gesammelte Aufsätze* II), München 1970, pp 69–92.

Bornkamm, G., 'Enderwartung und Kirche im Matthäusevangelium,' in: *Überlieferung und Auslegung im Matthäusevangelium,* G. Bornkamm, G. Barth and H. J. Held, 6th edn, Neukirchen-Vluyn 1970, pp 13–47.

Bornkamm, G., 'Die Sturmstillung im Matthäusevangelium,' in: *Überlieferung und Auslegung im Matthäusevangelium,* G. Bornkamm, G. Barth and H. J. Held, 6th edn, Neukirchen-Vluyn 1970, pp 48–53.

Bousset, W., *Der Religion des Judentums in späthellenistischen Zeitalter, Tübingen* 1966.

Branscomb, B. H., *Jesus and the Law of Moses,* New York 1930.

Braun, H., *Spätjüdisch-häretischer und frühchristlicher Radikalismus* II, Tübingen 1957.

Braun, H., 'Qumran und das Neue Testament, Ein Bericht über 10 Jahre Forschung (1950–1959),' *ThR* 28, 1962, pp 95–233.

Braun, H., *Jesus,* Stuttgart 1969.

Broadus, J. A., *Gospel of Matthew,* Valley Forge, Pa. 1886.

Broer, I., 'Die Antithesen und der Evangelist Mätthaus. Versuch, eine alte These zu revidieren,' *BZ* 19/1, 1975, pp 50–63.

Brooks, E. W., *The Book of Joseph and Asenath,* Translations of Early Documents II, 6, New York 1918.

Brown, F., Driver, S. R. and Briggs, C. A., *Hebrew and English Lexicon of the Old Testament,* Oxford 1962.

Brown, J. P., 'Synoptic Parallels in the Epistles and Form-history,' *NTS* 10, 1963–64, pp 27–48.

Bruce, F. F., *Commentary on the Book of Acts,* Grand Rapids, Mich. 1954.

Bruce, F. F., *Jesus and Paul,* Grand Rapids, Mich. 1974.

Brun, L., *Segen und Fluch im Urchristentum,* Oslo 1933.

Bruppacher, H., 'Was sagte Jesus in Mätthaus 5,48?' *ZNW* 58, 1967, p 145.

Bryant, H. E., 'Matthew 5:38,39,' *ET* 48, 1936–37, pp 236–7.

Büchsel, F., *Theologie des Neuen Testaments,* Gütersloh 1935.

Bultmann, R., *Der Stil der paulinischen Predigt und die kynisch-stoische Diatribe,* FRLANT 13, Göttingen 1910.

Bultmann, R., 'Das religiöse Moment in der Unterweisung des Epiktet und das Neue Testament,' *ZNW* 13, 1912, pp 97–110, 177–91.

Bultmann, R., 'Das Problem der Ethik bei Paulus,' *ZNW* 23, 1924.

Bultmann, R., *Theology of the New Testament,* 2 vols, New York E.T. (I) 1951, (II) 1955.

Bultmann, R., 'The Sermon on the Mount and the Justice of the State' in: *Existence and Faith,* selected essays translated by S. Ogden, Cleveland 1960.

Bultmann, R., *The History of the Synoptic Tradition,* Oxford E.T. 1968.

Bultmann, R., *Jesus,* München 1970.

Bultmann, R., 'Die Bedeutung des geschichtlichen Jesus für die Theologie des Paulus,' in: *Glauben und Verstehen* I, 7th edn, Tübingen 1972, pp 188–213.

Bultmann, R., 'Das christliche Gebot der Nächstenliebe,' in: *Glauben und Verstehen* I, 7th edn, Tübingen 1972, pp 229–44.

Burchard, C., *Untersuchungen zu Joseph und Aseneth,* WUNT 8, Tübingen 1965.

Burchard, C., 'Das doppelte Liebesgebot in der frühen christlichen Überlieferung,' in: *Der Ruf Jesu und die Antwort der Gemeinde. Festschrift für J. Jeremias,* E. Lohse (ed.), Göttingen 1970, pp 39–62.

Burney, C. F., *The Poetry of our Lord,* Oxford 1925.

Campenhausen, H. von, 'Die Christen und das bürgerliche Leben, nach den Aussagen des Neuen Testaments,' in: *Tradition und Leben, Kräfte der Kirchengeschichte,* Tübingen 1960, pp 180–202.

Carrington, P., *The Primitive Christian Catechism,* Cambridge 1940.

Cerfaux, L., 'Die Tradition bei Paulus,' *Catholica* 9, 1953, pp 94–104.

Charles, R. H. (ed.) *The Apocrypha and Pseudepigrapha of the Old Testament* I, II, Oxford 1913.

Charles, R. H., *Religious Development between the Old and New Testaments,* London 1914.

Christ, W. von, *Geschichte der griechischen Literatur,* Part 2, 1st half, 6th edn, München 1959.

Conzelmann, H., *The Theology of St Luke,* London E. T. 1961.

Conzelmann, H., *Der erste Brief an die Korinther,* MK, 11th edn, Göttingen 1969.

Conzelmann, H., *An Outline of the Theology of the New Testament,* New York E.T. 1969.

Cranfield, C. E. B., *A Commentary on Rom 12–13,* Scottish Journal of Theology Occasional Papers 12, Edinburgh 1965.

Cullmann, O., *Christ and Time,* Philadelphia E.T. 1950.

Cullmann, O., *Die Tradition als exegetische, historisches und theologisches Problem,* Zürich 1954.

Cullmann, O., *Salvation in History,* London E.T. 1967.

Cullmann, O., 'Out of Season Remarks on the "Historical Jesus" of the Bultmann School,' in: *In Search of the Historical Jesus,* H. K. McArthur (ed.), London 1970.

Dabney, R. L., *Discussions: Evangelical and Theological* I, London 1967.

Dahood, M. J., 'Two Pauline Quotations from the Old Testament,' *CBQ* 17, 1955, pp 19–24.

Dalman, G., *Die Worte Jesu,* Leipzig 1930.

Dana, H. E. and Mantey, J. R., *A Manual Grammar of the Greek New Testament,* New York 1927.

Daube, D., *The New Testament and Rabbinic Judaism,* London 1956.

Daube, D., 'Participle and Imperative in I Peter,' appended note in: *The First Epistle of Peter,* E. G. Selwyn, London 1969.

Davenport, Gene L., *The Eschatology of the Book of Jubilees,* Leiden 1971.

Davies, W. D., *Paul and Rabbinic Judaism,* London 1948.

Davies, W. D. 'Reflections on a Scandinavian Approach to "the Gospel Tradition",' in: *Neotestamentica et Patristica. Freundesgabe für O. Cullmann,* W. C. van Unnik (ed.), Leiden 1962, pp 14–34.

Davies, W. D., *The Setting of the Sermon on the Mount,* Cambridge 1966.

Degenhardt, H-J., *Lukas, Evangelist der Armen,* Stuttgart 1965.

Delling, G., *Das Zeitverständnis des Neuen Testaments,* Gütersloh 1940.

Denis, A-M., *Introduction aux Pseudepigraphes Grecs de l'ancien Testament,* Leiden 1970.

Derrett, J. D. M., *Law in the New Testament,* London 1970.

Dibelius, M., *Geschichte der urchristlichen Literatur* II, Berlin 1926.

Dibelius, M., 'Zur Formgeschichte des Neuen Testaments ausserhalb der Evangelien,' *ThR* NS 3, Tübingen 1931, pp 207–42.

Dibelius, M., *An die Thessalonicher I, II, an die Philipper,* HNT 11, Tübingen 1937.

Dibelius, M., *Der Brief des Jacobus,* MK, Göttingen 1964.

Dibelius, M., *Jesus,* 4th edn, Berlin 1966.

Dibelius, M., *From Tradition to Gospel,* New York E.T. n.d.

Dietzfelbinger, C., 'Das Gleichnis vom erlassenen Schuld. Eine theologische Untersuchung von Mt 18:23–35,' *EvTh* 32, 1972, pp 437ff.

Dietzfelbinger, C., *Die Antithesen der Bergpredigt,* München 1975.

Dihle, A., *Die goldene Regel. Eine Einführung in die Geschichte der antiken und frühchristlichen Vulgarethik,* Studienhefte zur Altertumswissenschaft 7, Göttingen 1962.

Dobschütz, E., *Thessalonicher-Briefe,* MK, Göttingen 1909.

Dobschütz, E., 'Matthäus als Rabbi und Katechet,' *ZNW* 27, 1928, pp 338–48.

Dodd, C. H., *The Epistle of Paul to the Romans,* London 1932.

Dodd, C. H., *The Parables of the Kingdom,* London 1935.

Dodd, C. H., *Gospel and Law: The Relation of Faith and Ethics in Early Christianity,* Cambridge 1951.

Dodd, C. H., 'ENNOMOS CHRISTOU,' in: *Studia Paulina. In Honorem Johannis de Zwaan,* J. N. Sevenster and W. C. van Unnik (eds.), Haarlem 1953, pp 96–110.

Dodd, C. H., 'The Primitive Catechism and the Sayings of Jesus,' in: *New Testament Essays, Studies in Memory of T. W. Manson,* A. J. B. Higgins (ed.), Manchester 1959, pp 106 -18.

Dodd, C. H., *History and the Gospel,* Digswell Place, England, 1960.

Dodd, C. H., 'Matthew and Paul,' in: *New Testament Studies,* Manchester 1967, pp 53–66.

Downey, G., 'Who is my Neighbor? The Greek and Roman Answer,' *ATR* 47/1, 1965, pp 3–15.

Dungan, D. L., *The Sayings of Jesus in the Churches of Paul*, Oxford 1971.
Dungan, D. L., 'Early Christianity minus Jesus,' *Interpretation* 28/1, 1974, pp 98–101.
Dupont-Sommer, A., *The Essene Writings from Qumran*, Oxford 1961.
Easton, B. S., *Christ in the Gospels*, New York 1930.
Easton, B. S., 'The New Testament Ethical Lists,' *JBL* 51, 1932, pp 1–12.
Edwards, P., 'Christian Hate,' *Way* 7/4, 1967, pp 300–8.
Eichholz, G., *Auslegung der Bergpredigt*, BSt, 2nd edn, Neukirchen-Vluyn 1970.
Eissfeldt, O., *The Old Testament: an Introduction*, New York E.T. 1965.
Ernst, J., 'Die Einheit von Gottes und Nächstenliebe in der Verkündigung Jesu,'
    ThGl 60, 1970, pp 3–14.
Fannon, P., 'Paul and Tradition in the Primitive Church,' *Scripture* 16, 1964, pp 47–56.
Feine, P., *Jesus Christus und Paulus*, Leipzig 1902.
Feine, P., *Der Apostel Paulus*, BFChTh 2nd series, Vol 12, Gütersloh 1927.
Fenton, J. C., *The Gospel of St Matthew*, Harmondsworth, Middlesex, England.
    1963.
Fichtner, J., 'Der Begriff des Nächsten im Alten Testament,' *Wort und Dienst, Jahrbuch
    der Theologie Schule Bethel* NS 4, 1955, pp 23–52.
Fiebig, P., 'Jesu Worte über die Feindesliebe im Zusammenhang mit den wichtigsten
    rabbinischen Parallelen eläutert,' *ThStKr* 91, 1918, pp 30–64.
Filson, F. V., 'The Christian Teacher in the First Century,' *JBL* 60, 1941, pp 317–29.
Filson, F. V., *The Gospel According to St Matthew*, London 1960.
Fjärstedt, B., *Synoptic Tradition in I Corinthians. Themes and Clusters of Theme
    Words in I Cor. 1–4 and 9*, Uppsala 1974.
Flender, H., *Heil und Geschichte in der Theologie des Lukas*, BEvTh 41, München
    1965.
Flender, H., *Die Botschaft Jesu von der Herrschaft Gottes*, München 1968.
Frame, J. E., *The Epistles of Paul to the Thessalonians*, ICC, Edinburgh 1912.
France, R. T., *Jesus and the Old Testament*, London 1971.
Fraser, J. W., *Jesus and Paul. Paul as Interpreter of Jesus from Harnack to Kümmel*,
    Appleford 1974.
Fuchs E., 'Was heisst? "Du sollst deinen Nächsten lieben wie dich selbst," ' in:
    Zur Frage nach dem historischen Jesus, 2nd edn, Tübingen 1965, pp 1–20.
Fuller, R. *The Mission and Achievement of Jesus*, London 1956.
Fuller, R. 'Das Doppelgebot der Liebe,' in: *Jesus Christus in Historie und Theologie*,
    G. Strecker (ed.), Tübingen 1975, pp 317–29.
Furnish, V. P. 'The Jesus -Paul Debate: From Bauer to Bultmann,' *Bulletin of the
    John Rylands Library* 47, 1965, pp 342–81.
Furnish, V. P., *The Love Command in the New Testament*, Nashville, Tenn., 1972.
Gaechter, P., *Das Matthäus-Evangelium*, Innsbruck 1963.
Gerhardsson, B., *Memory and Manuscript: Oral Tradition and Written Transmission
    in Rabbinic Judaism and Early Christianity*, Copenhagen 1964.
Gerhardsson, B., *Tradition and Transmission in Early Christianity*, Lund 1964.
Gesenius, F. H. W., *Hebrew Grammar*, 2nd edn, Oxford 1910.
Gloege, G., *Aller Tage Tag*, Stuttgart 1960.
Glover, R., 'The Didache's Quotations and the Synoptic Gospels,' *NTS* 5, 1958,
    pp 12–29.
Goldschmidt, L., (ed.), *Der babylonische Talmud*, Berlin 1967.
Goppelt, L., *Christentum und Judentum im ersten und zweiten Jahrhundert*, Gütersloh
    1954.

Goppelt, L., 'Tradition nach Paulus,' *KuD* 4, 1958, pp 213–33.

Goppelt, L., *Jesus, Paul and Judaism,* New York E.T. 1964.

Goppelt, L., *Christologie und Ethik: Aufsätze zum Neuen Testament,* Göttingen 1968.

Goppelt, L., *Typos,* Darmstadt 1969.

Goppelt, L., *Apostolic and Post-Apostolic Times,* New York E.T. 1970.

Goppelt, L., 'Jesus und die "Haustafel"-Tradition,' in: *Orientierung an Jesus. Für Joseph Schmid,* P. Hoffmann (ed.), Freiburg 1973, pp 93–106.

Goppelt, L., *Theologie des Neuen Testaments: I Jesu Wirken in seiner theologischen Bedeutung, II Vielfalt und Einheit des apostolischen Christuszeugnisses,* Göttingen, 1975, 1976.

Goppelt, L., *Der erste Petrusbrief,* MK 12, Göttingen 1978.

Grabner-Haider, A., *Paraklese und Eschatologie bei Paulus. Mensch und Welt im Anspruch der Zukunft,* NTA NS 4, Münster 1968.

Grant, F. C., 'Ethics and Eschatology in the Teaching of Jesus,' *JR* 22, 1942, pp 359–70.

Grant, F. C., 'The Impracticability of the Gospels' Ethics,' in: *Aux sources de la tradition chrétienne,* O. Cullmann and P. Menoud (eds.), Paris 1950, pp 86–94.

Grässer, E., *Das Problem der Parusieverzögerung in den synoptischen Evangelien und in der Apostelgeschichte,* Berlin 1957.

Grundmann, W., *Das Evangelium nach Matthäus,* THNT 1, 2nd edn, Berlin 1971.

Grundmann, W., *Das Evangelium nach Markus,* THNT 2, 5th edn, Berlin 1971.

Grundmann, W., *Das Evangelium nach Lukas,* THNT 3, 6th edn, Berlin 1971.

Guelich, R., *Not to Annul the Law, Rather to Fulfill the Law and the Prophets,* Dissertation, Hamburg 1967.

Guelich, R., 'The Antitheses of Matthew 5:21–48: Traditional and/or Redactional?' *NTS* 22/4, July 1976, pp 444–57.

Haas, H., *Idee und Ideal der Feindesliebe in der ausserchristlichen Welt,* Leipzig 1927.

Haenchen, E., 'Matthäus 23, *ZThK* 48, 1951, pp 38–63.

Haenchen, E., *Die Apostelgeschichte,* MK, 15th edn, Göttingen 1968.

Hammond, N. G. L. and Scullard, H. H. (eds.), *The Oxford Classical Dictionary,* 2nd edn, Oxford 1970.

Hanson, R. P. C., *Tradition in the Early Church,* London 1962.

Häring, B., 'The Normative Value of the Sermon on the Mount,' *CBQ* 29/3, 1967, pp 375–85.

Harrelson, Walter, 'Patient Love in the Testament of Joseph,' in: *Studies on the Testament of Joseph,* George W. E. Nickelsburg (ed.), Missoula, Montana 1975, pp 29–36.

Hasler, V., *AMĒN,* Stuttgart 1969.

Heinemann, J., 'Nochmals Matt. 5,42ff,' *BZ* 24, 1938–39, pp 136–8.

Heitmüller, W., 'Zum Problem Paulus und Jesus,' in: *Das Paulusbild in der neuren deutschen Forschung,* K. H. Rengstorf (ed.), Darmstadt 1969, pp 124–43.

Held, H. J., 'Matthäus als Interpret der Wundergeschichten,' in: *Überlieferung und Auslegung im Matthäusevangelium,* G. Bornkamm, G. Barth and H. J. Held, 6th edn, Neukirchen-Vluyn 1970, pp 155–284.

Hengel, M., 'Leben in der Veränderung,' *EK* 3, 1970, pp 647–51.

Hengel, M., *War Jesus Revolutionär?,* Stuttgart 1970.

Hoffmann, P., 'Die Stellung der Bergpredigt im Mtevangelium = Auslesung der Bergpredigt I,' *BL* 10, 1969, pp 57–65.

Hoffmann, P., 'Die bessere Gerechtigkeit,' *BL* 10, 1969, pp 264–75.

Hoffmann, P., 'Die Anfänge der Theologie in der Logienquelle,' in: *Gestalt und An-*

spruch des neuen Testaments, J. Schreirer (ed.), Würzburg 1969, pp 134–52.

Hoffmann, P., *Studien zur Theologie der Logienquelle,* Münster 1972.

Holtzmann, H. J., *Lehrbuch der neutestamentlichen Theologie* II, Tübingen 1911.

Holzmeister, U. 'Vom Schlagen auf die rechte Wange (Mt. 5,39),' *ZKT* 45, 1921, pp 334–6.

Hübner, Hans, *Das Gesetz in der synoptischen Tradition,* Witten 1973.

Hultgren, A., 'The Double Commandment of Love in Mt. 22:34–40, Its Sources and Compositions,' *CBQ* 36/3, 1974, pp 373–8.

Hummel, R., *Die Auseinandersetzung zwischen Kirche und Judentum im Matthäus-evangelium,* BEvTh 33, München 1963.

Hunter, A. M., *Paul and His Predecessors,* rev edn, Philadelphia 1961.

Jeremias, J., *Jesus als Weltvollender,* Gütersloh 1930.

Jeremias, J., 'Zur Hypothese einer schriftlichen Logienquelle Q,' *ZNW* 29, 1930, pp 147–9.

Jeremias, J., 'Zum Gleichnis zum verlorenen Sohn, Lk 15,11–32,' *ThZ* 5, 1949, pp 228ff.

Jeremias, J., *Die Bergpredigt,* Calwer Heft 27, Stuttgart 1970.

Jeremias, J., *Die Gleichnisse Jesu,* 8th edn, Göttingen 1970.

Jeremias, J., *Neutestamentliche Theologie,* Part 1, Gütersloh 1971.

Jeremias, J., *New Testament Theology: The Proclamation of Jesus,* New York E.T. 1971.

Jervell, J., 'Ein Interpolator interpretiert,' in: *Studien zu den Testamenten der Zwölf Patriarchen,* W. Eltester (ed.), Berlin 1969, pp 30–61.

Jonge, M. De, *The Testaments of the Twelve Patriarchs,* New York E.T. 1953. (*Testaments*).

Jonge, M. De, *Studies on the Testaments of the Twelve Patriarchs,* Leiden 1975 (*Studies*).

Jülicher, A., *Die Gleichnisreden Jesu,* 2 vols, Tübingen 1910.

Jüngel, E., *Paulus und Jesus,* Tübingen 1962.

Juncker, A., *Die Ethik des Apostels Paulus,* 2 vols, Halle (I) 1904, (II) 1909.

Käsemann, E., *Exegetische Versuche und Besinnungen* I, Göttingen 1960.

Käsemann, E., 'Gottesdienst im Alltag der Welt (zu Rm 12),' Beiheft *ZNW* 26, 1960, pp 165–71.

Käsemann, E., *An die Römer,* HNT 8a, 2nd edn, Tübingen 1974.

Kamlah, E., *Die Form der katalogischen Paränese im Neuen Testament,* WUNT 7, Tübingen 1964.

Kattenbusch, F., 'Über die Feindesliebe im Sinne des Christentums,' *ThStKr* 89, 1916, pp 1–70.

Kelly, J. N. D., *The Epistles of Peter and Jude,* New York 1969.

Kissenger, Warren S., *The Sermon on the Mount: A History of Interpretations and Bibliography,* ATLA Bibliography Series, No 3, Metuchen, New Jersey 1975.

Kittel, G. and Friedrich, G., *Theological Dictionary of the New Testament,* 9 vols, Grand Rapids 1964–73.

Klassen, W., 'Coals of Fire: Sign of Repentance or Revenge?' *NTS* 9, 1963, pp 337–50.

Klassen, W., 'Love Your Enemy: A Study of New Testament Teaching on Coping with an Enemy,' in: *Biblical Realism Confronts the Nation,* Paul Reachey (ed.) Scottsdale, Pa., 1963, pp 153–83.

Klassen, W., 'Love in the New Testament,' in: *IDB Supplementary Volume,* pp 557f.

Klausner, J., *Jesus of Nazareth,* London 1925.

Klostermann, E., *The Sources of the Synoptic Gospels*, 2 vols, Cambridge 1957.

Klostermann, E., *Das Matthäusevangelium*, HNT 4, 4th edn, Tübingen 1971.

Knox, W. L., *Some Hellenistic Elements in Primitive Christianity*, London 1944.

Knox, W. L., *The Sources of the Synoptic Gospels: II St Luke and St Matthew*, Cambridge 1957.

Köster, H., *Synoptische Überlieferung bei den apostolischen Vätern*, TU 65, Berlin 1957.

Kümmel, W. G., 'Jesus und die Rabbinen,' in: *Heilsgeschehen und Geschichte*, Marburg 1933, pp 1–14.

Kümmel, W. G., *Promise and Fulfilment*, London E.T. 1961.

Kümmel, W. G., 'Jesus und Paulus,' in: *Heilsgeschehen und Geschichte*, Marburg 1965, pp 439–56.

Kümmel, W. G., *Introduction to the New Testament*, New York E.T. 1966.

Kümmel, W. G., *Die Theologie des Neuen Testaments nach seinen Hauptzeugen Jesus. Paulus. Johannes* III, Göttingen 1969.

Kuhn, H-W., 'Der irdische Jesus bei Paulus,' *ZThK* 67, 1970, pp 295–320.

Kuhn, K. G., 'The Lord's Supper and the Communal Meal at Qumran,' in: *The Scrolls and the New Testament*, K. Stendahl (ed.), New York 1957, pp 65–93.

Kuss, O., *Die Briefe an die Römer, Korinther und Galater*, Regensburg 1940.

Ladd, G. E., *Jesus and the Kingdom*, New York 1964.

Larsson, E., *Christus als Vorbild*, Uppsala 1962.

Lewis, C. S., *The Weight of Glory*, Grand Rapids 1965.

Liechtenhahn, R., *Gottes Gebot im Neuen Testament*, Basel 1942.

Lietzmann, H., *The Beginnings of the Christian Church*, London 1949.

Lilly, J. L., 'Missal Epistles from Romans,' *CBQ* 6, 1944, pp 94–8.

Linnemann, E., *Gleichnisse Jesu*, Göttingen 1961.

Linton, O., 'St. Matthew 5:43,' *StTh* 18/1, 1964, pp 66–79.

Lohmeyer, E., *Das Evangelium des Markus*, MK, 17th edn, Göttingen 1967.

Lohse, E., 'Lukas als Theologe der Heilsgeschichte,' *EvTh* 14, 1954, pp 256ff.

Lohse, E., 'Paränese und Kerygma im ersten Petrusbrief,' *ZNW* 45, 1954, pp 68–89.

Lohse, E., *Die Briefe an die Kolosser und an Philemon*, MK, 14th edn, Göttingen 1968.

Lohse, E., 'Ich aber sage euch,' in: *Der Ruf Jesu und die Antwort der Gemeinde. Festschrift for J. Jeremias*, E. Lohse (ed.), Göttingen 1970, pp 189–203.

Luck, U., 'Kerygma, Tradition und Geschichte Jesu bei Lk,' *ZThK* 57, 1960, pp 51ff.

Lührmann, D., *Die Redaktion der Logienquelle*, WMANT 33, 1969.

Lührmann, D., 'Erwägungen zur Geschichte des Urchristentums,' *EvTh* 32, 1972, pp 452–67.

Lührmann, D., 'Liebet eure Feinde,' *ZThK* 69, 1972, pp 412–38.

Lünemann, G., *Briefe an die Thessalonicher*, MK, Göttingen 1878.

Lütgert, W., *Ethik der Liebe*, Gütersloh 1938.

Luz, U., 'Einige Erwägungen zur Auslegung Gottes in der ethischen Verkündigung Jesu,' in: *Evangelisch-Katholischer Kommentar zum Neuen Testament, Vorarbeiten* II, E. Schweizer (ed.), Zürich 1970, pp 119–30.

Machen, J. G., *The Origin of Paul's Religion*, Grand Rapids 1965.

Machoveč, M., *Jesus für Atheisten*, Berlin 1972.

Manek, J., 'On the Mount – On the Plain (Mt v,1 – Lk vi,17),' *NovTest* 9/2, 1967, pp 124–31.

Manson, T. W., *The Sayings of Jesus*, London 1949.

Manson, T. W., *The Teaching of Jesus,* 2nd edn, Cambridge 1967.

Marshall, I. H., *Luke: Historian and Theologian,* Devon 1970.

Martin, C., 'Imprecations in the Psalms,' *PTR* 1 (1903) pp 537–53.

Marxsen, W., *Mark the Evangelist,* E.T. Nashville 1969.

Mendenhall, G., *Law and Covenant,* Pittsburg 1955.

Merkel, F., Georgi, D. and Baltzer, K., 'I Pet. 3,8f,' *Göttinger Predigt Meditationen* 16, 1961/62, pp 231ff.

Metzger, B. M., *A Textual Commentary on the Greek New Testament,* London 1971.

Michel, O., 'Der Lohngedanke in der Verkündigung Jesu, ' *ZSTh* 9, 1932, pp 47–54.

Michel, O., 'Das Gebot der Nächstenliebe in der Verkündigung Jesu,' in: *Zur sozialen Entscheidung: Vier Vorträge,* Tübingen 1947, pp 53–101.

Michel, O., *Der Brief an die Römer,* MK, 13th edn, Göttingen 1966.

Michl, J., 'Apokalypse/Apokryphe,' in: *Sacramentum Mundi* I, K. Rahner (ed.), Freiburg 1967, columns 214–23.

Milik, J. T. 'Le Testament de Lévi en Araméen,' *RB* 62, 1955, pp 398–406.

Moe, O., *Paulus und die evangelische Geschichte,* Leipzig 1912.

Moffatt, J., *Love in the New Testament,* London 1921.

Molin, G., 'Matthäus 5,43 und das Schrifttum von Qumran,' in: *Bibel und Qumran,* S. Wagner (ed.), Berlin 1968, pp 150–3.

Montefiore, C. G., *The Synoptic Gospels* II, 2nd edn, New York 1968.

Montefiore, C. G., *Rabbinic Literature and Gospel Teachings,* New York 1970.

Moore, G. F., *Judaism in the First Centuries of the Christian Era,* Cambridge 1927.

Morenz, S., 'Feurige Kohlen auf dem Haupt,' *ThLZ* 78, 1953, pp 187–92.

Morgenthaler, R., *Kommendes Reich,* Zürich 1951.

Moule, C. F. D. 'The Use of Parables and Sayings as Illustrative Material in Early Christian Catechesis,' *JTS* NS 3, 1952, pp 75–9.

Moule, C. F. D., 'Obligation in the Ethic of Paul,' in: *Christian History and Interpretation: Studies Presented to John Knox,* W. R. Farmer, C. F. D. Moule and R. R. Niebuhr (eds.), Cambridge 1967, pp 389–406.

Moulton, W. F. and Geden, A. S., *A Concordance to the Greek New Testament,* Edinburgh 1963.

Murray, J., *The Epistle to the Romans,* 2 vols, Grand Rapids 1959, 1965.

Nauck, W., 'Freude im Leiden,' *ZNW* 46, 1955, pp 68–80.

Neil, W., *The Epistle of Paul to the Thessalonians,* MNTC, London 1950.

Neugebauer, F., 'Geistessprüche und Jesuslogien. Erwägungen zu der von der formgeschichtlichen Betrachtungsweise R. Bultmanns angenommenen grundsätzlichen Möglichkeit von einer Identität von prophetischen Geistessprüche mit Logien des irdischen Jesus,' *ZNW* 53, 1962, pp 218–28.

Neuhäusler, E., *Anspruch und Antwort Gottes,* Düsseldorf 1962.

Neuhäusler, E., 'Beobachtungen zur Form der synoptischen Jesusethik,' *LZ* 1/2, 1965, pp 91–102.

Nieder, L., *Die Motive der religiös-sittlichen Paränese in den paulinischen Gemeindebriefen,* München 1956.

Niederwimmer, K., *Jesus,* Göttingen 1968.

Nissen, Andreas, *Gott und der Nächste im antiken Judentum. Untersuchungen zum Doppelgebot der Liebe,* WUNT 15, Tübingen 1974.

Noll, P., *Jesus und das Gesetz,* Tübingen 1968.

Norquist, N. L., *The Transmission of the Ethical Tradition in the Synoptic Gospels and the Writings of Paul,* Dissertation, Hartford Seminary Foundation 1956.

Oepke, A., Der Brief des Paulus an die Galater, THNT 9, 2nd edn, Berlin 1957.

Oepke, A., 'Die Briefe an die Thessalonicher,' in: *Die kleineren Briefe des Apostel Paulus*, NTD 8, G. Friedrich (ed.), Göttingen 1972, pp 162–81.

Oyen, H. v., *Botschaft und Gebot*, Gütersloh 1962.

Percy, E., *Die Botschaft Jesu*, Lund 1953.

Perrin, N., *Rediscovering the Teaching of Jesus*, London 1967.

Pesch, W., *Der Lohngedanke in der Lehre Jesu*, München 1955.

Pesch, W., *Matthäus der Seelsorger*, Stuttgart 1966.

Philonenko, M., *Les Interpolations chrétiennes des Testaments des Douze Patriarches et les Manuscrits de Qoumrân*, Paris 1960.

Philonenko, M., *Joseph et Asenath*, Leiden 1968.

Philonenko, M., 'Joseph and Asenath,' in: *Encyclopaedia Judaica* X, Jerusalem 1971, columns 223f.

Pines, S., 'Slavonic Book of Enoch,' in: *Encyclopaedia Judaica* VI, Jerusalem 1971, columns 798f.

Piper, J., "Deciding What We Deserve," *Christianity Today* 22/2, Oct. 21, 1977, pp 12–15.

Plöger, O., 'Henochbücher,' in *RGG* III, K. Galling (ed.), 3rd edn, Tübingen 1957ff, columns 224f.

Plummer, A., *The Gospel According to Saint Luke*, Edinburgh 1922.

Pohlenz, M., 'Paulus und die Stoa,' in: *Das Paulusbild in der neueren deutschen Forschung*, Darmstadt 1969.

Preisker, H., *Das Ethos des Urchristentums*, 2nd edn, Darmstadt 1968.

Rad, G. von, *Old Testament Theology*, 2 vols, New York E.T. 1962, 1965.

Radlinger, S., *Die Fiendesliebe nach dem natürlichen und positive Sittengesetz*, Paderborn, 1906.

Ratschow, C. H., 'Agape, Nächstenliebe, und Brüderliebe,' *ZSTh* 21, 1950, pp 160–82.

Rausch, J., 'The Principle of Non-Resistance and Love of the Enemy in Mt 5:38-48,' *CBQ* 28, 1966, pp 31–41.

Reicke, B., *The Epistles of James, Peter and Jude*, The Anchor Bible, New York 1964.

Rengstorf, K. H., *Das Evangelium Lukas*, NTD 3, Göttingen 1969.

Rengstorf, K. H. (ed.), *Das Paulusbild der neuren deutschen Forschung*, Darmstadt 1969.

Ridderbos, H., *Paul and Jesus*, Philadelphia E.T. 1958.

Ridderbos, H., *The Coming of the Kingdom*, Philadelphia E.T. 1962.

Ridderbos, H., *Paulus*, Wuppertal 1970.

Riesenfeld, H., *The Gospel Tradition and its Beginnings*, London 1957.

Riesenfeld, H., 'Vom Schätzesammeln und Sorgen - ein Thema urchristlicher Paränese,' in: *Neotestamentica et Patristica. Eine Freundesgabe für O. Cullmann*, W. C. van Unnik (ed.), Leiden 1962, pp 47–58.

Riessler, P., *Altjüdisches Schrifttum ausserhalb der Bibel*, Darmstadt 1966.

Riessler, P., 'Joseph und Aseneth,' *ThQ* 103, 1922, pp 1–22, 145–83.

Rieu, E., *The Four Gospels: A New Translation from the Greek*, London 1953.

Robertson, A.T., *A Grammar of the Greek New Testament in the Light of Historical Research*, Nashville, Tenn., 1934.

Robinson, J. M. and Köster, H., *Trajectories through Early Christianity*, Philadelphia

Robinson, W. C., *Der Weg des Herrn. Studien zur Geschichte und Eschatologie im Lukas-Evangelium*, Hamburg 1964.

Roloff, J., *Das Kerygma und der irdische Jesus*, Göttingen 1970.

Rost, L., *Einleitung in die alttestamentlichen Apokryphen und Pseudepigraphen einschliesslich der grossen Qumran Handschriften*, Heidelberg 1971.

Sanday, W. and Headlam A., *The Epistle to the Romans*, ICC, Edinburgh 1902.

Sander, Reinhold, *Furcht und Liebe im palästinischen Judentum*, Stuttgart 1935.

Sanders, E. P., *The Tendencies of the Synoptic Tradition,* Cambridge 1969.

Sanders. J., 'Ethics in the Synoptic Gospels,' *BR* 14, 1969, pp 19–32.

Schelkle, K. H., *Die Petrusbriefe. Der Judasbrief,* HThK 13, 3rd edn, Freiburg 1970.

Schelkle, K. H., *Theologie des Neuen Testaments:* III Ethos, Düsseldorf 1970.

Schenk, W., *Der Segen im Neuen Testament,* Berlin 1967.

Schlatter, A., *Die Geschichte des Christus,* Stuttgart 1921.

Schlatter, A., *Die Theologie der Apostel,* 2nd edn, Stuttgart 1922.

Schlatter, A., *Gottes Gerechtigkeit,* Stuttgart 1935.

Schlatter, A., *Jesus and Paulus,* 3rd edn, Stuttgart 1961.

Schlatter, A., *Der Evangelist Matthäus,* 6th edn, Stuttgart 1963.

Schlatter, A., 'The Theology of the New Testament and Dogmatics,' in: *The Nature of New Testament Theology,* Robert Morgan (ed.), SBT 2nd series 25, Naperville 1973, pp 117–66.

Schlier, H., 'Die Eigenart der christlichen Mahnung nach dem Apostel Paulus,' in: *Besinnung auf das Neue Testament. Exegetische Aufsätze und Vorträge* II, Freiburg 1964, pp 340–57.

Schlier, H., *Der Brief an die Galater,* MK, 14th edn, Göttingen 1971.

Schlink, E., 'Gesetz und Paraklese,' in: *Antwort. Karl Barth zum 70. Geburtstag,* E. Wolf, Ch. von Kirshbaum and R. Frey (eds.), Zürich 1956, pp 323–335.

Schmauch, W., *Das Evangelium des Matthäus,* MK, 4th edn, Göttingen 1967.

Schmidt, H. W., *Der Brief des Paulus an die Römer,* THNT 6, Berlin 1963.

Schmidt, L., *Die Ethik der alten Griechen* II, Stuttgart 1964.

Schmithals, W., 'Paulus und der historische Jesus,' *ZNW* 53, 1962, pp 145–60.

Schnackenburg, R., *Die Sittliche Botschaft des Neuen Testaments,* 2nd edn, München 1962.

Schnackenburg, R., *Gottes Herrschaft und Reich,* 4th edn, Freiburg 1965.

Schnackenburg, R., 'Mitmenschlichkeit im Horizont des N.T.' in: *Die Zeit Jesu. Festschrift für Heinrich Schlier,* G. Bornkamm and K. Rahner (eds.), Freiburg 1970, pp 70–91.

Schniewind, J., 'Zur Synoptiker-Exegese,' *ThR* NS 2, 1930, pp 127–89.

Schniewind, J., 'Die Botschaft Jesu und die Theologie des Paulus,' in: *Nachgelassene Reden und Aufsatze,* E. Kähler (ed.), Berlin 1952, pp 16–37.

Schniewind, J., *Das Evangelium nach Matthäus,* NTD 2, Göttingen 1964.

Schniewind, J., *Das Evangelium nach Markus,* München 1968.

Schoeps, H. P., *Paul, The Theology of the Apostle in the Light of Jewish Religious History,* Philadelphia E.T. 1961.

Schottroff, L., 'Das Gleichnis vom verlorenen Sohn,' *ZThK* 68, 1971, pp 27–52.

Schottroff, L., 'Gewaltverzicht und Feindesliebe in der urchristlichen Jesustradition Mt 5,38–48; Lk 6,27–36,' in: *Jesus Christus in Historie und Theologie,* G. Strecker (ed.), Tübingen 1975, pp 197–221.

Schrage, W., 'Zur formalethischen Deutung der paulinischen Paränese,' *ZEE* 4, 1960, pp 207–33.

Schrage, W., *Die konkreten Einzelgebote in der paulinischen Paränese,* Gütersloh 1961.

Schrage, W., 'Zur Ethik der neutestamentlichen Haustafeln,' *NTS* 21/1, 1974, pp 1–21.

Schroeder, D., *Die Haustafeln des Neuen Testaments,* Dissertation, Hamburg 1959.

Schüller, B., 'Zur Rede von der radikalen sittlichen Forderung,' *ThP* 146, 1971, pp 321–339.

Schürer, E., *Geschichte des jüdischen Volkes* III, 4th edn, Leipzig 1909.

Schürmann, H., 'Die vorösterlichen Anfänge der Logientradition,' in: *Der historische Jesus und der kerygmatische Christus,* H. Ristow and K. Matthiae (eds.), 2nd edn, Berlin 1960, pp 342–70.

Schürmann, H., 'Eschatologie und Liebesdienst in der Verkündigung Jesu,' in: *Vom Messias zum Christus.* K. Schubert (ed.), Wien 1964, pp 203–32.

Schürmann, H., 'Die Warnung des Lukas vor der Falschlehre, in der "Predigt am Berge" Lk 6,20–49,' *BZ* NS 10, 1966, pp 57–81.

Schürmann, H., *Das Lukasevangelium,* Part 1, HThK 13, Freiburg 1969.

Schürmann, H., *Ursprung und Gestalt,* Düsseldorf 1970.

Schütz, F., *Der leidende Christus,* Stuttgart 1969.

Schulz, S., *Q, Die Spruchquelle der Evangelien,* Zürich 1972.

Schweitzer, A., *Das Messianitäts- und Leidensgeheimnis,* Tübingen/Leipzig 1901.

Schweitzer, A., *Paul and his Interpreters,* London E.T. 1912.

Schweitzer, A., *Geschichte der Leben-Jesu Forschung,* 6th edn, Tübingen 1951.

Schweizer, E., 'Zur Frage der Lukasquellen, Analyse von Lk 15,11–32,' *ThZ* 4, 1948, pp 469ff.

Schweizer, E., 'Observance of the Law and Charismatic Activity in Matthew,' *NTS* 16/3, April 1970, pp 213–30.

Scott, C. A. A., *Christianity According to St Paul,* Cambridge 1927.

Seeberg, A., *Der Katechismus der Urchristenheit,* 1903, reprinted München 1966.

Seitz, O. J. F., 'Love Your Enemies,' *NTS* 16, October 1969, pp 39–54.

Selby, D. J., *Toward the Understanding of St Paul,* Englewood Cliffs, N. J., 1962.

Selwyn, E. G., *The First Epistle of Peter,* London 1969.

Sevenster, J. N., *Paul and Seneca,* Leiden 1961.

Smith, C. W. F., *The Jesus of the Parables,* Philadelphia 1948.

Smith, M., *Tannaitic Parallels to the Gospels,* Philadelphia 1951.

Smith, M., 'Mt 5:43: Hate thine Enemy,' *HTR* 45, 1952, pp 71–3.

Smothers, E. R., 'Give Place to Wrath,' *CBQ* 6, 1944, pp 205–15.

Soiron, T., *Die Bergpredigt Jesu,* Freiburg 1941.

Spicq, C., 'Die Liebe als Gestaltungsprinzip der Moral in den synoptischen Evangelien,' *FZTP* 1, 1954, pp 394–410.

Spicq, C., *Agape in the New Testament,* 3 vols, St Louis E.T. 1966.

Stählin, H., 'Die Früchte der Umkehr,' *StTh* 1, 1947, pp 54–68.

Stanley, D. M., 'Become Imitators of Me: the Pauline Conception of Apostolic Tradition,' *Biblica* 40, 1959, pp 859–77.

Stanley, D. M., 'Pauline Allusions to the Sayings of Jesus,' *CBQ* 23, 1961, pp 26–39.

Stanton, *Jesus of Nazareth in New Testament Preaching,* SNTS Monograph Series 27, Cambridge 1974.

Stauffer, E., *Jesus: Gestalt und Geschichte,* Bern 1957.

Steele, J., 'Heaping Coals on the Head (Pr 25:22; Ro 12:20),' *ET* 44, 1932–33, p 141.

Stendahl, K., 'Hate, Non-Retaliation and Love: 1QS 10:17–20 and Rom 12:19–21,' *HTR* 55, 1962, pp 343–55.

Stendahl, K., *The School of St Matthew,* 2nd edn, Lund, n.d.

Stern, J. B., 'Jesus' Citation of Dt 6:5 and Lv 19:18 in the Light of Jewish Tradition,' *CBQ* 28, 1966, pp 312–16.

Stonehouse, N. B., *Origins of the Synoptic Gospels,* Grand Rapids 1963.

Strack, H. L. and Billerbeck, P., *Kommentar zum Neuen Testament aus Talmud und Midrasch,* München 1969.

Strecker, G., *Der Weg der Gerechtigkeit. Untersuchung zur Theologie des MtEvangeliums*, FRLANT 82, Göttingen 1962.

Strecker, G., 'Die historische, theologische Problematik der Jesusfrage,' *EvTh* 29, 1969, pp 453-76.

Streeter, B. H., *The Four Gospels*, London 1924.

Stuhlmacher, P., 'Kritische Marginalien zum gegenwärtigen Stand der Frage nach Jesus,' in: *Fides et Communicatio. Festschrift für Martin Doerne*, Göttingen 1970.

Suggs, M. J., *Wisdom, Christology and Law in Matthew's Gospel*, Cambridge, Mass., 1970.

Suggs, M. J., 'The Antitheses as Redactional Products,' in *Jesus Christus in Historie und Theologie*, G. Strecker (ed.), Tübingen 1975.

Sutcliffe, E. F., 'Not to Resist Evil (Mt 5:39).' *Scripture* 5, 1952, pp 33-5.

Talbert, C. H., 'Tradition and Redaction in Romans 12:9-21,' *NTS* 16, October 1969, pp 83-93.

Taylor, V., *The Formation of the Gospel Tradition*, London 1964.

Taylor, V., *The Gospel According to Mark*, 2nd edn, New York 1966.

Theissen, G., 'Wanderradikalismus,' *ZThK* 70, September 1973, pp 245-71.

Thielicke, H., *Theological Ethics* I, London E.T. 1968.

Thomas, J., 'Aktuelles im Zeugnis der Zwölf Väter,' in: *Studien zu den Testamenten der Zwölf Patriarchen*, W. Eltester (ed.), Berlin 1969, pp 62-150.

Traub, F., 'Das Problem der Bergpredigt,' *ZThK* 17, 1936, pp 193-218.

Trilling, W., *Das wahre Israel*, 3rd edn, München 1964.

Trilling, W., 'Weisung und Anspruch (Mt 22,34-46),' *Am Tisch des Wortes* 5, 1965, pp 26-37.

Trilling, W., *Fragen zur Geschichtlichkeit Jesu*, Düsseldorf 1967.

Trilling, W., *Christusverkündigung in den synoptischen Evangelien*, Leipzig 1968.

Unnik, W. C. van, 'Die Motivierung der Feindesliebe in Lukas vi, 32-35,' *NovTest* 8, 1966, pp 284-300.

Vögtle, A., *Die Tugend- und Lasterkataloge im Neuen Testament*, NTA 14 (4/5), Münster 1936.

Völkl, R., *Die Selbstliebe in der Heiligen Schrift*, München 1956.

Waldmann, M., *Die Feindesliebe in der antiken Welt und im Christentum*, Wien 1902.

Walker, R., *Die Heilsgeschichte im ersten Evangelium*, FRLANT 91, Göttingen 1967.

Warnach, V., *AGAPE: Die Liebe als Grundmotiv der neutestamentlichen Theologie*, Düsseldorf 1951.

Wegenast, K., *Das Verständnis der Tradition bei Paulus und in den Deuteropaulinen*, WMANT 8, Neukirchen 1962.

Weidinger, K., *Die Haustafeln, Ein Stück urchristlicher Paränese*, UNT 14, Leipzig 1928.

Weiser, A., *Die Psalmen*, ATD 14/15, Göttingen 1966.

Weiss, B., *Die paulinischen Briefe und der Hebräerbrief*, Das Neue Testament 2, 2nd edn, Leipzig 1902.

Weiss, J., *Predigt Jesu vom Reich Gottes*, Göttingen 1900.

Weiss, J., *Das Urchristentum*, Göttingen 1917.

Wendland, H. D., *Die Eschatologie des Reiches Gottes bei Jesus*, Gütersloh 1931.

Wendland, H. D., 'Gibt es eine Sozialethik im NT?' in: *Botschaft an die soziale Welt*, Hamburg 1959, pp 68-84.

Wendland, H. D., *Ethik des Neuen Testaments*, NTD Ergänzungsreihe 4, Göttingen 1970.

Werner, M., *Die Entstehung des christlichen Dogmas,* Bern 1941.

Wibbing, S., *Die Tugend - und Lasterkataloge im Neuen Testament,* BZNW 25, Berlin 1959.

Wilckens, U., 'Hellenistische-christliche Missionsüberlieferung und Jesustradition,' *ThLZ* 89, 1964, pp 517–20.

Wilder, A. N., *Eschatology and Ethics in the Teaching of Jesus,* New York 1950.

Windisch, H., 'Das Problem des paulinischen Imperativs,' *ZNW* 23, 1924.

Windisch, H., 'Die Sprüche von Eingehen in das Reich Gottes,' *ZNW* 27, 1928, pp 163–92.

Windisch, H., *Der Sinn der Bergpredigt,* Leipzig 1929.

Windisch, H., *Die katholischen Briefe,* Tübingen 1951.

Wohlenburg, D. G., *Der erste und zweite Thessalonischerbrief,* 2nd edn, Leipzig 1909.

Woude, A. S. van der, *Die messianischen Vorstellungen der Gemeinde von Qumran,* Assen 1957.

Wrege, H. T., *Die Überlieferungsgeschichte der Bergpredigt,* Tübingen 1968.

Yoder, J. H., *The Politics of Jesus,* Grand Rapids 1972.

Young, J. E., 'Heaping Coals of Fire on the Head,' *The Expositor* 3rd series 2, 1885, pp 158–9.

Ziener, G., 'Synoptische Frage,' in: *Gestalt und Anspruch des Neuen Testaments,* Würzburg 1969, pp 173–85.

Zyro, F., 'Über Röm 12,19: *dote topon tē orgē,*' *ThStKr* 18, 1945, pp 887–92.

INDEX OF PASSAGES CITED

I. The Old Testament

Genesis
1:27	89
2:24	89, 90
4:9	90
29:31ff	28
44:4	182n20

Exodus
12:19	31
12:45ff	182n27
20:6	27
20:13	90
21:23	90
21:24	68, 89, 182n28
23:4f	34, 48
23:4	28
23:5	28, 39
23:22	28
23:27	28
34:12	32

Leviticus
17:8	182n27
17:9	182n27
17:10	182n27
19	31, 32
19:10	182n27
19:16–18	30
19:17	28, 32
19:18	30, 31, 32, 37, 47, 68, 91, 92, 93, 94, 95, 112, 147, 148, 152, 189n117, 208n110
19:34	31, 32, 48
22:18	182n27
24:10	182n28
24:20	89
23:35ff	182n27
25:47ff	182n27

Numbers
30:2f	188n99
30:2	90

Deuteronomy
4:42	28
5:10	27
5:26	207n96
6:4	94
6:5	28, 92, 93, 95, 152, 208n110
7:1	32
7:2	32
7:7	31
7:8	31
7:9	27
10:12	27
10:15ff	31
10:18	28, 31, 34
10:19	28, 31, 34
11:1	27
11:13	27
11:16	207n96
11:22	27
14:1	193n164
18:12	32
19:9	28
19:21	89, 90, 182n28
19:30	28
20:18	32
21:15–17	28
22:13	28
23:3–6	32
23:21	90
23:22f	188n99
24:1–3	28
24:1	89
25:17–19	32
32:35	27, 37, 112

Joshua
6:15	182n29
8:1	182n29
8:18	182n29
10:8	182n29
10:11	182n29
10:14	182n29

Joshua (*cont.*)

10:30	182n29
10:32	182n29
10:42	182n29
11:8	182n29
13:6	182n29
22:5	28
23:5	182n29
23:10	10, 32
23:11	28

I Samuel

24:17–18	182n30
25:26	182n30
25:33	182n30

II Samuel

1:26	28
13:15	28
19:6	32
22:9	115
22:13	115

I Kings

2:5–9	182n30
3:3	27
3:10ff	29, 34

II Chronicles

19:2	32

Ezra

5:41	218n82
7:9	218n82
7:16	218n82
8:58	218n82

Nehemiah

1:5	27

Job

1:1	38
22:29	125
31:12	115

Psalms

5:4–6	182n31
9:8	216n58
9:16	216n58
11:5	182n31
18:9	115
18:13	115
18:27	201n56
31:6	182n31
33:8LXX	64
33:13–17 LXX	122, 123
33:15LXX	13, 14, 57, 64, 112, 180n24
33:16LXX	215n52
34	5, 63, 124, 127, 218n88, 218n89
34:12–16 (LXX33)	27, 34, 215n47

Psalms (*cont.*)

34:12	218n89
34:15	112
34:13–17	123, 124
35	34
35:1	34
35:12–14	34
41:7	28
50:14	188n99
69:21–28	41, 180n24
69:22	184n54
69:23	184n54
69:25	184n54
72:4	216n58
109	33, 41
109:4	33, 190n130
109:5	33, 190n130
109:21	33
109:22	33
139:3	33
139:4	33
139:17	33
139:18	33
139:19–22	28, 33, 41
139:21	183n33
139:23	33
139:24	33
140:11	115
143:11f	216n58
143:11	216n59

Proverbs

3:4LXX	6, 27, 112, 179n23
3:7	27
3:32	182n31
3:34LXX	125
6:16ff	182n31
6:27–29	115
11:31LXX	215n47, 217n78
17:3	182n20
17:13	27, 34, 49, 64
20:22	182n20
24:17	29:34
24:18	29, 34
24:29	28, 34, 182n20
25:21f	27, 30, 34, 112, 215n45
25:21	48, 61
25:22	116

Song of Solomon

8:6f	28

Isaiah

5:21	27
29:19LXX	230n109
33:24	83
53:5f	83

Isaiah (*cont.*)
56:6	27
61:1-3	201n56
61:1	83
65:19	83

Jeremiah
2:2	28
31:31ff	206n96, 207n96
31:31-34	90
31:33	28, 90
31:34	83, 90
32:37ff	90

Ezekiel
11:19	28, 90
34:25	207n96
34:31	187n87
36:22ff	206n96
36:25ff	207n96
36:25-27	83
36:25	90
36:26	90, 207n97
36:27	90
37:26	207n96

Daniel
9:4	27
9:16-19	216n59

Hosea
6:6	152
9:15	182n31

Jonah
	34
4:2	29
4:4	29

Zephaniah
3:17	83

Zechariah
13:1	83

Malachi
1:3	28

II. The New Testament

Matthew
1:23	151
4:17	71, 79, 200n48
4:23	141
5-9	141
5-7	141, 153
5:1	141
5:1f	153
5:3-12	49
5:3	60, 77, 197n24, 197n26
5:4-9	197n26
5:7	189n118, 197n28
5:8	145, 205n89
5:9	60, 64, 77, 180n26, 189n118, 197n24

Matthew (*cont.*)
5:10ff	220n27, 227n66
5:10-12	224n35, 225n39
5:10	77, 162, 190n123, 197n24, 197n26
5:11	162, 189n118, 190n123, 206n91, 224n35, 227n65
5:12	60, 162, 190n123, 193n155
5:13-15	199n42
5:16	78, 88, 143, 144, 199n42
5:17ff	89
5:17-19	151, 210n119, 228n76
5:17	152
5:18	152, 210n119
5:19	152, 204n80, 226n52
5:20ff	149
5:20	55, 59, 146, 206n91, 220n7, 226n54
5:21-7:11	204n80
5:21-48	146
5:21f	51, 145, 188n102, 188n103, 204n83, 206n90
5:21	52, 225n51
5:22	62, 119, 210n125
5:23f	143, 197n28
5:23	204n80, 226n52
5:24f	188n98
5:27f	51, 145, 188n102, 188n103, 204n83, 206n90
5:27	52, 225n51
5:28	205n89
5:29f	62, 188n98
5:31f	188n100
5:31	51, 52, 188n100
5:32	51, 204n83, 223n32
5:33ff	90
5:33-37	51, 206n90
5:33f	91
5:33	52, 205n90, 206n90, 225n51
5:34	51, 52, 53, 97, 204n83, 205n90, 206n90
5:37f	90
5:37	180n98
5:37b	206n91
5:38ff	206n94
5:38-48	49, 50, 54, 98, 99, 134, 135, 136, 137,

Matthew (*cont.*)

	141, 142, 145, 146, 148, 171, 186n79
5:38f	38, 51, 90, 91, 151, 204n83
5:38	51, 52, 53, 56, 89, 97, 98, 135, 210n120
5:38b	89
5:39–42	88, 89, 136, 137, 148, 191n141
5:39–41	98
5:39f	188n98, 191n138
5:39	51, 52, 53, 56, 58, 119, 136, 143, 150, 156, 188n107, 206n91
5:39bff	58
5:39b–47	50
5:39b–42	52, 54, 55, 56, 58, 135, 188n107
5:39b–41	191n140, 192n142
5:39b	135, 191n138
5:40	58, 135, 150, 156, 191n138
5:41	58, 89, 135, 136, 156, 191n135, 191n136, 191n138, 231n125
5:42–48	194n172
5:42	58, 89, 150, 157, 188n107, 191n138, 191n140
5:42b	59, 157, 191n136, 230n107
5:43–48	51, 68, 72, 87, 94, 143, 146
5:43–47	146
5:43–44	51
5:43f	91, 151
5:43	51, 53, 54, 55, 135, 148, 207n99, 225n51, 226n62
5:44–48	54, 193n154
5:44–47 par	95
5:44 par	133
5:44f	46, 197n25
5:44	25, 51, 53, 54, 55, 56, 91, 98, 135, 136, 142, 143, 144, 146, 162, 189n117, 189n118, 215n47
5:44b	135, 136, 190n127, 220n7, 225n39
5:44b–48	56
5:45–47	146

Matthew (*cont.*)

5:45	26, 54, 60, 61, 62, 76, 87, 135, 136, 146, 150, 197n24, 220n5
5:46f	76, 77, 136, 146, 149, 190n127, 226n54
5:46	54, 59, 135, 136, 148, 156, 189n118, 225n41
5:47	59, 87, 135, 136, 142, 144, 146, 149, 150, 156, 190n127, 194n170, 206n91, 220n7, 225n41
5:48	26, 50, 63, 87, 135, 136, 146, 148, 193n162, 194n171, 206n93, 204n80, 220n7, 225n49, 226n52
6:1ff	77, 88
6:1–6	149
6:2ff	145
6:2	204n80, 225n43, 226n52
6:3	199n42
6:5f	143, 144
6:5	225n43
6:7f	149
6:7	59, 149, 150, 192n153, 226n54
6:8	149, 150, 204n80, 226n52
6:9–13	143
6:9	143, 204n80, 226n52
6:9b par	88
6:10	224n37
6:11	224n37
6:12	143
6:13	143, 200n49, 224n37
6:14f	197n28
6:16–18	149
6:16	225n43
6:19–21	232n131
6:19–20	232n131
6:20 par	88
6:21 par	77
6:21	205n89
6:22	204n80, 226n52
6:23	204n80, 206n91
6:24 par	179n14
6:25ff	60
6:25–33	232n131
6:25	224n37

Matthew (*cont.*)

6:27	200n51
6:30–33	88
6:30	150
6:31f	150
6:31	204n80, 226n52
6:32	78, 149, 150, 226n54
6:32b	150
6:33	158, 193n155, 224n37
6:34	204n80, 226n52
7:1–5	50
7:5	225n43
7:11	88, 150, 204n80, 206n91, 226n52
7:12	147, 148, 152, 204n80, 226n52, 228n73
7:13	204n80
7:15–20	50
7:15	224n37
7:17	199n42
7:18	61, 145, 225n46
7:21–27	50
7:21	144, 173, 224n37
7:23	144
7:24	173, 204n80, 225n42, 226n52
7:26f	144
7:26	145, 225n42
7:28f	141
8–9	141
8:4 par	179n16
8:18–22	149
8:19f	149
8:23–27	149
8:23	227n67
8:24	149
8:25	227n67
8:34	226n52
9:4	205n89, 206n91
9:10–13	152
9:13	227n62
9:35	141
10:10	194n174
10:17ff	227n66
10:18	227n65
10:20	227n72
10:22	227n65
10:23	162, 190n123
10:25	149
10:28	62
10:29	227n72
10:31	227n72

Matthew (*cont.*)

10:34	204n79, 231n125
10:37	198n32
10:39	198n36, 227n65
11:2ff	79
11:2–6	88
11:2–4	81
11:5f	202n68
11:5	79, 81
11:5b	83
11:6	81
11:19	81, 194n167, 201n54
11:20–24	200n51
11:20–22 par	119
11:21	200n48
11:25–27	198n34
11:25 par	77
11:25	202n69
11:27	151
11:28	151
12:1–8	152
12:7	152, 227n62
12:12	57
12:34	205n89
12:35	206n91
12:39	88, 206n91
12:41f	200n51
12:41	200n48
12:45	206n91
12:46–50	151
12:49	151
12:50	151, 191n138
13:9	206n91
13:12	191n138, 192n150
13:15	205n89
13:24–30	216n64
13:30	34
13:32f	88
14:20	192n150
14:28–33	227n68
15:7	225n45
15:8	205n89
15:19	145, 205n89, 206n91
16:4	206n91
16:24ff	227n66
16:25	227n65
18:3	60
18:10	179n16
18:14	227n72
18:17	59, 149, 192n153
18:21	190n129
18:23ff	85, 203n72
18:23–35	84
18:23–25	60, 119

Matthew (*cont.*)

18:33	84
18:34	84
18:35	84, 197n28, 205n89, 225n47
19:1	226n56
19:3–12	226n56
19:8	90
19:13–15	226n56
19:16–22	147, 226n56
19:16	147
19:17–21	227n62
19:17f	147
19:17	147, 148, 227n62
19:18f	147, 148
19:18	226n58
19:19	147, 148, 152, 223n32, 226n62
19:20	147
19:21	63, 146, 147, 148, 220n7, 225n49
19:22–24	147
19:22	147
19:23–30	226n56
19:29	87, 193n155, 191n138, 227n65
19:30	87
20:8ff	193n156
20:16	87
21:28–31	194n167
21:31	81
21:33	191n138
22:2	86
22:8	225n43
22:10	206n91
22:21	158
22:37	147, 205n89
22:39	148, 152
22:40	94, 152
23:1ff	204n83
23:3	89
23:12	88, 125, 191n138
23:13	225n43
23:14	225n43
23:15	225n43
23:17	210n125
23:23	152
23:25–28	205n89
23:25–26	225n44
23:25	225n45
23:26	145, 225n44, 225n45
23:32	227n66
23:34	162
23:35	216n64

Matthew (*cont.*)

24:4 par	179n16
24:9	227n65
24:12f	61
24:12	144, 152
24:17	190n123
24:48	205n89
24:51	205n43
25:26	206n91
25:29	192n150
25:31–46	193n155
25:31f	200n51
25:34ff	193n156
25:35f	143
25:40	197n28
25:44	86
25:45	197n28
27:26	231n126
27:32	229n105
27:55	191n138
28:18–20	149
28:20	142

Mark

1:15	79, 200n48
1:21	204n83
1:38	201n60
1:44	89, 204n83, 209n118
2:15–17 par	81
2:15–17	201n54
2:17	81, 192n152, 194n167, 201n60
2:18–3:6	204n83
2:19	86, 221n14
3:4	57
3:7–12	153
3:13–19	153
3:31–35	151
3:34	151
4:10	155
4:24 par	179n16
4:25	192n145
5:17	226n52
5:18	97
6:20	201n60
6:43	192n150
7:5	204n83
7:8	91
7:9–13	204n83
7:9	89, 91
7:11	205n84
7:13	89, 205n84
7:21f	145
7:33	230n110
8:15	155

Mark (*cont.*)

8:34f par	78
8:35	198n36
9:15	192n145
9:33–37	86
9:35	197n28
9:50	64, 180n26
10:1ff	208n118
10:1	226n56
10:2ff	204n82
10:2–12	89, 97, 205n86, 207n97
10:2–9	89, 97, 205n86, 207n97
10:2	89
10:3	89
10:4	89
10:5	89, 90, 91, 204n83
10:6–8	89
10:9	89
10:11f	194n174
10:11	223n32
10:13–16	226n56
10:15	79
10:17ff	202n69
10:17–22	77, 198n30, 226n56
10:17	77, 198n38
10:18 par	89
10:18	147
10:21	77, 147, 148, 197n28, 199n42
10:23–31	226n56
10:23–28	77
10:23–27	198n30
10:23	77
10:24	77
10:27	77, 199n42, 202n69
10:30	193n155
10:31	87
10:42ff	77
10:42	87, 88
10:43f	86
10:43	86, 203n76, 219n95
10:44	86, 203n76
10:45	86, 87
11:15–18	210n125
11:25	197n28
12:17	133, 210n120
12:28–31	114
12:28	92, 93
12:29	92, 93
12:30f par	92
12:30f	93
12:31	92

Mark (*cont.*)

12:32–33	208n107
12:33	93, 208n108
12:34	94
12:35	145
12:38–40	155
14:20	158
14:21	158
15:15	231n126
15:18	192n145
20:30f	87
22:22	158

Luke

1:32	193n162
1:35	193n162
1:76	193n162
2:9	233n134
2:14	233n134
2:20	233n134
3:1–6	154
3:7–18	154
3:8	160
3:9	163
3:11	160
3:17	163
3:21f	154
4:1–6:11	154
4:18	79, 81
5:25f	233n134
5:25	162
5:30	42, 192n148
6:3ff	159
6:3	159, 230n114
6:5	159, 230n114
6:9	57
6:12–49	154
6:12:20	154
6:12–15	153
6:12	153
6:13	154
6:15	60
6:16	159, 230n114
6:17–35	50
6:17–19	153
6:17	153, 154, 229n98
6:17b	154
6:18	153, 155
6:20–49	153, 154
6:20–26	153, 229n99
6:20–23	49, 158
6:20f	162
6:20	60, 81, 153, 154, 155, 158, 163, 233n145
6:20b	158
6:21	158, 160, 163, 169

Luke (*cont.*)

6:21b	158, 167
6:22f	163
6:22	189n118, 190n126
6:22b	189n118
6:23	60, 169, 193n155, 233n145
6:24–26	50, 155, 158
6:24f	159, 163
6:24	158, 160, 162, 169, 230n109
6:24b	230n114
6:25	160
6:26	163, 190n126
6:27–46	136, 153
6:27–45	153, 229n101
6:27–38	229n101
6:27–36 par	187n90
6:27–36	49, 50, 51, 52, 54, 56, 98, 134, 135, 136, 141, 156, 157, 171, 194n172
6:27ff	194n169
6:27	17, 53, 54, 55, 56, 58, 63, 135, 136, 158, 189n116, 189n117, 189n118
6:27b–31	136
6:27b	57, 135, 190n126
6:27c	135
6:27d	135
6:28	25, 56, 57, 58, 172, 190n126, 190n127, 195n174, 215n47, 224n35
6:28b	189n118
6:29f	58, 135, 230n106
6:29	52, 54, 55, 135, 156, 191n140, 230n106, 230n107
6:29b	191n136
6:30	52, 54, 55, 135, 159, 160, 162, 191n140, 192n144, 227n71, 230n109
6:30b	59, 157, 191n136, 230n107
6:31	54, 226n52
6:32–36	68
6:32–34	54, 55, 59, 79, 135, 136, 156, 163, 189n116
6:32f	76, 232n131
6:32	59, 192n143
6:33	59, 63, 180n25, 192n143

Luke (*cont.*)

6:34f	160
6:34	59, 158, 191n136, 192n144, 230n109, 232n133
6:35	25, 54, 55, 57, 59, 63, 76, 136, 157, 158, 159, 162, 163, 167, 169, 180n25, 189n114, 189n116, 191n136, 193n162, 194n169, 230n109
6:35b	61, 135, 136, 168, 189n114, 192n146
6:35c	60, 136
6:36–42	50
6:36	63, 87, 135, 136, 146, 161, 168, 170, 189n118, 193n162, 194n169, 194n171, 220n5
6:37ff	194n171
6:37f	163, 193n159
6:37	194n169, 197n28
6:39–45	229n101
6:39	229n101
6:40	149, 229n101
6:41	229n101
6:43–45	50
6:43f	229n101
6:43	169, 175
6:45	145, 175, 206n91, 229n101
6:46–49	50, 153, 163
6:46	229n99
6:47	225n42
6:49	170, 225n42
7:1	154, 155
7:16	233n134
7:22	81
7:30ff	202n61
7:34	192n148
7:37ff	202n69
7:37	201n58
7:41ff	85
7:45ff	83
8:1	79
8:9	155
8:10	155
8:14	162, 169
8:16	229n100
8:18	165
8:26	227n71
9:24	163
9:26	164, 233n134
9:54–56	87

Luke (*cont.*)

9:57–69	149
10:5	225n40
10:13f	164, 230n113
10:13	200n48
10:19	47
10:21–24	155
10:21	198n34
10:22	198n34
10:25	164, 168
10:26	204n83
10:28	164
10:29–37	93, 94, 95, 159, 162, 190n129
10:29	56, 95
10:30	231n123
11:4	164
11:20 par	88
11:20	79, 81, 197n24
11:29	88
11:31f	164
11:32	200n48
11:33	229n100
11:39–41	225n44
11:41	225n44
11:42	228n79
11:49	231n125
11:50	216n64
12:1	155
12:4f	164
12:5	62
12:6f	164
12:8–10	164
12:13–21	232n131
12:15	162
12:18	227n71
12:20f	164, 200n51
12:20	157
12:21	169
12:22ff	164
12:22–32	232n131
12:30	192n148
12:31	158, 164
12:32f	232n131
12:32	79, 164, 168
12:33f	232n131
12:33	164, 167, 168, 169, 174, 197n28, 231n122
12:34	161
12:37	86, 164
12:45f	164
12:51–53	88
12:51	231n125
12:57ff	197n28

Luke (*cont.*)

13:3f	200n48
13:5	164
13:13	233n134
13:24	164
13:27f	164
13:30	87
14:1	161
14:7–14	86
14:7–11	86, 169
14:7	86
14:11	86, 87, 125, 165, 203n76
14:12–14	86, 161, 162, 190n129, 232n134
14:13f	163, 165, 167, 232n133
14:13	162
14:14	161, 167, 232n133
14:24	164
14:25	77
14:26	77, 161, 198n32, 205n88, 221n14
14:31	227n71
14:34	165
15	81, 82, 194n167
15:1–3	82
15:1f	83
15:1	192n148
15:2	42, 81
15:7	83, 200n48
15:10	83, 200n48
15:11–13	82
15:11–24	81
15:21f	169
15:21	168
15:25–32	81, 83
15:27	230n110
15:28–32	83
15:29	202n63
16:1–8	197n132
16:1	167
16:8	227n7
16:9	162, 165, 167, 169, 174, 232n132
16:11f	165
16:11	170
16:14f	160
16:15	169
16:17	97, 210n119
16:18	223n32
16:19–31	159, 160, 162
16:19	159
16:20f	159
16:20	162

Luke (*cont.*)

16:22	160
16:23	160, 231n118
16:24	160
16:25	160, 163, 165, 167, 169, 230n110
16:26	160
16:29	231n118
16:30	160, 200n48
17:1f	230n113
17:2	165
17:3	200n48
17:8	86
17:9	192n146
17:10	78, 168, 169
17:15	233n134
17:18	233n134
17:20	88, 227n71
17:21	79, 88, 197n24
17:33	198n36
18:9–14	77, 88, 198n33
18:33	168, 169
18:14	87, 125, 165, 167, 233n142
18:18	169
18:25	210n119
18:29f	165
18:30	169, 193n155, 230n110
18:43	233n134
19:1–10	231n120
19:7	42, 201n58
19:8	83
19:26	165, 192n150
19:27	165
19:37	229n98
19:38	233n134
20:15f	165
20:20	231n126
20:26	231n126
20:28	193n155
20:45	155
20:46f	165
20:46	169
21:12	190n123, 231n125
21:17–19	165
22:27	86
22:38	99
22:51	99
23:2	231n126
23:5	231n126
23:13–16	231n126
23:18f	231n126
23:23	231n126
23:25	231n126
23:29	191n135

Luke (*cont.*)

23:30	191n135
23:34	190n129, 191n131, 231n125
23:36	191n135
23:41	230n110
23:47	233n134

John

3:3–8	119
3:17–21	216n61
5:44	78, 88
6:44	202n69
6:45	202n69
9:31	38
12:25	198n36
13:23	231n119

Acts

1:20	184n54
2:42	221n14
2:44f	231n122
4:32–37	231n122
6:4	221n14
7:48	193n162
7:56	200n51
7:60	191n131
9:21	217n76
12:12	231n122
13:7	231n126
13:12	231n126
16:16ff	231n126
16:39	231n126
18:15–17	231n126
19:23	231n126
19:35–41	231n126
23:29	231n126
25:25	231n126
26:32	231n126
27:9	176nl
27:22	176nl
28:30f	231n126

Romans

1:1	34
1:2	34
1:5	109
1:11–14	212n26
1:16f	216n58
1:16	117, 121
1:18	25, 216n58
1:27	230n110
2:4f	118
2:4	118
2:5	118
2:6–8	117
2:6	118
2:8	34

Romans (*cont.*)

2:10	63, 191n132
3:31	114
4:4	106
4:23	114
4:24	117, 121
5	113
5:5ff	106
5:5–10	104
5:5–8	121
5:5	103, 106
5:6–8	61
5:6	104
5:7	104
5:8	103, 104
5:10	103, 104, 117, 119
6	104
6:4	106, 121
6:6	106
6:11	121
6:12	104
6:13	104, 121
6:14	106, 120
6:17	121, 213n32
6:18	106
6:22	106, 213n32
8:4–7	193n160
8:9f	107
8:11	117, 121
8:17	125
8:24	117, 119, 120
9–11	41
9:2	41
9:3	41, 215n47
9:13	41
9:16	108
10:1	41, 215n47
10:17	41, 117
10:23	109
11:9	184n54
11:10	184n54
11:22	193n160
12	8, 9, 103, 104, 109, 191n141, 211n14, 212n15
12:1–13:7	111, 113
12:1f	41, 212n15
12:1	24, 102, 103, 104, 105, 119, 121, 212n15, 212n19, 212n22
12:2	24, 39, 103, 104, 105, 106, 122, 128, 133, 212n16
12:3–13:7	103, 105

Romans (*cont.*)

12:3–8	5, 103
12:3	109, 213n29
12:6	213n29
12:7	86, 109
12:9–21	5, 8, 103, 176n1, 212n21
12:9–19	178n7
12:9–13	8, 132, 211n13
12:9	11, 15, 34, 104, 105, 129, 130, 180n24, 188n109, 212n16, 212n21
12:9b	9
12:10–16	137
12:10	7, 13
12:11	129
12:11b	9
12:12f	127
12:12	9, 11, 129, 211n13
12:12c	9, 11
12:13	17, 104, 105
12:14ff	178n7
12:14–21	14, 15, 179n23, 211n13
12:14–20	137
12:14–17	16
12:14	4, 5, 6, 7, 15, 16, 17, 25, 41, 57, 63, 102, 103, 104, 114, 116, 117, 118, 121, 129, 132, 171, 172, 190n123, 190n126, 195n174, 215n47
12:15–16	132, 211n13
12:15	15, 24, 211n13
12:16–21	15
12:16–19	24
12:16	8, 13, 15, 16, 24, 211n13
12:16b	7, 27
12:17ff	104, 121
12:17–21	16, 17, 102, 103, 132, 211n13
12:17–20	4, 111, 114, 171
12:17f	215n47
12:17	5, 6, 7, 8, 9, 11, 13, 14, 15, 16, 17, 27, 34, 38, 39, 49, 53, 57, 64, 112, 113, 132, 178n7, 178n8, 182n20, 184n46, 212n16
12:17b	13, 15, 27, 112, 114, 179n23
12:18	7, 9, 13, 15, 17, 64, 112, 180n24,

Romans (*cont.*)

	180n26
12:19–21	215n47
12:19f	15, 114, 116, 118, 127
12:19	6, 8, 34, 36, 46, 59, 62, 112, 113, 115, 117, 194n172, 194n173
12:19b	27, 112, 115
12:20	27, 30, 34, 61, 112, 114, 115, 116, 117, 118, 129, 132, 194n173, 215n52
12:20b	115
12:21	15, 212n16, 224n38
13	103, 211n14, 212n15, 214n39
13:1–7	5, 103, 132, 210n124
13:1	131
13:3	63, 180n25, 191n132, 212n16
13:4	131, 212n16
13:8–10	114, 131, 211n14
13:8	13
13:9	214n39
13:10	211n16, 219n98
13:11–14	211n14
14:3	109
14:9	217n76
14:19	64, 180n26
14:26	109
15:3	62
15:4	113, 114
15:7	62
15:13	126
15:14	109
15:15	109
15:26–28	105
15:29	129
15:30	103, 212n19
16:17	42

I Corinthians

1:9	127
1:26	179n16
3:5	86
3:10	109, 179n16
3:16	109
4:12	16, 17, 57, 63, 129, 132, 171, 190n123
4:14	16
4:16	16, 103
4:17	16
5:13	188n109
6:7	59

I Corinthians (*cont.*)

6:11	106
6:12	109
6:19	110
7:10	111, 194n174, 214n35
7:15	127
7:40	107
8:9	12, 179n16
9:5	221n14
9:9	129
9:10	113, 114
9:14	194n174, 214n35
9:19ff	118
9:24	232n132
10	113
10:2	12
10:12	179n16
10:23	213n28
10:27	42
10:32f	180n23
11:1	62
11:2	211n11
11:23ff	214n35
11:23	211n11
12:3	213n29, 214n35
12:5	86, 219n95
12:13	109
12:27	213n29
12:31ff	132
12:31–13:13	131
12:31	130
13	130
13:4	24, 179n14
13:5	219n96
13:6	118
14:1	213n29
14:3	213n29
14:20	63
14:21	112
14:37	111
15:2	117
15:3	211n11
16:10	179n16
16:14–16	131
16:14	130
16:15	131
16:16	131, 132

II Corinthians

1:20	113
2:9	217n76
2:16	118
3:8	107
3:14	114
3:17	110, 212n18
4:6	108, 109

II Corinthians (*cont.*)

4:9	63, 190n123
4:16	108
4:17	108
5:7	133
5:17	106, 121
5:18	121
5:19–20	212n26
5:20	108, 109, 121
6:14–18	42
8	104, 105
8:4	105
8:5	105
8:8	105
8:9	105
8:19f	105
8:21	112, 179n23
8:24	105
9	104, 105
9:1	105
9:5	105
9:8	105
9:12	105
10:1	212n19

Galatians

1:15	108
2:9	109
2:11	53
2:14	192n53
2:20	106, 133, 219n95
3:2	41
4:5	230n110
5:5b	61
5:11	63, 190n123
5:13	212n18
5:14	114
5:15	12, 179n16
5:18	106
5:21	61
5:22	106, 212n18
6:10	42, 63, 179n21, 191n132, 219n98
6:12	63, 190n123
6:15	106, 121

Ephesians

2:8	108
3:2	109
3:7	109
4:1	103
4:19	158
4:22f	211n8
4:25	211n8
4:32–5:2	62
4:32	63
5:5	193n160

Ephesians (*cont.*)

5:7	42
5:15	179n16
5:21	211n8
6:8	63, 191n132
6:11	211n8
6:13	53
6:18	211n8

Philippians

1:1f	212n19
1:28	118
1:29	117
2:1	63
2:5ff	62
2:17	212n22
2:29	219n94
3:10	127
3:15	63
3:18f	117
4:4	11
4:5–8	11
4:5	11, 13
4:6	11
4:8	11
4:9	179n15, 211n11

Colossians

1:4f	117
1:4	120
1:13	111
1:28	63, 213n33
3:8	211n8
3:9f	211n8
3:10	121
3:12	63
3:13	179n20
3:14	219n97
3:15	127
3:16	109, 110
3:18f	219n96
3:18	211n8
3:19	219n96
3:20	219n96
3:24	230n110
4:2	211n8
4:5	180n23
4:12	63, 211n8
4:17	179n16

I Thessalonians

1:3	61
1:4	211n12
1:5	108
1:6	62, 110
2:2–3	212n26
2:9–14	212n26
2:9	10

I Thessalonians (*cont.*)
2:12   10, 61
2:13   39, 61, 211n11, 211n12
3:12   13, 42, 61, 110
3:13   211n12
4:1   110
4:2   110
4:6   61, 193n160
4:7   127
4:9   106, 110
4:11f   179n12
4:11   10, 12
4:12   180n23
4:15   214n35
5   8, 9, 12
5:1–10   34
5:8   120
5:12–22   8
5:12   12, 131
5:13–22   178n7
5:13   9, 17, 64, 130, 131, 180n26
5:14–22   10
5:14–21   11
5:14–18   8, 9
5:14   9, 10, 12, 13, 179n11, 179n12, 179n14
5:14d   11
5:15–22   176n1
5:15   5, 6, 8, 9, 10, 11, 12, 15, 17, 25, 38, 39, 42, 49, 53, 57, 63, 64, 110, 112, 129, 132, 137, 171, 178n7, 178n8, 179n11, 180n24, 182n20, 184n46, 191n132, 211n12, 219n98
5:15b   13, 179n23
5:16ff   5, 10
5:16–22   11
5:16–21   11
5:16   9, 11, 13
5:17   9, 11, 13
5:18   11, 13
5:19   9
5:21f   180n24
5:21   9, 11, 13
5:22   13, 188n109

II Thessalonians
1:6–8   115
1:6   116
2:15   211n11
3:6   9, 42, 179n13, 211n11

II Thessalonians (*cont.*)
3:7   9, 179n13
3:11   9, 179n13

I Timothy
1:12   192n147
2:1   190n131
5:17   219n94
6:17–19   232n132

II Timothy
1:3   192n147
3:12   63, 190n123
3:16   114
4:13   210nl

Titus
1:9   179n14
3:5   119
3:10   42

Hebrews
3:12   179n16
5:14   63
10:30   112, 113
10:34   232n132
12:1   211n8
12:9   211n8
12:14   64, 180n26
12:17   127, 218n82
12:25   179n16
12:28   192n147
13:1–3   8
13:4   193n160
13:17   211n8, 219n94

James
1:4   63
1:18f   211n8
1:18   119
1:21   211n8
2:8–10   114
3:2   63
3:9–12   57
4:7   53, 211n8
5:6   53

I Peter
1:3ff   120
1:3–12   120
1:3–9   125, 126
1:3–5   61
1:3   39, 119, 120, 121, 122, 126, 217n67, 218n85
1:4f   128
1:4   125, 126
1:5   120, 121, 122, 125, 126, 217n67, 217n70
1:6f   125, 126
1:6   217n71

I Peter (*cont.*)

1:7	125, 126, 217n70
1:9	120, 122, 125, 126, 217n67, 217n70
1:13	34, 120
1:14f	26
1:14	122
1:15	194n168, 217n74
1:17	124, 217n67
1:18–21	61
1:18f	125
1:18	218n85
1:19	121, 122
1:21	120, 121, 126, 217n67
1:22	120, 211n8, 218n85
1:23–25	120
1:23	39, 61, 119, 120, 121, 126, 218n85
1:25	119, 121, 211n8
2:1ff	120
2:1	121, 211n8
2:2	120, 121
2:3	64, 121, 180n24, 218n88
2:4	180n24, 218n88
2:5	122
2:6	217n67, 217n70
2:9f	34
2:9	217n74, 218n85
2:12	129, 180n23, 217n71
2:13–3:12	132
2:13ff	210n124
2:13–17	5, 132
2:13	211n8
2:14f	63
2:14	180n25, 191n132, 217n71
2:15	180n25, 191n132, 215n52
2:18–25	5, 132
2:18	217n67
2:19f	192n146, 195n175
2:20	59, 63, 156, 180n25, 191n132
2:21–25	120
2:21	62, 121, 124, 127
2:23	119
2:24	61, 121, 122, 218n85
3:1–7	5, 132
3:1	8, 225n38
3:2	217n67
3:6	63, 180n25, 191n132
3:8–12	178n7

I Peter (*cont.*)

3:8f	8, 178n7
3:8	5, 7, 132
3:9–12	113, 117, 122, 124, 127, 132, 137, 194n173
3:9	5, 6, 7, 8, 11, 13, 14, 15, 16, 17, 25, 38, 39, 49, 53, 57, 61, 64, 112, 122, 125, 126, 127, 128, 129, 132, 171, 173, 178n7, 182n20, 184n46, 215n52, 217n76
3:9b	123, 124
3:10–12	27, 34, 57, 61, 64, 123, 124, 127, 215n47
3:10	61, 124
3:11	7, 13, 17, 63, 64, 127
3:12	61, 124, 193n161, 215n52, 218n79
3:13	63, 180n25
3:15	217n67, 217n71
3:16	57, 191n132, 215n52
3:17f	121
3:17	63, 180n25, 191n132
3:18	61, 120, 121, 218n85
4:4	129, 217n71
4:6	123, 124
4:7	211n8
4:9	13
4:12–16	126
4:12	125, 217n71
4:13–16	126
4:13	125, 126
4:14	125
4:16	125
4:18	215n47, 217n78
4:19	61, 63, 180n25, 191n132
5	125
5:5	13, 211n8
5:5b	125
5:6	125
5:8	211n8
5:9f	126
5:9	53, 120, 122, 211n8, 217n67, 217n70, 217n71, 218n81
5:10	217n74

I John
2:13f	188n109
3:1–3	194n168
3:8	217n76
3:9	119
4:7–9	194n168
5:8	119

II John
8	179n16, 230n110
10	42
11	63, 180n25

III John
7	192n153
11	191n132

Revelation
2:6	129, 183n33
12:13	63, 190n123
18:9	218n81
18:18	218n81
20:9	34
20:15	34
21:7	193n160
21:8	193n160

III. Extra-Biblical Literature of Antiquity
A. *Jewish* (alphabetically)

Aristeas
187–294	35
200	35
207	36
211	35
220	35
222	35
225	36
227	36
232	36
235	35
256	35

Baruch
4:1	210n119

II Baruch (= Syriac Apocalypse of Baruch)
55:8	218n82
77:15	210n119

I Enoch (Ethiopic)
45:4f	218n82
103:10	230n109

II Enoch (Slavonic)
30:13	183n39
44:4	37
44:5	37
50:3	36
51:2	37
51:3	36
51:59	183n39
51:61	183n39

II Enoch (Slavonic) (*cont.*)
51:62	183n39
51:68	183n39
60:1	36
61:1	37

IV Ezra
9:37	210n119
12:7	233n142

Joseph and Asenath
23–29	37
23:9	37
28:4	16, 37, 38, 64
28:12	38
28:14	38
29:3	38

Josephus
Against Apion
II, 123	46
II, 145f	186n80
II, 183	47
II, 190	93
II, 209f	47
II, 211f	47
II, 261	47

The Jewish War
II, 157	232n134
III, 10	208n100
IV, 397	230n109
V, 354	230n109

Jubilees
20	185n69
20:2	185n56
22:16	42
36	185n69

IV Maccabees
2:9	36
2:10–12	36
2:13	36
2:14	36

Qumran Documents
Damascus Document (CD)
6:20–21	184n52

Hymn Scroll (1QH)
15	184n53

Manual of Discipline (1QS)
1:2	40
1:4	40
1:9	32, 40
1:10	32, 40, 41, 91, 215n54
1:11	41
3:25	41
4:1	41
9:21	215n54
10:9–13	32

Manual of Discipline (1QS) *(cont.)*
10:17–19   40, 182n20
10:18–20   216n54
11:9–10   40
11:10   41
Philo
  De agricultura
    110   184n49
  De migratione Abrahami
    128   39
  De plantatione
    49   39
  De specialibus legibus
    II,63   93
  De virtutibus
    116–18   39
Rabbinic Literature
  Aboth de Rabbi Nathan
    16:7   48
  Babylonian Talmud
    Kiddushim
      36a   193n164
    Pesahim
      113b   186n85
    Yebamoth
      60b   187n87
  Midrashim
    Numbers Rabbah
      2.138b   187n85
  Mishnah
    Aboth
      1:12   48
      2:11   48
  Targums
    Onkelos   113
    Pseudo Jonathan
      Lev. 22:28   194n170
  Tosephta
    Sanhedrin
      13:2   186n87
Sirach (Ecclesiasticus)
  4:7–10   186n78
  8:10   115
  11:32   115
  12:1–7   45
  12:1–6   194n172
  12:1   192n147
  12:6f   46
  28:1–7   186n78
Testaments of the Twelve Patriarchs
  Benjamin
    3:6   190n130
    4:2f   44
  Dan
    5:3   93

Gad
  5:9–11   185n75
  6:7   45
Issachar
  5:2   93
  7:6   44
Joseph
  18:1–4   45
  18:2   44, 45
Levi   43
  6:7   185n75
Naphtali   43
Reuben
  69   44, 45
Zebulun
  6:6   45
  7:2–4   44
  8:3   45
  8:5–9:2   44, 45
Tobit
  1:6   210n119
  4:14–17   35
Wisdom of Solomon
  3:14   192n147

B. *Christian*
Didache
  1:3   156
  11:5f   221n14
I Clement
  17:3   38
  59:3   230n109
Gospel according to the Hebrews
  13:1393–4   226n60
Ignatius to Polycarp
  2:1   192n147
Polycarp to the Philippians
  2:2   17

C. *Greek and Roman*
Epictetus
  Discourses
    I.22   25
    I.25   26
    I.29   26
    I.36   25
    III.4   25
    III.9   25
    III.13.11   26
    III.13.13   26
    III.20.9   25
    III.22.54   26
    III.22.81   26
    III.22.82   26
    III.22.82   26

Epictetus (*cont.*)
  Discourses (*cont.*)
    III.22.90-2   182n17
    III.22.100-3 182n17
    IV.1.79   229n105
    IV.5.28   182n16
    IV.5.32   181n14
  Encheiridion
    1   181n15
    20   182n16
    33.9   181n14
    42   25
Seneca
  De beneficiis
    IV.26   21
    IV.26.1   62
    VII.28.3   181n10
    VII.30.2   21
    VII.30.5   21
  De constantia
    2:1   181n11
    2:3   181n11
    3:3   181n11
    4:1   23

Seneca (*cont.*)
  De constantia (*cont.*)
    5:4   23
    7:2   23
    12:3   24
    13:1   24
    14:3   181n9
  De ira
    II.32   22
    II.34.5   181n10
    III.5.8   23
    III.25.3   23
    III.39.4   24
    III.40.5   24
    III.42.3   22
    III.42.4   22
    III.43.1   22
    III.43.2   22
  De otio
    1:4   21
Tacitus
  Histories
    V.5   208n100

INDEX OF MODERN AUTHORS

Althaus, P., 191n133, 215n50
Augstein, R., 201n54
Augustine, 199n40

Baltzer, K., 218n84
Bammel, E., 222n23
Banks, R., 187n88, 190n122, 205n86,
   210n119, 226n61
Barrett, C. K., 138, 191n133, 200n51,
   212n18, 216n58, 222n17
Barth, G., 151, 204n80, 226n55, n59,
   227n63, n69, 228n75, n80
Barth, P., 180n1, 184n48
Bartsch, H. W., 153, 154, 156, 228n84
Batiffol, P., 184n40
Bauer, W., 116
Baumbach, G., 153, 154
Bayer, O., 197n25
Beare, F. W., 7, 177n3, 187n93, 194n170
Becker, J., 43, 44, 45, 185n75, 190n130
Behm, J., 200n48
Best, E., 179n18, 184n43
Beyer, H., 87
Bjerkelund, C., 212n17
Black, M., 194n170, 198n33
Bolkestein, H., 180n2, 231n117
Boman, T., 195n179
Bonhoeffer, A., 25, 27, 180n5
Bornemann, W., 179n17
Bornkamm, G., 94, 148, 149, 195n179,
   196n17, n19, n22, 199n45, 224n36,
   227n71, 228n75, n79, 232n129
Bonsett, W., 184n40
Braun, H., 70, 71, 75, 85, 192n142,
   197n28, 201n54, 202n68, 207n98,
   n99, 209n111, n112, 224n36
Broer, I., 206n90
Brooks, E. W., 184n40
Brown, J. P., 211n11, 221n12
Bruce, F. F., 231n126
Büchsel, F., 198n39, 203n72, 217n67

Bultmann, R., 51, 52, 53, 54, 56, 70, 73,
   74, 75, 76, 81, 82, 84, 158, 181n12,
   187n95, 188n102, n105, 189n114,
   192n142, 193n166, 194n170,
   195n179, 196n17, 198n30, n32,
   199n45, 200n47, 201n60, 202n68,
   203n79, 204n82, 205n84, n86, n90,
   207n98, 209n112, 210n119,
   216n63, 219n90, 224n36, 232n132,
   n134
Burchard, C., 92, 93, 94, 183n40,
   184n46, n47, 208n106, n107, 209n111
Burney, C. F., 191n137

Calvin, J., 218n83
Carrington, P., 101, 102, 178n7, 211n8
Cervaux, L. 211n11
Charles, R. H., 43, 183n38, 185n56
Conzelmann, H., 153, 168, 213n28
Cranfield, C. E. B., 115, 178n7, 191n133,
   211n13, 215n50
Cullmann, O., 200n46, 206n90, 211n11

Dabney, R. L., 185n54
Daube, D., 8, 14, 177n5, 180n23, 188
   n110, 211n13
Davenport, G. L., 185n55
Davies, W. D., 102, 177n5, 190n121,
   195n178, 213n30, 223n25
Degenhardt, H. J., 154, 230n115
De Jonge, M., 43, 44, 45, 186n76
Delling, G., 200n46, 220n99
Denis, A. M., 43, 183n36, n39, n40
Dibelius, M., 9, 11, 86, 101, 102, 136,
   176n1, 178n10, 179n22, 199n44,
   203n72, n74, 211n10, 224n24
Dietzfelbinger, C., 206n90
Dihle, A., 210n5
Dobshütz, E., 179n19, 188n102
Dodd, C. H., 8, 102, 116, 137, 138,
   177n4, n5, 191n133, n141, 195n178,

199n46, 211n9, n13, 213n31, n34
Dungan, D., 177n7, 195n178, 211n11, 221n15
Dupont-Sommer, A., 43, 185n55

Easton, B. S., 191n137
Eissfeldt, O., 35, 183n37, n39, 185n55, 186n77
Ernst, J., 290n111

Fannon, P., 195n178, 211n11
Feine, P., 195n178
Filson, F., 137, 211n11, 221n13
Fjörstedt, B., 195n178, 211n11, 222n18
Flender, H., 86, 155, 187n95, 195n179, 200n48, 229n100
Frame, J. F., 179n11
France, R. T., 195nl
Fraser, J. W., 195n178, 211n11
Fuchs, E., 202n65
Fuller, R. H., 199n45, 209n113
Furnish, V., 1, 2, 204n80, 212n15, 218n80, 224n38, 228n73

Gaechter, P., 55, 191n136, 207n99
Georgi, D., 218n84
Gerhardsson, B., 138, 210nl, 211n11, 221n14, 222n24, 223n25
Glover, R., 187n93
Goppelt, L., 67, 75, 83, 131, 134, 171, 172, 177n1, 187n95, 188n105, 193n159, 194n167, 195n174, n178, 197n26, n28, 203n70, n74, 204n82, 205n89, 206n93, 207n97, n99, 209n115, n117, 210n120, 211n11, 214n35, n36, n38, 215n44, 217n71, 219n95, 220n99, 222n24, 223n30, 227n62, n73, 228n75, 234n2
Grabner-Haider, A., 107, 176n1, 212n26, 216n57
Grant, F. C., 200n51
Grässer, E., 199n45
Grundmann, W., 158, 187n91, 191n136, n137, 192n147, 198n32, n33, 199n40, n42, 202n68, 204n79, 207n99, 209n117, 216n63, 229n101, 230n115, 232n131
Guelich, R., 187n95, 189n120, 204n82, 205n90, 206n90, n91, 207n99, 226n62, 228n75
Gutbrod, W., 205n88, 206n94

Haas, H., 195n176
Haenchen, E., 228n79

Hafemann, S., xi
Hahn, F., 101
Hanson, R. P. C., 211n11
Harrelson, W., 185n75
Hasler, V., 189n117
Headlam, A., 212n15, n18
Heitmüller, W., 195n179
Held, H. J., 226n57
Hengel, M., 80, 98
Hirsch, E., 158
Hoffmann, P., 98, 139, 188n107, 207n99
Hübner, H., 188n110, 190n122
Hultgen, A., 208n104
Hummel, R., 216n64
Hunter, A. M., 177n5, 198n178, 210n5, 211n10, n11

Jeremias, J., 51, 52, 55, 66, 81, 84, 86, 89, 137, 182n26, 188n99, n110, 191n136, 193n159, 194n170, 198n33, n34, 199n41, 201n55, n57, n59, 202n68, 204n83, 205n86, 206n90, 207n99, 220n2, n8, 227n73, 231n118, n119, n123, 232n132, 233n142
Jervell, J., 43, 185n58
Jülicher, A., 82
Juncker, A., 195n178
Jüngel, E., 202n62, 202n65

Kamlah, E., 210n5
Käsemann, E., 115
Kelly, J. N. D., 123, 177n2, 178n7
Kirkpatrick, 218n89
Kissenger, S., 209n117
Klassen, W., 176n3, 195n176
Klostermann, E., 84
Knox, W. L., 187n93, 198n34
Köster, H., 214n35
Kühl, E., 211n13
Kümmel, W. G., 158, 179n13, 193n158, 197n28, 200n46, 200n51, 203n72, 228n78, 231n126
Kuhn, K. G., 183n40, 184n40, 195n179

Ladd, G. E., 199n44, 203n72
Lagrange, M. J., 211n13
Lang, F., 216n60
Larsson, E., 221n15
Lewis, C. S., 166
Liechtenhahn, R., 199n40, 203n72, 206n95
Lietzmann, H., 107
Linnemann, E., 84, 202n65

Lohmeyer, E., 198n30, n31, 201n60, 208n107, 209n111
Lohse, E., 120, 177n5, 178n7, 187n95, 204n82, 216n57, 217n69, 218n78
Lührmann, D., 38, 49, 52, 55, 56, 59, 60, 70, 73, 75, 135, 184n42, 187n90, n93, 190n126, n127, 191n134, n136, n139, 192n144, n146, 193n162, n163, 194n171, 196n6, n15, 207n98
Lünemann, G., 179n18
Luz, U., 201n52

Machovevč, M., 69, 70, 71, 74, 75, 85, 196n7, n8, 203n69
Manson, T. W., 167, 168, 188n110, 191n134, n137, 195n4, 198n34, n36, 223n31, 232n131
Marshall, I. H., 222n24, 223n26
Martin, C., 185n54
Mendenhall, G., 228n77
Merkel, F., 218n84
Michel, O., 16, 27, 28, 104, 113, 179n23, 196n22, 198n32, 201n59, 208n108, 209n111, 211n13, 212n15, n21, 215n52, n53
Michl, J., 183n39
Milik, J. T., 184n50
Moe, O., 195n178
Moffatt, J., 1
Montefiore, C. G., 183n32, 186n81, n84
Morenz, S., 115
Morgenthaler, R., 200n46
Moule, C. F. D., 191n141
Murray, J., 185n54

Neugebauer, F., 214n35
Neuhäusler, E., 187n93, 192n146, 195n179, 203n72
Nieder, L., 215n50
Niederwimmer, K., 70, 72, 75, 85
Nissen, A., 187n88, 208n105, n106, n110
Noll, P., 208n102

Oepke, A., 179n12

Percy, E., 55, 188n110, 189n116, 199n43, 207n99
Perrin, N., 193n154, 203n76, 206n91, 223n30
Pesch, W., 196n22
Philonenko, M., 43, 44, 183n40, 185n65
Pines, S., 183n39
Piper, J., 210n120
Plöger, O., 183n39

Pohlenz, M., 20
Preisker, H., 116, 117, 203n74

Quell, G., 27, 28

Rad, G. v., 206n96, 216n58
Rengstorf, K. H., 158, 187n90, 191n136, 209n112, 217n66, 223n31, 229n101, 230n115, 231n124
Ridderbos, H., 191n133, 195n178, 196n23, 199n43, 201n56, 205n87 221n15, 232n131
Riesenfeld, H., 138, 139, 211n11
Robertson, A. T., 217n76
Robinson, J. M. 214n35
Roloff, J., 220n1, 230n108
Rost, L., 43, 183n35, n36, n37, n39, 185n55, 186n77

Sanday, W., 212n15, n18
Sanders, E. P., 138, 210nl, 222n18
Schelkle, K. H., 177n2, 178n7, 216n56, 217n71, n78
Schenk, W., 217n77, 218n82, n86
Schlatter, A., 3, 84, 90, 119, 186n79, 187n90, n94, 191n138, 192n152, 195n3, 202n61, n65, 203n78, 207n99, 214n37, 216n60, 229n101, 232n131
Schlier, H., 176n1, 193n160, 212n17
Schlink, E., 176n1
Schmauch, W., 28, 187n90, 190n130, 192n147, 193n156, 225n40
Schmidt, L., 180n2, 191n133
Schmithals, W., 195n179
Schnackenburg, R., 196n20, 199n40, 200n50, n51, 209n111, 224n36
Schniewind, J., 77, 83, 193n156, 195n178, 197n27, 198n31, n38, 199n42, 202n65, n68, 208n99, 209n118, 216n63
Schoeps, H. P., 195n179
Schottroff, L., 82, 98, 99, 207n98, 210n124, 224n88
Schrage, W., 101, 107, 131, 177n1, 195n179, 212n24, 214n43, 219n93, n96, n97
Schroeder, D., 220n99
Schulz, S., 56, 181n91, 189n117, 190n123, n128, 191n136, n138, 192n145, n146, 193n162, n163, 194n171, 209n119
Schürer, E., 184n40
Schürmann, H., 55, 153, 154, 187n95, 189n115, n118, 190n127, 191n135,

n136, 192n144, 194n169, 197n24, n28, 200n46, 229n95, n98, n101
Schütz, F., 223n26
Schweitzer, A., 195n179, 199n45
Schweizer, E., 81, 204n82, 228n80
Scott, C. A. A., 195n178
Seeberg, A., 101, 102
Seitz, O. J. F., 56, 182n26, 189n117, 207n99
Selby, D. J., 194n174, 195n178
Selwyn, E. G., 101, 102, 177n2, 178n7, 180n23, n24, 195n175, 212n21, 217n66, n71, n72, 218n88, n89
Sevenster, J. N., 180n6, 181n7, n12, 215n50
Smith, C., 82
Smith, M., 188n110
Soiron T., 199n40, 203n72, 209n116, n117
Spicq, C., 1, 115, 176n3, 204n82, 226n60
Stanton, G. N., 222n24, 230n108
Stauffer, E., 199n46
Stendahl, K., 215n47
Strecker, G., 206n91, 207n99, 223n32, 224n34, 225n44, n45, 228n79, n80
Suggs, M. J., 188n105, 189n110, 206n90

Talbert, C., 9, 14, 15, 18, 177n5
Taylor, V., 191n137, 198n30, n36,

201n60, 205n84, n86, 209n111, 229n106
Theissen, G., 221n14
Thielicke, H., 209n117, 225n48
Thomas, J., 39, 49, 186n75
Trilling, W., 151, 189n111, 210n119, 223n33, 224n34, 226n53, 227n70, 228n74, n76

Unnik, W. C. van, 156, 159, 192n143, n147, 195n175, 230n116

Vögtle, A., 210n5

Warnach, J., 1
Wegenast, K., 211n11
Weidinger, K., 210n5
Weiser, A., 218n89
Weiss, J., 195n179, 199n45
Wellhausen, J., 202n62
Wendland, H. D., 199n40, n44, 203n72, 204n82, n83, 209n117, 212n15, 219n97
Werner, M., 199n45
Wibbing, S., 210n5
Wilckens, U., 195n179
Wilder, A. N., 199n44, 200n51
Windisch, H., 197n24, 218n80
Woude, A. S. van der, 43
Wrege, H. T., 156, 187n90, 192n147, n149, n150

INDEX OF SUBJECTS

Antitheses, 51–5
   and the law in Mt, 151f
Atheism, 70–2
Authenticity of synoptic tradition, 66f;
   see also historicity

Beatitudes in Lk, 158
Body of Christ and ethics, 109f, 213n31

Catechism, early Christian structure,
   211n8
Condition
   for entering Kingdom, 76–80, 203n70
   for inheritance of blessing, 122–6
   for perfection, 148f
   for salvation, 173
Conversion of enemy, 98f, 143f, 215n47

Discipleship in Mt, 148f
Double love command, 92–5

Enablement of love command; *see* motivation
   in Jesus' teaching, 60f, 77–85,
      202n69, 203n72, 204n80
   in paraenesis, 211n12, 213n32
   through love of God, 203n70
Enemy love
   and blessing, 130
   and society's institutions, 130–3
   'command of', 176n2
   involving hate, 129
   practical features in Lk, 157–62
   practical features in Mt, 142–5
   practical features in paraenesis, 128–30
   see also love command
Eschatological tension, 97, 133, 174,
   199n46
Eschatology
   and wisdom, 196n24
   consistent, 199n45
   realized, 199n46

Faithfulness of God, 117f, 149–51
Forgiveness
   as part of enemy love, 225n47
   of tax collectors and sinners, 81–5
   not automatic, 202n61, n69

Generosity, 104f
Gesinnungsethik, 96
God
   his faithfulness, 117f
   his hate of evildoers, 182n31
   his judgment, 114–19, 217n58, n64
   his love, 103f, 203n70
   his mercy, 102–6
   his righteousness, 118, 216n58, n59
   his vengeance, 114–19
   his wrath, 216n58, n64
   imitation of, 21, 31, 41, 46, 49, 62
   in relation to Jesus' commands, 75, 85
Golden rule, 35, 37
Gospel tradition
   definition, 134
   how it differs from paraenetic tradition,
      137
   of enemy love, 134–6
   relation to paraenetic tradition, 136–9
   Sitz im Leben, 136–9
   transmission, 221n14, 222n18

Hardness of heart, 89–91, 206n95, n96,
   n97
Hatred
   God's, of evildoers, 182n31
   hating what God hates, 183n33
   in Psalms, 33f, 41
   meanings in OT, 27f
   of Jews for others, 208n100
Haustafel, 5, 131–3, 177n1
Hellenizing of love command tradition,
   156
Hermeneutical problems, 66f
Historicity of gospel tradition; *see* authen-

ticity
  Mt's attitude toward, 141f
  Lk's attitude toward, 153–7, 170
Holy Spirit, 103f, 106–10, 212n24,
    213n29, n30
Hope, 120; *see also* reward

Imitation
  of God, 21, 31, 41, 46, 49, 62
  of Christ, 62
Imperative participle, 8, 177n5
Indicative-imperative tension, 108
Institutions of society and enemy love,
    130–3
Interim ethic, 96

Jesus' teaching
  as criterion of paraenesis, 64, 138,
    172, 233n1
  authenticity, 66–8
  authoritative for Paul, 111
  in paraenetic tradition, 58, 64f
  relation to Paul, 195n178, n179,
    214n35
  theological structure preserved in
    paraenesis, 128
Judgment of God, 114–19, 217n58, n64

Kerygma and paraenesis, 101f, 120–2
Kingdom of God
  condition of entering, 76–80
  future, 76–80
  in recent studies, 69
  its sign in love command, 86–8,
    203n74
  love command as a sign of, 86–8
  present, 79–85
  present–future tension and *lex
    talionis*, 97

Law
  abolition or abiding validity of, 89,
    95–8
  and love command, 89–99
  and the antitheses in Mt, 151f
  Jesus' attitude toward, 264n83
Law of Christ, 213n34
Lex talionis
  abolished?, 95–8
  dam against violence, 90, 206n95
  foundation of civil order, 96, 209n115
  in OT, 182n28
  vs. non-resistance, 89
Lord's prayer, 143, 224n37
Love; *see* enemy love, love command

meanings in OT, 27f
  of God 103f, 149–51, 203n70
Love command
  and service, 86f
  as canon of OT interpretation in MT,
    152
  as condition of salvation, 76–80, 122–6,
    148f
  as criterion of paraenesis, 64, 100,
    138, 172, 233n1
  as sign of the Kingdom, 86–8, 203n74
  as summons to transformation, 85
  authenticity, 56–63
  common features of interpretation,
    173–5
  destructive function of, 208n102
  not absolute prescription, 99
  phrase 'command of enemy love,'
    176n2
  practical features of obedience,
    128–30, 142–5, 157–62
  why Christians need the command,
    106–10

Marxists, 69–71
Motivation of love; *see* enablement
  by rewards in Lk, 162–70
  christological in Mt, 145–9
  in paraenesis, 101–26
  role of Holy Spirit, 106–10
  role of imperatives, 106–10, 213n34,
    219n90
  role of OT, 114–19, 122–6
  theological in Mt, 149–51, 204n80
Mystery religions, 119

Neighbor love, 30–2, 47f, 91–5, 148
New birth, 119f
New covenant, 206n96
Non-resistance, 95–9, 131, 209n116,
    210n120, 219n97

Old Testament
  as background of paraenesis, 27–35
  use in explicating love command,
    111–14
  use in motivating love command,
    114–19
Oral tradition, 8, 18, 100, 122, 126f
  two streams, 134

Paraenesis; *see* paraenetic tradition
  and parousia, 107, 214n43
  definition, 102f, 176
  relation to kerygma, 101f, 120–2

style, 8
Paraenetic tradition of love command
contents, 17f, 63f
existence of ?, 7–8
relation to gospel tradition, 136–9
relation to Jesus' words, 58, 64f
Paraklēsis, 109, 176n1, 212n17
Parousia and Paraenesis, 107, 214n43
Paul
as bearer of tradition, 211n11
motivation of love command, 102–18
relation to Jesus' teaching, 195n178,
n179, 214n35
Perfection, 146–9
Persecutions in I Pt, 217n71
Possessions, use of in Lk, 157–62
Prayer for enemies, 142–5
Psalms
use of in paraenetic tradition, 13f
imprecatory 33f, 41, 185n54

Q, Sermon on the Mt, 49f
Qumran, 39–41

Reciprocity, denunciation of in Lk,
159–61
Redaction; *see* redaction criticism
in I Thess, 8–13
in Rom, 14–17
Lk's use of love command, 153–70
Mt's use of love command, 141–52
Redaction criticism
Lk's attitude to historicity of
tradition, 153–7, 170
Mt's attitude to historicity of tradition,
141f
our approach, 139–41
Repentance, 79f

Jesus' call to, 155, 173
vocabulary of, 200n48
Rewards
as motive in Lk, 162–70
as motive in paraenesis, 122–6,
216n57
existential interpretation of, 232n134
in Jesus' teaching, 60f, 76f, 80,
196n22, 197n28
Righteousness of God, 114–19, 216n58,
n59
Rules in guiding behavior, 219n90, n91

Sermon on the Mt in Q, 49f
in Lukan setting, 153–5
in Q, 49f
Service and the love command, 87f
'Sinners', 201n58
Sitz im Leben of gospel tradition, 136–9
Sojourner, 31, 48, 182n27
Stoicism, 20–7, 35f, 39
difference from NT paraenesis, 24–7
Subjection, 131–3, 220n99
Systematizing, validity of, 67f

Tradition
in NT, 211n11
oral, 8, 18, 100, 122, 126f
two streams, 134, 222n24
written, 210n1

Vengeance of God, 114–19

Wisdom and eschatology, 196n24
Wissenschaft defined, 187n94
Woes in Lk, 158
Wrath of God, 114–19, 216n58, n64

Zealots, 98f